SPECTRUM

KOREA JOONGANG DAILY
in association with The New York Times

The Best **리딩**스펙트럼 **컴팩트**

홍준기 지음

Jonghap Books

INTRODUCTION

■ 머리말

　이 책은 이미 잘 알려진 「리딩 스펙트럼」 총 4권(인문, 문화 · 예술, 과학 · 기술, 사회과학)의 또 다른 버전(version)으로, 이 책에서는 기존 「리딩 스펙트럼」 1권당 100개씩 구성된 원문(지문)에서 분야별로 지문 20개씩을 선정하여 총 80개의 소재들로 꾸몄다. 이렇게 한 이유는 첫째, 그동안 기존의 4권으로 구성된 「리딩 스펙트럼」 독자들이 시리즈 전체 범위에서 각 20개씩을 추려내어 한 권으로도 만들면 어떨까하고 간간이 필자나 출판사로 제안해왔다. 둘째, 종래의 책으로 강의해온 선생님들도 이 책을 방학특강용으로 한 권 정도 분량으로 꾸며 활용하면 좋겠다는 요청을 몇 번 받았다고 출판사 측에서 알려왔다. 마지막으로 성격이 다른 하나는 중등교사 임용시험 영어전공 일반영어 과목에 글을 읽고 영어로 짧게 정리(Summary & Paraphrase) 하는 유형의 문제가 나오는데, 이 시험을 준비하는 학생들이 「리딩 스펙트럼」 원문을 소재로 연습할 수 있기를 수업 중에 꾸준히 요구해왔다. 결국 위의 두 가지와 세 번째 임용시험에 따른 독자의 요청을 포함하여 이를 계기로 코리아중앙데일리 그리고 출판사 측과 의논을 한 뒤 이 책을 만들게 되었다.

　한편, 다음 페이지의 학습방법에도 언급하겠지만 이 책으로 공부하는 독자들은 지문을 읽고 문제를 풀고 난 후, 그 내용을 상기하면서 핵심 부분을 추려 영어로 요약 · 패러프레이즈를 하여 필자의 요약문과 비교 · 확인해 봄으로써 더욱 도움이 되리라 본다. 각자 바라보는 관점에서 약간의 차이가 있긴 하겠지만 지문을 읽고 요약하는 것이므로 큰 틀에서는 맞춰볼 수 있을 것이다. 참고로 해당 코너의 영어 요약문은 필자가 작성하였으며, 원어민 교수의 영문 교정·교열을 거쳤다.

　끝으로 처음에는 크게 어려운 작업이 아닐 거라 생각했는데, 하다 보니 그렇게 만만하지만은 않아서 생각보다 시간이 오래 걸렸다. 필자 입장에서는 지문 하나하나가 모두 중요하다보니 각 분야에서 지문 20개씩을 추리는 것도 쉽지 않았을 뿐더러, 모범이 될 수 있는 요약문을 만드는 것 역시 쉬운 일은 아니었다. 하지만 「리딩 스펙트럼」 시리즈를 선호하는 여러 독자들에게 또 다른 효과적인 교재를 안겨주고자 하는 마음으로 나름 열심히 노력했는데, 독자들의 평가가 어떨지…. 모쪼록 뜻한 바 큰 성과가 따르기를 기대한다.

홍 준 기

■ 이 책의 성격과 학습방법

1. '인문, 문화·예술, 과학·기술, 사회과학' 4개 분야를 한 권에…!

이 책은 기존 「리딩 스펙트럼」 각 권에 있는 4가지 분야의 주제를 한 권에 압축시켰다. 이 한 권을 통해 다방면에 걸친 다양한 주제의 내용을 두루 접함으로써 유연하고 균형 잡힌 학습을 할 수 있도록 구성하였다. 만약 글을 읽고 배경지식이 필요하면 백과사전 등을 참조하여 관련지식을 하나씩 쌓아가는 것도 좋은 영어 학습법이다. 우리가 새로운 언어를 공부하는 것도 궁극적으로는 새로운 지식을 습득하고자 하는 것이기 때문이다. 영어로 된 배경지식이 쌓이면 자신의 의견을 회화로든 글로든 영어로 피력할 수 있는 능력이 생기므로 가능하면 영어로 된 배경지식을 쌓기를 권한다. 참고로 이 책은 각 분야를 모두 망라하지는 못하기 때문에 전체 분야의 다양한 글을 읽고자 하는 독자들에게는 「리딩 스펙트럼 시리즈」(전 4권)를 추천한다.

2. 철저한 감수 과정을 거친, 확고한 신뢰가 보장되는 코리아중앙데일리 콘텐츠!

이 책은 중앙일보의 주요 뉴스와 논평을 엄선하여 영어로 번역한 기사에 외국인 편집자가 참여하는 '코리아중앙데일리'의 고급 콘텐츠를 활용하였다. 원문의 단어, 문장 하나하나까지 원어민 에디터들의 철저한 감수 과정을 거쳐 신뢰할 수 있는 콘텐츠 중 가급적 독자들의 입맛에 맞는 소재들로 발췌하여 내용을 꾸몄다.

3. 완결성 있는 지문으로 독해뿐만 아니라 작문실력까지 높일 수 있는 최적의 교재!

이 책은 기존 일반 독해 교재와는 달리 하나의 지문 자체가 완결적이어서 논리성을 가지고 있다. 이러한 지문을 바탕으로 공인영어시험에 자주 나오는 유형의 문제를 풀어보고 원활한 학습을 위한 매 지문(원문)의 어휘해설, 해석과 함께 중요 구문 및 각 문제별 해설을 다뤘다. 또한 지문을 활용하여 요약, 패러프레이즈까지 연습한다면 독해는 물론 작문실력까지 두 마리 토끼를 동시에 잡을 수 있을 것이다. 이러한 구성은 심도 있는 독해 연습을 원하는 사람은 물론, 중등교사 임용시험 일반영어 과목을 공부하는 수험생에게도 최적의 교재가 될 것이다. 다시 말해서 이를 위해 별책에 〈Summary&Paraphrase〉 코너를 두어 모범 요약문 격인 영문과 한글 해석, 그리고 연습(practice) 란을 함께 달아놓았다. 영어로 요약해서 발표하거나 핵심적인 부분을 패러프레이즈 하는 연습에 적당할 것이다. 더불어 한글 해석을 바탕으로 영문을 작성해 보고 비교해 보는 연습을 한다면 영어실력, 특히 영작실력 향상에 많은 도움이 될 것이다. 한 가지 팁을 말하면 한글을 영어로 옮길 때 한글의 의미가 애매하면 먼저 자신이 표현하고자 하는 한글을 명확한 의미로 바꿔서 영어로 옮기는 연습을 하는 것이 좋을 것이다.

CONTENTS

Part 1 인문

Unit 01	Rumors: society's cancerous tumors 사람 잡는 루머	10
Unit 02	'Social proofs' on the Web 인기 검색어	12
Unit 03	Give us hope! 피그말리온	14
Unit 04	Waiting for the cargo 카고 컬트(Cargo-Cult)	16
Unit 05	Lost in translation 오역	18
Unit 06	Surviving stress 스트레스	20
Unit 07	Fanning fears 도시의 전설	22
Unit 08	Diamonds are forever 다이아몬드	24
Unit 09	Straw-man logic 허수아비 논법	26
Unit 10	When 'smaller is better' is not '축소 지향' 일본의 그릇된 역사 인식	28
Unit 11	The Republic of Complex 콤플렉스	30
Unit 12	Irrational minds 선택적 지각	32
Unit 13	How accidents shape history 우연과 필연	34
Unit 14	No pain, no gain on literary road 작가의 각오	36
Unit 15	When the masses silent the wise 집단사고	38
Unit 16	Moving to the left 사회주의에 빠진 20/30대	40
Unit 17	Is the law the problem? 법이 문제인가?	42
Unit 18	Not a curse, but still weighty issue 비만 할증료	44
Unit 19	Maternal instincts 부계 불확실성	46
Unit 20	The return of Machiavelli? 마키아벨리	48

Part 2 문화·예술

Unit 01	Mansplaining 잘난 척하는 남자들	52
Unit 02	Battling it out on the football pitch 전쟁과 축구	54
Unit 03	An addiction we can't afford 명품 프렌들리	56
Unit 04	Growing old peacefully 100세의 실종	58
Unit 05	The text generation 텍스트 세대	60
Unit 06	Memories of Mozart 모차르트	62
Unit 07	Leaping tall buildings 수퍼맨	64
Unit 08	Epicurean bean paste 칙릿	66
Unit 09	The essence of consumption 반소비	68
Unit 10	When the internet splits 인터넷 분열화	70
Unit 11	Barbie does Freud 키덜트	72
Unit 12	Is a college degree necessary? 대학 졸업장이 꼭 필요한가?	74
Unit 13	Sheep astray 학위 효과와 학력 검증	76
Unit 14	Get fathers involved '출산 보이콧'을 막으려면	78
Unit 15	The right to be forgotten online 잊혀질 권리	80
Unit 16	No such thing as a free bribe 스폰서	82
Unit 17	A different perspective on love 진정한 사랑에 대하여	84
Unit 18	Playing with blocks 테트리스	86
Unit 19	Cyberbullying is a crime 악플은 범죄다	88
Unit 20	A war over religious rights 부르카 전쟁 인권과 종교의 자유	90

Part 3 과학·기술

Unit 01	Racing toward a dissonant drive 전기자동차와 소음	94
Unit 02	Written in wrinkles 보톡스	96
Unit 03	Always polite, never complaining 밤새 일하고도 불평 없는 그 직원	98
Unit 04	Flying pandemics 조류 인플루엔자	100
Unit 05	Unfounded fears 공포의 문화	102
Unit 06	Insane or sane? 정신분석 요법의 귀환	104
Unit 07	The silent organ 간	106
Unit 08	History in color 피부색	108
Unit 09	Addicted to speed 속도	110
Unit 10	Under the microscope 다이옥신	112
Unit 11	Weather not an exact science 수치예보	114
Unit 12	A different side to drones 드론	116
Unit 13	Wrangling with nuclear risk 핵실험	118
Unit 14	A high-tech, brain-shrinking future 진화하는 인간	120
Unit 15	Painful patent protection 특허의 역설	122
Unit 16	Statistics use and misuse 통계의 사용과 오용	124
Unit 17	Autonomous driving dreams 자율주행차의 꿈	126
Unit 18	Repent, ye carbon emitters 환경 면죄부	128
Unit 19	Turn off the lights 빛 공해	130
Unit 20	Kimchi in space 우주식품	132

Part 4 사회과학

Unit 01	At Google, there is no manual "구글에는 매뉴얼이 없습니다"	136
Unit 02	Candidate games 딜레마	138
Unit 03	Progress over product GDP	140
Unit 04	Respecting privacy v. Public interests 사생활 보호 v. 공익	142
Unit 05	Just give them some fish 물고기를 줘라	144
Unit 06	Dollar envy 시뇨리지	146
Unit 07	More Sea Story blame game 정보의 비대칭성	148
Unit 08	Hierarchical incompetence? 피터원리	150
Unit 09	Broken items 깨진 유리창	152
Unit 10	Demonstrators in the dark 합리적 무시	154
Unit 11	An unbroken union 월마트	156
Unit 12	How the strong grew weak 강한 정부의 역설	158
Unit 13	A crime of passion '제2의 스위스' 된다는 영국의 망상	160
Unit 14	A rational vote 투표의 경제학	162
Unit 15	In the interest of whom? 수쿠크	164
Unit 16	NGO: A dearth of humility 인본주의가 결여된 NGO	166
Unit 17	Populism's persuasiveness 상황주의	168
Unit 18	Korea lacks basic values 스마트 기업 50	170
Unit 19	Like Robin Hood, tax up to no good 부유세	172
Unit 20	America's risky pot experiment 아슬아슬한 미국의 마리화나 실험	174

Humanities

Part 1 인문

UNIT 01 Rumors: society's cancerous tumors
사람 잡는 루머

| 인간과 심리 |

On Dec. 7, 1941, aircraft and submarines of the Imperial Japanese Navy attacked Pearl Harbor. As news of the Japanese assault spread, chaotic rumors began to circulate among the American public. Then President Franklin Roosevelt repudiated the rumors, setting the facts straight: During the attack, 2,340 American men were killed and 1,100 injured. Only three American ships deployed in the harbor area were damaged beyond repair. It was untrue that the U.S. lost over 1,000 jets. Japan did not know how many jets they destroyed, and Roosevelt did not divulge that information. He did, however, inform the public that the number of Japanese jets destroyed was far greater than the American losses. Roosevelt also entreated the public not to believe in all the rumors blindly, but to verify the information first. He knew that rumors could be a cancer that could bring down the people's morale and ultimately undermine the nation itself. His actions are an example of how a leader should stand against rumors in times of national crisis.

Rumors are like the tail of a lizard. Even when you sever them, they grow back. Oftentimes, they put innocent people in danger. Why do we accept rumors? In his book "On Rumors: How Falsehoods Spread, Why We Believe Them, What Can Be Done," Harvard Professor Cass Sunstein described one of the reasons as the "social waterfall effect." When we make a judgment, we have a tendency to depend on the thoughts and actions of others. That's why when the majority of the people you know believe in a rumor, you also start to believe it. The second reason is "group polarization." When people with the same thought get together to talk, they end up with a far more extreme version of that thought than before. And yet, they still believe themselves to be reasonable.

1. Choose the word that best replace the underlined repudiated.
   (a) addressed
   (b) heard
   (c) denied
   (d) acknowledged

2. What does the phrase "social waterfall effect" mean according to the passage?
   (a) Rumors are like waterfalls, they spread over a long distance.
   (b) The more people that believe in and propagate a rumor the more powerful it becomes.
   (c) The higher up a rumor comes from socially the more it is believed.
   (d) Rumors spread like water over a large area.

3. What is the most likely topic of the next paragraph?
   (a) The consequences of such things as social waterfall effect and group polarization on populations
   (b) How Roosevelt prevented such things as group polarization
   (c) Why the Japanese lied and spread rumors about the attack on Pearl Harbor?
   (d) How to determine what is and isn't a rumor

4. Which of the following is not true according to the passage?
   (a) Rumors are like a cancer in a society.
   (b) Rumors can become very dangerous when they become believed by many.
   (c) There is a discrepancy between the American and Japanese accounts.
   (d) Roosevelt lied to the American public to maintain moral.

| WORDS & PHRASES |

submarine *n.* 잠수함   chaotic *a.* 혼돈 상태인   repudiate *v.* (공시적으로) 부인하다   divulge *v.* 폭로하다, 밝히다   bring down 낙담시키다, 무너뜨리다, 떨어뜨리다   lizard *n.* 도마뱀   sever *v.* 자르다   polarization *n.* 극단(화)   discrepancy *n.* 차이, 불일치
moral *n.* 도덕, 교훈, 윤리

| 문장분석 |

■ He knew ①that rumors could be a cancer ②that could bring down the people's morale and ultimately undermine the nation itself. ➔ ①의 that은 know동사의 목적어를 이루는 목적절이며, ②의 that은 a cancer를 선행사로 하는 주격 관계대명사이다.

What Is Social Proof?

UNIT 02 'Social proofs' on the Web
인기 검색어

| 심리 |

One day, a man looked up at the sky in the middle of a street in New York City. Most people just passed him by, but about 4 percent of passersby also looked up to see what was going on. As the number of people looking up increased, more people noticed them and followed. When five people looked up, 8 percent of the passersby followed, and when 15 people gazed at the heavens, 40 percent of the people walking down the street stopped and looked up to see what they were staring at. That was a famous experiment on the phenomenon of social proof. People tend to think that by imitating a social proof, or behavior of the majority, they can reduce mistakes. Therefore, they follow what others do. The laugh tracks inserted into a comedy on television and the advertisements emphasizing that a book is a bestseller are exploiting the phenomenon of social proof. Even though the fake laughs sound artificial and silly, the viewers laugh more frequently and find the program more entertaining if they hear other people laughing. At a charity event, a list of donors is often made public and an offering box is passed around at a church, exploiting people's behavior.

But social proofs are not always the truth. In fact, they often go against the truth. In modern days, the grounds to manipulate public opinion by the media or advertisements are the effect of social proofs. Social proofs can be found at Internet portal sites. Popular search keywords, which greatly influence the setting of social agendas and forming public opinion, are one of the examples of social proofs on the Web. Popular search keywords are positioned to stand out, and the list changes in real time, adding a sense of urgency and drama. While many of the keywords are inaccurate and lead to bad information or provocative subjects, they have a strong impact as a social proof the minute they show up on the popularity list. When a strange name or a word is on the list, people become curious about why it became popular and click on it. Although it is not my concern, it is what other people, or society, are interested in. Then the ranking of the word rises. It does not matter whether it has a valuable piece of information or not. Moreover, it is not important whether many people were actually curious about it or not.

1. What is the phenomenon of social proof?
(a) Human desire to be the same as everyone else.
(b) By raising someone's curiosity about a subject, he or she is more likely to research it.
(c) If one person likes something, everyone likes it.
(d) People follow the behavior of others because they think it is the norm.

2. What can you infer about Internet search engines?
(a) They are manipulated to control what people search for.
(b) They reflect the interests of society.
(c) Many companies use the information to come to conclusions about specific people.
(d) They are geared to send people to adult sites.

3. Which of the following is false?
(a) Books that are advertised as bestsellers do not sell better than other books.
(b) People want to follow the majority so as not to make mistakes.
(c) Laughter tracks on TV shows make viewers laugh more.
(d) Internet users are tempted to search for something strange that others have searched for.

4. What was the result of the social experiment in New York City?
(a) Whether people mimicked or not depended on the appearance of the leaders.
(b) When a large group gathered, people thought a demonstration was occurring.
(c) The more people that looked up, the more people that joined them.
(d) A small group was laughed at; a large group was taken seriously.

| WORDS & PHRASES |

social proof 사회적 증거   laugh track 가짜 웃음   make public 공표하다   stand out 두드러지다   the minute ~하자마자
norm *n.* 규범   gear (to) *v.* (계획이나 요구에) 맞게 조정하다

| 문장분석 |

■ While many of the keywords ①are inaccurate and ②lead to bad information or provocative subjects, they have a strong impact as a social proof the minute they show up on the popularity list.

→ 부사절의 many of the keywords가 공통관계로 ①과 ②동사의 주어이다. 주절의 they는 many of the keywords를 의미하며, the minute는 '~하자마자'의 의미로 뒤에 절이 따라온다.

UNIT 03 Give us hope!
피그말리온

|문학|

Pygmalion, King of Cyprus, who appears in Greece myth was phobic of women. He had no confidence in his looks and believed that women were destined to have many flaws. He thought that he would not be able to fall in love with a woman in this mundane world. That is why he concentrated on sculpting his ideal figure in ivory. Instead of abandoning love, he craved vicarious satisfaction.

Since Pygmalion was a talented sculptor, the ivory statue was beautiful. He cherished it, bringing it flowers and even embracing and stroking it. During these moments, he began to have hope. He started to dream that the sculpture would come alive. On one festival day he visited the temple of Aphrodite, the goddess of beauty. Pygmalion prayed earnestly for the sculpture to become his wife. Then a miracle happened — the sculpture began to breathe. Pygmalion married this woman, and had a daughter named Paphos. His views on women also started to change.

The phrase "Pygmalion effect" comes from this story. When one has dreams or hopes, real life changes. Edward Burne-Jones, a British painter in the 19th century, painted this myth. The four images in "Pygmalion and the Image" hang inside the Birmingham Museum in England. Before starting the painting, Burne-Jones said, "I want to draw a masterpiece that would make everyone exclaim 'wow' and leave them breathless." Burne-Jones' wish has also come true like Pygmalion's — many people today view his drawings full of wonder.

|문장분석|

■ Pygmalion, King of Cyprus, who appears in Greece myth was phobic of women. ➡ Pygmalion과 King of Cyprus는 동격이며, who 이하는 관계대명사의 계속적 용법으로, 피그말리온은 그리스 신화에 나오는 인물인데, 여성기피증이 있었다고 해석하면 된다.

1. What can be inferred from the passage?
    (a) It's possible to bring statues to life sometimes.
    (b) Desire can help a person to achieve their goals.
    (c) Drawings fill people with a sense of wonder.
    (d) Festivals are the proper time to attempt the impossible.

2. Which of the following is not true according to the passage?
    (a) Pygmalion knew he would find love someday.
    (b) Burne-Jones and Pygmalion were both talented.
    (c) Myths are fictional stories.
    (d) Statues cannot be brought to life.

3. What is another way of saying that you are "phobic" of something?
    (a) You forget about it.
    (b) You are happy with it.
    (c) You are bored by it.
    (d) You are afraid of it.

4. What is the main purpose of the passage?
    (a) To explain the best way to get a wife
    (b) To show people how to be happy with life
    (c) To illustrate how important it is to want to achieve something in life
    (d) To demonstrate how people inspire each other

| WORDS & PHRASES |

phobic *n.* (병적) 공포증의 사람 *a.* 공포증의   **mundane** *a.* 평범한, 실제의, 이승의, 현세의   **crave** *v.* 갈망하다, 추구하다
stroke *v.* 쓰다듬다, 어루만지다   **exclaim** *v.* 감탄하다   **breathless** *a.* 숨을 죽인, 숨도 못 쉴 정도의

UNIT 04 Waiting for the cargo
카고 컬트(Cargo-Cult)

| 철학 |

After World War II ended, the native people living in the numerous islands of the Pacific Ocean began a unique custom. They started to make sloppy runways and control towers, copying the U.S.-built supply bases. Some tribes even patrolled near the runways, wearing coconut helmets and holding wooden rifles in their hands. Their unusual customs attracted interest from anthropologists and people who studied religion.

The native tribes believed that if they made runways like the U.S. troops did, planes loaded with supplies would come to their island. It must have been hard for the people to turn back to their living standards after their sudden affluence that came from U.S. supply boxes that were either airdropped by mistake or swept on to their shore. The tribes were not an exception to the "Ratchet Effect," an economics rule which says that it is hard to lower the consumption level once it has increased, even if earnings have decreased.

However, despite their earnest wish, no more supply boxes came to their islands. They had made the error of what people who study logic call, "post hoc, ergo propter hoc." They had confused the simple sequential order of events. In short, they thought a specific event was the cause of another event, just because it happened before the other event.

In late 1945, an Australian magazine called "Pacific Islands Monthly" named this custom of the Papua New Guinea tribes the "Cargo-Cult." Later, that phrase was used to describe native tribes that copy foreign systems and things without knowing the reason for it. The "Cargo-Cult" later developed to mean "pseudo-science" and "shams." It means things that look similar outwardly but have inferior functions, or studies with no academic essence.

| 문장분석 |

■ It <u>must have been</u> hard for the people to turn back to their living standards after their sudden affluence ①<u>that</u> came from U.S. supply boxes [②<u>that</u> were <u>either</u> airdropped by mistake <u>or</u> swept on to their shore.]

→ must have been은 '~이었음이 틀림없다'라는 뜻이다. ①의 that은 their sudden affluence를 선행사로 받는 주격 관계대명사이고, ②의 that은 U.S. supply boxes를 받는데, [ ] 안의 내용은 전부가 U.S. supply boxes를 수식한다.

1. What can be inferred from the passage?

(a) Cargo-cults are all made up of individuals with problems accepting reality.
(b) Not all things that happen together are necessarily related.
(c) World War II caused massive damage to the Pacific oceans islands.
(d) Events that coincide are by nature related to one another.

2. What is the main purpose of the passage?

(a) To explain the odd behavior of island people
(b) To illustrate the negative impact the U.S. military had on the Pacific islands
(c) To prove that it is possible to imitate Americans
(d) To explain how the concept of cargo-cults came about

3. What is the most likely topic of the next paragraph?

(a) An example and discussion of a pseudo-science or a sham
(b) What the American government did to aid the islanders
(c) To explain why these people were left without their supplies they were waiting for
(d) A further detailed discussion on the ratchet effect

4. Which of the following is not true according to the passage?

(a) The Papua New Guinea tribes eventually received supplies from U.S. planes.
(b) Islander pretended to be American soldiers at an air strip.
(c) Islanders thought they would continue to receive cargo.
(d) An Australian magazine coined the phrase Cargo-Cult.

| WORDS & PHRASES |

sloppy *a.* 엉성한   runway *n.* 활주로   control tower *n.* 관제탑   rifle *n.* 소총   ratchet effect 톱니바퀴 효과
post hoc ergo propter hoc 그것 다음으로, 그러니까 바로 그렇기 때문에 (전후관계와 인과관계의 오류)   pseudo-science *n.* 사이비 과학
sham *n.* 모조품   air strip 간이 활주로

UNIT 05 Lost in translation
오역

| 언어 |

Wrong translations can be found everywhere. The Bible is one example: And again I say unto you, it is easier for a camel to go through the eye of a needle, than for a rich man to enter into the kingdom of God. Here, in the original Aramaic, the word gamta, meaning rope, was wrongly translated as gamla, a camel. But instead of destroying the original meaning, the translation was evaluated as having expressed it better.

Misinterpretation can happen in translation from one language to another. A prime example is a July 1945 press conference held by Japanese Premier Kantaro Suzuki, when Japan was ready to surrender to Allied forces. However, he had decided to delay formally announcing it until Allied forces had been notified through official channels. He wanted to buy time to negotiate the terms of surrender. However, the prime minister made a mistake at the press conference. To the Postdam Declaration that demanded unconditional surrender, he responded ambiguously, "The cabinet holds that it will ignore [mokusachu] the declaration." He meant to say that he would for now defer from responding. However, the word mokusachu can be interpreted as either to "ignore" or "refrain from commenting." Japanese media and the Tokyo English Broadcast interpreted it as the former — that the cabinet would reject the Postdam Declaration. Three days later, U.S. President Harry Truman signed the order to drop the atomic bomb on Japan. Had it not been for the misunderstanding and misinterpretation, the atomic bombing might have been avoided.

| 문장분석 |

■ <u>Had it not been for</u> the misunderstanding and misinterpretation, the atomic bombing might have been avoided. ➡ 〈if it had not been for〉에서 if가 생략된 후 도치된 가정법 과거완료의 표현으로, '~이 없었더라면'의 뜻이다. 가정법 과거완료이므로 주절에서는 〈might have p.p.〉의 형태인데, 여기에서는 수동형이기 때문에 might have been avoided가 되었다. '생기지 않을 수 있었을 텐데'의 의미이다.

18 Part 1 인문

1. What is the passage mainly about?
   (a) The misunderstandings that can come from translating a language
   (b) Errors that cause major disasters
   (c) The surrender of the Japanese army after the atomic bomb was dropped
   (d) The true meaning of one part of the Bible

2. Which of the following is incorrect according to the passage?
   (a) The words of the Japanese prime minister were misunderstood.
   (b) The atomic bombing was purely the result of a misunderstanding.
   (c) There is at least one translation error in the Bible.
   (d) Misinterpretation is something that occurs from time to time.

3. Which of the following means the same as "it is easier for a camel to go through the eye of a needle."?
   (a) Camels are smaller than something else.
   (b) Camels are more patient and obedient than other animals.
   (c) It is impossible for this to happen.
   (d) The needle will need to be very large.

4. What can be inferred from the passage?
   (a) The Americans made a mistake.
   (b) Misunderstanding differences in language can have varying results.
   (c) The Bible has many very strange analogies.
   (d) Translators do very poor work on important things.

| WORDS & PHRASES |

Aramaic *n.* 아람어(아람어 원어)   misinterpretation *n.* 오역   buy time 시간을 벌다   ambiguously *ad.* 애매하게   defer from -ing ~을 못하게 하다   ignore *v.* 무시하다   refrain from -ing ~을 삼가다

UNIT 06 Surviving stress
스트레스

| 심리 |

"We cannot possibly avoid stress and stress is not necessarily bad," said stress expert Bruce McEwen of Rockfeller University. Hormones secreted when you are under stress heighten your awareness of your environment, improve eyesight and hearing and help muscle movement. We can drive in busy streets without causing accidents thanks to these secretions. Stress helps us address life's demands. It is said that those who are successful or hold positions of power have higher levels of stress hormones, such as cortisol, than those with more lowly lots in life.

McEwen said, "Stress protects the body. People under stress are vigilant about their environment and plan to avoid danger. On the other hand, happy, laid-back people are not aware that they are falling into traps." Evolutionary psychology assumes people who are more susceptible to stress are people who manage better in the competition for survival, and are thus believed to be our ancestors. In early civilization, people who were insecure, highly suspicious and anticipated the worst were believed to have been naturally stronger.

If so, we must ask: While the living environment was harsh for primitive people, why do people still have stress in modern society, when lifespan has increased and there is material abundance? Is stress a physical reaction to basic insecurity and fear? It is said that the main reason for more stress in modern society is the media. Stress researcher Joseph E. LeDoux of New York University said insecurity is due to exaggerated headlines. "In ancient times, people were stressed by things they encountered personally. It is different nowadays. Everyone knows the atrocities happening in the world and potential dangers. Things to worry about have increased dramatically."

1. What can be inferred from the passage?
    (a) Stress is essential to a productive life.
    (b) Stress is a part of life that will always be with us.
    (c) People without stress historically can't survive.
    (d) The media is the cause of all stress in society.

2. What are the positive aspects of stress according to the article?
    (a) Increased vigilance and insecurity
    (b) Better sight and heightened aggression
    (c) Increased worry and health problems
    (d) Hyper awareness and better coping abilities

3. What can be said about stress in regard to our past according to the article?
    (a) Those who experienced higher levels of stress were most likely those that survived.
    (b) People with low stress tend to have had happier lives.
    (c) People became stressed about large social issues.
    (d) Stress caused unfounded fear which lead to unhappiness.

4. What is the next paragraph most likely about?
    (a) The personal stress of people
    (b) How people used to deal with stress
    (c) How people now cope with the new stressors that exist in modern life
    (d) How to deal with stress in your daily life to become more productive

| WORDS & PHRASES |

secrete *v.* 분비하다   address *v.* (문제를) 다루다, 처리하다   be susceptible to ~에 손상받기 쉽다, 해를 입기 쉽다
laid-back *a.* 느긋한, 태평한   insecure *a.* 불안한

| 문장분석 |

- Evolutionary psychology assumes (that) people and are thus believed to be our ancestors.
  S   V   S'   V2
  [who are more susceptible to stress] are people
                                        V1   C'
  [who manage better in the competition for survival],

  → that절 안의 주어 people은 두 개의 동사를 받는다. 절 내에서 앞의 people은 주어, 뒤의 people은 보어로 쓰였다.

UNIT 07 Fanning fears
도시의 전설

| 사회 |

"A report on gang initiation: new gang members have been told to commit murder. At night, they ride through the streets with the car lights out and search for victims. If an oncoming car flicks its lights to inform the gangsters that their lights aren't switched on, then the gang members follow the car and kill those inside. Two families have already died as a consequence. Never flick your car lights at another car." The above is a summary of a fax message from the Illinois State police that made Americans shiver in fear in 1993. ____①____ the Illinois State police said it was a false alarm, the fear did not subside easily. This rumor became popular again, slightly changed, as an e-mail in 2006. A Web site specializing in rumors, Snopes.com, studied it and defined it as an urban legend. "They are legends that people believe in, but which contain weird and surprisingly false facts." In Korea, it would be something like a popular superstition.

There is a disgraceful phenomenon that has become internationally famous. The online dictionary Wikipedia defines "fan death" as a South Korean urban legend. The story goes like this: "The Korean government and media believe in fan death. However, no one in any other country has ever died from fan exposure. Causes of death are cited as a drop in body temperature and breathing difficulties. ____②____, body temperature cannot drop below 27.7 degrees Celsius (82 degrees Fahrenheit) in mid-summer even with a fan. If we can die from moving air, why don't motorbike riders die? The real causes of death are heart and cerebral blood vessel problems or alcoholism in people who happened to have their fans on."

| 문장분석 |

■ If an oncoming car flicks its lights to inform <u>the gangsters</u> that <u>their lights aren't switched on</u>, then the gang members follow the car and kill those inside.

→ 〈if ~ then …〉 구문으로 '만약 ~한다면, 그렇다면…'라는 의미이다. to 이하는 to 부정사의 부사적 용법이며, inform은 4형식 동사로 뒤에 간접목적어(the gangsters)와 직접목적어(that their lights aren't switched on)가 왔다.

1. *What's the overall topic of the passage?*
    (a) Whether fan death is real or not
    (b) Is it urban legend or truth?
    (c) The involvement of the media in the circulation of urban legends
    (d) How to avoid being targeted by gangs

2. *What can you infer about fan death?*
    (a) Fan death is medically possible according to some doctors.
    (b) There have been a number of cases of fan death reported in many countries, indicating that fan death is spreading.
    (c) It is possible to die from riding a motorbike too fast.
    (d) The fan death explanation covers up the real causes of death.

3. *Which of the following is true?*
    (a) The Illinois State police had arrested many gang members who testified that this initiation was real.
    (b) Snopes.com has been identified as the culprit in spreading the gang initiation rumor.
    (c) Snopes.com said that the gang rumor was true and not an urban legend.
    (d) The rumor of the gang initiation was not forgotten quickly by the general public.

4. *The most appropriate words for the blanks ① and ② would be*
    a) Unless - Nevertheless
    b) Since – In addition
    c) even though - However
    d) As long as - Therefore

| WORDS & PHRASES |

flick *v.* 깜빡거리다　　**shiver in fear** 공포에 떨다　　**urban legend** 도시 괴담(근거없이 마치 사실처럼 떠도는 놀라운 이야기)　　**weird** *a.* 이상한　　**cerebral blood vessel** 뇌혈관　　**cover up** 숨기다, 은폐하다

UNIT 08 Diamonds are forever
다이아몬드

| 역사 |

Humans began to use diamonds first as an abrasive. Traces of ruby and sapphire were discovered in a Chinese stone ax from the Neolithic era 4,500 years ago, its surface polished smoothly like a mirror. A research team from Harvard University concluded in 2005, "This could not have been done without using diamonds as an abrasive." Diamonds were also once used as a charm for sorcery. Around 7 B.C., the king and soldiers of the Dravida Kingdom in India believed that "the hardest stone in the world" had a magical power to protect the person wearing it. This is exactly in line with the origin of the word diamond, which comes from the Greek adamas, meaning "untamable, invincible." During the Middle Ages and the Renaissance in the West, kings and the nobility possessed diamonds to ____①____ disease and avoid calamity.

Diamonds began to be regarded as jewels around the 15th century, after a grinding method was discovered. A poor young man who practiced metalcraft in Venice was in love with his master's daughter, and asked to marry her. The father set an impossible condition: "If you find a way to grind diamonds, I will give you my daughter's hand." After much deliberation, the young man found the answer. Rubbing diamonds against each other produces a microscopic powder that can be used as an abrasive. Nowadays, diamond jewelry is mainly used for wedding gifts. Thanks to the advertising slogan "A diamond is forever," it has become a symbol of eternal love. The advertisement used by De Beers has so dominated the world diamond market that it is considered one of the most successful in history.

| 문장분석 |

■ The advertisement [used by De Beers] has **so** dominated the world diamond market **that** it is considered one of the most successful in history. → used by De Beers는 the advertisement를 수식하고 있으며, 〈so ~ that …〉 구문을 사용하였다.

1. *Which of the following purposes have diamonds not been used for, according to the passage?*
   (a) Diamonds have been used as talismans by important people to provide protection.
   (b) Diamonds have been a symbol of eternal life to the person who possesses it.
   (c) Diamonds have been used as abrasives due to their quality of being the hardest stone in the world.
   (d) Diamonds are a common theme in the design of wedding jewelry.

2. *How did the young man gain his desired wife's hand in marriage?*
   (a) He worked hard to buy a diamond ring to propose to his loved one.
   (b) He gave the father of his love the secret of how to turn metal in diamonds.
   (c) He thought for a long time about the right thing to do, finally deciding to propose marriage.
   (d) He discovered the method of rubbing diamonds against each other to produce an abrasive powder.

3. *What can you infer from the passage?*
   (a) A couple who exchange diamond wedding rings have a good chance at a prosperous marriage.
   (b) The first use of diamonds by humans was not as decoration, but as a tool.
   (c) The origin of the word diamond is still unknown as its existence was kept a secret for so many years by those in the Dravida Kingdom.
   (d) Humans were at first unaware of the potential uses of the diamond and preferred to gaze at it instead.

4. *Which of the following fits the blank ①?*
   a) call off
   b) ward off
   c) put off
   d) kick off

| WORDS & PHRASES |

abrasive *n.* 연마재   ax *n.* 도끼   neolithic *a.* 신석기의 (cf. paleolithic 구석기의)   charm *n.* 주문   sorcery *n.* 마법
in line with ~와 긴밀히 연결되는   invincible *a.* 정복할 수 없는   ward off 막다, 피하다   calamity *n.* 재앙   metalcraft *n.* 금속 세공
give one's hand to ~와 결혼하다   microscopic *a.* 미세한   powder *n.* 가루

UNIT 09 Straw-man logic
허수아비 논법

Setting up a "straw-man argument" means creating a vulnerable fictitious persona and pulverizing it with one swift blow. After setting up the opposition's supposed position, it is refuted in a one-sided attack, and the attacker then acts as if the opponent's actual position has been refuted.

An example of a straw-man fallacy is to refute the assertion, "Children must not run into busy streets" with, "It would be unreasonable to lock children up all day." Insinuating the argument is much more draconian than it really is, the refuter has side-stepped the issue, and any response sounds like an excuse. For this reason, anybody who becomes entangled in this war of words has a difficult time escaping unscathed.

President George W. Bush is famous for setting up straw-man arguments. As soon as the opposition suggested considering withdrawal from Iraq in 2005, President Bush immediately said, "There are some people who want our troops to leave immediately" and concluded that withdrawing troops "would be a big mistake." After misrepresenting a "consideration of troop withdrawal" with "immediate and absolute withdrawal," he concluded that it would be "a grave mistake." Someone suggesting troop withdrawal is in danger of being labeled unpatriotic, against the war on terror and irresponsible enough to disregard the safety of American troops.

Setting up a straw-man argument misrepresents the opposition's position and prevents genuine dialogue; it misleads and manipulates people into believing its fabricated conclusions. For this reason, the study of logic points to this technique as an unethical error in logic. Although the argument at hand may be won, everybody loses in the end.

| 문장분석 |

■ Insinuating the argument is **much more** draconian **than** it really is, the refuter has side-stepped the issue, and any response sounds like an excuse.

→ 허수아비 주장과 원래 화자가 의도했던 주장을 비교하고 있다. much는 비교급을 수식하는 부사로 more를 수식한다.

1. What's the main purpose of the passage?
   (a) To encourage the use of more straw-man arguments in politics, since they have been successful in the past
   (b) To criticize straw-man arguments on the basis that they destroy any chance of reasoned debate on issues
   (c) To teach somebody how to carry out straw-man arguments effectively and win them
   (d) To argue against the withdrawal of U.S. troops from Iraq

2. Which of the following is true about straw-man arguments?
   (a) Straw-man arguments cause problems because they address the core of the issue.
   (b) Straw-man arguments often cause scandals to be unearthed.
   (c) Straw-man arguments are extremely difficult to argue against.
   (d) President Bush didn't like the use of straw-man arguments since this method twisted his words.

3. What can be inferred from the passage?
   (a) President Bush wanted immediate withdrawal of troops from Iraq.
   (b) Straw-man arguments are used primarily by those without satisfactory debating skills.
   (c) Using straw-man arguments is a way to resolve an issue fairly.
   (d) Those pushing for troop withdrawal were labeled unpatriotic and uncaring of American troops.

4. How does a straw-man argument work?
   (a) The refuter accuses the opponent of lying.
   (b) The refuter first agrees with the original statement, then later on changes their position.
   (c) The refuter makes the original statement sound much harsher than it was intended.
   (d) None of the above.

| WORDS & PHRASES |

straw-man argument 허수아비 논법   fictitious *a.* 가공의   pulverize *v.* 가루로 만들다, 분쇄하다   insinuate *v.* 암시하다, 넌지시 말하다
draconian *a.* 매우 엄격한, 가혹한   side-step *v.* 회피하다   unscathed *a.* 다치지 않은, 아무 탈 없는   withdrawal *n.* 철수
misrepresent *v.* 잘못 전하다, 와전하다   genuine *a.* 진정한   fabricated *a.* 조작된   address *v.* (문제) 제기하다   unearth *v.* 찾다, 밝혀내다   twist *v.* 왜곡하다

UNIT 10 When 'smaller is better' is not

'축소 지향' 일본의 그릇된 역사 인식

| 역사 |

The former culture minister, Lee O-young explained in his book "Smaller is better" that the Japanese people were deeply rooted in culture and that the "smaller is better" tendency could be evidenced even in everyday items like folding fans, bonsai trees, flower arrangements, lunch boxes and portable radios. Recently, I was once again marveled by this acute insight. It also appears to apply to Japan's historical awareness and the extent to which it realizes how much it harmed its neighbors during the colonial period and during World War II.

Japan protested when historical documents detailing the Nanjing Massacre in China were added to the UNESCO Memory of the World Register. It claimed that the number of the victims killed in the six-week bloodbath carried out by Japanese forces occupying Nanjing in December 1937 was inaccurate and refused to acknowledge the decision by the Nanjing Military Tribunal in 1947 that more than 300,000 people were killed. Tokyo slammed China for making what it said was a unilateral claim and asserted that UNESCO had been played. Until 10 years ago, it was widely accepted in Japan that the victims of the Nanjing massacre numbered at least 200,000. In 2005, an approved high school Japanese textbook stated that it was likely to be more than 200,000, then it was reduced to 100,000. Now, Tokyo again wants to drastically reduce the number of casualties, to about 20,000 to 40,000 victims. While the Japanese government's official position is that the civilian killings during that time were undeniable, its demands for revision indicate that it wants to distance itself — even deny — its historical responsibility.

The "smaller is better" instinct can also be seen in its attitude toward Korea's "comfort women," the young women and girls the Imperial Japanese Army forced into sexual slavery. Prime Minister Shinzo Abe and his administration continues to deny that these women were forcibly taken and moved into military brothels. They advocate for a future-oriented relationship in a weak bid to improve the bilateral relationship with Korea. Tokyo's tactic is to waste time, to wait until the witnesses and the evidence have disappeared. But this cannot make a dark past disappear and it will resurface someday. Japan must sincerely apologize and repent.

1. What is the message of the passage?
(a) Japan should face up to its past and acknowledge it publicly before everyone will move on.
(b) Japan should be given a break and allowed to forget something in its past that is shameful.
(c) Japan is making its victims suffer even more than they already have by its denial.
(d) Japan has a point when it says that data has been exaggerated to fit a pre-determined narrative.

2. Which sentence best complete the passage?
(a) We cannot allow Japan to get off lightly.
(b) Only then, can there be a future for us.
(c) When apologies are made, everyone will forget.
(d) It is strongly being encouraged not to, however.

3. What can be inferred about Japan?
(a) It truly doesn't believe that as many people died in Nanjing as is claimed.
(b) It still doesn't think that it did anything wrong during the wars.
(c) It doesn't understand the full extent of what it has done to others.
(d) It wants to let the passing of time erase the memory of what it did.

4. What does the underlined mean?
(a) Members of UNESCO had a secret goal to discredit Japan and boost china's image.
(b) China had deliberately tried to hurt Japan just as Japan had hurt it in the past.
(c) China and Japan had been getting along better than ever before this was brought up again.
(d) UNESCO had been deceived by the lies of the Chinese into saying what they did.

| WORDS & PHRASES |

tendency *n.* 경향   portable *a.* 휴대 가능한   marvel *v.* 놀라다   acute *a.* 날카로운; 격심한; 민감한   awareness *n.* 의식, 관심
victim *n.* 피해자   bloodbath *n.* 대학살   carry out 실행하다   slam *v.* 비방하다, 혹평하다   unilateral *a.* 일방적인
massacre *n.* 대학살   casualty *n.* 사상자, 희생자; 사고, 재난   civilian *n.* 민간인   undeniable *a.* 부정할 수 없는
advocate *v.* 옹호하다; 옹호자   bilateral *a.* 쌍방의   repent *v.* 반성하다   get off 손 떼다, 그만하다

| 문장분석 |

■ Tokyo slammed China for making what it said was a unilateral claim and asserted that UNESCO had been played. ➡ slam A for B: B란 이유로 A를 비난하다. making은 전치사의 목적어 자리 동명사, what it said was~ 이하는 명사절로 동명사 making의 목적어이다. 이때, what 뒤 it said는 삽입으로, what [it said] was a unilateral claim로 분석하면 된다. and asserted는 동사 slammed와 동사 병치 구조를 이룬다. that UNESCO had been played는 asserted의 목적어 자리 명사절이다.

UNIT 11 The Republic of Complex
콤플렉스

| 심리 |

The word "complex," when used with reference to psychology, refers to unconscious thoughts and feelings as a source of human actions. Although analytical psychologists such as Sigmund Freud and Carl Jung coined the term, it is a combination of two Latin words, "com" and "plectere," which mean to weave together and refer to something woven or complicated. Freud uses the term to describe the tension between taboo and desire. It is a combination of repressed feelings due to morality, ethics and conscience, and it establishes the foundation of the human mind in tandem with the id, ego and superego. Variations of complex include the Oedipus and Electra complexes, which a young child feels about his or her opposite sex parent. Jung said complex is the central node of one's psychological life and a prototype of human feelings, perceptions and desires.

In a more popular sense, a complex is a feeling of inferiority. The term "inferiority complex," coined by Alfred Adler, has spread to the general public. Once a student of Freud, Adler opposed the Freudian theory that hinges upon sexuality and desire as a conclusive factor of almost everything and instead provided a sound perspective on the human mind that overcomes feelings of inferiority. According to Adler, being human is tantamount to realizing the inferiority of one's person. Yet this inferiority also becomes a motivation for human behaviors. It is a powerful locomotive since humans also have a desire to be superior. For instance, a child experiences weakness, helplessness and dependency compared to an adult, but these feelings motivate the child to grow up. Adler emphasized rising above one's feelings of inferiority. He cited the examples of Demosthenes, an ancient Greek orator who overcame a speech impediment, and former U.S. president Roosevelt who overcame his physical weakness. Adler also said if inferiority is not overcome in a constructive way one might have psychological distress or become a criminal.

1. What's the main idea of the passage?
   (a) Using the word complex to talk about the link between taboo and desire and, furthermore, feelings of inferiority
   (b) The scholarly rivalry of Freud and Adler
   (c) How to be human by your actions and attitudes to things
   (d) The etymological origin of the word complex and its evolution into a different word today

2. What is Adler's theory about humanity?
   (a) Every human is born and dies with an inferiority complex.
   (b) All humans are motivated to become more virtuous in their lives.
   (c) Those who cannot overcome their inferiorities may develop psychological problems.
   (d) Those who recognize their inferiorities and endeavor to overcome them live better lives.

3. What can you infer about the inferiority complex?
   (a) The inferiority complex is only present in those children who will grow up to be criminals.
   (b) The inferiority complex motivates humans to improve themselves and seek superiority over others.
   (c) The inferiority complex can be overcome by confronting one's Oedipus complex.
   (d) A child with an inferiority complex usually has a hard time in school and achieveing things.

4. Which of the following is incorrect?
   (a) An Oedipus complex refers to a child's unnatural attitude to his or her parent.
   (b) Freud believed that sexuality and desire were evident in most human behavior.
   (c) Adler and Freud had many of the same opinions over the role of sexuality and desire in human life.
   (d) The term inferiority complex has become popular and is used in everyday language.

| WORDS & PHRASES |

repress *v.* 억압하다   in tandem with ~와 나란히, 동시에   prototype *n.* 원형   perception *n.* 지각   inferiority *n.* 열등감   hinge upon 전적으로 ~에 달려있다   sound *a.* 건전한   tantamount to (효과가) 마찬가지인, 상당하는   motivation *n.* 동기   locomotive *n.* 기관차, 추진력   orator *n.* 웅변가   impediment *n.* 장애   distress *n.* 고통, 곤경   etymological *a.* 어원상의

| 문장분석 |

■ Once a student of Freud, Adler opposed the Freudian theory [that hinges upon sexuality and desire as a conclusive factor of almost everything] and instead provided a sound perspective on the human mind [that overcomes feelings of inferiority.]
  → that은 주격 관계대명사로 the Freudian theory를 선행사로 한다. Adler는 opposed와 provided를 본동사로 한다.

UNIT 12 Irrational minds
선택적 지각

| 심리 |

Psychologists do not believe that people are inherently rational. They use a psychological term "selective perception" to explain why people don't perceive external information as it is. Instead, they frame it selectively so that it exists in harmony with their own beliefs, and often to their own advantage. There is a similar term. It's called the "cocktail party effect," which is when people hear their names at a party even if they are standing in the middle of a noisy room.

Selective perception undergoes the following steps: selective exposure, attention and understanding. The term was originally used in cognitive psychology, but it is now a major concept in advertising and marketing. No matter how much money is spent on an ad, it will be useless if it fails to grab consumers' selective perception. According to research, we're exposed to 1,500 advertising messages every day. But we only notice around 70 of them, and we can remember only about 10. Selective perception can be also experienced in our everyday lives. A person of low self-esteem has a tendency to misinterpret other people's unintentional behavior as a threat, while patients plagued by delusion are a perfect example of selective perception.

Advertisers tend to generate well-coordinated ad campaigns based on the theory of selective perception, so the question of what people believe to be true is largely irrelevant. There is also a term known as "cognitive dissonance." When there's inconsistency between a person's attitude and behavior, he or she tries to bring them together to eliminate any feeling of uneasiness. When such a discrepancy exists, people usually change their attitude to accommodate their behavior.

| 문장분석 |

- No matter how much money is spent on an ad, it will be useless if it fails to grab consumers' selective perception.
  → 양보구문으로 '아무리 많은 돈을 광고에 쏟아 붓는다 하더라도'의 의미이다.

1. What will be the most likely topic of the next paragraph?

(a) The process involved in cognitive dissonance
(b) How the cocktail party effect influences cognitive dissonance
(c) Why people are inherently rational
(d) How selective perception can influence decision making

2. What can be inferred from the passage?

(a) Most people will have internal conflicts that they will resolve or go insane trying to.
(b) People will alter their own reality to maintain a sense of rationality within their environment.
(c) People block out all the irrational things they see as a coping mechanism.
(d) If conflicts are not resolved between attitude and behaviour people will become irrational.

3. Which of the following is not true according to the passage?

(a) People with low self-esteem are inherently violent towards others.
(b) Advertising companies use psychology to make their ads more effective.
(c) Selective perception allows people to hear what they want to hear.
(d) Cognitive dissonance allows people to resolve internal vs. external conflict.

4. What is the main purpose of this passage?

(a) To show how media companies manipulate people
(b) To explain why people are considered to be rational
(c) To explain how people maintain their rationality in their society
(d) To talk about how people resolve conflict when they have low self-esteem

---

| WORDS & PHRASES |

selective perception 선택적 지각   delusion *n.* 망상   cognitive dissonance 인지 부조화   go insane 돌아버리다, 미쳐버리다

UNIT 13 How accidents shape history
우연과 필연

| 역사 |

The French philosopher Blaise Pascal remarks in his book "Pensees" that seemingly trivial occurrences we might not even be aware of affect geopolitical events. He famously wrote, "Cleopatra's nose, had it been shorter, the whole face of the world would have been changed." Those who support the historical view that history is the continuation of accidents based on causality rather than reason often side with Pascal. Had it been shorter, the thinking goes, Mark Antony would not have fallen in love with Cleopatra, deserting his family; the Battle of Actium between the forces of Octavian and the combined forces of Mark Antony and Cleopatra would not have taken place; and Octavian could not have consolidated enough power to be enthroned as the first emperor of the Roman Empire. These events, and their subsequent ramifications, were conjured into existence because a man fell in love with an Egyptian queen.

Of course, it is not possible to explain history through accident alone. If we inquire into antecedents, accidents are prone to be the product of causality. Therefore, E. H. Carr, who said history was an endless dialogue between the past and the present, rejected the view that emphasized the role of historical accidents in his renowned work, "What is History?" However, accidents certainly play a role in history. For example, the 14th-century Ottoman Sultan Bajazet stopped his expedition to central Europe because he was afflicted with gout. Historian Edward Gibbon wrote that the incident showed that a tumor on one's muscle could prevent or postpone the miseries of a people.

Then there's the fall of the Berlin Wall, which was detonated by a slip of the tongue by a spokesman of the East German Communist Party. When reporters asked the spokesman when East Germans would be free to travel to West Germany, he inadvertently said, "Right now." The East Berlin residents rushed to the wall with hammers and axes, bringing the wall down. Of course, the fall of the Berlin Wall must have a historical inevitability, but it was due to a historical accident that the wall came down on that day in such a dramatic way. And this is the reason why history is so fascinating. How boring history would be if it were not for historical accidents, instead running only on necessity.

1. What can not be inferred from this passage?

(a) Events cannot be predicted accurately due to the possibility of unforeseen accidental events.
(b) Nothing can be inferred from the passage as things are inherently unpredictable.
(c) Without the mistaken comment made by the East German spokesman the two halves of the country would have never become reunited.
(d) Most theories about history are contradictory in nature, and no one knows the real truth of historical events.

2. Which of the following is the main idea of the passage?

(a) Democratic freedom in East Germany took a long time to occur, but once it began it did so rapidly.
(b) Cleopatra and Mark Anthony were lovers by mere chance.
(c) There are many factors to consider when one is developing theories of how historical events have unfolded.
(d) The democratic movement in the world and how one person sparked a country into revolution.

3. Which of the following is not correct according to the passage?

(a) Cleopatra would have rather been with Octavian but Mark Anthony would not have cooperated if she had done so.
(b) East and West Germans became able to travel back and forth even if it did not happen perfectly according to plan.
(c) The French philosopher Blaise Pascal didn't believe in just necessity controlling history.
(d) Many factors contributed to the historical events, not just one event made the difference.

4. What is a good title for the passage?

(a) How accidents shape history
(b) A brief look at the historical struggles of the Korean democratic movement
(c) The political upheaval created by individuals that make mistakes when speaking to the public
(d) The differing factors that contribute to the final history that becomes recorded

---

| WORDS & PHRASES |

causality *n.* 인과 관계   consolidate *v.* 굳히다, 강화하다, 통합하다   enthrone *v.* 왕좌에 앉히다   ramification *n.* 영향, 파문
antecedent *n.* 선행 사건   be prone to ~하기 쉽다   afflict *v.* 괴롭히다, 피해를 입히나   gout *n.* 통풍   detonate *v.* 폭발하다
a slip of the tongue 실언   inadvertently *ad.* 무심코, 부주의로, 우연히   inevitability *n.* 필연   back and forth 왔다갔다
make the difference 영향이 있다, 차별을 두다

| 문장분석 |

■ The French philosopher Blaise Pascal remarks in his book "Pensees" that seemingly trivial occurrences [we might not even be aware of] affect geopolitical events. → that 이하는 목적절이며, that절 안에서 [ ]는 형용사절로 trivial occurrences를 수식한다.

UNIT 14 No pain, no gain on literary road
작가의 각오

|문학|

The cities and countryside have been devastated, the survivors forced to attack each other and steal what precious little food remains. Living just one day in this cold environment is such insufferable torture that a father and his young son set out on a road to find a new beginning. "The Road," a 2007 Pulitzer Prize-winning novel, describes sufferings of biblical proportions, similar to the Book of Revelation. A detailed description of starvation and pain in the depth of winter's darkness heightens the reader's sense of reality. The detail in the narration reflects the poverty that the book's author Cormac McCarthy suffered in his early years, living in a barn for eight years without enough money to even buy toothpaste. Since escaping such miserable hardship, McCarthy has refused to give lectures or interviews that would net him a huge payday. Instead, he has absorbed himself in his writing, without associating with other writers. His rare appearance on a television talk show was attributed to Oprah Winfrey's constant persuasion. On refusing interviews, he said, "I preferred to do things my way."

Kenji Maruyama is considered Japan's most notable reclusive writer. He left Tokyo after receiving the prestigious Akutagawa Prize at the age of 22. He has since lived in his hometown with his wife and devoted himself to writing. He decided against having children. He thought a child would interfere with the structured life he needs for writing. Maruyama continues to live with such determination and discipline, his head shaven as if he were a monk. "Creation is an effort of penetrating into the depth of a spirit in a solitary manner," he said. "As soon as I subordinate myself into literary circles and accommodate myself to popular tastes, my novels will be nothing but useless trash."

| 문장분석 |

■ On refusing interviews, he said, "I preferred to do things my way." → 여기서 on은 이유를 타나낸다. 즉 '인터뷰를 거부한 것에 대해'의 뜻이다. ⟨on -ing⟩(~하자마자) 구문으로 혼동하면 안 된다.

1. What is the passage mainly about?

(a) Authors who decide to live a monk-like existence to get material for their writing
(b) The relationship of Cormac McCarthy and Kenji Maruyama in relation to their backgrounds
(c) The damage the literary circle can do to your self-confidence
(d) Authors who reject the fame circuit that would bring wealth to concentrate instead on their writing

2. Which of the following is correct, according to the passage?

(a) McCarthy took the same journey along The Road to gain first-hand experience of it before writing.
(b) The refusal of McCarthy to give interviews or lectures was so that he didn't embarrass his parents.
(c) McCarthy's childhood provided him with the ability to write accurately about hardships.
(d) Maruyama and his wife were unable to have children, but decided not to pursue fertility treatment.

3. What can you infer from the passage?

(a) The authors write because it is their passion, rather than for money or fame.
(b) Both authors have been striving to win a literary prize to no avail so far.
(c) Maruyama and his family will follow the lifestyle of monks to prepare for his new novel.
(d) The style of McCarthy and Murayama is one which an increasing number of writers are following in order to gain a new sense of perspective.

4. Which of the following most closely resembles Murayama's philosophy in writing?

(a) You can get inspiration every day, even in doing mundane things.
(b) By going alone into the spirit and world of the novel, one can reach the destination of true creativity.
(c) Association with other authors will bring ideas and thoughts that were hitherto undiscovered.
(d) A disciplined life will bring joy in your life and pleasure in the world.

| **WORDS & PHRASES** |

the Book of Revelation 계시록, 묵시록　　starvation *n.* 기아　　barn *n.* 헛간　　escape *v.* 벗어나다　　net *v.* 순이익을 주다
absorb oneself in = devote oneself to ~에 헌신하다, 몰두하다　　reclusive *a.* 은둔하는　　structured *a.* 절제된
accommodate *v.* 영합하다　　fertility treatment 불임치료　　to no avail 헛되이, 보람 없이

UNIT 15 When the masses silent the wise
집단사고

| 심리 |

The failure of the Bay of Pigs invasion remains as a lasting blot on U.S. President John F. Kennedy's profile. Fresh into his presidency, Kennedy approved a Central Intelligence Agency-planned military campaign to sabotage and overthrow the new socialist government led by Fidel Castro. The CIA naively believed that it could disguise the invasion as an anti-Castro guerilla activity. But as soon as the 1,400-man invading force landed on the beaches of the Bay of Pigs, they were swamped and defeated by heavily armed Cuban combatants. The Kennedy administration immediately came under fire for unsophisticated military maneuvering at home and abroad during the tenuous and sensitive Cold War period.

Arthur Schlesinger, a historian who served as special assistant to Kennedy during the period, recalled later that although he opposed the plan as it could "fix a malevolent image of the new administration in the minds of millions," he held back his opinion lest he undermine the president's desire for a unanimous decision. Following the plan's failure, he lamented, "I can only explain my failure to do more than raise a few timid questions by reporting that one's impulse to blow the whistle on this nonsense was simply undone by the circumstances of the discussion."

Shouting "no" when everyone else is saying "yes" requires enormous courage and responsibility. Such hasty, uncritical reasoning toward faulty decision-making is termed as "groupthink," as identified by psychologist Irving Janis. In his 1972 book "Victims of Groupthink," Janis singled out the Vietnam War and Bay of Pigs invasion as particularly compelling examples of how a group of smart people can make collectively foolish decisions. Desire for unanimity and conformity, repulsion against outside opinions and panic in a state of emergency all can motivate a faulty "groupthink." Such circumstances leave no room for in-depth discussions and the voice of reason is easily silenced by the multitude's louder noise.

1. What is the best definition of "groupthink"?

(a) An idea that is made into a concrete choice because no other option is available
(b) A swift decision that is made by a group without thinking the issue through or debating its merits and demerits
(c) A thorough debate on a matter by a group of smart people
(d) A series of deliberations that reach no definite conclusion because there are too many people involved

2. Which of the following is incorrect, according to the passage?

(a) It is a difficult task to stand up to and question the authority of a group of people who are united.
(b) The disaster of groupthink concerning the Bay of Pigs motivated Kennedy to follow a different tactic.
(c) Cuba was ready for the supposedly covert American invasion and successfully repelled them.
(d) Arthur Schlesinger spoke his mind to Kennedy and his aides who ignored his warning unanimously.

3. What is the main topic of the passage?

(a) Another failure of the CIA
(b) The unknown role of historians in government
(c) An example of American expansionary techniques
(d) The importance of questioning groupthink decisions

4. What can you infer from the passage?

(a) Groupthink is still used in many governments today.
(b) The success of groupthink relies on intimidation and fear of standing alone from a group.
(c) Kennedy averted nuclear conflict by his smart thinking at the Bay of Pigs.
(d) Groupthink shows that foolish people can get into power.

| WORDS & PHRASES |

blot *n.* 얼룩, 오점   **profile** *n.* 평판, 이미지   **sabotage** *v.* 파괴하다, 방해하다   **disguise** *v.* 감추다, 꾸미다   **swamp** *v.* 압도하다, 침몰시키다   **tenuous** *a.* 미묘한   **malevolent** *a.* 사악한, 해악을 끼치는   **hold back** 감추다, 비밀로 하다   **blow the whistle on** ~을 밀고하다   **groupthink** *n.* 집단사고   **compelling** *a.* 설득력 있는   **conformity** *n.* 순응   **repulsion** *n.* 격퇴, 물리치기   **deliberation** *n.* 심사숙고, 궁리   **covert** *a.* 암암리에, 위장된

| 문장분석 |

■ Arthur Schlesinger, a historian who served as special assistant to Kennedy during the period, recalled later that although he opposed the plan as it could "fix a malevolent image of the new administration in the minds of millions," he held back his opinion lest he undermine the president's desire for a unanimous decision. ➡ Arthur Schlesinger 뒤에 동격이 나오고, that 이하 목적절에서 although 이하는 양보를 나타내는 부사절로 쓰였고, 주절에서는 he가 주어이다. 여기에서 lest ~ (should)는 '~하지 않도록'을 뜻하는 표현이다.

UNIT 16　Moving to the left
사회주의에 빠진 20/30대

| 문화 현상 |

Alex McIntyre, a 19-year-old college student in Brighton, England, became a socialist after he realized he could not afford to rent a flat near his school. He also needed to pay back a loan of £46,500 ($60,741) after graduation. His health was declining because he worked from midnight to 8 a.m. as a kitchen helper. When he found out most of his coworkers were college graduates, he wasn't confident he would find a decent job even after earning a college degree. He participated in protests calling for a minimum wage increase, went to an anti-capitalism workshop and joined a Marx reading club. That's how The New York Times described _____.

Western societies, especially Britain and the United States, are seeing a trend of millennials becoming enamored with socialism. Thirty years after the fall of the Berlin Wall and the Soviet Union's dissolution, we thought capitalism had triumphed over socialism and that the ideological debate was over. Yet socialism is back. A 2018 U.S. Gallup poll showed 51 percent of the respondents in age 18 to 29 viewed socialism positively. It was the first time more people felt more positive about socialism than about capitalism.

There are many reasons for this. Even as the U.S. economy is thriving with its lowest unemployment rate in a half century, young people's lives remain difficult. It seems social discontents over economic disparities have encouraged favorable views of socialism. This is most evident among young people, who are the first generation to be less well-off than their parents. It may also be due to their ignorance. In a survey in Australia, 58 percent of respondents said they prefer socialism, but only 26 percent knew who Lenin was, 34 percent knew Stalin and 21 percent knew Mao Zedong.

Alexandria Ocasio-Cortez, who, at 29, became the youngest person in U.S. history to be elected to Congress, is a self-proclaimed "democratic socialist." She advocates that the highest earners should be taxed by 70 percent and the state should provide jobs and welfare benefits to all. It is a sweet theory, but raising taxes on the rich alone cannot maintain a welfare system. Enhanced market control by the state will inevitably lead to regression of democracy and competition. The economy would lose vitality. Former British Prime Minister Margaret Thatcher said that when low-income families buy leases in public housing, they are a part of capitalism. When more young people expect that they won't be able to buy a home, capitalism loses its influence.

1. What is the passage mainly about?
   (a) The phenomenon of Alexandria Ocasio-Cortez.
   (b) The modern rise of socialism.
   (c) The discontent of young people with their parents' generation.
   (d) The lack of political awareness amongst the young.

2. Which of the following is correct?
   (a) The US economy is doing well right now.
   (b) Young people favor capitalism over socialism.
   (c) Ocasio-Cortex believes taxes should be higher for all.
   (d) This trend is happening all over the world.

3. According to the passage, why are young people favoring socialism?
   (a) They feel that society is leaving them behind and does not care about their welfare and prospects.
   (b) They are feeling the effects of the irresponsible attitude their parents' generation took towards the economy.
   (c) Although unemployment is dropping, their lives are not improving, and they are less well-off than their parents.
   (d) They have little idea of the history of socialism and why their parents' generation rejected it so strongly.

4. Which best completes the sentence?
   (a) how a young man became a socialist
   (b) what's wrong with young people today
   (c) what sent this man with prospects over the edge
   (d) what left Alex disappointed into politics

| WORDS & PHRASES |

kitchen helper *n.* 주방 보조   decent *a.* 괜찮은   anti-capitalism *n.* 반자본주의   dissolution *n.* 해체   discontent *n.* 불만
disparity *n.* 불평등   democratic socialist 민주주의적 사회주의자   welfare benefits 복지 혜택   regression *n.* 후퇴
vitality *n.* 활력   public housing 공공주택   over the edge 벼랑 끝으로

| 문장분석 |

■ **It seems** social discontents over economic disparities have encouraged favorable views of socialism. → It seems 다음에 목적절의 접속사 that이 생략되었고, that절 안의 주어는 social discontents (over economic disparities)이므로 주어 동사 수일치를 통해 have encouraged가 동사로 쓰였다.

UNIT 17 Is the law the problem?
법이 문제인가?

| 역사 |

Marcus Tullius Cicero compiled the universal principles of Roman law, the basis of Western modern law. In "De Legibus" (On the Laws), he wrote, "Salus populi suprema lex esto," which means "The health of the people should be the supreme law."

Roman law gained the spirit of justice from Cicero. The modern enlightenment and the philosophy of natural law are also his legacy. It means that the principle to believe that human nature is right is higher than the law made by humans and that the law needed to be just.

But Cicero himself did not practice his philosophy. While he is praised as a lawyer and philosopher who took Roman law to another level, he impeached Catilina through a means beyond the law. When he was accused four years later, he fled using a legal loophole.

As the wealth accumulated in Western society after the Renaissance, Roman law was highlighted again, mostly to define the property rights of the church, kings and aristocrats. The spirit of the law was to protect people's rights, but it was abused. When Spain established colonies in the 16th century, the infringement of native people's property rights became controversial. The church and the royal family argued that refusing free travel was against natural law and that property was based on civic community and society, which the native community did not establish, therefore they could not claim property rights.

After hundreds of years of trial and error, modern law was completed. It is still far from the definition of the natural law, but _____. While they may have different legal systems, consensus close to natural law is created through precedents and agreements in a civic society.

1. What's the passage mainly about?
   a) The abuse of natural law by those through history.
   b) The evolution of democratic law from Roman times.
   c) The agreement that must be the cornerstone of natural law.
   d) The creation of a civic society that follows the rules of law.

2. What can be said about Cicero?
   a) He didn't practice what he preached.
   b) He knew more about law than anyone else.
   c) He didn't trust human nature.
   d) He believed himself to be above the law.

3. Choose the false statement from the following.
   a) The church, kings, and aristocrats pretended that they were trying to help others.
   b) Cicero worked inside the law to bring about the downfall of Catilina.
   c) The native community in the Spanish colonies were accused of not being civic-minded.
   d) Spain abused the law to enable them to legally take property from others.

4. Which best completes the sentence best?
   a) modern law isn't made to benefit anyone but those who created it
   b) conflict resolution is something that doesn't come naturally to humans
   c) when countries embrace democracy there is no limit to what they can do
   d) the laws of the countries with a long history of democracy don't differ much

| WORDS & PHRASES |

supreme *a.* 최고의 enlightenment *n.* 계몽, 교화 natural law 자연법 legacy *n.* 유산 impeach *v.* 탄핵하다 loophole *n.* 허점, 흠결 accumulate *v.* 축적하다, 쌓다 aristocrat *n.* 귀족 infringement *n.* 법규 위반, 침해 controversial *a.* 논란이 되는, 논쟁적인 property rights 재산권 trial and error 시행착오 consensus 합의, 동의 precedent *n.* 판례, 선례 downfall *n.* 몰락

| 문장분석 |

■ It means that the principle to believe that human nature is right is higher than the law made by humans and that the law needed to be just. ➜목적절인 that절이 두 개이고, 첫 번째 that 안에서 the principle (to believe that human nature is right)가 주어이고 is higher than이라는 비교급을 활용하였다. 비교 대상은 the principle과 the law (made by humans)가 된다.

UNIT 18　Not a curse, but still weighty issue
비만 할증료

| 문학 (신화) |

　　In Greek mythology, you can find Erysichthon, who was cursed with hunger. Erysichthon cut down a tree in the sacred garden of the goddess Demeter and killed Demeter's beloved nymph. The enraged goddess cursed him with insatiable hunger so that he could never be full, no matter what he ate. He quickly ate everything he could find and even sold his beloved daughter as a slave in exchange for food. Finally, he realized that he could never satisfy his endless appetite, so he ate his own body starting with his limbs. He could free himself from the terrible curse only after he killed himself.

　　The pain from irresistible appetite is not limited to mythologies. It is a reality for the patients who suffer from Prader-Willi syndrome, which recalls the hunger Erysichthon was stricken with. It is a very rare disease caused by a genetic disorder or malfunction in a certain part of the brain. The patient suffers from insatiable appetite. Naturally, it causes obesity, cardiac disease, high blood pressure and other complications. As dietary control, which is essential to human life, is not easy for them, patients suffer from many complications.

　　While being overweight is not a curse or a disease, it is obviously a source of agony for many people. In the 2001 film, "Bridget Jones's Diary," Bridget agonizes over whether to wear a sexy panty or underwear that covers up her big paunch before she goes out for a date. Moviegoers might find her underwear dilemma charming, but being too overweight can be a big problem that can hurt one's health and pocketbook. It is reported that Air France imposed an "obesity premium" for overweight passengers started on April 1. In the United States, a similar controversy arose when ambulance companies began charging higher rates — up to two times the regular fare — for overweight patients in October of last year.

1. *What's the topic of the passage?*
    (a) An obesity tax
    (b) Bridget Jones' fans
    (c) Greedy people
    (d) Being overweight

2. *What is Prader-Willi syndrome?*
    (a) When someone never feels satisfied or full
    (b) A brain disorder that affects emotions
    (c) A glandular disease that determines weight
    (d) A heart problem from eating too much red meat

3. *Which of the following is incorrect, according to the passage?*
    (a) It's expensive to be overweight.
    (b) Erysichthon's appetite eventually killed him.
    (c) People who are overweight are unhappy.
    (d) Erysichthon gave up his daughter for food.

4. *What can you infer from the passage?*
    (a) Ambulance workers sustained injuries from lifting overweight people.
    (b) Air France is deliberately trying to discriminate against fat people.
    (c) Viewers said they would have preferred Bridget Jones to have been thinner.
    (d) The weight of Bridget Jones worked to comedic effect on the big screen.

| WORDS & PHRASES |

mythology *n.* 신화　　curse *v.* 저주하다　　sacred *a.* 신성한　　nymph *n.* 요정　　enraged *a.* 분노한　　irresistible *a.* 주체할 수 없는, 억누를 수 없는　　stricken with ~에 걸린　　disorder *n.* 질병　　insatiable *a.* 만족할 줄 모르는　　complication *n.* 병, 합병증　　agony *n.* 고뇌　　paunch *n.* 올챙이 배, 튀어나온 배　　pocketbook *n.* 지갑, 재력　　impose *v.* 부과하다

| 문장분석 |

■ It is a very rare disease caused by a genetic disorder or malfunction in a certain part of the brain. ➜ disease와 caused 사이에 which is가 생략된 형태로 '주격 관계대명사와 be동사'는 생략될 수 있다.

UNIT 19 Maternal instincts
부계 불확실성

"Paternity uncertainty" refers to men who are unsure they are the father of a child. The British journal "Proceedings" published fascinating research that revealed people feel closer to their mothers because they harbor some degree of paternity uncertainty. According to the research, more respondents said they were likely to run into a burning house and save a cousin on their mother's side. Researchers explained this as the psychological mechanism of altruistic behavior towards maternal relatives because of paternity uncertainty.

The Mosuo tribe living near Yunnan, China is a rare empire of women. Living in the heart of a mountain 2,700 meters above sea level, they have maintained a maternal society for nearly 1,500 years because of a unique tradition called "zou hun" or "walking marriage." When a girl reaches her thirteenth birthday, they hold a coming of age ceremony for her and she can select multiple sex partners. The men live with their mothers and visit the woman only when engaging in sexual relations. Naturally, nobody knows who the real father is. The women raise the children. Words like "father," "husband," or "getting married" do not exist. When necessary, the maternal uncle plays the minimal role of father. The woman is the head of the household. This custom formed as a result of paternity uncertainty.

Closer examination reveals that paternity uncertainty forms the root of family relations in a patriarchal society. As people living in agricultural societies started accumulating wealth, the patriarchal system was created as men wanted to bequeath their assets to their real son in a desire for self-preservation. In a paternal-centric system, married women become their husband's property; assets and the family line are passed to the son; and women are obligated to maintain their chastity. The research states that although paternity uncertainty may have established a paternal society, perhaps people have long yearned for maternal rights and "maternal assurance."

1. All of the following are incorrect except ...
(a) The 'walking marriage" takes place on top of a mountain 2,700 meters above sea level and then the tribe returns to a lower location.
(b) In paternal-centric societies women retain much freedom while being able to have many sexual partners.
(c) Men wanted to pass along their possessions, including their women, to their sons to prevent women from any wrongdoing.
(d) In dire situations when a male figure is needed for a child of the Mosuo tribe, the maternal uncle will stand in as father.

2. What can you infer about the research findings of the journal "Proceedings"?
(a) Most people do not know who their real fathers are.
(b) People naturally feel closer to their maternal relatives because there is often a degree of paternity uncertainty.
(c) Respondents were aware that they preferred their mother but could not explain the reason why.
(d) Respondents were more sympathetic to their maternal relatives because they had a bond from childhood.

3. Which of the following is true about the Mosuo tribe?
(a) The girls get married on their thirteenth birthdays to multiple men.
(b) Men only have contact with their partners to perform sexual intercourse.
(c) Men live with their mothers until they get married and then move into the family home of their wife.
(d) Nobody knows who the father of the child is so all men care for all the children of the tribe.

4. What's the passage mainly about?
(a) The last remaining matriarchal society in the world
(b) Differences between matriarchal and patriarchal societies
(c) The influence of paternity uncertainty in modern family relationships
(d) The increase in paternal-centric societies throughout the world

| WORDS & PHRASES |

uncertainty *n*. 불확실성   fascinating *a*. 놀라운   respondent *n*. 응답자   altruistic *a*. 이타주의적   rare *a*. 드문, 진기한
unique *a*. 독특한   engage in ~에 참여하다, 관여하다   patriarchal *a*. 가부장적인   bequeath A to B A를 B에게 유증하다
property *n*. 재산   be passed to ~에게 내려가다, 전수되다   be obligated to ~할 의무가 있다

| 문장분석 |

■ According to the research, more respondents said they were likely to run into a burning house and save a cousin on their mother's side. → said 뒤에 명사절을 만들어 주는 that이 생략이 된 형태이다. 원래 형태는 said that ~이다. 또한 동사가 and를 중심으로 병치가 되고 있다. 즉 likely to run의 run 부분과 save가 병치가 되고 있다.

UNIT 20 The return of Machiavelli?
마키아벨리

| 역사 |

The Basilica di Santa Maria del Fiore, which stands in the center of Florence, Italy, was the first octagonal stone tower built in the West. It is the symbol and the pride of Florence, the city of flowers. It is also the place where the young lovers of the novel and film "Between Calm and Passion" met to keep the promise they had made 10 years before. The basilica had a particular meaning for Niccolo Machiavelli (1469-1527), too. Nanami Shiono, author of "The Story of the Romans," wrote, "Reminded of the surging anger that Machiavelli might have directed toward himself while watching the basilica from a mountain cabin not far from Florence after he was inexplicably expelled from his government post, I made up my mind." It is said that Machiavelli, who hailed from Florence, lived his life while sharing highs and lows with the basilica. As he loved "his fatherland more than his soul," he must have thought, while writing his life's masterpiece "The Prince," that the duty of the monarch was to defend the basilica from outside invasion.

It is rare to find someone like Machiavelli, who continues to be the subject of controversy even 500 years after his death. He was considered a cold-hearted theorist who advocated an autocratic monarchy. He was also regarded as the incarnation of all sorts of trickery. One representative example is the fox and the lion metaphor. He emphasized that "the Prince should have both the power of the lion and the slyness of the fox." He also suggested that "the Prince should be able to conduct an evil act if necessary" and recommended that he make use of the weaknesses of the human psyche. At the time, Florence was only a small city-state that agonized over its own survival, as it was threatened by the powers around it. Therefore, Machiavelli thought that strong leadership was necessary to build a modern state. He did not intend to evaluate the autocratic monarchy. The Prince discusses the ways and means of winning and managing power in a monarchy.

1. What's the topic of the passage?
(a) Nanami Shiono
(b) The Prince
(c) The Basilica di Santa Maria del Fiore
(d) Machiavelli

2. Why was Machiavelli fired from his job in the government?
(a) It is unclear why he lost his job.
(b) He spent his time writing.
(c) He was not suited to a government post.
(d) He had plotted against the government.

3. Which of the following could be used to describe Machiavelli?
(a) Unemotional
(b) A daydreamer
(c) A communist
(d) Lithe

4. What can you infer about Machiavelli?
(a) He meant well, but usually came out of situations looking bad.
(b) He agonized over whether he was doing the right thing in life or not.
(c) He got close to the monarchy in Florence in order to exploit it.
(d) He felt that a true leader should be able to do both good and bad deeds to cement his power.

| WORDS & PHRASES |

octagonal *a.* 팔각형의   surging *a.* 들끓는   inexplicably *ad.* 이유 없이   autocratic monarchy 전제군주   incarnation *n.* 화신
trickery *n.* 권모술수   weakness *n.* 나약함   agonize *v.* 고민하다   evaluate *v.* 평가하다, 찬양하다   lithe *a.* 유연한

| 문장분석 |

■ It is rare to find someone like Machiavelli, who continues to be the subject of controversy even 500 years after his death.   ➔ 가주어와 진주어 구문으로 to ~ 이하가 진주어이다. who 이하는 Machiavelli를 받는다.

Culture & Arts

Part 2
문화·예술

UNIT 01 Mansplaining
잘난 척하는 남자들

| 문화 |

In time for International Women's Day, "mansplaining" has been discussed on social media. A combination of "man" and "explaining," the term was selected as Macquarie Dictionary's Word of the Year for 2014. But what does it mean? According to the Oxford English Dictionary, mansplain means, "(a man) explaining (something) to someone, typically a woman, in a manner regarded as condescending or patronizing." It basically means, "You wouldn't know much about this, as you are a woman, so let me explain it to you."

The word was first used in cultural columnist Rebecca Solnit's 2008 blog post published in the L.A. Times, "Men Explain Things to Me; Facts Didn't Get in Their Way." She wrote about her conversation with a man several years earlier. When she introduced herself as the author of a book on Eadweard Muybridge, a photographer known for "The Horse in Motion," the man cut her off and said, "And have you heard about the very important Muybridge book that came out this year?" Only after her friend told him several times, "That's her book," did he understand the situation. It turned out that he hadn't read the book, but had just read about it in a New York Times review.

While Solnit's story may be dramatic, it is not so rare. To a different degree, many women experience similar situations in their everyday lives. Solnit wrote, "Some men. Every woman knows what I mean." It doesn't remain an individual situation. It affects women's rights. Depending on where you stand, you see a different world. We don't even need to go into gender inequality. <u>How about men start looking at the world from a woman's position, and vice versa?</u>

| 문장분석 |

■ Only after her friend told him several times, "That's her book," did he understand the situation. ➡ only와 시간 표현이 함께 오면 문장에서 도치가 일어난다. 그러므로 only after ~ did he understand가 되는 것이다. 정상적인 어순이라면 He understood the situation only after her friend told him several times, "That's her book."이 된다.

1. *What's the main idea of the passage?*
    (a) Why it is important to understand 'mansplaining'.
    (b) When it is necessary to call out 'mansplaining'.
    (c) How the term 'mansplaining' came about.
    (d) The effect of 'mansplaining' on women.

2. *Which of the following is incorrect about Solnit's encounter?*
    (a) The man ignored the fact that she had written the book.
    (b) Another person had to convince him of her credentials.
    (c) The man was also an authority of Muybridge.
    (d) The man had not even read the book he was recommending.

3. *What can be inferred from the passage?*
    (a) Mansplaining has arisen from the fact that women know less about certain things than men.
    (b) Women also speak in such a way to other women, but it isn't focused on.
    (c) All men are guilty of mansplaining at some point in their lives.
    (d) Nearly every woman has been on the receiving end of mansplaining.

4. *What does the underlined mean?*
    (a) Both men and women need to start stepping into the shoes of the other.
    (b) If men realized how the world is for women, they might act differently.
    (c) Men and women do not understand each other very well at all.
    (d) The world benefits the men more than it does women.

| WORDS & PHRASES |

social media 소셜 미디어   typically *ad.* 전형적으로   cut off 자르다, 막다, 차단하다   gender inequality 성차별
credential *n.* 자격, 인증, 자질   authority *n.* 권위자   on the receiving end of 불쾌한 일로 영향을 받다
benefit *v.* 이득을 보다, 이익이 되다

UNIT 02 Battling it out on the football pitch
전쟁과 축구

| 스포츠 |

The War of the Triple Alliance which took place between 1864 and 1870 was instigated by the ambitious Paraguayan dictator Francisco Solano Lopez, who thought of himself as a Latin Napoleon. After Brazilian troops invaded Uruguay, Lopez decided to declare war on both Brazil and Argentina. While the well-prepared Paraguayan military fought well against the two nations early on, Lopez lacked diplomatic skill and managed to turn Uruguay against him. Instead of having to fight against just two nations, Paraguay had to face the Triple Alliance of Brazil, Argentina and Uruguay.

In 1869, Paraguay's capital of Asuncion fell into the hands of the Triple Alliance, and the war ended in 1870 when Lopez was shot to death as he fought alongside the remnants of his army on the northern frontier of Paraguay. The result of Lopez's reckless war was devastating. Between 90,000 and 100,000 soldiers and civilians were killed on the Alliance's side, and the population of Paraguay, which was 520,000 before the war, was reduced to 220,000 by its end. Most of Paraguay's male population was killed. Historians estimate that after the war only 28,000 males were left. As I watched the South American teams compete in the World Cup, I couldn't help thinking about the War of the Triple Alliance. The aggressive competition and nationalism that permeated the matches left me thinking that the footballers were re-enacting their historic conflicts on the pitch.

American anthropologist Richard Sipes said in 1973 that sports games like football could be used as an alternative to war, as they could reduce tensions between the main agents of aggressive conflicts. In the 1970s, the United States and China benefited from such thinking. The U.S. administration's strategy of "Ping Pong Diplomacy," which involved American table tennis players competing in China, led to a thaw in U.S.-China relations during the Cold War. We should remember the many lives lost to senseless conflicts the next time tensions rise, and consider the benefits of battling it out on the pitch.

1. What's the main topic of the passage?
   (a) The conflicts of South America
   (b) Senseless conflicts and ways to avert them
   (c) The use of sport in deciding who is dominant
   (d) Gender imbalances in South America

2. What can be inferred about Ping Pong Diplomacy?
   (a) It can reduce tensions between countries.
   (b) It can end a war quickly.
   (c) It is only used by the U.S.
   (d) It does not stop war, just slows it down.

3. What was the result of the War of the Triple Alliance for Paraguay, according to the passage?
   (a) It lost credibility in South America.
   (b) It lost most of its male population.
   (c) It lost its football stars.
   (d) It lost many relationships globally.

4. Choose the incorrect one from the following statements.
   (a) Lopez saw himself as the Napoleon of South America.
   (b) Paraguay enjoyed successes early on in the war.
   (c) Lopez was a skilled diplomat but this skill was not enough to save Paraguay.
   (d) Lopez's death marked the end of the war and the defeat of Paraguay.

| WORDS & PHRASES |

the Triple Alliance 삼국동맹   instigate v. 선동하다, 부추기다   invade v. 침략하다   declare war on ~에 선전포고 하다
early on 초기에   diplomatic a. 외교의   face v. 직면하다, 출동하다, 맞서다   fall into the hands of ~의 손에 넘어가다
remnant n. 잔여, 나머지   aggressive a. 공격적인   alternative n. 대안   senseless a. 어리석은, 몰상식한, 분별이 없는

| 문장분석 |

■ The War of the Triple Alliance which took place between 1864 and 1870 was instigated by the ambitious Paraguayan dictator Francisco Solano Lopez, who thought of himself as a Latin Napoleon.

➡ which가 주격 관계대명사로서 앞의 War를 수식하고 있다. 두 번째 줄의 who는 앞에 나와 있는 Solano Lopez를 수식하고 있으며 동사는 think 이다. think 동사는 이 문장에서 think of A as B의 형태로 사용되어 'A를 B로서 생각하다'라고 해석된다.

UNIT 03 An addiction we can't afford
명품 프렌들리

| 문화현상 |

Aboard the U.S.S. Missouri in Tokyo Bay on Sept. 2, 1945, Gen. Douglas MacArthur signed the Japanese Instrument of Surrender, which was first agreed upon by representatives from Japan on behalf of the Allied Powers. It was a historic scene that ended the Pacific War. But the attention of the people was focused on something else. "What is the brand name of General MacArthur's pen?" they asked. In response, the Parker Pen Company admitted that his writing instrument was theirs.

Years later, the image of Marilyn Monroe standing over a subway grate, holding down her dress as it blew up above her knees, made the film "The Seven Year Itch," more famous for this iconic image than for the plot itself. When the film came out, however, the attention of the women in the audience was focused on something else. They all wanted to know what brand of shoes Monroe was wearing. They were Ferragamos, and Monroe's sexy stand turned the company into a designer label.

In Japan, Burberry remains an icon of luxury. Trench coats made by the clothier became popular among civilians after World War I. At one stage, more than one half of the company's product line was sold in Japan, where Japanese housewives are said to have helped save Burberry from financial difficulty. Recently, The Wall Street Journal declared that Korea is, "emerging as one of the most 'luxury-friendly' places in the world." It reported that 46 percent of survey respondents said they spent more on luxury goods in the past year than before. It also said that those who said they felt guilty about how much they spent on luxury items totaled less than 5 percent.

| 문장분석 |

■ Years later, the image of Marilyn Monroe standing over a subway grate, holding down her dress as it blew up above her knees, made the film "The Seven Year Itch," more famous for this iconic image than for the plot itself.

➡ standing과 holding은 Marilyn Monroe를 수식하고 있으며 as는 접속사로서 when의 뜻으로 사용되었다. 주절의 동사는 made이며 5형식으로 사용되고 있고 목적어는 the film인데 The Seven Year Itch가 동격으로 수식하고 있다. 목적 보어는 그 뒤에 나와 있는 famous이다.

1. What's the idea of the passage?
   (a) Luxury goods used by celebrities
   (b) Luxury items in history
   (c) The use of luxury goods in Asia
   (d) The rise of luxury goods

2. What effect did Japanese housewives have on the Burberry company?
   (a) Sales to Japanese housewives saved the company from economic ruin.
   (b) Their fashion sense made others want to buy from the company again.
   (c) Burberry sales went down because the company had lost its luxury image.
   (d) They ensured Burberry was the number one luxury good company in Japan.

3. How do Koreans feel about luxury goods?
   (a) They feel that luxury goods make them more attractive.
   (b) They want luxury goods to appear better than their friends and neighbors.
   (c) They don't feel the need to buy designer products these days.
   (d) They are buying more and more of them without feeling guilty about the cost.

4. Choose the incorrect one from the following.
   (a) Ferragamo was considered a designer label even before Marilyn Monroe wore them.
   (b) Mac Arthur signed the Japanese Instrument of Surrender aboard a ship.
   (c) The Seven Year Itch was mostly forgotten as a movie, but remembered as a fashion moment.
   (d) Even today, Burberry is a sought-after designer brand in Japan.

| WORDS & PHRASES |

instrument *n.* 법률 문서   representative *n.* 대표   historic *a.* 역사적인   hold down 아래로 내리다   turn A into B A를 B로 변화시키다   financial difficulty 재정난   luxury-friendly *a.* 명품에 호의적인   guilty *n.* 죄책감   total *v.* 합계 ~이 되다   sought-after *a.* 수요가 있는, 인기가 있는

UNIT 04 Growing old peacefully
100세의 실종

| 사회문제 |

The Hunza Valley in the northern area of Pakistan is famous for mysteriously beautiful scenery that has been preserved since ancient times. The valley was the inspiration for Shangri-La in James Hilton's novel "Lost Horizon." It is also the backdrop for "Nausicaa of the Valley of the Wind," a manga series and animated feature by Hayao Miyazaki. The Hunza Valley is not only famous for its natural scenery, but also for residents who live very long lives. Along with Aphasia in the Russian Caucasus and Vilcabamba in Ecuador, the Hunza Valley is known as one of the three places for longevity in the world. Situated amid large mountain ranges, they all have access to clean air and fresh water.

Although it is an island, Okinawa in Japan is also a place of longevity. Among its 1.3 million inhabitants, there are more than 700 senior citizens over the age of 100. In Okinawa, they say that a septuagenarian is a child and an octogenarian is a youth. There is even an old saying: "If your ancestors call you to heaven when you reach 90, tell them to wait and that you'll think about it when you're 100." There was even an "Okinawa program" in which people could follow the lifestyle of the Okinawans. The island's residents consume 18 kinds of food, 78 percent of which are vegetables. Their staple foods are grain, vegetables and seaweed. When they do cook meat, it is not roasted or grilled.

Although all kinds of people have dreamt of eternal youth since ancient times, no one can stop the passage of time or prevent hair from turning gray. Thus, the only thing we can do is grow old gracefully. And we can take a cue from people who live in villages known for the longevity of its citizens — they all live lives of leisure. Instead of going against time, they advise us to get used to it. Probably for that reason, people use well-aging, not anti-aging, cosmetics these days.

1. *What is the passage's main topic?*
   (a) Why Asians live longer
   (b) Anti-aging ideas
   (c) Living a long and healthy life
   (d) How to be healthy inside and out

2. *According to the passage, which of the following is NOT something the Hunza Valley is famous for?*
   (a) The setting for a Mayazaki manga comic
   (b) The backdrop to an epic movie
   (c) Living a long time
   (d) Being the motivation for creating for Shangri-La

3. *Which best paraphrases the underlined Okinawan saying?*
   (a) Do not accept death early at the age of 90 — wait until you are at least 100.
   (b) If you die early, you lived a misguided life.
   (c) It is not your time to die unless you receive word from your ancestors.
   (d) A 90-year old person has lived a long and rewarding life.

4. *What is the best subject for the next paragraph?*
   (a) The advantages to never wearing make-up
   (b) The benefits of well-aging cosmetics
   (c) New technologies in make-up
   (d) Cosmetics cover up your skin's problems

| WORDS & PHRASES |

scenery *n.* 광경, 풍경, 배경   since ancient times 고대 이래   inspiration *n.* 영감   longevity *n.* 장수   (be) situated *a.* ~에 위치한
have access to ~에 접근이 가능하다   inhabitant *n.* 거주자   eternal *a.* 영원한   go against time 시간(자연의 흐름)을 거스르다

| 문장분석 |

■ The Hunza Valley is not only famous for its natural scenery, but also for residents who live very long lives.

➡ not only ~ but also 구문이 들어가 있다. 전치사 for가 병치되고 있음을 볼 수 있다. not only ~ but also 구문에서 only는 merely, simply, just, alone으로 대체될 수 있으며, also는 생략이 가능하다.

Good morning! We can discuss what has already been done at the end of the week

Аня

I'm too lazy for typing, I will say it, I hope you do not mind, so listen, you just won't believe it, it all started yesterday...

UNIT 05 The text generation
텍스트 세대

| 문화현상 |

"The English textbook is 10 years old, but high school English teachers ask to make it easier since students have a hard time studying it," said a man who works at a publisher of English reading materials. Everyone paid attention to his remarks at the meeting. High school students today must be better in English than before. Then why the difficulty understanding an older textbook?

He came up with an unexpected answer: "It is not about English proficiency. The ability to read and understand long texts has diminished, whether it is English or Korean." A Korean language teacher didn't seem surprised. "So many students don't understand the text on Korean tests. Some get things wrong because they don't understand the question, not the text. If the question asks to choose 'something farthest,' they don't know what 'farthest' means."

Another debater asked, "If kids have a hard time reading, why do YouTube videos have so many subtitles? It is painful to read subtitles with typos." The Korean language teacher summed it up. "They are the 'text generation,' communicating on KakaoTalk since childhood," he said. The text generation, who cannot read long sentences and understand abstract expressions, has been born.

Maryanne Wolf, an advocate for children and literacy around the world, discussed a surprising result in her book "Reader, Come Home." She referred to the "deep reading circuit," which allows readers to understand long and complicated sentences. It doesn't last long, and readers with a substantial intelligence level would return to beginner-level reading _____. How much immersed reading experience do you get?

60　Part 2 문화·예술

1. *What is the main idea of the passage?*
    (a) The difficulty of high school English tests in Korea.
    (b) The problematic nature of studying English comprehension.
    (c) The drop in reading skills among young people.
    (d) The joys of learning to read when young.

2. *What can be inferred from the passage?*
    (a) Young people focus on the things that are important in life rather than advancing their reading skills.
    (b) Reading long and advanced texts comes more naturally to young people than it does to adults.
    (c) Teenagers want to read long texts, but they are unable to because of their education.
    (d) The more one engages in immersion reading, the more skilled at reading one gets.

3. *According to the passage, which of the following is true?*
    (a) Young people have an easier time understanding English texts than Korean texts these days.
    (b) Students are struggling with the length and complexity of both Korean and English texts.
    (c) The addition of subtitles on online videos has helped the reading skills of many teenagers.
    (d) The new English text that students are using is much harder than that of a decade ago.

4. *Which best completes the sentence?*
    (a) if they lose the experience of immersion in reading
    (b) as a result of their heightened academic abilities
    (c) when they have no interest in doing any advanced reading
    (d) without enough reading instruction

| WORDS & PHRASES |

pay attention to 주의를 기울이다   proficiency *n.* 숙달, 능숙   sum up 요약하다

abstract *a.* 추상적인   immerse *v.* 몰두하다, 열중하다

| 문장분석 |

■ It doesn't last long, and readers with a substantial intelligence level <u>would return</u> to beginner-level reading if <u>they</u> lose the experience of immersion in reading. ➡ it이 지칭하는 것은 deep reading circuit이며, readers (with a substantial intelligence level) would return to beginner-level reading if they lose the experience of immersion in reading.에서 문장구성은 if 절은 조건문 현재이고, 주절은 가정법 과거로 쓰인 혼합가정법 문장이 된다..

UNIT 06 Memories of Mozart
모차르트

| 예술/음악 |

In Philippe Sollers' book "Mysterieux Mozart," the author writes, "Every modern person lives with Mozart's music." On cellular phones, elevators and in shopping malls, Mozart's music is there. Speaking extremely, people are born having listened to Mozart's "Die Zauberfloete" while inside their mothers' wombs, go on dates with "Le Nozze di Figaro" as their theme music and are buried to the sound of "Requiem." It is not an exaggeration that Mozart could buy all of Austria if he was alive today and able to receive copyright royalties on all his music.

However, when Mozart was alive he was always pressed for money. His worst year was 1789. A letter he wrote to his fellow Freemason Johann Michael Puchberg details his needy circumstances as follows. "If you, as a close friend and brother of mine, discard me, then my poor and sick wife, all my children and I will have no other way to survive. Sadly, I am a very unlucky person and whatever I do, it is hard to earn any money. I have passed out a reservation list of a recital for 14 days, but Swieten was the only one who wrote his name on the list."

Although he was poor when alive, today Mozart feeds practically all of Salzburg. In that city, almost everything from t-shirts, pencils, ashtrays, cigarette lighters to even beer and golf balls has a Mozart brand. The famous Kugel chocolate, with Mozart's face on the wrapping, has sold over one hundred million pieces overseas, which is 58 billion won ($59.5 million) worth. Salzburg has evaluated the brand value of Mozart at 5.4 billion euro or 6.4 trillion won. That is higher than the brand value of Phillips — 4.9 billion euro — and Volkswagen at 4.6 billion euro.

The brand power of Mozart comes from familiarity. It is different from Beethoven's music, which is strict, or Bach's devout music. Mozart's music is bright, easy, fun and sweet. It fits well with the brand awareness of modern people. Mozart is like a friend or lover that it is hard to separate from. Albert Einstein described Mozart as follows. "When someone dies, it means that person can no longer listen to Mozart's music."

1. *What does the phrase "Every modern person lives with Mozart's music" mean according to the passage?*
   (a) Everyone loves to listen to his music.
   (b) His music is used in every form of advertising, movie, or show.
   (c) There is at least one of his songs in every home.
   (d) His music has become very commonplace in today's society.

2. *Which of the following is true of Mozart according to the passage?*
   (a) He was unlucky in life, never able to do well financially.
   (b) Mozart was part of a secret society that protected him.
   (c) People love and have always loved his music.
   (d) He always had sold out recital performances.

3. *What would be the best title for this passage?*
   (a) How to survive as a struggling musician
   (b) The life and times of Mozart
   (c) The Mozart legacy
   (d) The love we have for Mozart

4. *What cannot be inferred from the passage?*
   (a) He had a difficult life even though he was very talented.
   (b) He didn't have a rich family to fall back on.
   (c) His music is possibly appreciated more now than it was while he lived.
   (d) Mozart's descendants have become wealthy from his music.

| WORDS & PHRASES |

womb *n.* 자궁　　exaggeration *n.* 과장　　be pressed for ~에 압박을 느끼다, 쪼들리다　　circumstance *n.* 환경　　discard *v.* 버리다
recital *n.* 독주회　　feed *v.* 먹여 살리다　　ashtray *n.* 재떨이　　evaluate *v.* 평가하다　　familiarity *n.* 친숙함　　awareness *n.* 인식

| 문장분석 |

■ Sadly, I am a very unlucky person and whatever I do, it is hard to earn any money.

➡ whatever는 복합관계대명사로서 '~하든지 상관없이'라고 해석하면 된다. 또한 명사절로, 혹은 부사절로 사용 가능한데 이 문장에서는 부사절로서 '내가 하는 것이 무엇이든지 상관없이'라고 해석하면 된다.

UNIT 07 Leaping tall buildings
수퍼맨

| 문화현상 |

The birth of Superman was in an American comic book in 1934. The immortal hero, who gave hope and courage to Americans during the Great Depression, later appeared in radio dramas, novels, animations, two television series and musicals. Christopher Reeve played Superman in four movies from 1978 to 1987. Later, a second television series was aired focusing on the childhood and romances of Superman. Superman was the origin of many "man" series, such as Batman, Spiderman and other superhero characters like Wonder Woman and the Incredible Hulk. Umberto Eco saw Superman as a "hero in whom viewers can embody a dream of authority in industrial society and easily regard themselves as the same person." In particular, the Superman of movies has become the icon of American heroes, leading the way to world peace as an American. Many people have criticized the image as tinged with racism and American superiority. Superman and supernatural heroes in general are nothing new. The journey of Superman is the same type of epic that Joseph Campbell studied in numerous myths, religions and legends. "Unusual birth, hardship during youth, coming across a helper, achieving miraculous power and return."

Then why is it that Americans are so enthusiastic about Superman? According to a recent analysis, it is said that to Americans, with only a short history of just over 200 years and no founding myth, Superman has become a mythical hero of the country. Superman is sent to Earth by his father, who is a leader of the planet Krypton's society, and saves the Earth. The plot centers on an alien from outer space who becomes an extraordinary hero. It overlaps with the self-image of American society which considers itself as the guardian of world peace. The new movie "Superman Returns" has opened. It emphasizes the messianic character of Superman and even uses the term "savior." The villains are intercepted by the power of Superman when trying to drown the American continent. Superman saves America, not the whole Earth. This "returned Superman" shows very well that Americans still long for super powers but must be justified and should even be holy. "Superman Returns" shows how badly Americans want to recover their moral compass despite its reaction to the Sept. 11 attacks. Director Bryan Singer himself also commented that Superman is "a figure who gives comfort and peace to a world in confusion after the Sept. 11 attacks." In short, it is a desire for a great power that is kind and self-sacrificing.

1. What can be inferred from the passage?

(a) Superman is akin to the growing of the American nation, from infancy to adulthood.
(b) Superman is the greatest super hero ever created.
(c) No other comic hero has had as much exposure or popularity as Superman has.
(d) Superman is the ultimate symbol for world peace and order.

2. What is the main theme of the passage?

(a) Superman and his history
(b) How all other super heroes are based on the theme of Superman
(c) The personal connection between Superman and New Yorkers
(d) Iconography of American society

3. Which of the following is correct according to the passage?

(a) Superman could have saved the towers on Sept. 11.
(b) The story of Superman resembles that of other mythic heroes.
(c) There are religions based on Superman as the savior.
(d) Joseph Campbell is still creating Superman comics.

4. What is the most likely topic of the next paragraph?

(a) Why Americans have or need to feel as though they have a great kindness and ability to sacrifice
(b) The next Superman movie that will be released
(c) How Superman maintains the moral compass of America
(d) Why America needs to use heroes like Superman to supplement their short history

| WORDS & PHRASES |

immortal *a.* 불사신의   the Great Depression 대공황   air *v.* 방송하다   embody *v.* 구체화하다   tinge with ~로 물들이다
superiority *n.* 우월성   hardship *n.* 고난   overlap with ~와 겹치다   messianic *a.* 메시아적인   long for ~을 갈구하다
justify *v.* 성낭화시키나   moral compass 도덕적 짓대   confusion *n.* 혼돈, 혼란   self-sacrificing *a.* 자기희생이
iconography *n.* 도해, 도상학

| 문장분석 |

■ Umberto Eco saw Superman as a "hero in whom viewers can embody a dream of authority in industrial society and easily regard themselves as the same person."

→ 목적격 관계대명사인 whom이 나와서 앞쪽의 hero를 수식하고 있다. 하지만 whom 앞에 쓰인 전치사 in으로 whom이 in whom의 형태로 관계부사가 되었다. 그러므로 뒷부분에는 완전한 문장이 나와야 한다. 그리고 and 뒤에는 regard A as B의 구문이 들어가 있다.

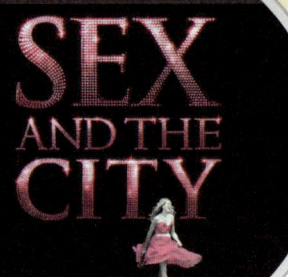

UNIT 08 Epicurean bean paste
칙릿

| 대중문화 |

"Chick-lit" is a genre of American and British popular fiction mainly targeting female readers in their 20s and 30s. Since the genre first emerged in Britain in the mid-90s, it has quickly spread across the United States, Asia and Eastern Europe. The heroes are usually young, urban female professionals in the media or fashion industry, who chat about sex, love and work. Topping bestseller lists around the world, chick-lit has established itself as a major genre, and movies and television series based on or influenced by the books have also been big hits: Witness the success of "Bridget Jones's Diary," "Sex and the City" and "Confessions of a Shopaholic." Chick-lit is not a mere literary subgenre but a major cultural phenomenon in the 21st century. "The Devil Wears Prada" and self-help books for single women are increasingly popular. Hollywood is taking note of "babebusters," blockbuster movie versions of chick-lit in which women rather than men are the leading characters.

While chick-lit books are often seen as being light reading with little substantial philosophy, feminists seem to approve of the genre. Chick-lit novels approach traditional feminine themes from a new angle, exploring the concept of "post-feminism." In short, it is given in the chick-lit novels that the heroines are modern women with completely different values on sex, consumption, desire and body image. Mallory Young wrote in "Chick Lit: the New Women's Fiction," that in a society where feminism has failed to take root, chick-lit satisfies both feminist liberty and post-feminist spending habits. On the other side of chick-lit are "lad-lit" novels focusing on the lives of contemporary young men. Nick Hornby, the leader in the genre, has written such popular novels as "High Fidelity" and "About a Boy," both of which have been made into films. If the girls in chick-lit unapologetically pursue worldly desires, the guys in lad-lit are often depicted as socially inept outsiders who are insensitive to trends and clumsy with relationships.

1. What is a typical chick-lit heroine like?
   (a) She is a feminist who cannot control her spending habits.
   (b) She is a young businesswoman whose main worries are sex, relationships and her career.
   (c) She is unhappy in her work and hopes to get a job in the media or fashion industries.
   (d) She is a mirror image of the men represented in lad-lit novels.
   (e) She doesn't care what anybody thinks of her.

2. What can you infer about lad-lit?
   (a) It is not very successful because men don't like to talk about their problems.
   (b) It appeals to women as much as to men.
   (c) It was created as a response to the success of chick-lit and to give a voice to men's issues.
   (d) The heroes of lad-lit are generally trying to get a girlfriend.
   (e) Men who read lad-lit have similar problems in their own lives.

3. Choose the correct statement from the following.
   (a) The main characters in chick-lit do not care about love and sex; they focus on their careers.
   (b) The genre, chick-lit, is still fighting to be taken seriously.
   (c) Chick-lit is at odds with feminism.
   (d) Chick-lit has its critics who believe it is demeaning to women.
   (e) The success of chick-lit movies has made Hollywood executives pay more attention to the genre.

4. Which is the best paraphrase of the underlined phrase?
   (a) Feminists demand that chick-lit books show the philosophy of being a woman.
   (b) Chick-lit is seen by feminists as a way to relax after a long day at work.
   (c) We might expect feminists to dismiss chick-lit, but instead they appear to endorse the genre.
   (d) Chick-lit is considered light reading because the issues involved are not important.
   (e) Feminists accept that not every woman wants to be a feminist.

| WORDS & PHRASES |

target *v.* 목표로 잡다, 겨냥하다   emerge *v.* 출현하다, 나타나다   top *v.* 선두에 서다, 정상을 차지하다   establish itself as ~로 정립하다
phenomenon *n.* 현상   leading *a.* 주도적인   contemporary *a.* 현대의   pursue *v.* 추구하다   worldly desire 세속적 욕망
clumsy *a.* 서투른

| 문장분석 |

■ Hollywood is taking note of "babebusters," blockbuster movie versions of chick-lit in which women rather than men are the leading characters.

→ 관계부사인 in which가 나왔다. 뒷부분에는 완전한 문장이 나와야 되는데 비교급 표현인 rather than이 수식을 하고 있다. A rather than B는 'B라기보다는 A이다'라고 해석하면 된다. 주어는 women이며 동사는 are이다.

UNIT 09 The essence of consumption
반소비

| 사회현상 |

Jean Baudrillard viewed ostentatiousness and waste as the distinguishing characteristics of modern consumption. He refers to the modern hero as "wasters." The standard of the modern hero is determined by the quantity of waste. People observe the grandiose lifestyles of rock, movie and sport stars with a sense of envy and surprise. Marcel Mauss wrote, "The waste of wealth provides the wasteful with special privileges and authority." According to Bourdieu, consumption serves as a demarcation of the social tiers. Buying luxury products is a voucher that shows one belongs in the upper class; the original meaning of "distinction," which connotes noble grace, refers to difference or discrimination. One can rise in social standing when adopting the spending style of the upper class; withstanding the economic strain, one buys luxury products or imitates the unbounded spending habits of the upper class. Woefully, there are <u>fake products</u>, as well. All this proves that the essence of consumption is ostentatiousness.

A dilemma forms: as society becomes wealthier, people pursue the upper class by mass consumption, which leads to the popularization of luxury products. When everybody carries around high-end products, the hierarchical distinctions of consumption become blurred, so the highest class chooses a strategy of "anti-consumption" or "underconsumption." Millionaires ride in compact cars or visit commonplace restaurants. Professor Park Chung-ja of Sangmyung University slams this in her book "Robinson Crusoe's Extravagance" writing, "If carrying a Luis Vuitton handbag is a sign of accession for middle class women in their 20s, class distinction for the owner of a jaebeol (large conglomerate) is eating sundubu (tofu soup), which costs 5,000 won ($5). This kind of underspending is an extreme display of power." Riesman makes a similar indictment: "The established upper class underspends to distinguish itself from the nouveau riche."

1. Which of the following is an example of underconsumption?

(a) A poor person working hard for a long time to save enough money to rent a large apartment
(b) A rich person staying in the penthouse suite of a luxury hotel while on vacation
(c) The president of a large international company wearing a cheap but well-made suit from a market
(d) A university student spending all of her money on clothes and accessories in order to attract a wealthy boyfriend

2. What's the main topic of the passage?

(a) A reversal in the ways that wealth is displayed by different classes of people
(b) The envy that society has for millionaires and those who show off their riches
(c) How to pass yourself off as a member of the nobility or the upper class
(d) The trend of modern society to follow consumption less aggressively than before

3. According to the passage, what happens when everybody purchases high-end products?

(a) An even higher product is looked for and the upper class spends even more money.
(b) The lines between social classes become less clear, causing the wealthy people to react and find a different way to distinguish themselves from the lower classes.
(c) Consumption continues increasing to an almost out of control level.
(d) Everybody lives together in a classless society, without distinction or hierarchy.

4. The underlined <u>fake products</u> means _____.

a) museum pieces
b) flagship
c) precious stone
d) knock-off

| WORDS & PHRASES |

ostentatiousness n. 과시   distinguishing a. 두드러지는   consumption n. 소비   refer to A as B A를 B로 간주하다
grandiose a. 웅장한, 숭고한   envy n. 질투   privilege n. 특권   demarcation n. 구분, 한계, 경계   voucher n. 상품권, 상환권
distinction n. 구별, 구분   connote v. 의미하다, 내포하다   withstand v. 저항하다, 견디다   unbounded a. 무절제한
spending habit 소비 습관   dilemma n. 난관   slam v. 혹평하다   conglomerate n. 대기업   indictment n. 기소, 고발
pass oneself off (as) (~로) 행세하다

| 문장분석 |

■ Buying luxury products is a voucher that shows one belongs in the upper class; the original meaning of "distinction," which connotes noble grace, refers to difference or discrimination.

➡ 동명사가 주어로 쓰일 때는 '~하는 것'이라고 해석하면 된다. 이 문장에서는 '사치품을 사는 것'이라고 해석하면 된다. 주격 관계대명사인 that과 which가 나와서 선행사인 a voucher와 the original meaning of distinction을 각각 수식하고 있다.

UNIT 10 When the internet splits
인터넷 분열화

| 문화현상 |

At the end of last month, Russia announced that it had successfully completed a test on the domestic network to replace the international internet. Russia had passed a bill to create its own exclusive internet network earlier last year. If the plan is implemented, Russians will be completely severed from the international internet that people around the world use, or can only access information approved by the Russian government. In other words, state's information control becomes easy.

Russia is not the only one. China has had the so-called "Great Firewall" policy of blocking foreign media as well as services like YouTube, Google search, Facebook, Instagram and Netflix. While nurturing its own internet industry, China blocks circulation of information that the government does not like. Countries like Iran and North Korea also use similar methods.

Experts are worried that these attempts limited to totalitarian countries in the past are developing into a global trend as "internet disintegration" or "Splinternet." While Western countries, as well as China and Russia, have mixed opinions on how to control the internet, the U.S.-inspired internet and the European-version are being created. The former focuses on national security and crime prevention while the latter is making new rules emphasizing privacy and personal protection.

When the internet has different standards and access levels depending on the country and region it is created, international finance and trade, as well as international information exchange, will be affected. One global internet that has been compared to an "ocean of information" that anyone can access in the past becomes _____.

1. What is the passage mainly about?

(a) The possible evolution of the internet from free global information to state-and region-controlled.
(b) The ongoing efforts of some countries to keep the internet free while others try to destroy it.
(c) The effect on the rest of world of Russia creating its own private internet for its citizens to use.
(d) The worrying trend of nations to try to control what their citizens do in their free time.

2. What do Russia and China hope to achieve?

(a) They think that a controlled internet will bring peace and reduced crime to their societies.
(b) Their governments wish to prevent their citizens from reading things that they do not approve of.
(c) They want to avoid being seen like other totalitarian countries by the West.
(d) They hope to increase their national security and prevent online terrorist attacks.

3. What can be inferred from the passage?

(a) Everyone wants to know exactly how China and Russia have managed to retain full control of their internet in this global society.
(b) The trend to control internet domestically is going to be used for nefarious deeds by wealthy and powerful corporations.
(c) Despite some nations ostensibly saying that the internet should not be controlled, they are doing the opposite behind the scenes.
(d) As soon as some nations have created their own private internet, every other nation must follow to remain equal.

4. Which best completes the sentence?

(a) a place that has no information at all
(b) an ocean that nobody can cross
(c) even bigger as more people start contributing to it
(d) a number of separate ponds of various sizes

| WORDS & PHRASES |

domestic *a.* 국내의, 가정의 bill *n.* 법안 exclusive *a.* 배타적인 sever *v.* 절단하다 nurture *v.* 양육하다, 육성하다
circulation *n.* 순환, 유포 totalitarian *a.* 전체주의의 nefarious *a.* 사악한 behind the scenes 비밀리의, 공개되지 않은

| 문장분석 |

■ While Western countries, as well as China and Russia, have mixed opinions on how to control the internet, the U.S.-inspired internet and the European-version are being created. The former focuses on national security and crime prevention while the latter is making new rules emphasizing privacy and personal protection. ➡
the former는 '전자'를 뜻하고, the latter는 '후자'를 뜻한다. 전자는 the U.S.-inspired internet을 의미하고, 후자는 the European-version을 의미한다.

UNIT 11 Barbie does Freud
키덜트

| 문화현상 |

Barbie was introduced to the world at the American International Toy Fair on March 9, 1959. Millions have been sold and her initial success was because she was an adult-bodied doll at a time when most children's dolls were based on infants. Mattel, the company which produced Barbie, made a fortune. Barbies have been made in many different nationalities and races and she has had many different careers. And Barbie got a family, too. She has friends and sisters. In fact it was Midge — a friend of Barbie — who was pregnant. Midge was designed to offset criticism that Barbie was just a sex symbol. Barbie has also sold related toy products, such as clothes and furniture. The world of Barbie is indeed limitless, including costumes, publications, stationery and electronic goods. Her career is an example of the present marketing trend, called "One Source Multi Use."

The recent changes in the traditional toy market are giving Barbie gray hair. Young teenagers no longer play with dolls so much. Girls nowadays want computer games, a video set, mobile phones, or an MP3 player, as soon as they enter a primary school. Thus the main market for traditional toys has narrowed to young children who have not yet gone to school. And many countries have a declining birth rate. Each of these aspects has worried traditional toy sellers. Toys "R" US, the world's leading toy retailer, has closed at least 70 stores in the United States. Some companies have been transformed into gift shops.

Sigmund Freud said, "What a distressing contrast there is between the radiant intelligence of the child and the feeble mentality of the average adult." Toy companies have taken this idea to heart. The biggest toy manufacturer in Japan, Bandai, has recognized that toys are not just for kids. The company has now developed dolls for retired people and adult females. Their new fashion doll, Sakurana, is an urban lady who has her own career. Bandai's marketing representative said Sakurana will appeal to an adult female's desire to identify with a successful looking doll and the company expects she will take care of her in the same way she takes care of herself. This is the newly emerging kidult (adults who are like kids) market. Even for Barbie, maniac adult collectors are the most important customers. Adults are grabbing the dolls kids have turned away from to extend their childhoods.

1. At what point do young girls start to want more adult products?
   (a) Before they even begin primary school
   (b) When they enter puberty and start to develop an interest in boys
   (c) The moment when they realize that Barbie is unrealistic
   (d) When they begin to attend primary school
   (e) When they see what their friends have

2. What's the passage mainly about?
   (a) Changes in the toy market involving type of products and target audience of each product
   (b) Attitudes to Barbie, ranging from affection to derision
   (c) A comparison of the marketing strategies of Toys "R" Us and Bandai
   (d) The emerging "One Source Multi Use" marketing trend
   (e) The place of Barbie in the contemporary world

3. What can you infer about Sakurana?
   (a) Sakurana is based on the traditional model of Barbie.
   (b) Sakurana has already become more popular than Barbie was in her early career.
   (c) Sakurana is aimed at retired people who want to feel young again.
   (d) She will appeal primarily to kidults who are looking for a way to return to their childhoods.

4. Which of the following is incorrect?
   (a) The Midge doll was an attempt to counteract the sexist criticism that Barbie was getting.
   (b) Barbie was a success because the proportions of her body were very attractive.
   (c) Toys "R" Us are being forced to close some locations due to the new face of the toy market.
   (d) The kidult market is an emerging but economically fruitful market.

| WORDS & PHRASES |

introduce *v.* 소개하다, 도입하다　　initial *a.* 초기의　　adult-bodied *a.* 성인을 닮은 몸을 가진　　nationality *n.* 국적　　offset *v.* 상쇄하다
stationery *n.* 문방구　　narrow to ~로 줄어들다, 협소해지다　　declining *a.* 감소하는　　career *n.* 직업, 경력　　maniac *a.* 마니아의
extend *v.* 확장하다, 연장하다　　rule out 배제하다

| 문장분석 |

■ Mattel, the company which produced Barbie, made a fortune.
➡ 주어를 the company가 동격으로 수식하고 있으며, 이것을 주격 관계대명사 which가 수식해주고 있다. 주절의 동사는 made이다.

UNIT 12 Is a college degree necessary?
대학 졸업장이 꼭 필요한가?

| 사회현상 |

"You should at least have a college degree to make a living." Korean parents have been saying this all the time, but I wonder if it is true. Every year, the number of unemployed college graduates is about 200,000. In reality, many young people cannot make a living even with a college degree. Also, it feels that the time has come when going to college is not a must, as creators and idol singers become role models.

A recent Wall Street Journal (WSJ) report gives me other ideas. The WSJ had an article titled "American Factories Demand White-Collar Education for Blue-Collar Work" on Dec. 9. The federal government data analysis shows that the percentage of college graduates among workers at manufacturing plants in the United States is the highest in history. The percentage went up from 29 percent in 2000 to 40.9 percent this year. In the same period, high school graduates fell from 53.9 percent to 43.1 percent. It is due to the facility automation and introduction of robots. From 2012 to 2018, total employment went down by 3 percent, but employment of workers who can handle complicated machines increased by 10 percent. Simple workers lost jobs, but college graduates trained for high-tech machines increased.

Korea's situation is not much different. Manufacturing companies replace human jobs with automated facilities and robots. While it seems that manufacturing jobs are decreasing, jobs dealing with high-tech machines are increasing. With the new industrial changes in the future, demands for an educated workforce will continue to grow for sure. Then, will it be the world where you need your college degree to make a living again? _____.

1. What's the passage mainly about?
    (a) Which college degrees are the best to guarantee employment.
    (b) Why college graduates are unable to find suitable work.
    (c) Why a college degree is necessary to find work.
    (d) How college graduates can improve their resumes.

2. Why do factories increasingly need college graduates as employees?
    (a) With automation, college graduates are the ones who are able to operate the high-tech machinery.
    (b) College graduates give the companies higher status and image.
    (c) If the employees have a college education, they are more responsible to be left alone to work.
    (d) There are many college degrees that teach how to be a better factory employee before starting work.

3. Which of the following statements is correct, according to the passage?
    (a) Simple human jobs in factories are not being replaced; rather, it is the office work that is disappearing.
    (b) The number of college graduates working in factories may well reach previous highs.
    (c) A college education is not necessary to work the complex factory machines.
    (d) Those with little education beyond high school are being laid off from factory work.

4. Which sentence best fits the blank?
    (a) Colleges and universities have already been preparing for an influx of freshman.
    (b) People with professional education for changes of industry will be competitive
    (c) Making a living is hard enough without having to worry about automation and robots.
    (d) Making sure you are employable is the top priority of college graduates.

| WORDS & PHRASES |

college degree 대학 학위 make a living 생계를 유지하다, 먹고 살다 white-collar 사무직 노동자 blue-collar 육체노동자
facility automation 설비 자동화 workforce n. 노동력 guarantee v. 보장하다 resume n. 이력서 lay off 해고하다

| 문장분석 |

■ Also, it feels that <u>the time</u> has come <u>when going to college is not a must</u>, as creators and idol singers become role models. ➡ that절 안을 살펴보면 the time when going to college is not a must has come의 문장인데, when 이하가 길어지면서 동사가 중간에 나온 구조이다. 그래서 when 이하를 the time에 붙여서 생각하고 "대학에 가지 않아도 되는 시절이 온 것"으로 해석하면 된다.

UNIT 13 Sheep astray
학위 효과와 학력 검증

| 사회현상 |

In any society, the higher a person's education, the more he or she gets paid. People who have spent more time and energy than others to get advanced degrees expect more compensation. For that correlation to continue, the premise that people with higher education work more competently must also prove to be true.

The problem occurs when one's educational background does not guarantee competence as an employee. If one has a high educational background but doesn't meet the expectations of him, his employer won't pay him more despite his background. In many fields, educational degrees are not considered important. In some jobs, employers do not even check the educational background of the new workers they hire.

Controversy arises when the difference in payment gets bigger along with the difference in educational backgrounds. In economics, this is called the sheepskin effect. According to that theory, a person with a higher degree gets paid a lot more even though he or she is not any more competent than other, less-educated people. If this persists, the demand for higher education will continue to increase.

Even though one's educational background does not guarantee competence, companies still look to applicants' educational backgrounds when they hire new workers. This is because there is no better way to differentiate applicants. When a job requires professional knowledge and skills, a higher educational background is required.

That is why, in the positions of researchers or professors, higher academic degrees and research papers are required. In these cases, academic degrees are not part of the sheepskin effect, but rather to show their competence. To be employed as a professor with a fabricated academic degree is the same as driving a car with a fake driver's license. It is more than a lie. It is a crime.

1. What's the passage mainly about?

(a) Valid reasons as to why some people get paid more than others for doing the same job
(b) The heinous crime of faking your academic degree
(c) The link, sometimes strong and sometimes weak, between educational background and competence
(d) The importance of gaining a higher education for all jobs

2. All of the following are correct except …

(a) Sometimes employers are not interested in job applicant's educational background.
(b) As people with higher education are given better jobs, the demand for higher education will increase.
(c) Educational background is often the only way for an employer to decide who will make the better employee.
(d) For researches and professors, academic degrees are not so important and many have fake degree certificates.

3. What is the sheepskin effect?

(a) When demand for higher education increases because demand for highly skilled workers has increased.
(b) When a competent employee gets paid more than an incompetent employee.
(c) When somebody gets paid a lot more money than an equally talented person simply because of their educational background.
(d) The demand for higher education is dependent on the demand for highly-educated people.

4. What can you infer about somebody with not much education?

(a) They wanted to enter the job market as soon as possible.
(b) They usually have a hard time getting a highly-paid job.
(c) They are likely to be more competent than somebody with higher education.
(d) They have the same skills and weaknesses as someone who has gone though higher education.

| WORDS & PHRASES |

compensation *n.* 보상   correlation *n.* 상관관계   premise *n.* 전제   competently *ad.* 유능하게, 적절하게   educational background 교육적 배경   guarantee *v.* 보장하다   expectation *n.* 기대   sheepskin *n.* 졸업증서   demand *n.* 요구, 수요   applicant *n.* 지원자   fabricated *a.* 조작된, 날조된   heinous *a.* 악랄한, 극악무도한

| 문장분석 |

■ For that correlation to continue, the premise that people with higher education work more competently must also prove to be true. ➡ to 부정사의 의미상의 주어를 이용한 문장이다. to 부정사는 원래 동사였으므로 주어가 있는데, 형태가 바뀌었으므로 주어의 형태도 바꾸어 주어야 한다. 주어의 모습은 for 목적격의 형태로 to 부정사의 주어로 사용한다. 해석을 주어와 동사의 해석으로 하면 된다. 또한 여기에서 that은 지시형용사로서 사용되고 있다. 주절의 주어인 the premise는 동격의 that으로 수식받고 있으며 주절의 동사는 must이다.

UNIT 14 Get fathers involved
'출산 보이콧'을 막으려면

| 사회현상 |

The National Health Insurance Service research shows that the insurance premiums were classified into five groups according to income levels. In the overall births, the portion of mothers in the two highest groups increased by 11.9 percent, from 39.2 percent in 2006 to 51.0 percent last year. In contrast, the mothers in the two lowest groups decreased by 11.3 percent, from 33.7 percent to 22.4 percent. The middle group remained almost the same, 26.2 percent to 26.0 percent. The age of birth inequality has come, as only the rich people get to have as many children as they want.

Another study released in June supports the claim. 44.6 percent of the women who decided to have no more children after having the first child say that childcare and educational expenses were the prime cause. Other reasons such as values (16.3 percent), work-life balance (15.4 percent) and unstable income and employment (10.1 percent) were far lower.

A low birth rate is not entirely a sign of despair. It has long been an established theory that when the national income grows, the overall birth rate of the country decreases. As women increasingly participate in society, _____.

However, in Norway and other Northern European countries, the birth rate has actually rebounded gently as the income continues to grow. Demographers call it "J curve." It does not appear in all European countries. In Southern Europe, such as Spain and Italy, fertility rate remains the same as income grows.

An Oxford University study shows that J curve does not appear in Southern Europe because of the clear distinction in gender roles, and men do not participate in housework and childcare. When husbands share housework, the birth rate increases as income goes up. Interestingly, in societies where wives are solely responsible for housework, more families decide to have only one child. Mothers feel burdened as fathers don't participate in childcare, and they refuse to have a second child.

1. What's the main idea of the passage?
   (a) Birth inequality looks set to stay.
   (b) A nation's wealth affects the raising of children.
   (c) Women need more encouragement to have babies.
   (d) A low birth rate can be turned around.

2. Which best completes the sentence?
   (a) the expense of raising a child and the cost for the mother surge
   (b) men find that they are being sidelined in areas they once took for granted
   (c) the government runs out of ways to encourage them to stay home
   (d) the birth rate increases along with more wealth

3. What does the underlined sentence mean?
   (a) Bearing children has become the sole preserve of the rich as birth inequality spreads.
   (b) Rich people have made sure that birth inequality helps them and hinders others.
   (c) It has been a long time coming, but we have finally reached a state of inequality of birth rights.
   (d) Birth inequality, where only the rich can afford to choose the size of their family, has arrived.

4. What can be inferred from the Oxford University study?
   (a) If countries want to increase their birth rate, men have to do their share of chores and help the mother.
   (b) Despite progress in gender equality, men are increasingly taking less interest in helping the mother of their children.
   (c) Gender roles have changed a lot, but society is beginning to react and stopping further change.
   (d) Societies that do not need any more children are the ones having them at a regular rate.

| WORDS & PHRASES |

insurance premium *n.* 보험료   classify *v.* 분류하다   income level 소득 분위   portion *n.* 일부, 부분   established *a.* 확립된
rebound *v.* 다시 튀어 오르다   demographer *n.* 인구 통계학자   fertility rate *n.* 출산율, 출생률   feel burdened *v.* 부담을 느끼다

| 문장분석 |

■ The age of birth inequality has come, <u>as</u> only the rich people get to have <u>as</u> many children <u>as</u> they want.   ➜ 주절은 The age of birth inequality has come, 첫 번째 as는 ~하면서 의 의미의 부사절 접속사, 두 번째 as ~ as는 비교급 as 구문이다.

UNIT 15 The right to be forgotten online
잊혀질 권리

| 인터넷 |

Just like a cavity or two, we all have a shameful part we want to hide. While it would have been nice to bury them in oblivion, it is no longer possible. The most shameful history can be exposed with a simple online search. That's what happened to Spanish attorney Mario Costeja González. In 1998, his foreclosed home was about to be auctioned, and unfortunately, the auction was published in a local newspaper. Soon, he paid his debt and saved his home, but the article on his foreclosure remained. When his name was searched online, the article on the auction and foreclosure came up. In May 2014, he sued Google and the local newspaper to remove the article, and the European Court of Justice ruled in favor of him. It was the first case in which "the right to be forgotten" was recognized.

After the ruling, Google received 210,000 requests for removals in 10 months. So many people wished some parts of their history forgotten. While the right to be forgotten was recognized recently, it is rapidly spreading in Europe, where the tradition of privacy is strong. On March 24, Google was fined 100,000 euros ($111,670) by the French authority as the right to be forgotten was not properly guaranteed. Recently, a software called Oblivion was developed to instantly remove all materials related to personal honor.

_____ When it is overly protected, the public's right to know may be infringed. In 2014, a British plastic surgeon wanted links on his medical procedures to be removed, and the request was accepted. However, the public outrage ended up canceling the delinking as they dealt with information on the doctor's poor surgery skills. The removal of such information helps prevent informed decisions for medical services. In the same year, Croatian pianist Dejan Lazic attempted a similar removal but failed. He asked the Washington Post to remove a negative review on his performance because the review was "defamatory, mean-spirited, opinionated, one-sided, offensive and simply irrelevant for the arts." But his request was not accepted because he was only trying to remove a fair review by a critic.

1. What is the main idea of the passage?

(a) The legal ramifications of removing everything related to a person from the internet.
(b) The fight in Europe for the right to have parts of one's history removed from Google searches.
(c) The arguments against removing information about people from the public domain.
(d) The fight over the relevance of certain information and whether the public needs to know it.

2. Which sentence best completes the blank?

(a) But the right to be forgotten is controversial.
(b) It doesn't matter how you look at it.
(c) Despite this, many have objections.
(d) Having said this, not everybody wants the same thing.

3. What can be said about both the British plastic surgeon and Dejan Lazic?

(a) They don't agree with what the other has done but they understand the other's situation.
(b) Both had had their lives negatively affected by the influence of a dissatisfied customer.
(c) Neither of them had actually done anything wrong, but the public thought that they had.
(d) They both sought to hide information that people might need to know to make a right decision.

4. What does the underlined mean?

(a) It's natural to have skeletons in your closet, but some have many more than others.
(b) Keeping things in your life secret is extra difficult if you happen to be famous.
(c) Nobody can truly understand what it is like to live in the public eye until you do.
(d) Everyone has something about themselves that they don't want others to know.

| WORDS & PHRASES |

cavity 충치   shameful 수치스러운   oblivion 망각   foreclose (문제 따위를) 처리하다, 끝맺다, 권리를 상실하게 하다   sue 고소하다, 소송을 제기하다   rule in favor of ~에 우호적으로 판결하다   infringe 위반하다   outrage 분노; 침해   opinionated 자기주장을 고집하는   one-sided 한쪽으로 치우친, 일방적인   ramification n. 파문, 영향   have skeletons in one's closet 감추고 싶은 비밀

| 문장분석 |

■ While the right to be forgotten was recognized recently, it is rapidly spreading in Europe, where the tradition of privacy is strong.

→ to be forgotten은 명사 the right을 수식하는 형용사구, where the tradition of privacy is strong은 장소관계부사의 계속적 용법으로 명사 Europe을 수식한다.

UNIT 16 No such thing as a free bribe
스폰서

| 예술/음악 |

German composer Richard Wagner is now lauded as a musical genius who took opera to new dramatic heights. But to his contemporary foes, he was a scandalous scrounger. Plagued for most of his life by debt, Wagner would often write to acquaintances asking for money. He was an expert in the field of solicited generosity. His friend Franz Liszt was also his father-in-law, and Wagner cunningly used his wife to encourage sympathy. "I would commit theft if I could make my wife happy," he said.

His financial dire straits, however, owed more to his expensive and fashionable taste rather than outright poverty. While working on his masterpiece, "The Ring of the Nibelung," Wagner spent a fortune to provide himself the perfect environment for composing, with specially tailored curtains to absorb noise and daylight, the best carpeting and silk clothes. He believed art could not be crafted with cheap liquor and a hard bed. Paul Johnson, in his book "Creators," called Wagner a hedonistic sponge.

Although not as extreme as Wagner, artists generally cannot seek excellence purely on their talent alone. Many famous artists were therefore born of the rich patronage for the arts. Joseph Haydn, known as the "Father of the Symphony," was given limitless freedom to experiment under the wings of Hungary's aristocratic Esterhazy family. Few composers enjoyed such luxury and support, as Haydn was free to choose any musician and rehearse as much as he wanted without financial worry. But there is always a price to pay. To satisfy his principal patron Prince Nikolaus, Haydn wrote 126 trios for the baryton, the prince's favorite string instrument, now rarely played.

Patronage sometimes can eat away at artistic freedom, which has led some artists to draw strict lines against sponsorship. The famous artistic couple Christo and Jeanne-Claude rely on bank loans to finance their mammoth environmental works, covering monumental landscapes and buildings with cloth, while rejecting sponsorships. To them, the only person authorized to offer a freebie is Santa Claus.

1. What's the main topic of the passage?
(a) A few famous European composers
(b) Why artists need to love so extravagantly
(c) The lifestyles and patronage of artists
(d) The best way to obtain artistic excellence

2. All of the following are incorrect according to the passage except …
(a) Haydn was born into a poor family and suffered extreme hardships until he met a member of a Hungarian aristocratic family.
(b) Wagner enjoyed a lavish lifestyle which he believed would enable him to produce the best work that he could.
(c) Christo and Jeanne-Claude produce their work with the help of sponsorship donations.
(d) Prince Nikolaus demanded that in return for his patronage symphonies be composed in his honor.

3. What does the underlined sentence refer to?
(a) Gifts will come to people at Christmastime with Santa Claus.
(b) If you believe in Santa Claus, you can enjoy the benefits that accompany this belief.
(c) Endorsement of the arts is an unimaginable luxury that most artists cannot dream of.
(d) Nobody should have the power to control artists with money in such a way as has been done in the past.

4. What can be inferred from the passage?
(a) Wagner would often take advantage of his wife's familial connections to bring in more money.
(b) Patronage is the worst thing that can ever happen to an artist.
(c) An artist must experience hardships to produce important works of art.
(d) Wagner was regarded as a child prodigy to his contemporaries.

| WORDS & PHRASES |

composer n. 작곡가   be lauded as ~로 칭송받다   genius n. 천재   foe n. 적   scandalous a. 소문이 나쁜
scrounger n. 구걸꾼   plague v. 괴롭히다   generosity n. 관대, 아량   father-in-law n. 장인   commit v. 저지르다
dire a. 비참한   strait n. (복수로) 곤란, 궁핍   outright a. 완전한, 철저한   poverty n. 빈곤   masterpiece n. 걸작, 명작
tailored a. 재단을 뜬   liquor n. 술   hedonistic a. 쾌락주의적인   seek v. 추구하다   limitless a. 무한의
under the wings of ~의 보호(후원)아래   financial worry 경제적 걱정   mammoth a. 거대한   monumental a. 대단히 큰

| 문장분석 |

■ Joseph Haydn, known as the "Father of the Symphony," was given limitless freedom to experiment under the wings of Hungary's aristocratic Esterhazy family. ➡ 주격 관계대명사인 who가 생략된 형태로 원래의 형태는 who was known as the "Father of the Symphony"이다. known은 뒤에 나오는 전치사에 따라서 그 의미가 바뀌는데, as는 '~으로 알려지다'(주어와 동격), for는 '~때문에 알려지다', to는 '~에게 알려지다', 그리고 by는 '~에 의해 판단되다'이므로 주의해서 해석한다.

UNIT 17 A different perspective on love
진정한 사랑에 대하여

| 사회현상 |

    The documentary "My Love, Don't Cross That River" garnered more than one million viewers, an unusual success for an independent film. The movie is about the love between an old couple who has lived together for 76 years. The seniors dress in matching traditional outfits, tease each other and make jokes like a young couple. When they part, the audience can't help crying. The film has become a landmark in movie history as it thrived among commercial blockbusters. It is loved not only by older audiences but also young Koreans, and has expanded the boundaries of documentaries.

    While some call it a senior version of a romantic fantasy about eternal love, this movie is not so simple. It is not about the greatness of love. It addresses the attitude of people in love. The 89-year-old wife constantly says, "Beautiful!" She is impressed by birds, wild plants and her 98-year-old husband wearing flowers behind his ear. She also likes to say, "Poor thing." She pities a stray dog and adopts him. When her husband passes away, she says with tears, "My poor love." She is not the kind of person to say cliched things like, "You left me all alone."

    The documentary shows that the essence of love is not the object of affection, but the attitude of the person in love. We often say that we can't find someone to love, or that someone is not worth loving. But true love comes from the mind-set to care and love one another, or from the attitude of love itself. And love begins from having sympathy and feelings for all the things in the world. Director Jin Mo-young said, "The couple has been caring for each other as a habit for 76 years. Their actions evoked love and affection from each other." In the movie, the husband says, "I've never complained about her food in my life. If something tastes good, I'd eat more. If I don't like something, I'd just eat little."

| 문장분석 |

■ It is loved not only by older audiences but also young Koreans, and has expanded the boundaries of documentaries. ➡ 주어는 It(이 영화)이고 동사는 is loved와 has expanded 두 개로 하나는 수동으로, 다른 하나는 능동으로 쓰였다. 더불어 앞부분에 not only A but also B의 상관접속사로 쓰인 구조이며, 이런 경우 양자를 긍정하지만 초점은 뒷부분에 가 있는 경우가 많다.

1. *Why does the audience have such feeling for the old couple in the movie?*
    (a) They spend all their time together every day, so death ultimately tears them apart.
    (b) Their relationship and behavior mirrors that of a young couple despite their advanced age.
    (c) They have such affection for each other's faults that we cannot help but admire them.
    (d) The audience can be reminded of simpler times when relationships were less complicated.

2. *According to the passage, why should modern people looking for love watch this film?*
    (a) They might find someone who also enjoyed this film and have something in common.
    (b) They will appreciate more those old people who try to give them romantic advice.
    (c) They may think twice about falling for and marrying the first person they come across.
    (d) They can learn that love is all about attitude as opposed to finding the perfect person of their dreams.

3. *Why is the success of the movie strange?*
    (a) Nobody likes to see films about love stories anymore; they want blockbusters.
    (b) Documentaries only appeal to a small community of people.
    (c) Stories about old people have never been successful in Korea before.
    (d) Independent films are usually not as popular as this one.

4. *Which sentence is the best to finish the passage?*
    (a) This considerate gesture is the very qualification of love.
    (b) He really didn't like her food very much.
    (c) She knew how he was, and loved him even the more for it.
    (d) It is this kind of gesture that led to his death.

| WORDS & PHRASES |

garner *v.* 모으다   independent film 독립영화   landmark *n.* 획기적인 사건   eternal *a.* 영원한   impressed *a.* 감명 받은, 감동 받은
thrive *v.* 번창하다, 번영하다   pity *v.* 불쌍히 여기다   cliched *a.* 상투적인   mind-set *n.* 사고방식   sympathy *n.* 동정, 연민
evoke *v.* 불러일으키다, 유발하다   affection *n.* 애정   complain *v.* 불평을 하다

UNIT 18 Playing with blocks
테트리스

| 오락 |

In 1988 when the video game universe was divided between Bubbles and Super Mario, a completely new engaging game consisting merely of blocks made a bombshell debut. The beloved Tetris is a video game puzzle in which seven types of blocks can be manipulated. The multicolored blocks rain down the screen to form horizontal rows, disappearing when they are complete. The completion of one playing field is celebrated with a dance by a wooden soldier to "Kalinka," a lively Russian folk tune.

The Russian touch is a tribute to the game's creator, Alexey Pajitov, a mathematician with an ardent love of puzzles, who designed and programmed the game while working for the Soviet Academy of Science in 1985. His idea originated from the square-block pentomino puzzle that dates back to ancient Roman times. Pentominoes are rectangular tiled boxes with 12 differing shapes of five unit squares. The Russian mathematician simplified the game to allow four unit squares making up seven blocks and named the video game after the Greek prefix tetra, meaning four.

The game, created to pass idle hours caused a sensation outside the Soviet Union when bundled on an IBM PC. In less than two years the game became a software blockbuster not only in Europe, but also in the United States and Japan. But its creator, stuck in communist USSR, was unable to cash in on the tremendous success. Because the former Soviet Union did little to claim copyrights, the game was locked in legal battles up to 1993. Moscow finally stepped in, but all Pajitov got in return was an IBM desktop. One can understand if Pajitov still bears some sore feelings, considering the game sold more than 70 million copies through the Nintendo Gameboy console alone.

What's surprising is that the game continues to draw players through evolutionary variations. Tetris is still a sought-after function in today's electronic devices like PDAs and mobile phones. The online game has hooked more than 500,000 in Korea alone. Tetris has also spawned an army of knockoffs and lookalikes. The game's biggest appeal lies in its simplicity. Anybody can take to it. One computer game magazine called the game "deceptively simple and insidiously addictive." Studies showed that the game boosts brain activity, helping to prevent memory loss and ease the ill effects of stress.

1. What's the main idea of the passage?
    (a) The career of Alexey Pajitov
    (b) The trial of Nintendo vs. Pajitov
    (c) Online game addiction started by Tetris
    (d) The history of Tetris

2. Tetris made "a bombshell debut". What does this mean?
    (a) Its success was quick and wide-reaching and this surprised people.
    (b) Players immediately became addicted to the block game.
    (c) Tetris attracted players from all over the world.
    (d) The debut was marred by the theft of Tetris from Pajitov by Nintendo.

3. What can you infer from the passage?
    (a) Pajitov still hasn't received the money or accolades that he rightly deserves.
    (b) Tetris had its day in the 1990s and these days it is considered more of a novelty.
    (c) Tetris is the only online block game of its kind in the world.
    (d) The Russian government profited from releasing Tetris to Nintendo.

4. All of the following are true, according to the passage, except …
    (a) Tetris became a hit in Europe, U.S.A., Asia and Africa.
    (b) When you complete a line, the line disappears.
    (c) The wooden soldier that dances is a tribute to the creator of Tetris.
    (d) The name 'Tetris' originated from a Greek word meaning four.

| WORDS & PHRASES |

universe *n.* 세계, 시장, 분야   engaging *a.* 매력적인   bombshell *n.* (폭발적인) 센세이션을 일으키는 것   manipulate *v.* 조작하다
completion *n.* 완성   wooden *a.* 나무로 된   folk tune 민요곡   touch *n.* 노래   ardent *a.* 열렬한   square-block *a.* 네모난 블록의
date back to ~까지 거슬러 올라가다   ancient Roman times 고대 로마시대   rectangular *n.* 직사각형   make up 구성하다
sensation *n.* 돌풍   tremendous *a.* 어마어마한   legal battle 법정 싸움   evolutionary *a.* 발달의, 발전의   variation *n.* 변화(물)
knockoff *n.* 복제품   lie in ~로 인한 것이다   deceptively *ad.* 믿지 못할 정도로   insidiously *ad.* 방심할 수 없게

| 문장분석 |

■ What's surprising is that the game continues to draw players through evolutionary variations.
→ What이 명사절을 이끌어 주고 있으며 이 명사절이 주절의 주어로 사용되고 있다. 또한 be동사 뒤에서 that 명사절이 나올시에는 '다음과 같다'로 해석하면 된다.

UNIT 19 Cyberbullying is a crime
악플은 범죄다

| 문화현상 |

In the overflowing news, it is regrettable that the shock of celebrity deaths is fading, but I pray for Choi Jin-ri and Koo Ha-ra, the late K-pop stars and actresses. Not so long after their deaths, even Pengsoo, a popular penguin character, began getting malicious comments. It is ludicrous that many trolls write malicious comments without giving much thought. In a recent survey by Incruit and Do It Survey 5 percent of 3,162 respondents said they had an experience of posting malicious comments. Fifty-five percent said it was out of anger, 16 percent blamed jealousy and envy. Fifteen percent said they wrote it to relieve stress, and 9 percent said it was a simple prank. So, one in five trolls hid behind anonymity to relieve stress or have fun. I don't expect some noble vision or _____ or Nobel Prize in Literature-worthy expressions from internet trolls, but this is too much.

Malicious online comments have become a global concern. Former U.S. President Barack Obama expressed opposition to the "cancel culture" of cyberbullying last month. Prince William of the United Kingdom has been leading an anti-cyberbullying campaign since 2017. Reporters Without Borders published a report on the harm of malicious comments. One third of the reporters in Sweden and Finland said they suffered from malicious comments. British journalist Jon Ronson wrote a book titled "So You've Been Publicly Shamed" about cases of online scandals and their devastating consequences. He interviewed not only the victims but the internet trolls as well. Most trolls said they did not know how things would blow up or that they wouldn't have done the same if they had known the victims in person. But cyberbullying is a crime that can take away a person's life.

1. What is the main idea of the passage?
    (a) The reasons why people engage in cyberbullying.
    (b) The methods that authorities use to catch cyber bullies.
    (c) The negative and serious effects of cyberbullying.
    (d) The causes of an increase in cyberbullying.

2. What did Jon Ronson's book tell us?
    (a) There would be more trolls if people knew those publicly shamed personally.
    (b) People troll because they can hide behind the anonymity of a keyboard.
    (c) Trolls know exactly the damage they are causing and revel in it.
    (d) Cyberbullying is annoying but doesn't have any significant consequences.

3. What cannot be inferred from the passage?
    (a) Jon Ronson wrote the book because he had firsthand experience of being publicly shamed.
    (b) Some people actually get enjoyment out of participating in cyberbullying of others.
    (c) When people engage in cyberbullying, they can use the anonymity of Internet.
    (d) There are so many celebrity deaths that we are becoming immune to the shock of them.

4. Which of the following best completes the sentence?
    (a) praise from those who agree with me
    (b) funding to fight the situation
    (c) delight in causing anguish to others
    (d) thorough analysis on the fate of the nation

| WORDS & PHRASES |

(internet) troll 악플러 malicious (online) comment 악플 ludicrous a. 어처구니없는, 터무니없는 prank n. 장난 anonymity n. 익명성 devastating a. 황폐화하는 take away 빼앗다 cyberbullying n. 사이버 폭력, 온라인 왕따 immune a. 면역된

| 문장분석 |

■ Most trolls said they did not know how things would blow up or that they wouldn't have done the same if they had known the victims in person. ➡ said 뒤에 that이 생략된 형태로 Most trolls said ① (that) hey did not know how things would blow up or ② that they wouldn't have done the same if they had known the victims in person. 즉 목적절이 두 개가 온 경우이다. ②의 경우에는 가정법 과거완료 문장으로 '과거 사실의 반대'를 뜻한다. '그들이 개인적으로 몰랐기 때문에 악플을 달았다'는 것을 '만약 알았더라면 악플을 달지 않았을 텐데'의 문장으로 나타낸 것이다.

UNIT 20 A war over religious rights
부르카 전쟁 인권과 종교의 자유

| 사회현상 |

Muslim women wear burqas, niqabs, hijabs or chador according to Islamic law. Among them, the burqa is the enveloping outer garment that covers the entire body with a veil over the eyes. Europe is having a debate over the ban of burqas and other face-covering attire in public.

France was the first country to ban the religious dress. Since the French Revolution in 1789, France has adhered to the strict principle of Laicite, or the separation of religion and the state. It is unconstitutional to display religious symbols in public places in France. The Christian cross is not to be displayed at schools and in public places.

But when France banned the wearing of religious clothing such as hijabs and burqas, Muslims fiercely protested that it is tantamount to religious persecution. In 2009, then-president of France Sarkozy said on burqas, "In our country, we cannot accept that women be prisoners behind a screen, cut off from all social life, deprived of all identity." A ban on burqas was legislated and enforced on April 1, 2011. A woman who violates the law and wears the full-body covering is subject to a fine of 150 euros ($204), and the law also penalizes anyone who forces women to wear the covering with a fine of up to 30,000 euros ($40,800).

Some Muslims brought the case to the European Court, arguing that the ban was discriminatory, but the EU Court upheld the French law earlier in July on grounds that the covering violates the human rights of women. After the decision, EU members like Germany and Austria, as well as non-EU member Switzerland, are preparing similar bans.

These countries receive many wealthy Muslim visitors who spend a fortune on tourism and shopping. Therefore, opponents argue that the law, which affects some 100 Muslims wearing burqas in the country, could hurt tourism income. But supporters claim that the human rights and dignity of women must be protected. They say people should be able to talk face to face, not through a veil.

1. What is the passage mainly about?
   (a) The link between religious identity and persecution.
   (b) Muslim women's fight against French persecution.
   (c) The French oppression of Muslims at all costs.
   (d) The bans against Muslim face coverings in France.

2. Why did the European Court uphold the law in France?
   (a) They felt that the most important point was the protection of women.
   (b) They wanted to take a stand against Islam's practices.
   (c) They believed that women were being oppressed more and more.
   (d) They heard the calls of women to allow them freedom from the veil.

3. What can be inferred from the passage?
   (a) The fear of Islam as a result of this ban is rising in those countries that want to have the ban.
   (b) Members of the Muslim world are planning to boycott countries that implement the ban.
   (c) There is a growing backlash against the ban that will win out in the end.
   (d) The bans that have been applied in France will continue to be implemented throughout Europe.

4. Which of the following is an argument mentioned in the passage that opponents of the ban use?
   (a) This ban is discrimination against some religions and not others that should be targeted.
   (b) France needs to realize that for some religion and state do mix.
   (c) Muslim tourists bring in a lot of money, so the economy will be affected with the drop in visits.
   (d) Women like wearing the veil or other coverings as it gives them a sense of religious identity.

| WORDS & PHRASES |

envelop *v.* 감싸다, 뒤덮다　　garment *n.* 의복, 옷　　debate *n.* 논쟁, 항의　　ban *n.* 금지　　attire *n.* 복장　　adhere *v.* 따르다
unconstitutional *a.* 헌법에 위배되는　　tantamount *a.* ~와 마찬가지의　　persecution *n.* 박해, 학대　　deprive *v.* 빼앗다, 박탈하다
legislate *v.* 법률을 제정하다　　penalize *v.* 처벌하다　　discriminatory *a.* 차별적인　　dignity *n.* 존엄성　　stoke *v.* 물을 때다, 더 부추기다
conservative *a.* 보수적인　　swing *n.* 흔들기, 변화, 변동

| 문장분석 |

■ Some Muslims brought the case to the European Court, arguing that the ban was discriminatory, but the EU Court upheld the French law earlier in July on grounds that the covering violates the human rights of women. ➡ arguing 이하는 분사구문으로 some muslims의 주장이다. but 이하에 문장이 이어지고 on grounds that은 조건을 나타내는 부사절이 뒤에 붙은 형태이다.

Science & Technology

Part 3
과학·기술

UNIT 01 Racing toward a dissonant drive
전기자동차와 소음

| 기술 |

The distinctive feature of Harley-Davidson motorcycles is the roaring sound of their engines. It is said that the cycle of engine combustion is built to match the rhythm of human heartbeats. As soon as the engine is started, it roars up like the heartbeat of a young person in love. Harley-Davidson Motor Company had even applied for a patent for its peculiar engine sound in 1944 but gave up on the idea because of the complicated paperwork. The engine sounds of Harley-Davidson bikes imported to Korea are adjusted to below 80 decibels in accordance with the local law. Therefore, it is not possible to hear the original roaring sound of its engine unless it's readjusted. The manufacturers of Ferrari, one of the most prominent sports-car makers, pay close attention to the roar of an engine as they put their final touches to a vehicle. Sports-car lovers will recognize a Ferrari's deep metallic growl and sigh in envy of the Italian marvel. Race fans will tell you that one of the most exciting moments of Formula One is hearing the deafening vroom of the racing cars.

Of course, engine noise has a practical purpose beyond its romantic charms. Luxury sedans are so quiet that drivers often make the mistake of thinking the engine is off and turning the key again. Jaguar has gotten around this problem by having the car play a tenor C note when the engine is turned on. Electric vehicles, on the other hand, do not make any noise because they run on electric motors, not combustion engines. They do not even make noise from the friction between the car wheels and the surface of the road when traveling at speeds less than 40 kilometers per hour (25 miles per hour). This lack of noise has proved dangerous to both car passengers and pedestrians. Other cars and people crossing the street cannot hear the car coming, so the chances of an accident occurring increases greatly. A quiet engine, once the source of pride of luxury carmakers, has become a safety problem. The United States Congress is even considering forcing carmakers to create vehicles with a minimum noise level.

1. What is the main idea of the passage?
    (a) Sound is important to those who deal with motor vehicles.
    (b) Harley Davidson motorcycles are too loud.
    (c) Congress doesn't want to have electric cars on the road.
    (d) Electric engines are better than regular combustion engines.

2. Which of the following is not untrue according to the passage?
    (a) Jaguar cars play a song in C major when the car starts.
    (b) Electric cars running below 40 kilometers per hour are nearly completely silent.
    (c) Electric car drivers cause many accidents due to their driving.
    (d) The best Formula One cars are made by Ferrari.

3. What is the most likely topic for the next paragraph?
    (a) The practical purposes for making cars sound loud.
    (b) How the car makers deal with cars that make either too much or too little noise.
    (c) The quietest cars in production today.
    (d) The new laws being proposed in Congress for electric cars.

4. What can be inferred from the passage?
    (a) Electric cars are plagued with safety issues.
    (b) There is a great importance to the level or lack of sound vehicles make.
    (c) Car makers will start making cars that are quieter.
    (d) Electric cars are not better than regular motor cars.

| WORDS & PHRASES |

distinctive *a.* 독특한   feature *n.* 특징   roaring *a.* 으르렁거리는, 굉음의   patent *n.* 특허   complicated *a.* 복잡한
paperwork *n.* 서류 작업   in accordance with ~에 맞춰   growl *n.* 으르렁거리는 소리   deafening *a.* 귀청이 터질 듯한
vroom *n.* (차량이 주행 중 내는 소리인) 부웅   combustion *n.* 연소   friction *n.* 마찰   pedestrian *n.* 보행자
plague with 성가시게 하다, 괴롭히다

| 문장분석 |

■ <u>As soon as</u> the engine is started, it roars up like the heartbeat of a young person in love.

➡ as soon as는 '~하자마자'라는 뜻의 구문으로 뒤에는 절이 온다. 비슷한 뜻을 지니는 the moment, the instant 등으로 대체할 수 있다.

UNIT 02 Written in wrinkles
보톡스

| 의학 |

These days, Botox is the most well-known substance of the anti wrinkle wonder drugs. Botox is a brand name but it often refers to all types of botulinum toxin cosmetic treatments. The problem is that this medicine is only effective for three to six months. A person who receives this treatment also has trouble making facial expressions. But Botox costs less than surgery and people now want to appear younger than they actually are, so the product is popular. Botox has a strong brand power, second only to Viagra.

The last syllable in Botox comes from toxin. Botulinum toxin occurs naturally and causes food poisoning. Dioxin is known to be the most poisonous artificial substance, and botulinum toxin is 100 times more toxic. Ordinary poisoning causes diarrhea and stomach ache but a botulinum poisoned patient has a 50 percent risk of death. In short, it is the most dangerous kind of poison.

Late last month, the U.S. Food and Drug Administration expressed concerns over the safety of Botox after the U.S. civic group Public Citizen announced that 16 people have died from side effects of Botox treatments since the drug was commercialized. The Korea Food and Drug Administration also took measures because it believes that an overdose of Botox might cause difficulty in breathing and swallowing food, thus putting lives at risk. The key word here is overdose. Most of the victims were cerebral palsy patients and they tried to temporarily ease muscle spasms with Botox. The injection they took was 28 times more than the amount used for cosmetic treatments.

Wrinkles on the face are traces of the person's life. In the late 20s, wrinkles start to form around people's eyes, then on the forehead in the late 30s and then around the mouth in the late 40s. There is a saying that wrinkles around the eyes form when a person starts to understand reason and rationality, on the forehead when he understands life and around the mouth when he grasps the laws of nature.

| 문장분석 |

■ A person who receives this treatment also has trouble making facial expressions. ➡ 〈have trouble -ing〉 구문은 '~하는 데 어려움을 겪다'는 뜻을 지닌다. 이때 trouble은 무관사 명사로 사용되어야 한다. 바로 뒤에 -ing 대신 명사가 나오는 경우 with를 사용해 〈have trouble with something〉 형태로 표현된다. 형태가 비슷하지만 뜻이 다른 경우로 〈have the trouble to do something〉이란 구문이 있는데, 이것은 '~하기 위해 무척 노력하다'는 뜻이 된다.

1. What's the passage mainly about?

(a) Growing old gracefully
(b) Why Botox has become so popular
(c) The toxicity and danger of Botox
(d) The future ban of Botox

2. Which of the following is true?

(a) Those who have died from Botox have mostly done so because they overdosed on the poison.
(b) The Korea Food and Drug Administration is unconcerned about Botox and supports its use for cosmetic procedures.
(c) Botulinum toxin is not very dangerous if you handle it with care.
(d) Deaths have occurred because the toxin is being sold to people who are not aware of the danger.

3. What can you infer about people who have Botox injected for cosmetic reasons?

(a) They don't have any of the side effects that are commonly reported.
(b) They put up with the sickness that comes with it, in order to look younger.
(c) They might delay wrinkles, but even more will appear when the toxin wears off.
(d) Their primary aim is to make wrinkles disappear and avoid the onset of aging.

4. What are the effects of injecting Botox?

(a) In most cases death, but usually just severe stomach cramps
(b) Wrinkles disappear temporarily as facial muscles cease moving
(c) The permanent removal of all facial wrinkles
(d) Sickness until the toxin wears off

| WORDS & PHRASES |

substance *n.* 물질   refer to ~을 지칭하다   toxin *n.* 독소   cosmetic *a.* 미용의, 화장의   facial expression 표정
food poisoning *n.* 식중독   artificial *a.* 인공적인   toxic *a.* 독성의, 유독한   diarrhea *n.* 설사   express concerns over ~에 대해 우려를 표명하다   civic group 시민단체   side effect 부작용   take measures 조치를 취하다   overdose *n.* 과다복용   swallow *v.* 삼키다
put ~ at risk ~을 위험에 처하게 하다   victim *n.* 희생자   cerebral palsy *n.* 뇌성마비   temporarily *ad.* 일시적으로   ease *v.* 완화시키다   muscle spasm *n.* 근육 경련   wrinkle *n.* 주름   trace *n.* 흔적, 자취   saying *n.* 속담   rationality *n.* 합리성, 순리성

UNIT 03 Always polite, never complaining
밤새 일하고도 불평 없는 그 직원

| 환경 |

The model employee is "always polite, they always upsell, they never take a vacation, they never show up late," Andrew Puzder, the former chief executive of CKE Restaurants, the parent company of Hardee's, said in an interview with a business magazine in 2017. The employee is the kiosk in front of the store. He also revealed his plan to try an "employee-free operation."

Humans are replaced by machines in places not exclusive to stores like Hardee's. In production lines, industrial robots _____. According to the World Robotics Report by the International Federation of Robotics, 381,000 industrial robots were sold worldwide in 2017. China's Changying Precision Technology replaced the workload of about 650 employees with 60 robots. As a result, its annual production of 8,000 units increased to 21,000 units, and the defect rate fell from 25 percent to 5 percent. If one robot can replace 10 workers, as in Changying's case, 3.81 million jobs would be replaced by robots around the world last year alone.

What choices do Korean chief executives have as they struggle with low labor flexibility? There are 631 robots per 10,000 workers in Korea, the highest in the world. It is over eight times the global average. Germany's ratio is 309 to 10,000 workers and Japan's is 303 to 10,000 workers. Chief executives cannot help but love robot workers that do not complain about overtime, do not go on a strike and do not take breaks.

About 100 years ago, the second industrial revolution was a revolution of mass production. Mass production was made possible by mass employment, so it was valid to hire tens of thousands of employees at once, train them and put them in the production line. The manufacturing industry that created jobs on a large scale is sending signals that it cannot hire as many people as in the past in the age of automation and industrial transformation. That is why the fourth industrial revolution is desperately needed as it will create new jobs for creative, young people.

1. Which quality does a perfect employee have, according to the passage?

a) They arrive at work when they feel like it.
b) They are honest with customers about their feelings.
c) They never try to convince customers to spend more.
d) They never take time off for themselves.

2. Which of the following is true, according to the passage?

a) Robots are a hit in Germany but in Japan and Korea humans remain the dominant employee.
b) Korean companies employ more robots per worker than other countries.
c) Korean chief executives do not tend to favor using robots.
d) Japan and Germany are much more reliant on robots than Korea.

3. Which best completes the sentence?

a) have been attempting to make sure they maintain the jobs they have now
b) have been trying to downplay how good they are
c) have been driving large-scale labor forces out of factories
d) have been showing what they can truly do in terms of creativity

4. Why is the fourth industrial revolution needed so badly?

a) There are not enough jobs for young people.
b) Innovation has slowed to a halt.
c) Creativity is seriously lacking in young people.
d) As young people desperately look for jobs, they will do anything.

| WORDS & PHRASES |

upsell *v.* (상품을) 사게 하다 production line 생산(제조)라인 defect rate 불량률 mass production 대량생산 automation *n.* 자동화 downplay *v.* 무시하다, 경시하다 take time off 휴가를 내다

| 문장분석 |

■ The manufacturing industry [that created jobs on a large scale] is sending signals that it cannot hire as many people as in the past in the age of automation and industrial transformation.

→ signal과 that은 동격 관계이다. it은 manufacturing industry를 가리킨다.

UNIT 04 Flying pandemics
조류 인플루엔자

| 의학 |

On March 11, 1918, a military hospital at Camp Funston in Fort Riley, Kansas, United States, treated an unusual number of patients who had similar symptoms all day long. "I feel a cold coming on," they said, by the hundreds. Some of them were shipped off to Europe a few days later to fight in the First World War. By May of that year, the flu had infiltrated the French army trenches. In June of that year, more than 8 million were brought down by influenza in Spain. It was referred to as "Spanish flu" by the French, while the Spanish called it the "French flu." Influenza was far more dreaded than the shells the French army rained down upon the German enemy. By the time that summer came to a close, influenza had overtaken the German barracks; at least 400,000 German civilians lost their lives. The disaster spread to Asia and swept India and China. The 1918 influenza pandemic, which continued into the following year, caused genuine panic throughout the world. The more surprising fact is that the memory of the calamity left people's minds so quickly. Many people know about the black plague, one of the deadliest pandemics during the Medieval Period, but have no idea about the "spanish flu," which broke out in the 20th Century. A major culprit behind the calamity was not a cold virus, but an influenza virus. In 2005, Dr. Jeffrey Taubenberger of the U.S. Armed Forces Institute of Pathology succeeded in mapping the genetic material of the virus that caused the devastating 1918 influenza pandemic. He is well-known for his work extracting samples of the 1918 virus from preserved tissue and sequencing its genome. He conducted an in-depth study on the corpse of an aboriginal man who died the same year as the flu pandemic and was buried in the ice for 80 years in Alaska. He initially believed a pig was the major culprit behind the epidemic; people and animals can be infected with the pig influenza virus. However, after a close investigation of virus genes extracted from corpses, he reached the conclusion that the disease originated from birds.

1. *What cannot be inferred from the passage?*
   (a) The influenza virus was a devastating disease.
   (b) Scientists eventually developed a cure for the influenza outbreak of 1918.
   (c) It would not have been as severe if there had not been a war.
   (d) It was shadowed by the tragedy of the war, while the black plague was not.

2. *What is the most likely reason the French called it the "Spanish Flu"?*
   (a) The Spanish actually gave them the flu.
   (b) A Spanish doctor was the first one to identify it.
   (c) They wanted to blame another country for the introduction of the flu to their people.
   (d) They were told it was called that by the German army.

3. *How did Dr. Taubenberger believe the flu was spread to humans?*
   (a) He believed it was transmitted from birds to people.
   (b) He believed it was a cold that new troops brought with them.
   (c) He thought it was contracted by being too close to pigs.
   (d) He felt it was spread through long times spent in trenches during the war.

4. *Which of the following is true according to the passage?*
   (a) The virus was first unlocked after it melted out of 80 year old ice.
   (b) The first person to die from the disease was an aboriginal man in Alaska.
   (c) The Spanish gave the flu to the French.
   (d) The genome of the 1918 influenza was discovered to be different from what was originally thought.

| WORDS & PHRASES |

symptom n. 증상   infiltrate v. 침입하다, 침투하다   trench n. 참호   A is referred to as B A가 B로 지칭되다   dreaded a. 두려운, 무서운   shell n. 포탄   overtake v. 불시에 닥치다   barrack n. 막사, 병영   civilian n. 민간인   disaster n. 재난   sweep v. 휩쓸다   pandemic n. 전국[전 세계]적인 유행병   calamity n. 재난, 재해, 참화   medieval a. 중세의   culprit n. 범인, 장본인   pathology n. 병리, 병리학   devastating a. 황폐시키는, 파괴적인   extract v. 추출하다   sequence v. 순서대로 나열하다   corpse n. 시체   aboriginal a. 원주민의   initially ad. 처음에는   originate v. 유래하다

| 문장분석 |

■ However, after a close investigation of virus genes extracted from corpses, he <u>reached the conclusion</u> that the disease originated from birds. ➡ 〈reach the conclusion that ~〉이라는 표현은 '결론에 도달하다'는 뜻으로, 동격의 that을 사용해 that 이하라는 내용의 결론에 도달한다는 뜻이 된다. '결론에 도달하다'는 다른 표현으로는 arrive at the conclusion, come to the conclusion 등이 있다.

UNIT 05 Unfounded fears
공포의 문화

| 의학 |

On April 19, 1982, U.S. TV network NBC aired a one-hour program called "DPT: Vaccine Roulette." It was a story about how the whooping cough vaccine could cause death by critically damaging the nerves. It was a story about a child with serious disabilities and his worried parents. The story was later featured on NBC's Today Show and in newspapers for several weeks. This led to mass phone calls to pediatricians nationwide, all because parents wanted to know whether their children would soon die.

In response, the U.S. Food and Drug Administration distributed a detailed 45-page document assuring that rarely does vaccination lead to death or complications. However, most news organizations ran condensed stories. In weeks, victims organized to systematically fundraise and publicize their anger. By 1984, unable to bear the demonstrations, testimonies of victims at public hearings and multiple litigations, two of the three DPT vaccine producers closed down. Years later, research on 1 million children showed that the threats had been hugely exaggerated.

The damage? In the U.S., parents feared having their children vaccinated, leading to an increase in the number of children with whooping cough. Be it vaccines or not, why are people so afraid even if the real threats are minimal? The American sociologist Barry Glassner, who wrote "The Culture of Fear" points to the "merchants of fear." Media organizations promote fear to increase sales of their newspapers and TV shows' ratings, politicians create a sense of fear to win votes and shift people's attention from really important issues and all kinds of groups use fear for their own marketing. All are responsible.

| 문장분석 |

■ This <u>led to</u> mass phone calls to pediatricians nationwide, all because parents wanted to know whether their children would soon die.

→ 〈A lead to B〉 구문은 'A라는 원인으로 B라는 결과가 발생하다'는 뜻으로 인과관계를 설명할 때 자주 사용되는 표현이다. 비슷한 표현으로는 앞서 나왔던 contribute to를 포함해 result in, cause, give rise to, translate to 등이 있다.

1. *What does the last portion of the passage on "Culture of Fear" mean?*
    (a) People grow up in a society that is based on fear of the unknown.
    (b) TV shows use fear to increase their ratings.
    (c) People are afraid of dangerous vaccines that are not tested properly.
    (d) Ordinary people are told partial truths to scare them into doing what others want them to do.

2. *What can be inferred from the passage?*
    (a) Vaccines are inherently dangerous and shouldn't be used.
    (b) Fear is an effective motivator to make people act in a certain way.
    (c) Fear is the best motivator to get things done.
    (d) Whooping cough is a very serious illness that cannot be prevented.

3. *Which of the following is true according to the passage?*
    (a) DPT was actually not as dangerous as it was made out to be.
    (b) The U.S. government uses fear to control its people.
    (c) DPT was one of the most dangerous vaccines made in recent history.
    (d) People only fear threats that are truly dangerous.

4. *What would be the best title for this passage?*
    (a) DPT; death by vaccine
    (b) Fear as a tool
    (c) Manipulation of mass media
    (d) The Whooping cough

| WORDS & PHRASES |

air *v.* 방영하다   whooping cough *n.* 백일해   nerve *n.* 신경   feature *v.* 특집 기사를 싣다   pediatrician *n.* 소아과 의사
assure *v.* 안심시키다   complication *n.* 합병증   condensed *a.* 압축된, 축약된   threat *n.* 위협   exaggerate *v.* 과장하다
minimal *a.* 최소의   sociologist *n.* 사회학자   promote *v.* 장려하다

UNIT 06 Insane or sane?
정신분석 요법의 귀환

| 의학 |

Is it possible for psychologists to accurately diagnose psychological disorders? In 1970, an unknown American psychologist conducted an experiment to test this. David Rosenhan and seven of his friends went to psychiatric hospitals all over the United States and falsely declared, "I hear voices and thudding sounds." By just stating this symptom, they were all hospitalized in psychiatric hospitals. But upon being hospitalized, they acted just like normal people, expressing their satisfaction and dissatisfaction with daily life to their doctors. By the end of the experiment, seven had been diagnosed with schizophrenia and one with bipolar disorder. After an average of 19 days, they were released from hospitals on the grounds that they had temporarily recovered upon treatment. Based on the experiment, Rosenhan published the paper, "On Being Sane in Insane Places." In reaction to the negative publicity, one psychiatric hospital challenged Rosenhan to send more pseudo-patients over the next three months, claiming "We will find them." Three months later, the hospital proudly declared that they had found 41 such patients. In reality, not a single pseudo-patient had been sent.

But perhaps this style of treatment could make a comeback. The Internet version of the New York Times on Oct. 1 carried the story "Psychoanalytic Therapy Wins Backing." According to the article, "Intensive psychoanalytic therapy, the 'talking cure' rooted in the ideas of Freud, has all but disappeared in the age of drug treatments and managed care. But now researchers are reporting that the therapy can be effective against some chronic mental problems, including anxiety and borderline personality disorder." The study, based on more than 1,000 patients, was published in the Journal of the American Medical Association on Friday. The return of psychoanalytic therapy must be proof that it has developed more effective methods after Rosenhan's attack. Just like civilization, doesn't science develop by taking up challenges?

1. What can you infer from the experiment of David Rosenhan?
    (a) The psychiatric hospitals were proven right in their diagnosis of their pseudo-patients.
    (b) Schizophrenia and bipolar disorder are much more common than previously thought.
    (c) Psychiatric hospitals and their employees have little knowledge of what they are doing and make mistakes.
    (d) Psychiatric doctors need to be more careful in prescribing drugs to patients.

2. How many pseudo-patients did the psychiatric hospital find?
    (a) None because the patients all acted like normal sane people.
    (b) All of them because it was obvious who was faking it.
    (c) None because there was none to find.
    (d) All 41 were found and sent away from the hospital.

3. According to the passage, what caused the disappearance of intensive psychoanalytic therapy?
    (a) The ideas of Freud brought about a change and intensive psychoanalytic therapy was used less and less.
    (b) The experiment of Rosenhan directly brought about a lack of trust in psychiatric hospital treatment.
    (c) People became more able to self-diagnose and self-treat themselves.
    (d) The global reliance on drug treatments rather than talking about what is wrong.

4. What's the main topic of the passage?
    (a) The attack on intensive analytic therapy in the 1970s and its subsequent evolution into a more reliable mode of therapy
    (b) The motivation of Rosenhan and his colleagues in conducting this experiment
    (c) The never-ending rivalry between psychoanalytic therapy and simple drug treatment
    (d) The change in civilization from the 1970s to present day and our attempts to keep up with it

---

| WORDS & PHRASES |

psychologist *n.* 심리학자   diagnose *v.* 진단하다   disorder *n.* 질병   conduct *v.* 실시하다   experiment *n.* 실험
psychiatric *a.* 정신 의학의, 정신 질환의   thud *v.* 쿵하고 떨어지다   symptom *n.* 증상   schizophrenia *n.* 정신분열증
bipolar disorder *n.* 조울증   on the grounds that ~라는 근거로   temporarily *ad.* 일시적으로   sane *a.* 제정신인   insane *a.* 미친
publicity *n.* 공개, 공표, 널리 알려짐   pseudo-patient *n.* 가짜 환자   backing *n.* 지원, 지지   intensive *a.* 집중적인, 철저한
all but 거의   chronic *a.* 만성의   borderline personality disorder *n.* 경계선 인격장애   take up a challenge 도전을 받아들이다

| 문장분석 |

■ But <u>upon</u> being hospitalized, they acted just like normal people, expressing their satisfaction and dissatisfaction with daily life to their doctors.

→ 〈on/upon -ing〉 구문은 '~하자마자'의 뜻을 지닌다. 앞서 나온 as soon as와 같은 의미를 지니지만, on -ing는 구로 사용되고 as soon as 뒤에는 절이 오는 차이가 있다.

UNIT 07 The silent organ
간

| 의학 |

According to a dissertation in Science magazine, Volume 276, the mythical story about Prometheus is an indication that ancient Greeks knew that the liver can regenerate itself if surgically removed or injured. The liver is one of a few internal human organs capable of natural regeneration of lost tissue; as little as 15 percent of a liver can regenerate into a whole liver in two or three months. Even if the liver is impaired by excessive drinking or hepatitis, it can be easily restored after a short period of abstinence or if the hepatitis is completely cured.

The adult human liver normally weighs 1.5 kilograms, the largest internal organ in the human body, and has several important functions. As we know, the liver is the key organ that metabolizes or breaks down alcohol; counteracting such poisoning is a process that transforms potentially toxic substances into less dangerous forms and pushes them out of the body. However, the liver is not able to detoxify or remove all toxic substances. It passes through hazardous substances that it is unable to neutralize.

The role of the liver in the human body can be compared to a link player in football. The food is broken down into the basic components, dextrose, amino acids and fatty acids, and gets fully digested in the body. All of these substances enter the liver via the portal vein and are changed into each required cell. When we do not have enough food to satisfy our appetite, the old axiom "Not the slightest hint to the liver," is actually scientifically accurate.

Unlike other organs that send distress signals directly, it serves well without uttering any complaints — until 70 percent of the liver is impaired, living up to its nickname, "the silent organ." Therefore, when the liver does give a cry of pain, it is likely to be already in an unrecoverable situation. We need to take care of it, before it sends a distress signal.

1. What's the topic of the passage?
(a) Why we should treat the human liver delicately
(b) How much poison the human liver can take
(c) The least important of the human organs
(d) An overview of the characteristics of the human liver

2. How did the liver receive the nickname "the silent organ"?
(a) The liver does not notify the body when it is becoming unhealthy until it is probably too late.
(b) The name is used ironically because the liver tells the body straight away when there is a problem.
(c) It can recover quickly from a poisonous substance.
(d) The liver works hard and never complains until the moment when it effectively stops functioning.

3. What cannot be inferred from the passage?
(a) The liver might be considered by some to be the hardest working organ in the human body.
(b) We shouldn't forget to take care of our liver because it is not going to warn us of ill-health.
(c) The liver will treat any substance that enters your body and neutralizes anything dangerous to health.
(d) You can treat your liver extremely badly and still it can repair itself given some time of healthy living.

4. Which of the following is false?
(a) The human liver has one function: to remove the toxins in alcohol from the human body.
(b) If you are not eating enough, your liver will be affected.
(c) Not all of the organs in the human body can regenerate.
(d) If your liver starts hurting, you need to see a doctor immediately.

| WORDS & PHRASES |

dissertation *n*. 논문   mythical *a*. 신화의   liver *n*. 간   regenerate *v*. 재생되다[재생시키다]   hepatitis *n*. 간염
abstinence *n*. (도덕·종교·건강상의 이유로 인한 음식·술·섹스의) 자제, 금욕   organ *n*. 장기   metabolize *v*. 대사 작용을 하다
toxic *a*. 유독한   detoxify *v*. 해독하다   hazardous *a*. 위험한   neutralize *v*. 중화하다   dextrose *n*. 덱스트로오스(포도당의 일종)
amino acid *n*. 아미노산   fatty acid *n*. 지방산   portal vein *n*. 간문맥   axiom *n*. 격언   live up to ~의 기대에 부응하다
distress signal 조난 신호   notify *v*. 알리다, 통지하다   straight away 즉시, 지체 없이

| 문장분석 |

■ <u>Unlike</u> other organs that send distress signals directly, it serves well <u>without</u> utter<u>ing</u> any complaints. ➡ 〈unlike + 명사〉는 '~와는 달리'라는 의미이며, 〈without -ing〉는 '~하는 것 없이'라는 뜻이다. unlike와 without이 모두 전치사이기 때문에 뒤에 모두 명사가 와야 한다는 것에 주의한다. without은 바로 뒤에 동사가 와야 할 때 명사가 위치해야 하므로 -ing 형태의 동명사가 오게 된다.

UNIT 08 History in color
피부색

Science explains that skin color depends principally on the following three elements: melanin, hemoglobin and carotene. Among them, carotene has a temporary effect on skin color. Excessive consumption of foods high in carotene, such as carrots and tangerines, may turn one's skin yellow for a short time. If hemoglobin is abundant on the surface of the skin, it may appear reddish. But the important factor in determining race and skin color is the amount of the dark brown pigment melanin in the skin. The number of melanin cells is not determined by race, but by the density of centrioles in a melanin cell.

The theory that skin color adapts to the level of ultraviolet radiation makes some sense. The ancestors of modern humans who lived predominantly near the equator in Africa had darker skin because it was more effective at reflecting heat, helping the body cool down and preventing the skin from receiving harmful ultraviolet rays. When receiving the same amount of sunlight, white people are 10 times more likely to develop skin cancer than black people. However, less exposure to ultraviolet rays can lead to a deficiency in vitamin D, also known as the "sunshine vitamin." This is the main reason why black people are at higher risk of contracting rickets, rheumatoid arthritis, cardiovascular diseases and colon, lung and prostate cancer, due to vitamin D deficiency.

After migrating from Africa and settling into areas of Asia and Europe, these humans may have needed to receive more vitamin D, thus their skin became yellow or white in order to survive. An exception to this theory are the original inhabitants of Alaska who had black skin, despite living in a polar area, which has scarce sunlight. Experts explained that their diet of fish high in vitamin D removed the need for their skin tone to lighten.

문장분석

■ When receiving the same amount of sunlight, white people are 10 times more likely to develop skin cancer than black people. ➡ 〈배수사 + 비교급 + than = 배수사 + as ~ as〉 구문에서는 배수사(0.5배, 3배, 10배 등)의 위치에 주의해야 한다. 원급 비교에서는 as ~ as 앞에 위치하며, 비교급에서는 비교급 바로 앞에 위치한다. 예문에서 be likely to는 '~할 가능성이 크다'는 의미이며, be more likely to ~ than이라고 하면 '~할 가능성이 …보다 더 크다'는 뜻이 된다. 이때 가능성이 몇 배가 더 크다고 표현할 때는 앞서 말한 위치에 배수사가 놓이게 된다.

1. Which of the following is not discussed in the passage?
   (a) The problems that can arise in the body as a result of not receiving enough vitamin D
   (b) The evolution of skin color to adapt to the environment
   (c) How melanin, hemoglobin and carotene affect the color of our skin
   (d) The effect that race has on skin color

2. What cannot be inferred from the passage?
   (a) A diet which contains a lot of fish will provide all of your vitamin D needs.
   (b) White people don't get diseases which are associated with vitamin D deficiency.
   (c) Darker skin can reflect heat better; therefore a darker skinned person will feel cooler in the desert than a white skinned person.
   (d) A temporary skin color change can come about from eating certain foods high in carotene.

3. What's the passage mainly about?
   (a) The reasons for the migration of African people to Asia and Europe
   (b) The importance of diet in choosing a skin color
   (c) The theory that skin color is determined directly by contact with ultraviolet rays, specifically vitamin D
   (d) What to eat to remain healthy

4. Choose the correct one from the following.
   (a) Alaskans retained their darker skin because their diet gave them the vitamin D that was missing from the atmosphere.
   (b) Everyone is at the same high risk of skin cancer regardless of skin color.
   (c) The skin of people who live far the equator is darker to protect it from dangerous rays and to keep the body cool more effectively.
   (d) Your race will have a direct correlation with your skin color because melanin appears in different numbers in different races.

| WORDS & PHRASES |

melanin *n.* 멜라닌 (색소)   hemoglobin *n.* 헤모글로빈, 혈색소   carotene *n.* 카로틴(당근 등에 들어 있는 적황색 물질)
temporary *a.* 일시적인   excessive *a.* 과도한   tangerine *n.* 탄제린(껍질이 잘 벗겨지는 작은 오렌지)   abundant *a.* 풍부한
factor *n.* 요인   pigment *n.* 색소   ultraviolet *a.* 자외선의   predominantly *ad.* 대개, 대부분   equator *n.* 적도   reflect *v.* 반사하다   exposure *n.* 노출   deficiency *n.* 부족   contract *v.* 병에 걸리다   rickets *n.* 구루병   rheumatoid arthritis 류머티즘 관절염
cardiovascular disease 심혈관 질환   colon *n.* 결장   prostate *n.* 전립선   inhabitant *n.* 거주자   scarce *a.* 부족한
come about 일어나다. 발생하다

UNIT 09 Addicted to speed
속도

|기술|

The world's fastest passenger rail service, Alstom's TGV Est, runs between Paris and Strasbourg at a top speed of 575 kilometers per hour (357 miles per hour). With its successful debut in April 2007, the upgraded French bullet train outshined its competitors, ICE of Germany and Shinkansen of Japan. In speed, Shinkansen still holds the world record of 581 kilometers per hour, set in 2003. But at that time it ran on the maglev system, which is impractical for commercial use due to engine overheating and weight problems. The French high-speed train normally shoots through Europe at 300 kilometers per hour.

The world's fastest car, the GTBO, is designed and manufactured by Britain's Acabion. The concept car showcased a top speed of 547 kilometers per hour in February. The 360-kilogram (794-pound) dolphin-shaped two-seater is capable of a scorching 480 kilometers in just 30 seconds, but remains out of reach for most petrol-heads at a price tag of over $2 million. In the sky, Lockheed's SR-71, or the Blackbird, stands out. The long-range strategic reconnaissance aircraft can reach a speed of Mach 3.3, (4,000 kilometers per hour for laymen) much faster than the Concorde's once-proud cruising speed of Mach 2.23.

The 21st century is an era of speed. History substantiates that speed corresponds with power. Genghis Khan built his Mongol Empire with the help of his efficient horseback archers while German military hero Erwin Rommel roamed North African deserts with his Afrika Korps tanks during World War II. Greater speed can take mankind to higher and farther places. We can attain more information and get more work done in less time. Speed can accelerate growth while growth presses on for more speed. Today some talk of a "speed virus." They complain that people having difficulty keeping up with society's obsession with speed are being left behind and neglected. Meanwhile, Mother Nature and her resources are falling victim to the human thirst for greater speed. One year's worth of global energy consumption eats up a 1-million-year accumulation of fossil fuel. Excessive consumption of fuels like oil and coal is fanning global warming.

1. What does the term "speed virus" not refer to, according to the passage?

(a) A quick acting virus that leaves people disabled and unable to keep up with others
(b) People's inability to keep up with the need for speed in today's society
(c) The need to keep going at a quicker and quicker pace that some cannot maintain
(d) The accelerated growth that presses us to work faster, doing more in less time

2. What cannot be inferred from the passage?

(a) People will eventually use up fossil fuels if they continue to use them at the rate they do.
(b) Speed has been the key element to many important events.
(c) The speed record set by the Japanese train will remain intact for the remainder of this century.
(d) Our obsession with speed will not end anytime in the near future.

3. Which of the following is not true, according to the passage?

(a) People like Rommel owe much of their achieved goals to their ability to utilize speed.
(b) Fossil fuels are used to a great degree and are causing environmental issues.
(c) The British made GTBO can travel faster than the average traveling speed of the French bullet train.
(d) The British have built the fastest passenger vehicle in the world.

4. What could be a possible subject for the next paragraph?

(a) How the French will succeed in developing a train faster than the Japanese
(b) Possible cures for those infected with the speed virus
(c) The alternative sources of fuel energy in the future to maintain our obsession with speed
(d) What will be the fastest machines in the next century

| WORDS & PHRASES |

bullet train *n.* 고속 열차   outshine *v.* ~보다 더 뛰어나다   competitor *n.* 경쟁자   maglev *n.* 자기 부상   showcase *v.* 나타내다, 전시하다, 진열하다   strategic *a.* 전략적인   reconnaissance *n.* 정찰   era *n.* 시대   substantiate *v.* 입증하다   roam *v.* 돌아다니다, 배회하다   attain *v.* 획득하다   keep up with (시류[유행]를) 뒤따르다   be left behind 뒤처지다   fall victim to ~의 희생물이 되다   thirst *n.* 갈증   accumulation *n.* 축적   fossil fuel *n.* 화석 연료   excessive *a.* 과도한   fan *v.* 부채질하다   intact *a.* (하나도 손상되지 않고) 온전한, 전혀 다치지 않은

| 문장분석 |

■ The long-range strategic reconnaissance aircraft can reach a speed of Mach 3.3, <u>much</u> faster than the Concorde's once-proud cruising speed of Mach 2.23.

→ 비교급을 강조할 때 흔히 사용되는 부사가 much이다. 이때 주의할 점은 비교급 앞에 more가 올 수 없다는 점이다. 그렇게 되면 비교급이 이중으로 들어가기 때문이다. much 말고도 even, still, far, a lot 등도 같은 의미로 사용될 수 있다.

UNIT 10 Under the microscope
다이옥신

| 건강 |

Our intellectual curiosity for the infinitesimal world is limitless. Scientific development satisfies our desire to seek knowledge. Viruses and prions are seen under an electron microscope. Extremely minute amounts of chemical substances can be analyzed by methods such as GC-MS or HPLC-MS. People in their 40s and over were interested to discover the concept of "micro". The "nano" terminology was popular in the '90s, while the scientific prefix "pico" has become familiar to us today.

Nowadays the food industry is under the microscope. They have to contend with vCJD, norovirus, dioxin and PCB, which were too small to be seen under detection technology in the past. In this context, the U.S. Food and Drug Administration abolished the 1958 Delaney Clause [of the Food, Drugs and Cosmetic Act of 1938], the zero cancer risk standard, on the sly.

With the development of analytical chemistry, the most hazardous substance revealed by the assessment processes was dioxin. Recently, some Irish pork has been found to contain dioxins. Toxins such as dioxin bio accumulate up the food chain so the dioxin levels for the final consumer are far higher than that of primary consumers. Organisms such as plankton can accumulate these toxic chemicals at much higher concentrations than are found in the water. As the plankton is eaten by fish, the toxic chemicals are further concentrated in the bodies of the fish.

Breast-fed infants are at the top of the food chain. Naturally, the highest level of dioxin is detected in breast milk, outside of man-made incidents including the Belgian dioxin crisis in 1999. However, despite the presence of dioxins in human milk, breast-feeding should be encouraged and promoted on the basis of convincing evidence of its benefits to the overall health and development of the infant.

1. What's the main topic of the passage?

(a) The presence of toxins, especially dioxins, in our food
(b) The ways that technology can eradicate toxins from our food and drink
(c) The importance of breast-feeding babies
(d) Hope for the future through the advances made in food science

2. Which of the following is incorrect?

(a) The U.S. Food and Drug Administration secretly tried to get rid of the Delaney Clause.
(b) These days the food industry has a lot to deal with, more than in the past.
(c) Dioxins increase as they pass up the food chain, becoming more dangerous to those who ingest it.
(d) Breast-feeding is being discouraged by the writer due to the dioxins present in it.

3. What has progress in analytical chemistry allowed us to do, according to the passage?

(a) We can now identify toxins which we were previously unable to pinpoint.
(b) We have discovered which foods are healthy to eat and which are not.
(c) It is possible to cause the decrease in dioxins in food through chemical processes.
(d) Food must be labeled to display its dioxin levels clearly to consumers.

4. What can we infer from the passage?

(a) Irish pork doesn't sell well throughout the world because of its association with dioxins.
(b) We are able to consume certain amounts of dioxin before any harm is done to our health.
(c) Dioxins are a main cause of death to plankton.
(d) We are going to find more hazardous substances in the future in our food.

| WORDS & PHRASES |

infinitesimal *a.* 극미한   prion *n.* 프리온   electron *n.* 전자   minute *a.* 미세한   terminology *n.* 전문 용어   prefix *n.* 접두사
contend with ~와 씨름하다   detection *n.* 탐지   abolish *v.* 폐지하다   on the sly 은밀히   hazardous *a.* 위험한
reveal *v.* 드러내다   assessment *n.* 평가   toxin *n.* 독소   accumulate *v.* 축적하다   concentration *n.* 농도
concentrate *v.* 농축시키다   convincing *a.* 확실한   eradicate *v.* 근절하다   get rid of ~을 없애다

| 문장분석 |

■ **People in their 40s and over** were interested to discover the concept of "micro." ➡ ⟨in the early/mid/late 40s⟩라는 표현은 나이가 40대임을 나타내는 말로, 40대 초반/중반/후반이냐에 따라 early/mid/late 등을 사용한다. 그리고 40대는 40~49까지의 숫자들이 모여서 하나의 단위를 이루고 있다고 생각해서 정관사 the(위의 예문처럼 소유격도 가능)와 복수의 s를 앞뒤로 사용해서 표현한다. 심슨 가족이라고 할 때 'the Simpsons'처럼 성을 이용해 the와 s를 붙이는 것과 같다고 할 수 있다. 마찬가지로 1990년대 혹은 2000년대도 같은 방식으로 the 1990s 혹은 the 2000s로 표현한다.

UNIT 11 Weather not an exact science
수치예보

|기상|

Increasing the accuracy of weather forecasts, is not a simple task because, fundamentally, weather forecasts are destined to be fallacious. The science of forecasting weather has been in existence for only a short time. Before people invented equipment that could accurately observe meteorological conditions, people predicted weather through experience and human senses. Galileo invented a crude thermometer in the early 1600s, and Benjamin Franklin discovered in 1773 that meteorological phenomena moved regionally. Weather charts that display expansive regional meteorological patterns were used in forecasting weather only after the wireless telegraph was invented in the 19th century. During the middle of the 20th century, high-tech meteorological equipment like artificial satellites and meteorological radar were invented, along with a supercomputer that could process vast amounts of meteorological information. The era of "numerical forecasting" began; forecasters used current meteorological data to calculate future weather.

Using a supercomputer to analyze the prodigious amount of information that can influence the weather to increase the accuracy of forecasts has its limits because of the so-called "butterfly" effect, a term coined in 1961 by American scholar Edward Lorentz. "The flap of a butterfly's wing in Brazil can set off a tornado in Texas." This suggests that small early meteorological conditions produce large variations. Regardless of how elaborate a weather forecasting model may be, if the initial data is slightly off, the forecast results will change dramatically. Augmentation of weather information and more elaborate models for forecasting do not guarantee weather forecasts that are more accurate. Precise numbers do not ensure precise forecasts. Human beings are left with the task of analyzing the numbers produced by computers and forecasting the weather.

1. What is the butterfly effect?

(a) Butterflies in Brazil are extremely intelligent and able to tell what weather is coming.
(b) Even small, and seemingly unimportant things, can produce enormous changes elsewhere.
(c) Weather conditions in one particular country can be duplicated almost exactly in another country at the same time.
(d) It is impossible to make weather forecasts accurately.

2. What jumpstarted the era of numerical forecasting?

(a) 20th century technology that could process larger than ever amounts of information and calculate future weather.
(b) The inventions of Benjamin Franklin in the field of meteorology.
(c) A change in attitudes that meant society was beginning to rely more heavily on human forecasters.
(d) There had been mistakes where society had wrongly trusted human senses, so people began looking for other ways to predict the weather.

3. What can you infer about the supercomputer used to forecast weather?

(a) It took many years and a lot of scientists to develop it.
(b) If used correctly it can predict the weather perfectly, but if used incorrectly it fails.
(c) The job of forecasting weather is done completely by the computer and humans do not have input.
(d) Despite all the data it uses, it cannot predict the weather exactly because there are unknown variables which affect it.

| WORDS & PHRASES |

accuracy *n*. 정확도   fundamentally *ad*. 근본적으로   be destined to ~로 운명 지어지다   fallacious *a*. 틀린
meteorological *a*. 기상의   crude *a*. 대강의, 대충 만든   thermometer *n*. 온도계   telegraph *n*. 전보   artificial *a*. 인공의
satellite *n*. 위성   prodigious *a*. 엄청난   coin *v*. 신조어를 만들다   set off 유발하다   variation *n*. 변화
regardless of ~와 관계없이   elaborate *a*. 정교한   augmentation *n*. 증가, 증대

| 문장분석 |

■ During the middle of the 20th century, high-tech meteorological equipment like artificial satellites and meteorological radar were invented, along with a supercomputer that could process vast amounts of meteorological information. ➡ along with는 '~와 함께, ~와 더불어'라는 뜻의 표현이며, 비슷한 표현으로는 together with, coupled with 등이 있다.

UNIT 12 A different side to drones
드론

| 기술 |

It seems like it is against the trend to oppose unmanned drones. You could look insensitive to technological advancement or you could be considered a skeptic. Holding a philosophical debate over drones is perhaps already meaningless. The market is already on the move, as regulations are expected to be lifted drastically. Drones are increasingly being used for positive purposes. Ambulance drones used in countries like the Netherlands arrive at the scene first and provide medical supplies. Compared to when their military uses were highlighted, people feel far less resistant to drones these days.

But the latest reports from the United States and Europe are casting concerns that we may be overly trusting the use of drones and the effectiveness of regulations on them. Reprieve UK claims that U.S. drone attacks on terrorist suspects in the Middle East have resulted in more than 1,000 civilian deaths. A U.S. drone struck a wedding in Yemen, killing 12 people including guests and the bride. A Federal Aviation Administration document reported by U.S. media is also noteworthy. In the last six months, there have been 25 cases of drones almost colliding with large aircraft. There have been 193 cases of passenger jet pilots spotting drones while flying and filing a report. And we need to think about terror threats as well as aviation safety.

The U.S. government's basic position is that meticulous regulation is possible. But optimism is not necessarily a good thing, as we have seen with gun control. Gun-related violence is practically impossible to prevent, so post-accident response capacity is improved as regulations are not effective when guns are already widely distributed. Drones are far more frightening than guns as weapons of destruction. In order not to follow the precedence of gun control, overly conservative reviews are necessary, which should not be swayed by economic theories or be swept up in optimism. The possibility of hacking and other technical discussions are also necessary. When the market moves first and regulations follow, it leads to a disaster. If the authorities are not confident in implementing perfect control, _____.

1. What is the overall tone of the passage?
    (a) Suspicion
    (b) Pessimism
    (c) Disappointment
    (d) Tension

2. What can you infer from the passage?
    (a) It is no longer worthwhile debating over the rights and wrongs of the existence of drones.
    (b) Drones are being increasingly used in terrorist attacks.
    (c) Staying out of the race to produce drones may be smarter than participating in the competition.
    (d) Drones are being used for more harm than good as regulations are being lifted.

3. Which of the following is true, according to the passage?
    (a) Drones are still viewed negatively even though they can be used in positive ways.
    (b) It has been proven impossible to hack into drone systems.
    (c) The last year has seen over two dozen collisions between drones and large aircraft.
    (d) Mistakes are sometimes made with drone use and innocent people are hurt.

4. Which of the following best completes the sentence?
    (a) tight restrictions could be a solution until thorough preparation is complete
    (b) the market will move on without the proper restrictions being put in place
    (c) no good can come of drone use in the long run
    (d) there will never be an appropriate time for implementing regulations

| WORDS & PHRASES |

insensitive *a.* 둔감한   skeptic *n.* 회의주의자   unmanned *a.* 무인의   on the move 이동 중인, 전진 중인   highlight *v.* 강조하다
noteworthy *a.* 주목할 만한   meticulous *a.* 꼼꼼한, 정교한   sweep up 들어 올리다, 쓸어 담다   implement *v.* 실행하다

| 문장분석 |

■ <u>In order not to</u> follow the precedence of gun control, overly conservative reviews are necessary, which should not be swayed by economic theories or be swept up in optimism. ➡ 〈in order not to〉는 목적을 나타내는 in order to의 부정 표현으로 부사적으로 쓰였고, overly conservative reviews가 주어이다. which는 앞 문장을 받는다.

UNIT 13 Wrangling with nuclear risk
핵실험

| 환경 |

The world's first atomic bomb was tested in Alamogordo, New Mexico, at 5 a.m. on July 16, 1945. The 20-kiloton device, code-named Trinity, left a large mushroom-shaped cloud over the desert. The explosive power of the bomb was confirmed in warfare within weeks of the test when Little Boy and the Fat Man were dropped on Hiroshima and Nagasaki, taking the lives of 200,000 people.

Tests of the United States' nuclear weapons technology peaked in the 1950s in the Cold War against the former Soviet Union. Tests were generally conducted in Nevada in the middle of the desert. It has been said that one of the nuclear tests caused the American movie star John Wayne to die. In 1954, Wayne was filming "The Conqueror," a movie about Genghis Khan, on the Utah plains. The location was 137 kilometers (85 miles) away from the nuclear test site. Over the next 30 years, 90 out of 220 of the film's cast and crew got cancer and 46 of them died, according to "Why John Wayne Died," a book by Japanese journalist Takashi Hirose. The figures are too high to deny the correlation with radioactivity. Wayne was diagnosed with lung cancer in 1964 but survived, before succumbing to stomach cancer in 1979. The film's director, Dick Powell, and its leading lady, Susan Hayward, also died of cancer.

America's first practical test of a thermonuclear hydrogen bomb was conducted on Bikini Atoll, part of the Marshall Islands, in 1954. The Japanese tuna fishing boat the Daigo Fukuryu Maru, or Lucky Dragon 5, was passing nearby when the bomb was detonated. It was exposed to the fallout, even though it was outside the safety line set by the U.S. Army. One sailor died and many complained of headaches and bleeding gums. After a series of accidents raised awareness of the danger of nuclear tests, countries signed an agreement to ban nuclear tests on the ground and in the water in 1963. But underground nuclear tests were excluded from the ban because they were thought to be unrelated to contamination of our air and oceans. But it is possible these tests contaminate our water and soil as well as cause earthquakes.

1. What is the main topic of the passage?

(a) The effectiveness of nuclear weapons throughout the 1940's, 1950's and into the 1960's
(b) The side effects of nuclear fallout from atomic bombs testing
(c) The truth behind the death of John Wayne and other actors filming in the Utah plains
(d) The history of the atomic bomb in America after the bombing of Hiroshima and Nagasaki

2. What can be inferred from the passage?

(a) John Wayne's last movie as the lead actor was "The Conqueror".
(b) Japan surrendered after Little Boy and Fat Man were dropped out of fear of further attacks.
(c) Scientists were not fully aware of all the effects of radiation during this time.
(d) The Utah plains are now the site for underground tests by the U.S. Army due to the ban on surface testing in the Marshall Islands.

3. Which of the following is false according to the passage?

(a) Nuclear tests were usually conducted in unpopulated areas like the Utah plains or the Marshall Islands.
(b) Scientists eventually became aware of the damaging effects of fallout from testing after side effects were noticed outside of safety lines.
(c) Nuclear testing is now done underground, but there may still be unknown side effects such as seismic activity.
(d) All the people exposed to radiation in the Utah Plains have died from cancer.

| WORDS & PHRASES |

mushroom-shaped *a.* 버섯 모양의   correlation *n.* 상관관계   radioactivity *n.* 방사능   be diagnosed with ~로 진단받다
succumb to ~에 굴복하다   hydrogen *n.* 수소   detonate *v.* 폭파시키다   fallout *n.* 낙진   gum *n.* 잇몸   exclude *v.* 배제하다
contamination *n.* 오염

| 문장분석 |

■ The figures are <u>too</u> high <u>to deny</u> the correlation with radioactivity. ➡ 〈too + 형용사 + to 부정사〉는 '~이하하기에는 너무(too) ~하다'는 뜻이다. 위의 예문을 보면 '그 수치는 방사능과의 상관관계를 부인하기에는 너무 높다'라는 뜻이 되며, 달리 말하면 '수치가 너무 높아 방사능과의 상관관계를 부인할 수 없다'는 부정의 의미를 내포하게 된다.

UNIT 14 A high-tech, brain-shrinking future
진화하는 인간

| 기술 |

Nowadays seeing a person walking down the street talking on a cell phone has become such a ubiquitous sight that a picture of modern man with one hand next to his ear should be painted next to the ape-like Cro-Magnon to depict the evolution of humans. According to recent press reports, American doctors are now warning of so-called "cell phone elbow" syndrome. It seems farcical that medical professionals are making such a fuss about this. Just like people who suffer daily from the constant pain of tennis elbow after playing tennis, cell phone gabbers complain of pain or numbness in the hand — especially the pinky and ring fingers.

We cannot avoid using cell phones, despite elbow pain and electromagnetic waves, as they empower humans to reach beyond geographical boundaries. In addition, human capabilities are much larger than a decade ago thanks to the emergence of laptop computers, wireless Internet and car navigation. Yet with all these portable digital devices, the memory devices they hold store much more information in a more precise manner than the human brain.

Recently, a new technology called brain-machine interface came into the spotlight. The technology is designed to control robots or machines by drawing on signals from the human brain. We cannot predict whether progress in genetic engineering, robotics engineering, information technology and nanotechnology will raise human capability to an even higher position. If such developments occur, we could live healthier and longer lives, and see huge progress in easily overcoming cultural and linguistic barriers. It is likely that a human with no need for sleep or food may emerge on earth.

However, it is a fact that we are deprived of true rest and spiritual freedom by cell phones ringing off the hook regardless of time or place. We have no need to use our brain due to calculators and dictionaries. Even the list of telephone numbers we remember is getting shorter. Research shows that as humans evolved from Australopithecus to Homo sapiens, the skull volume expanded. However, the size of the human brain has seen a 10 to 15 percent decrease over the past 30,000 years. While relying more on equipment or social systems, the role of the brain might be on the decrease.

Humans are slowly evolving toward becoming cyborgs. However, naturally born humans, the underprivileged who possess no cutting-edge portable digital devices, are unlikely to win in a battle of the species. We worry that the situation might be even worse than projections of the future.

1. What is the correct definition of "cell phone elbow"?
(a) A pain in the upper arm because of the long periods of time holding the cell phone to the ear
(b) Pain in all fingers of the hand that sends text messages
(c) Pain in the elbow of the arm that lifts the cell phone to the ear
(d) Some kind of pain in the hand that holds the cell phone after prolonged use of it

2. What can you infer from the passage?
(a) The need for the human brain will become obsolete and information we need will be stored on a chip.
(b) If a battle between naturally-born humans and cyborgs took place, humans would not see a favorable result.
(c) Cell phones are enabling humans to advance in ways that were hitherto unseen, such as spiritually and socially.
(d) Brain-machine interface makes the human brain unnecessary and relies on an electromagnetic brain.

3. What is the best title for this passage?
(a) A high-tech, brain-shrinking future
(b) The war between nature and technology
(c) The reduced need for the human brain
(d) How much memory can a human brain hold

4. What would be most appropriate for the next paragraph?
(a) Ways in which we don't need to use our brains anymore
(b) New technology that will open up possibilities about how our brain's abilities can be expanded
(c) Common theories about our future society and existence
(d) Some ailments that have arisen from using modern gadgets

| WORDS & PHRASES |

ubiquitous *a.* 어디에나 있는, 아주 흔한   ape-like *a.* 유인원과 같은   depict *v.* 묘사하다   evolution *n.* 진화   farcical *a.* 웃음거리가 된
make a fuss 크게 떠들어대다, 소란 피우다   gabber *n.* 수다쟁이   pinky finger 새끼손가락   empower *v.* 권한을 주다
emergence *n.* 출현   portable *a.* 휴대[이동]가 쉬운, 휴대용의   draw on 이용하다   linguistic *a.* 언어의   barrier *n.* 장벽
be deprived of ~을 빼앗기다   ring off the hook 연속으로[쉴 새 없이] 울리다   regardless of ~와 관계없이   be on the decrease 줄어들다
underprivileged *a.* (사회·경제적으로) 혜택을 못 받는   cutting-edge *a.* 최첨단의   projection *n.* 예상, 추정
obsolete *a.* 더 이상 쓸모가 없는, 한물간, 구식의

| 문장분석 |

■ However, naturally born humans, <u>the underprivileged</u> who possess no cutting-edge portable digital devices, are unlikely to win in a battle of the species. ➔ ⟨the + 형용사⟩라는 형태로 사용되면 '~하는 사람들'을 의미한다. 예를 들어 the rich는 '부자들'을, the poor는 '가난한 사람들'을 의미하며, 예문과 같이 the underprivileged라고 하면 '경제적 혜택을 못 받는 사람들'이 된다. 주의할 것은 이때 의미가 복수형이기 때문에 동사의 수의 일치도 '복수'로 해야 한다는 점이다.

UNIT 15 Painful patent protection
특허의 역설

| 발명 |

The Rhine River, the longest river in Germany, was the most important waterway for European trade in the Middle Ages. Merchant ships paid tolls as they passed each state along the Rhine, in return for the Holy Roman Empire's protection. But in line with the decline of the empire in the 13th century, barons peppered the riverside with hundreds of castles to claim tolls from passing ships. Their toll demands became so audacious that merchants gave up ventures down the Rhine altogether. The trade business along the Rhine collapsed, bringing down the sponging barons along with it.

Such nibbling away at a public property or resource can in the end compromise its existence and make everyone worse off. Columbia Law School professor Michael Heller calls this effect the "tragedy of the anticommons." The waste of unclaimed property can be ruinous, but self-serving and expansive fights over a property can be equally disastrous, as seen in the Rhine River example. Heller, in his book "The Gridlock Economy: How Too Much Ownership Wrecks Markets, Stops Innovation, and Costs Lives" argued that overly fragmented property rights and broad ownership can eventually trap the industry and market in a dead end.

There is an overabundance of patents in the biotech industry right now. Patents licensed over the last 30 years associated with DNA alone top 40,000 cases. Pharmaceutical companies must go through numerous patent holders and negotiate terms before marketing a new drug. Many tests fail to go beyond the labs for fear of litigation backlashes from reclusive patent owners. The same problems interfered with the development of a vaccine against SARS during the outbreak.

The genetically engineered golden rice, developed to help millions of children in Africa and other impoverished areas suffering from vitamin A deficiency, also might have never seen daylight, if not for humanitarian relief efforts. Scientists who developed the miracle crop in 1999 were walled in by more than 70 patent rights. They were finally freed to hand out the grain after companies redefined the rice as having a "humanitarian use of license."

| 문장분석 |

■ The genetically engineered golden rice, … also might have never seen daylight, if not for humanitarian relief efforts. ➡ 〈if it were not for something, if it had not been for something〉은 가정법으로 '~이 없었다면'의 뜻이다. 예문에서는 이를 줄여서 if not for로 표현했으며, 예문 주절에 'might have never been'이라는 가정법 과거완료의 표현이 있으므로 if it had not been for something을 줄여서 만든 것이라는 사실을 알 수 있다.

1. What can you infer from the passage?

(a) Greed is at the root of all human problems.
(b) Disputes over property are disadvantageous in the short run but have positive effects in the long run.
(c) Patent issues are impeding the progress of science and medicine.
(d) The SARS vaccine was delayed because of the inability of research scientists to deal with lawyers.

2. Which of the following is incorrect?

(a) Loss of activity on the part of the merchants on the Rhine, damaged both themselves and the barons who controlled the waterway.
(b) It is much easier to get a patent for a new product these days than 50 years ago because the process has been speeded up.
(c) The biotech industry is suffering over a lack of knowledge about patents on the part of the scientists.
(d) Genetically engineered rice was eventually given to African children after its use was renamed as humanitarian.

3. According to the passage, what is the problem with releasing a new drug on the market?

(a) There are obstacles in the form of patent holders and terms must be agreed upon whereby all parties are satisfied.
(b) About 40,000 patent holders are waiting to claim some money from profits of the new drug.
(c) There is a struggle between those who wish to use new drugs for personal profit and those who have more humanitarian concerns.
(d) Having to undergo numerous tests and trials to ensure the safety of the new drug.

4. What is the best title of the passage?

(a) The economic downturn as a result of the overabundance of patents
(b) Technological advances being hindered as a result of debate among scientists
(c) Giving humanitarian aid through medical research
(d) An economy and society at a standstill through extensive ownership

---

| WORDS & PHRASES |

waterway *n.* 수로   in line with ~에 따라, ~와 함께   baron *n.* 남작   pepper *v.* 뿌려대다, 퍼붓다   audacious *a.* 대담한
collapse *v.* 붕괴하다   sponge *v.* 뜯어먹다, 빌붙다   nibble away 조금씩[야금야금] 먹다   compromise *v.* ~을 위태롭게 하다
worse off 더 가난한, 더 못한   unclaimed *a.* 주인이 나서지 않는   ruinous *a.* 파괴적인, 파멸을 가져올   self-serving *a.* 자기 잇속만 차리는
fragmented *a.* 분열된   dead end *n.* 난관   overabundance *n.* 과잉, 과다   patent *n.* 특허   top *v.* 능가하다, 더 높다
pharmaceutical *a.* 제약의   term *n.* 계약 조건   litigation *n.* 소송   backlash *n.* 반발   reclusive *a.* 은둔의   outbreak *n.* 발생
impoverished *a.* 빈곤한, 가난해진   deficiency *n.* 부족   humanitarian *a.* 인도주의적인   standstill *n.* 정지, 멈춤

123

UNIT 16 Statistics use and misuse
통계의 사용과 오용

| 통계 |

If Austrian priest Gregor Mendel (1822-1884) had stopped his preoccupation with garden peas at breeding and experimenting, his work [1] may not have had the same impact on the world of genetics. Mendel studied pea plants for 15 years to expand on his hypothesis that certain traits in these plants follow particular laws of inheritance. He recorded his findings of variations in numerical order for statistical analysis. His findings went largely unnoticed by his contemporaries [2] who were ignorant of statistics.

But scientists rediscovered his ideas at the turn of the 20th century, posthumously giving him the title "the father of modern genetics." The principle of heredity was not the only thing Mendel's followers uncovered from his studies. They discovered disparity in the result ratios, raising suspicion that Mendel may have censored his experiments to validate his hypothesis or excluded results that [3] will contradict his earlier belief.

English mathematician Charles Babbage in his 1830 book "Reflection on the Decline of Science in England," said there were three kinds of fraud scientists can commit: cooking, trimming and forging. In "cooking," scientists take in only the results that fit their theory, discarding others. "Trimming," which Babbage considered more evil, is an act of smoothing irregularities in order to make the data appear extremely accurate and precise. Such fabrication and rounding of numbers until they fit the desired result are rampant in social statistics.

Kevin Phillips, who served as an economic brain in the Richard Nixon administration, exposed the Nixon government for excluding food and energy prices in calculating the consumer price index in order to report a more positive economic indicator. Economist Steven Levitt in his best-selling nonfiction book "Freakonomics" cites a cheating incident in Chicago schools. Due to the city government's policy of punishing teachers with pay and promotion disadvantages based on school reports, the teachers [4] fabricated students' test results.

1. What's the main topic of the passage?
    (a) A discussion of scientific forgery and its effects
    (b) Mendel's breeding and experimentation of garden peas
    (c) Cooking, Trimming, Forging!
    (d) The study of Freakonomics

2. Which of the following is grammatically incorrect among [1] – [4]?
    (a) [1]   (b) [2]   (c) [3]   (d) [4]

3. According to the passage, each of the following is true except …
    (a) Mendel was named as the father of modern genetics by other scientists.
    (b) Of cooking, trimming and forging, trimming and forging are the most alike.
    (c) Kevin Phillips became a whistleblower on the Nixon administration.
    (d) Chicago's education policy caused its teachers to forge students' test results.

4. Which of the following can be substituted for the underlined rampant?
    (a) extensive
    (b) exasperating
    (c) insane
    (d) shocking

| WORDS & PHRASES |

priest *n.* 사제   preoccupation *n.* 몰두; 집착   genetics *n.* 유전학   hypothesis *n.* 가설   trait *n.* 특징   inheritance *n.* 유전, 상속   statistical *a.* 통계의   contemporary *n.* 동시대 사람   posthumously *ad.* 사후에   heredity *n.* 유전   disparity *n.* 차이   suspicion *n.* 의혹   censor *v.* 검열하다, 검열하여 삭제하다   validate *v.* 입증하다   contradict *v.* 모순되다; 부정하다, 반박하다   fraud *n.* 사기   trim *v.* 다듬다, 손질하다   forge *v.* 위조하다   irregularity *n.* 불규칙한 것, 고르지 못한 것   fabrication *n.* 위조, 꾸며낸 것   round *v.* 둥글게 하다; 반올림하다   rampant *a.* 만연하는, 걷잡을 수 없는   cite *v.* 예로 들다   promotion *n.* 승진   whistleblower *n.* 밀고자

| 문장분석 |

■ His findings <u>went</u> largely <u>unnoticed</u> by his contemporaries who were ignorant of statistics. ➡ 〈go + 형용사〉는 '(시간이 감에 따라) ~이 되다'는 뜻을 지닌다. '가다'는 의미의 go가 아니라는 점에 주의한다. go bad는 '음식 등이 상하다'는 뜻이며, go bankrupt는 '파산하다'는 뜻이며, go wild는 '난폭해지다'는 뜻이다. 좀 덜 친숙한 표현들로는 go green, go nuclear, go public 등이 있는데, 각각 '친환경적으로 되다', '핵보유국이 되다', '상장 회사가 되다'는 뜻으로 사용된다. 위의 예문에서의 'went largely unnoticed'는 그가 발견한 것이 대체로 (사람들의) 주목을 받지 못하게 됐다'는 뜻이다.

UNIT 17 Autonomous driving dreams
자율주행차의 꿈

| 의학 |

"Where is it easier to apply fully autonomous driving, in a passenger car or a cargo truck?" an AI expert asked in a lecture a few years ago. Most of the audience chose the cargo truck, because even if it gets into a car accident, there will be no casualty. But the answer was the opposite. The expert explained that in an unexpected situation, like running into debris on the road, a passenger can respond, but an unmanned cargo truck can do nothing.

From November, roads in Sejong will be open for a pilot run of autonomous driving buses. They will run level three autonomous driving with a driver, and once they are verified as safe, they'll be upgraded to level four, without a driver. The age of completely autonomous driving is almost here.

The changes brought about by autonomous cars will be revolutionary. A businessman running a parts supplier is agonizing over how to respond. The biggest challenge is the rapid drop in new car sales. The concept of cars will change from individuals owning a car to sharing self-driving taxis. The number of new car sales will drop to less than half and the one fortunate thing is that the lifespan for parts will be shortened as cars will run further.

The insurance industry is also in trouble. In the age of self-driving cars, traffic accidents will drastically decrease. It will be good news for the automobile insurance in the short term. But low accident risk means that insurance is useless. Automobile insurance will fade into history and product liability insurance will remain.

A completely new car interior without a driving seat can be imagined. What passengers will do during the ride will be a key topic in the content industry. Employment issues as taxi and bus drivers become superfluous are inevitable, along with ethical and security concerns.

While I imagine this future, _____. An auto insurance expert projects that many small streets have no clear distinction between the sidewalk and the road, so it will take considerable time before fully self-driving cars can realistically move around the streets of Korean cities. It may even be impossible.

1. What is the passage mainly about?

   a) A new concept of autonomous vehicles intended to be safer for humans.
   b) The inherent problems associated with the introduction of autonomous vehicles.
   c) The next generation of autonomous vehicles and who is behind it.
   d) The future of autonomous vehicles and the effects that will come with them.

2. Which of the following is incorrect, according to the passage?

   a) Level three autonomous driving has already proved successful, so they are moving on to level four.
   b) Initially, drivers will accompany the autonomous vehicles for safety purposes.
   c) Private car ownership may decrease as shared autonomous taxi services increase.
   d) If public transportation has no need for drivers, many people will find themselves out of work.

3. How will the insurance industry be affected?

   a) The significant drop in accidents and claims will bring stability to the industry.
   b) Many drivers will stop buying insurance and continue to drive around illegally.
   c) If nobody is having accidents, driver's insurance will become unnecessary.
   d) They will have to drop prices in order to stay competitive, and even that may not be enough.

4. Which best completes the sentence?

   a) other cities around the world have already made this a reality
   b) realistic analysis throws a cold blanket over my dreams
   c) the reality of the situation is that people are still wary of self-driving cars
   d) real life is very different, and the costs will outweigh the advantages.

| **WORDS & PHRASES** |

cargo truck 화물차 **casualty** 사상자 **debris** 파편, 부스러기 **pilot run** 시범 주행 **autonomous driving bus** 자율주행버스 **agonize** *v.* 고민하다, 고뇌하다 **product liability insurance** 제조물책임보험 **superfluous** *a.* 과잉의, 불필요한 **security concern** 보안문제

| 문장분석 |

■ The number of new car sales will drop to less than half and the one fortunate thing is that the lifespan for parts will be shortened as cars will run further.

➡ the number of는 '~의 수'를 뜻하며, a number of는 '수많은'의 뜻이다. as는 접속사로 '~함에 따라'의 뜻이다.

UNIT 18 Repent, ye carbon emitters
환경 면죄부

| 환경 |

An indulgence for the modern era has emerged, and this one ostensibly forgives the sin of carbon dioxide emission. The so-called carbon-offset system demands investment in environmentally friendly projects to compensate for the excessive emission of carbon dioxide. They are mainly bought by people who travel on airplanes, which emit more carbon gases than other forms of transportation. In addition to airfare, they pay $10 to $40 more for apparently contributing to planting trees in Africa and constructing hydroelectric power plants in Brazil. Thanks to the demand spurred by people's desire to rid themselves of a guilty conscience, the amount earned from the carbon-offset system worldwide has reached a couple million dollars.

But there are strong criticisms of the system, which is also known as carbon credit or cap and trade. As the indulgence in the Middle Ages allowed people to commit crimes and still have peace of mind, the carbon-offset system also encourages people to travel more frequently and consume more.

Environmental specialists point out that emissions trading, which has been partly regulated since 2005 by the Kyoto Protocol, simply exacerbates global warming. They say that the system, which allows countries that have exceeded their limit of greenhouse gas emissions to buy the right to emit from countries that have not crossed the limit, only results in indulging the countries that consume more and emit more, and that the effect of gas reduction is meager. James Hansen, a climatologist at NASA in the U.S., lamented to the Times of London, "They are selling indulgences there. The developed nations want to continue basically business as usual so they are expected to purchase indulgences to give some small amount of money to developing countries. They do that in the form of offsets and adaptation funds".

| 문장분석 |

■ Thanks to the demand spurred by people's desire to <u>rid</u> themselves <u>of</u> a guilty conscience, the amount earned from the carbon-offset system worldwide has reached a couple million dollars.

→ 〈rid/clear/deprive/rob A of B〉 표현은 모두 기본적으로 'A에(게)서 B를 제거하다/빼앗다'는 뜻이다. A는 대상이 오고, B에 제거할 내용이 온다는 점에 유의한다.

1. *What is a true statement about the carbon credit system according to the passage?*
    (a) It is an effective system for stopping greenhouse gases.
    (b) There are no other possible solutions.
    (c) It allows developed countries to maintain their current way of life.
    (d) In time all countries will produce less carbon emissions using this system.

2. *What can be inferred from the passage?*
    (a) The current carbon system needs to be replaced.
    (b) People don't really believe in the system.
    (c) No one ever gets the money that people pay into the system.
    (d) There are no winners in the carbon offset system.

3. *Why do climatologists compare the carbon credit system to indulgences of the middle ages?*
    (a) They can find no other way to explain it.
    (b) Because it has the same premise.
    (c) There are some who do, others disagree.
    (d) None of the above.

4. *What is the best title for the passage?*
    (a) Carbon offset system
    (b) The increase of transportation
    (c) The carbon savings program
    (d) The indulgence of carbon

| WORDS & PHRASES |

indulgence *n.* 면죄부; 하고 싶은 대로 함[하게 함]   ostensibly *ad.* 외면상, 표면상   carbon-offset system 탄소 상쇄 제도
environmentally friendly 환경 친화적인   compensate *v.* 보상하다   emit *v.* 방출하다   hydroelectric *a.* 수력 전기의
carbon credit = cap and trade 탄소배출권   regulate *v.* 규제하다; 조절하다   exacerbate *v.* 악화하다   lament *v.* 한탄하다

UNIT 19 Turn off the lights
빛 공해

| 조명 |

In July 1938, physiologist Nathaniel Kleitman of The University of Chicago emerged from a cave with an overgrown beard, after having spent 32 calendar days underground. During this time he tried living on a 28-hour cycle but failed to adapt himself to the new biorhythm, indicating that the human body contains a powerful clock clinging to the 24-hour cycle.

Plants and animals, as well as humans, are strongly influenced by sunlight. Paddy rice, perilla and cosmos require daily exposure to sunlight to bloom and bear fruit during autumn. Last March, teams from the Roslin Institute in Britain and Japan's Nagoya University found that birds begin to sing more often to attract potential ___(A)___ partners in the spring, when they receive more light. Some birds, such as quails, burst into song in the spring, because cells on the surface of the brain trigger hormones when the days get longer, expanding male testes as a result.

The average temperature of the Earth's surface is around 15 degrees, and plants go through the process of photosynthesis, thanks to light ___(B)___ from the sun. However, night is also important to living organisms. In the dark, male fireflies expose themselves to females. Small and weak animals hunt at night to hide from their predators.

Human-made light sources also impact the order of the night. As seen from a satellite, the strong light from the Earth's night dazzles our eyes. Living organisms are used to day and night, and seasonal ___(C)___ throughout the long history of the Earth, but if they receive more light at a strange season or time, they will naturally fall into confusion.

Artificial light is a murky subject for humans as well. Perhaps two-thirds of the world's population can no longer see the Milky Way at night. Australia is losing sight of the Southern Cross. The stars depicted on its flag are no longer visible to the naked eye. Last February, a new study by Israeli researchers revealed that females exposed to artificial lighting such as lamps or television screens at night have a 37 percent higher risk of breast cancer than females living in the dark with no lamps.

1. What can be inferred from the passage?

    (a) Exposure to light effects most life on Earth.
    (b) People can change their internal clock.
    (c) Light is the only factor to consider when studying behavior.
    (d) The Earth is moving further away from the Milky Way and other stars.

2. Which of the following is incorrect according to the passage?

    (a) Many plants require sunlight for blooming.
    (b) Animals react to exposure to light levels.
    (c) Artificial light can affect human life.
    (d) Exposure to light has no effect on health.

3. What does the underlined phrase mean?

    (a) Shoot drugs in the body
    (b) Produce chemicals in the body
    (c) Start using drugs to feel better
    (d) The brain creates new signals

4. Which words best complete the passage?

    (a) (A) mating   (B) energy   (C) change
    (b) (A) energy   (B) night   (C) visible
    (c) (A) visible   (B) change   (C) mating
    (d) (A) mating   (B) energy   (C) important

| WORDS & PHRASES |

emerge *v.* 나타나다   overgrown *a.* 다 지란   beard *n.* 수염   adapt oneself to ~에 스스로 적응하다   cling to ~을 고수하다, ~에 매달리다   paddy rice *n.* 벼   perilla *n.* 들깨   exposure *n.* 노출   bloom *v.* 꽃이 피다   quail *n.* 메추라기   trigger *v.* 작동시키다, 촉발시키다   photosynthesis *n.* 광합성   firefly *n.* 개똥벌레, 반딧불   predator *n.* 포식자   dazzle *v.* 눈이 부시게 하다   confusion *n.* 혼란   artificial *a.* 인공적인   murky *a.* 흐린, 탁한   lose sight of ~이 더 이상 안 보이게 되다   depict *v.* 묘사하다   naked eye 육안

| 문장분석 |

■ Living organisms <u>are used to</u> day and night. ➡ ⟨be used/accustomed to -ing⟩라는 표현은 '~(하는 것)에 익숙하다'는 뜻 이다. 이때 to가 전치사이기 때문에 뒤에는 명사나 동명사가 와야 한다.

UNIT 20 Kimchi in space
우주식품

| 우주 |

John Glenn, the first American to orbit the Earth, carried semi-fluid applesauce aboard Friendship 7 in 1962. In space, people eat three balanced meals a day. A daily diet totaling between 2,000 and 2,200 calories is given to male and female astronauts, respectively. The taste falls below most standards. The first requirement in the manufacturing of space food is that it be light in weight. Dragging 1 kilogram of food to outer space costs 50 million won ($51,250). Freeze-drying and pulverization of the space food are mandatory to reduce the production costs. Additionally, it is of great importance to give sanitation due consideration in the production of space foods. Since Columbus (the International Space Station module) is not equipped with a refrigerator, it is too difficult to store up large stocks of food for a long period. The Hazard Analysis and Critical Control Point is an internationally recognized system to ensure food safety and protect consumers. Its origin is deeply rooted in the beginnings of space exploration, to manage the preparation of food for manned space flights. The lack of a refrigerator on the ISS module is mainly due to a lack of electricity.

The United States and Russia share the responsibility of providing astronauts with space food. Records show that the United States and Russia listed 200 and 130 food and beverage items, respectively, as of January 2008. Even though there are no differences in their menus, they differ in packaging materials and container openings. The Americans use light disposable packaging materials, such as aluminum foil, while the Russians use transparent packaging. The dispensers for American products remind us of gas valves on LPG vehicles, while Russian products resemble the valves of gasoline-powered vehicles. The American space foods are better equipped with airtight containers than the Russians'. As shown in these cases, the preparation of space foods has greatly contributed to improving the container and packaging technologies of foods on Earth.

| 문장분석 |

■ The first <u>requirement</u> in the manufacturing of space food is that it <u>be</u> light in weight. ➡ 〈insist/demand/require/recommend that 주어 + (should) 동사원형〉 구문을 설명 한 바 있다. 동사뿐만 아니라 requirement와 같은 명사의 경우에도 뒤의 that 절에 should가 들어오거나 생략된다는 것을 예문을 통해 알 수 있다.

1. What is the best title for the passage?

　　(a) Dining in space
　　(b) Food restrictions
　　(c) Space food
　　(d) Eating in space

2. What can be inferred from the passage?

　　(a) U.S. space food will probably be used more than Russian space food.
　　(b) Russian research is slower than the U.S.
　　(c) No other countries have the technology to produce space food.
　　(d) Refrigerators will soon be on the space station.

3. What is not a difference between the U.S. and Russian foods according to the passage?

　　(a) Packaging
　　(b) Valves
　　(c) Number of items available
　　(d) Preparation standards

4. How has space exploration helped improve things on Earth according to the passage?

　　(a) New foods are being developed.
　　(b) Container and packaging technology
　　(c) Gas technology for cars
　　(d) Food safety standards

| WORDS & PHRASES |

semi-fluid *a.* 반 액체의　　astronaut *n.* 우주비행사　　respectively *ad.* 각각　　outer space 우주　　pulverization *n.* 가루로 만듦, 분쇄
mandatory *a.* 의무적인　　sanitation *n.* 위생　　due consideration 충분한 고려　　ensure *v.* 보장하다, 확실히 하다　　exploration *n.* 탐험
disposable *a.* 사용 후 버리게 되어 있는, 일회용의　　transparent *a.* 투명한　　dispenser *n.* 용기　　airtight *a.* 밀폐된

Social Science

Part 4
사회과학

UNIT 01 At Google, there is no manual
"구글에는 매뉴얼이 없습니다"

| 경제/경영 |

Here, you can taste delicacies from around the world prepared by top chefs at 11 restaurants. Not only employees but also their families and visitors can dine for free. Unlimited fresh fruit and drinks are provided. Personal trainers are available at the gym, and there is a swimming pool, massage rooms and a spa. No one cares if you take a walk or sunbathe during work hours or if you bring your pet to the office — because you're at the Googleplex in Mountain View, California.

The arrangement is not to encourage employees to relax and do whatever they want. Google's Vice President Megan Smith says that when employees are provided with a workplace that allows them to work freely, they find answers and ideas that are beyond their normal imagination. Google's management knows very well that enhancing concentration and satisfaction is directly related to productivity.

This environment leads to a creative corporate culture. A meeting at Google is always filled with bold questions and passion. An entry-level employee can freely express their ideas to the managers. Google encourages employees to allocate 20 percent of their working hours on the things that are irrelevant to the job and that they like to do. Ideas from the 20 percent project has led to innovative projects such as Gmail and AdSense.

Google's management philosophy is simple: autonomy and openness. They believe that talented employees can fulfill their job 100 percent and display creativity, passion and ownership without surveillance or control. The corporate culture of keeping employees satisfied has made Google an icon of innovation and it became the true competitive edge of the company.

| 문장분석 |

■ The corporate culture of keeping employees satisfied has made Google an icon of innovation and it became the true competitive edge of the company.

➡ "keep + 목적어 + p.p. 구문"으로 근로자들이 계속 만족하는 상태에 놓이게 된다는 의미로 결국 The corporate culture of keeping employees satisfied(근로자를 만족시키는 조직문화)가 주어이며 made는 5형식동사이고 Google이 목적어, an icon of innovation이 목적보어가 된다. and는 접속사이고 it은 the corporate culture of keeping employees satisfied를 받으며, became은 2형식동사이다.

1. What is the passage mainly about?
   (a) The corporate culture that Google fought against and won.
   (b) The innovation that has upped Google's productivity and success.
   (c) The rate of employee satisfaction at Google.
   (d) The belief it took for Google to relinquish control over its employees.

2. Which of the following is correct, according to the passage?
   (a) Your ranking in the Google career ladder has no relevance on your ability to do your job well.
   (b) When Google wanted to improve its productivity, it knew it needed to hire a new Vice President.
   (c) Some of the most successful of Google employees' ideas have come from their free working time.
   (d) Google's employees are encouraged to ignore things that are irrelevant and focus on tech stuff.

3. What can you infer from the passage?
   (a) Google believes that if you hire talented people and let them work in their own way, they will prosper.
   (b) Google believes that it can take any employee, give them independence to think, and success will follow.
   (c) The 20 percent innovation has proven so efficacious that other companies are considering using it.
   (d) Google is so liberal with its employees because it has such talented individuals and cannot afford to lose them to their rivals.

4. The underlined can be best paraphrased by which of the following?
   (a) When you attend a Google meeting, you must be prepared to show your ideas.
   (b) Google has lively meetings where people keenly contribute their ideas and questions.
   (c) Those who attend Google meetings are the cream of the crop in terms of creativity.
   (d) If you don't have any good ideas, you shouldn't care about.

| WORDS & PHRASES |

concentration *n.* (업무) 집중   bold *a.* 거침없는, 대담한   allocate *v.* 배정하다   autonomy *n.* 자율   openness *n.* 개방
surveillance *n.* 감시   up *v.* 가격을 올리다   relinquish *v.* 포기하다, 내주다   keenly *ad.* 날카롭게, 열심히, 강렬하게

UNIT 02 Candidate games
딜레마

| 경제 |

  A dilemma is a situation in which you have to choose between difficult alternatives. The "Prisoner's Dilemma," the most famous among dilemmas, is a game theory. Two players in a critical situation tend to make the worst choice possible due to their own doubts and selfishness. The police don't have enough evidence for a conviction. Thus, having separated both prisoners, they offer each of them the same deal: If one testifies for the prosecution against the other and the other one remains silent, the betrayer goes free and the silent accomplice receives a 10-year sentence. If both stay silent, both prisoners are sentenced to only 1 year in jail. If each betrays the other, each receives a 5-year sentence. However, either prisoner can choose to confess and receive five years in jail.

  The prisoner's dilemma provides the basis to explaining the development of the nuclear arms race between the United States and the Soviet Union during the Cold War. The rival military powers' competition drove them to build more and more nuclear weapons, mainly out of mutual distrust and fear, even though they were well aware that the other country would stop building new nuclear weapons if they did. Like the prisoner's dilemma, the game of chicken is an important model for a diverse range of human conflicts. The adolescent game of chicken came to the public's attention in the 1955 movie "Rebel Without a Cause". The game consists of two boys simultaneously driving their cars toward the edge of a cliff, jumping out at the last possible moment. The boy who jumps out first is "chicken" and loses. The only way they would not be called a loser or chicken is to die together.

| 문장분석 |

■ A dilemma is a situation in which you have to choose between difficult alternatives. ➔ in which는 a situation을 선행사로 하는 관계대명사 which 앞에 전치사 in이 추가되어 있는 형태로, in the situation이란 의미를 지닌다. 그리고 전치사와 관계대명사는 합쳐서 관계부사로 변경이 가능하며, 이 경우 장소와 관련이 있으므로 관계부사 where로 바꿔 사용할 수 있다.

1. What can be inferred from the passage?
    (a) That criminals will always do what is in their own best interest.
    (b) People have a desire to be in a position that is either inferior or equal to their rival.
    (c) The arms race during the cold war was an inevitable event.
    (d) The only way to preserve yourself and your way of life is to not be a chicken.

2. What is the reason that the prisoner's dilemma works according to the passage?
    (a) A person's greed
    (b) Fear of others
    (c) Self-preservation
    (d) Misplaced anger

3. Which of the following is not an example of the prisoner's dilemma according to the passage?
    (a) Students being threatened with expulsion by the principal of a school if they do not confess
    (b) A standoff between two people with guns
    (c) Two people trying to prove who can drink the most
    (d) A person deciding who can get into a life boat on a sinking ship

4. Which of the following would be the best title for the passage?
    (a) Why we don't back down
    (b) The reason for the cold war
    (c) How to play chicken
    (d) The new prisoner's dilemma: Volunteer's Dilemma

| WORDS & PHRASES |

alternative *n.* 대안   **critical** *a.* 중요한, 위급한   **tend to** ~하는 경향이 있다   **evidence** *n.* 증거   **conviction** *n.* 유죄 선고[판결]
deal *n.* 제안   **testify** *v.* 증언하다   **prosecution** *n.* 기소   **betrayer** *n.* 배신자   **accomplice** *n.* 공범   **sentence** *n.* (형의) 선고
arms race *n.* 군비 경쟁   **mutual** *a.* 상호의   **distrust** *n.* 불신   **diverse** *a.* 다양한   **rebel** *n.* 반항아, 반대자   **without a cause** 이유 없는   **consist of** ~로 구성되다   **simultaneously** *ad.* 동시에   **chicken** *n.* 겁쟁이   **standoff** *n.* 대치 상황, 교착 상태
back down (주장 등을) 굽히다; 패배를 인정하다; 양보하다, 철회하다, 포기하다   **play chicken** 담력겨루기를 하다

UNIT 03 Progress over product
GDP

| 경제 |

In March 1989, the Alaskan oil tanker Exxon Valdez ran aground and leaked 40,000 cubic meters of oil. Around 2,000 kilometers of seashore was polluted and many people crowded to Prince William Sound near Anchorage to help clean up the mess. The restaurants, hotels, gas stations and stores in the remote location were suddenly full of people, stimulating an unprecedented business boom. The gross domestic product of Alaska increased, too. Could it be said that Alaska improved because its GDP increased, even though countless species of seabirds and whales died?

The GDP is an index that evaluates total production volume with a market value standard. All things produced are, of course, presumed to be good products. It does not differentiate between sustainable and non-sustainable products, nor does it differentiate between economic activities that actually improve living standards and those that do not. Even if nature is depleted by the excavation of resources and reckless deforestation, GDP can still increase. This leads to the criticism that GDP is a calculator that only knows how to add and does not know how to subtract.

GDP was created by the U.S. Department of Commerce during the Great Depression in the 1930s, and it was used as a guideline for measuring economic revival. However, even Simon Kuznets, the economist who created the GDP, warned against misuse of the measure idea, saying, "There are hardly any cases where the welfare conditions of a country can be inferred from total national profits." With the problems with the GDP rising to the surface, there are efforts to develop a new index to replace the GDP. One of the major new indexes proposed recently is the Genuine Progress Indicator. GPI measures factors that are not included in the GDP, such as reduction of resources, pollution, long-term environmental damage and domestic chores.

| 문장분석 |

■ This leads to the criticism that GDP is a calculator that only knows how to add and does not know how to subtract.

→ 〈A lead to B〉 구문은 'A가 B로 이어지다'는 의미로, A라는 이유로 인해 B라는 결과가 생긴다는 인과관계를 설명하는 구문이다. 비슷한 뜻으로 result in, cause, contribute to 등이 있다.

1. What's the passage mainly about?

    (a) Ways that recognition of GDP can improve a country's image in the eyes of the world
    (b) The rise and fall of the GDP index
    (c) The different ways of interpreting the GDP
    (d) The mass use of the GDP index and why it was so popular

2. Which of the following is correct?

    (a) The GPI considers the ecological harm that the country sustains while developing economically.
    (b) The GDP differentiates between economic progress that helps living standards for the normal person and that which doesn't.
    (c) Pollution is not forgotten when creating a country's GDP and GPI.
    (d) The GDP takes into account the welfare conditions of a country in deciding its' index.

3. How did the oil tanker disaster help Alaska?

    (a) The volunteers in the clean-up created a kind of tourism business in the country.
    (b) When the volunteers arrived, they realized how beautiful Alaska was and encouraged others to come.
    (c) The volunteers from the big cities demanded modern and international cuisine.
    (d) Inter-marriage of Alaskans and tourists brought a new character to the country.

4. What can't you infer from the passage?

    (a) GPI is considered a more accurate gauge of a country's situation than the GDP.
    (b) The Exxon Valdez spill contributed to the extinction of many species of animals.
    (c) Pursuit for economic development is causing the destruction of the natural world.
    (d) Alaska now ranks very high in the world rankings of GDP, alongside other developed countries.

| WORDS & PHRASES |

run aground 배가 좌초하다　leak *v.* 새다　cubic meter *n.* 세제곱미터　seashore *n.* 해안　stimulate *v.* 자극하다
unprecedented *a.* 유례없는　boom *n.* (경제) 호황　gross domestic product 국내 총생산 (= GDP)　countless *a.* 무수히 많은
index *n.* 지표　evaluate *v.* 평가하다　presume *v.* 가정하다　differentiate *v.* 구별하다, 차별화하다　sustainable *a.* 지속 가능한
deplete *v.* 대폭 감소시키다, 격감시키다　excavation *n.* 발굴　reckless *a.* 무모한　deforestation *n.* 삼림 벌채　subtract *v.* 빼다
the Great Depression 대공황　misuse *n.* 오용, 남용　welfare *n.* 복지, 복리후생　infer *v.* 추론하다　long-term *a.* 장기적인
domestic *a.* 집안의; 국내의

UNIT 04 Respecting privacy v. Public interests
사생활 보호 v. 공익

| 경제 |

The Japanese government does not release information on Covid-19 cases in detail. Only the district-level residential information and age group are made public, without stating where patients visited and when. Some local governments specify neighborhoods. Some cases could have remained secret if the companies did not post them on their websites. Publishing the information is completely at the discretion of the companies or individuals.

The justification is "protection of personal information." When information about them is released, the individual or company could suffer reputational damage. There was a news story about female students at a school with Covid-19 patients being called "corona." The Japanese government's default stance is not to release the information. It chose to keep the majority of people in the dark. In Japan, the government's surveillance of people's mobile phone information is considered untouchable, because it is associated with totalitarian policies.

The direction is the opposite from Korea. When a case was confirmed at a club in Itaewon, the city of Seoul checked the communications information from the mobile phones of 10,000 people who had been in the area that day. While some identifying information was released, and a certain individual had been criticized, the spread of the virus has slowed. As a result, Korea has been far more successful in tracing the chains of infections than Japan.

Every country is contemplating the limits placed on government surveillance and control of information. Citizens' voluntary sacrifices to live in a safer and more pleasant community are creating a healthy, supervised society. Many countries have joined the trend. <u>Instead of debating whether to allow surveillance, it's time to talk about creating a system to use information for public interests that prevents the abuse of information.</u>

1. What's the main idea of the passage?
   a) How to prevent governments from taking control in a pandemic.
   b) The use of personal information in the time of Covid-19.
   c) Working together with governments to solve the Covid-19 crisis.
   d) A lack of understanding about how the government will use our private information.

2. Which of the following is true, according to the passage?
   a) Companies that have seen an infection have no choice but to let other patrons know.
   b) The Japanese government releases the names of business where infected people have visited.
   c) The more people make an effort to protect their personal data, the faster the infections will stop.
   d) Due to the ease of accessing private data, Korea could trace infections better than Japan.

3. What does the underlined mean?
   a) In an age of surveillance, the pressure to conform to the government system that spies on everyone at all times is massive.
   b) It's about time that the government created a system to collect individuals' private information without them knowing about it.
   c) As the increase in invasions of privacy continues to worry society, it is on us now to come up with a way to combat such a system.
   d) To avoid the government simply taking our personal information, we should find a way to share relevant information for everyone's protection.

4. What can be inferred from the passage?
   a) The Japanese government cares more about privacy and reputation than its citizens' health.
   b) Japan looked to the successful situation in Korea in order to find ways to combat Covid-19.
   c) Those countries where people are more open about their movements are seeing better situations.
   d) No more than the age and location of infected people is needed to trace the chain of infections.

| WORDS & PHRASES |

in detail 세부적으로 make public 공표하다. 발표하다 discretion n. 자유재량 justification n. 정당화, 명분 default stance 기본 입장 surveillance n. 감시 infection n. 감염 contemplate v. 심사고하다 no choice but to ~하지 않을 수 없다 no more than 단지 ~에 지나지 않다. ~일 뿐(only)

| 문장분석 |

■ The Japanese government's default stance is not to release the information.
　　　　　　　S　　　　　　　　　　　V SC

앞에 not을 위치시킨다. default stance는 기본적인 입장을 뜻하는데, 그 이유는 default가 값을 지정하지 않았을 때 저절로 지정되는 초기값을 뜻하기 때문이다.

➜ to 부정사가 보어로 쓰인 경우이며, to 부정사의 부정은 to 부정사

UNIT 05 Just give them some fish
물고기를 줘라

| 정치/사회 |

"If you give someone a fish, he will be full for a day. If you teach him how to fish, you will make him full for life." You've heard this before. As a mantra for many missionaries and nongovernmental groups, it means that aid and welfare should bring changes in life rather than temporary gifts.

But is it right? American anthropologist James Ferguson wrote in his book "Give a Man a Fish: Reflections on the New Politics of Distribution" that the saying is no longer valid, considering today's fishing industry, for instance. The fishing industry now uses "floating factories" that no longer need people to actually catch fish in the ocean. He argues that teaching someone how to fish today will only produce an unemployed fisherman or a novice in the already saturated market.

As things have changed, the world doesn't need the labor of poor people today. They cannot use the skills they learn from vocational training. With globalization and digitization, _____. So, some argue that poor people should be given money for basic income.

As basic income accompanies tremendous psychological resistance, the traditional leftists especially feel appalled. It goes against the philosophy of "those who don't work should not eat." Karl Marx criticized the class who does not engage in proper production activities but wishes to become rich, calling it the "lumpenproletariat." He thought that the lumpenproletariat not only interferes with a proletariat revolution, but also participates in reactionary conspiracy. The traditional leftists reject basic income, as giving cash would bring people into the world of neoliberal market exchange.

| 문장분석 |

■ Karl Marx criticized the class [who does not engage in proper production activities but wishes to become rich], calling it the "lumpenproletariat." → who 이하의 관계대명사절은 the class를 꾸미며, calling 이하는 분사구문으로 Karl Marx가 call의 주체이다. 그러므로 calling으로 쓰였다.

1. What's the passage mainly about?
- a) The effect of globalization on poor people around the world.
- b) The validity of poor people's jobs in a world where AI is more efficient.
- c) The need for the rich to understand what kind of employment poor people can do.
- d) Time to change the system for the poor people: basic income debate

2. What does the opening mantra of the passage mean?
- a) When helping someone, you should aim to provide longer-lasting help rather than something short-term.
- b) If you want to help someone for real, it is necessary to look at what they already have and go from there.
- c) The kind of help that well-meaning groups often end up giving is useless to those that are in need of welfare.
- d) Giving gifts to someone to help them is frowned upon by welfare groups and charities as it doesn't teach the recipient anything.

3. Which of the following is incorrect, according to the passage?
- a) It is a waste of time to learn any kind of vocational training as digitization is easily able to replace people.
- b) Traditional leftists would not wish to see a basic universal income as it rewards those who don't work.
- c) Traditional fishermen find it hard to make ends meet as they are being superseded by fishing factories.
- d) Karl Marx thought that a basic universal income would solve many problems that beset the proletariat.

4. Which best completes the sentence?
- a) full employment has become a nearly impossible goal
- b) nobody is earning as much as they used to
- c) those who have undertaken vocational training are thriving
- d) a basic income has become a controversial subject

| WORDS & PHRASES |

mantra *n.* (기도·명상 때 외는) 주문, 문구 missionary *n.* (외국에 파견되는) 선교사 anthropologist n 인류학자 novice n 초보자 saturated *a.* 포화된 vocational training 직업훈련 appalled *a.* 간담이 서늘한, 끔찍해 하는 lumpenproletariat 계급의식과 연대의식이 없는 최하층 프롤레타리아 계급

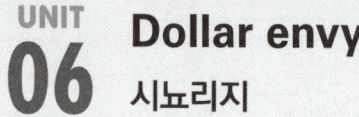

UNIT 06 Dollar envy
시뇨리지

| 경제 |

In 1999, the United States government began to issue commemorative coins of each of its 50 states, which became the most successful coinage program in history. The U.S. Mint issued five different 25 cent coins with designs that symbolized a particular state each year. The quarters put into circulation at the face value of the coin were extremely popular. The U.S. Mint calculated that about half of the U.S. population collected these coins. All 50 coins went into circulation in 2008.

This makes us ask: "How much did the U.S. government earn from issuing these coins?" It costs less than five cents to produce a 25 cent commemorative coin. As of the year of 2008, revenue from the coins has already amounted to $4.6 billion. The profit that the government or the central bank earns from issuing currency is called seigniorage. If coins, like the commemorative state quarters, are collected and are not circulated in the market, the difference between the face value of the coin and the cost of issuing it becomes seigniorage. However, the calculation is different when bank notes circulated in the market become worn out and are discarded. The financial capital's profit earned by the central bank issuing and circulating cash becomes seigniorage. The total annual seigniorage is calculated by subtracting the cost of issuing and circulating the cash from the market interest, multiplied by the amount of cash currently in circulation.

Seigniorage is also called "inflation tax." If more cash is supplied for circulation and brings about inflation, the real value of the cash diminishes and that wealth is transferred to the central bank. If this happens only domestically, then the total amount of wealth does not change. However, the U.S. dollar is different as it's the key currency of international financial transactions. If the U.S. issues more cash, the resulting drop in the real value of the world's holdings of the dollar due to inflation is transferred to the U.S. Federal Reserve. The seigniorage that the U.S. has earned since the dollar became the international currency after World War II must be astronomical. On Monday, the U.S. and European central banks declared they would release unlimited amounts of U.S. dollars in order to supply flexibility to financial corporations. The U.S. Federal Reserve intends to issue enough dollars as necessary and unlimitedly expand the currency exchange ceiling between central banks. We envy the seigniorage effect and the international currency, the U.S. dollar.

1. Which is the best definition of seigniorage?
   (a) Seigniorage is the revenue that a government earns from making and circulating money.
   (b) Seigniorage is the profit that the government collects if more cash is being circulated than is needed.
   (c) Seigniorage is the money that the government earns from currency exchange dealings.
   (d) Seigniorage is the income that the government gets from making commemorative coins that are not for everyday use, but instead for collectors.

2. What is the passage not about?
   (a) The ability for profit that commemorative coins bring about
   (b) The intention of the U.S. government to help weaker currencies to become stronger
   (c) How to calculate seigniorage of a government
   (d) The link between the seigniorage effect of U.S. dollar and international markets

3. What can't be inferred from the passage?
   (a) The seigniorage effect is something quite positive for a government.
   (b) Commemorative coins are just one way that seigniorage can be increased.
   (c) Becoming the international currency has a disappointing effect on an economy and causes losses.
   (d) The U.S. Federal Reserve gains from inflation.

4. According to the passage, what could be a cause of inflation in the U.S.?
   (a) A change in the material used by the U.S. Mint to produce coins or bills
   (b) People collecting coins or bills as commemorative memorabilia rather than using them
   (c) The state of the economy in countries that use U.S. dollars
   (d) A sharp rise in the currency exchange of U.S. dollars

| WORDS & PHRASES |

commemorative *a.* 기념하는   coinage *n.* 주화   symbolize *v.* 상징하다   face value *n.* 액면가   diminish *v.* 줄어들다
domestically *ad.* 국내에서   astronomical *a.* 천문학적인   declare *v.* 선언하다   flexibility *n.* 유연성   ceiling *n.* 한도, 천장

| 문장분석 |

■ The seigniorage [that the U.S. has earned since the dollar became the international currency after World War II] must be astronomical.
➜ 주어는 The seigniorage, 동사는 must be이다. 동격인 명사절(that) 안에서도 since가 이끄는 부사절이 있기 때문에 긴 주어 형태이다.

UNIT 07 More Sea Story blame game
정보의 비대칭성

| 경제 |

No matter how democratic and transparent a society might be, there remain unfair situations. Among things unfair, the most serious and hard to solve problem might be the distribution of information. In real life there are many problems due to incomplete and unfair distribution of information, which is also known as information asymmetry. A classic example is when buying a used car. The seller of the used car knows far more than the person who is willing to buy the used car. In a situation where the buyer does not know much about the quality of the used car, it is hard for the seller to get over the temptation of selling the car for a higher price than its actual value. The sellers overcharge the buyers. But when this kind of incident repeats itself, buyers no longer remain silent. They even refuse to make deals with a seller with a bad reputation. In some cases, the sellers will have to shut down their stores. They may have some fun using their position for a competitive advantage, but they cannot cheat the customers forever.

George Arthur Akerlof, who served on President Bill Clinton's Council of Economic Advisors, received the Nobel Prize for Economics with his theory, Market for Lemons, which is based on information asymmetry. Lemon refers to products that just look fancy on the outside, like a shiny used car that may be worthless on the inside. The scenario where information asymmetry results in a serious problem is in an owner-agent relationship. As the society gets more complex, people entrust experts to make judgments and decisions. One of the well-known relationships is the one between stockholder and CEO. But there is no guarantee that the agent will be loyal and work sincerely for his owner. The owner who entrusted the agent with the work lacks knowledge related to the field compared with the agent, so it is hard for the owner to observe and supervise the agent. This is where the moral hazard occurs among the agents. It means that the agent has a high chance of hurting the owner's profit by putting his own profit motive in front of him.

1. *What's the main topic of the passage?*
    (a) How to cheat your boss for you own gains
    (b) The moral questions of buying and selling cars
    (c) The problem of information asymmetry
    (d) The distribution of information through society

2. *What can you infer about car sellers?*
    (a) They never change the correct price to suit their own needs.
    (b) If they want to be successful, they can't cheat every customer out of money.
    (c) They participate in criminal activity to become rich.
    (d) They do not have long careers.

3. *Where does the problem lie in the relationship between owner and agent?*
    (a) The owner doesn't usually trust the agent to put the owner's interests first.
    (b) The owner tries to closely supervise the agent but doesn't have the time to fulfill this duty fully.
    (c) The owner is at a disadvantage because they lack expertise in the field that the agent knows well.
    (d) The agent will charge more money for a job that costs little.

4. *All of the following statements are true, except one. Which one?*
    (a) If the reputation of a car seller is damaged, he might lose his business.
    (b) A lemon refers to a person who does not understand what job they have to do.
    (c) A car seller might be tempted to overcharge a buyer who doesn't know about the quality of the car.
    (d) Stockholders and CEOs have a close owner-agent relationship.

| WORDS & PHRASES |

democratic *a.* 민주주의의   transparent *a.* 투명한   distribution *n.* 분배   information asymmetry 정보의 비대칭성
overcharge *v.* 바가지 씌우다   competitive advantage 경쟁우위   entrust *v.* 맡기다   guarantee *n.* 보증   sincerely *ad.* 진심으로
supervise *v.* 감독하다   moral hazard *n.* 도덕적 해이

| 문장분석 |

■ In real life there are many problems due to incomplete and unfair distribution of information, which is also known as information asymmetry.

➡ which는 distribution of information을 선행사로 하는 관계대명사의 계속적 용법이다.

UNIT 08 Hierarchical incompetence?
피터원리

| 경영 |

There is an old saying that the position in which an individual is seated makes the person. Unless the person's skill level is very low, most people are capable of a position when they receive it. However, if a person is placed in a position that is far beyond his ability level, it becomes a totally different story. That person will have a hard time trying to handle a position that is far beyond his capability, and other employees may have to struggle to tolerate the misery of the mismatch. Of course, the organization that seated the incapable person in the first place should pay for the inefficiency of its mistake. There are rumors during the season of promotions that incapable people are always on the list to be promoted. Why is this the case?

Laurence Peter discovered that the promotion of incapable people in a hierarchical society is very common. He came to this conclusion after researching hundreds of cases since 1969. "In a hierarchy every employee tends to rise to his level of incompetence," he said. This is the Peter Principle. According to this principle, each employee in a hierarchy keeps rising to a higher position until he reaches the final level of incompetence. An employee who has been promoted to a level beyond his ability senses by instinct that it will be his last position.

However, he never admits this fact or relinquishes the position voluntarily. Instead, he tries various things to cover up his incompetence. The common symptoms of this cover-up are many. He may include paper phobia, evidenced by cleaning one's desk compulsively; piling up stacks of documents to give the impression of busy-ness; long, meaningless conversations; endless walking around; phone addiction and table addiction, where every outcome has to be shown visibly.

| 문장분석 |

■ There is an old saying that the position in which an individual is seated makes the person.

→ an old saying과 명사절인 that은 동격으로 쓰이고 있으며 명사절 안에서의 주어는 the position, 동사는 makes이다. which는 목적격 관계대명사이고 전치사의 목적어인 position을 선행사로 받고 있다.

1. What's the passage mainly about?

(a) Being able to admit when you've made a mistake
(b) How incapable people cover up their incompetence
(c) The research of Laurence Peter
(d) Incapable people reaching positions above their level of competence

2. What did Laurence Peter discover about a hierarchical society?

(a) It takes a long time to discover those people who are incompetent at their jobs.
(b) Every member of a hierarchical society is incompetent at low levels.
(c) Every employee will keep rising up through positions until he reaches the level where he is incompetent.
(d) Hierarchy in society existed up until 1969 but is less common now.

3. What can you infer about somebody who is in a position for which he is incompetent?

(a) He doesn't care who knows he is incompetent as long as he can get a paycheck.
(b) He'll remain there until somebody finds out he is incompetent.
(c) He will try to learn new things to become competent.
(d) He doesn't realize that he is incompetent.

4. Which of the following is false?

(a) Employees have a tough time accepting the incompetence of a co-worker who gets a promotion.
(b) On every list of promotion there are a few people who are incompetent.
(c) A person in a position which they are unable to perform competently will relinquish the job readily.
(d) Moving things around on your desk is a method of creating the appearance of busy-ness.

| WORDS & PHRASES |

capability *n.* 능력   struggle *v.* 고투하다   tolerate *v.* 참다   misery *n.* 고통   mismatch *n.* 부조화   incapable *a.* 무능한
inefficiency *n.* 비능률   hierarchial *a.* 계층의   incompetence *n.* 무능   relinquish *v.* 포기하다   compulsively *ad.* 강제적으로
addiction *n.* 중독

UNIT 09 Broken items
깨진 유리창

| 경제 |

A hooligan passing by a bakery broke a window. The startled owner ran out and went after the man, but the hooligan ran away and the damage was not serious. The owner just covered the broken window with paper. A few days later, garbage piled up in front of the bakery and scribbling appeared on the wall. Customers started to decrease. Soon, the area became a place where the hooligans fought each other. American criminal psychologists James Wilson and George Kelling focused on increasing crime rates in the city and published the thesis "Broken Windows," in 1982. It says that if the building owner neglects minor damage, such as a broken window, then larger and more serious crimes such as theft and violence occur. People who see the broken window feel the landlord has given up the building. The theory is that if we take small disorders and crimes lightly, they eventually become a serious matter.

Michael Levine, an expert in marketing and promoting, applied this theory in business management and introduced the Broken Windows Theory. If a company ignores a minor mistake or loophole, then it will bring unexpected losses and a critical failure of management later on. When paint chips off walls, toilets get dirty, and when employees are allowed to have unkind attitudes, it could lead to the fall of a great company. The message is, whether in criminology or business management, we should fix the broken windows at once.

Early in the 19th century, there was already a debate about broken windows in economics. M. de Saint-Chamans, a member of the committee to reconstruct France, said replacing the broken window brings a loss to the bakery owner, but since the window shop owner gains that much, there is no loss for the nation. He even said that due to the window shop owner's consumption, new income is created — so it is desirable to break windows. In contrast, Claude Frederic Bastiat, a liberal economist, said if the window had not been broken, the money would have been used elsewhere. Therefore, the profit of the window shop owner is just a loss of opportunity for another person. Bastiat argued that wealth created through damage is false, trapped in the error of the broken window.

1. What is the main idea of the passage?

(a) How to limit your business competition
(b) What to do in case of vandalism at your place of work
(c) The effect of uncorrected outside influences on an existing situation
(d) How vandalism encourages other crimes acting as a gateway crime

2. What can be inferred from the passage?

(a) Criminology has become very adept at predicting what crimes cause further crimes.
(b) A positive effect from a negative situation is still a negative.
(c) America has one of the highest rates of crimes causing minor damage.
(d) Economists all agree that the broken window theory is a positive one.

3. Which of the following is true according to the passage?

(a) Economists have differing opinions on the effect of the broken window.
(b) Bakery owners always try to replace broken windows.
(c) Loopholes are not a serious problem for most businesses.
(d) Dirty toilets are responsible for the downfall of several major companies.

4. Which of the following is a simple explanation of the broken window theory?

(a) A person throws a rock, a window breaks.
(b) Broken windows cost money to replace.
(c) If a window is broken a person must decide to replace it or just cover it over.
(d) If there is a problem you must fix it or it will cause more problems.

| WORDS & PHRASES |

hooligan *n.* 깡패, 불량배   startled *a.* (깜짝) 놀란   go after 뒤쫓다   pile up 쌓이다   scribbling *n.* 낙서
psychologist *n.* 심리학자   thesis *n.* 학위 논문   landlord *n.* 주인   take ~ lightly ~을 경시하다, 무시하다   loophole *n.* 구멍
criminology *n.* 범죄학   desirable *a.* 바람직한   trap *v.* 가두다   uncorrected *a.* 교정되지 않은   downfall *n.* 몰락

| 문장분석 |

■ In contrast, Claude Frederic Bastiat, a liberal economist, said if the window had not been broken, the money would have been used elsewhere. ➡ 〈if had p.p., 주어 + would have p.p.〉 형태의 가정법 과거완료 용법이 쓰였다.

UNIT 10
Demonstrators in the dark
합리적 무시

| 경제 |

In 1845, the French economist Frederic Bastiat wrote a parody lampooning protectionism. In his story, candle makers submit a petition to the Chamber of Deputies of Third Republic. "We are suffering from the ruinous competition of a rival," they say, "who apparently works under conditions so far superior to our own for the production of light that he is flooding the domestic market at an incredibly low price... This rival, which is none other than the sun, is waging war on us mercilessly." The French candle makers demanded legislation banning not only the import of foreign candles but also natural lighting. They asked the Chamber of Deputies to prevent "artificial" competition and boost demand. However, the Chamber of Deputies turned down the petition, for it ignored the interests of consumers.

The American economist and social scientist Mancur Olson theorized in his book, "The Logic of Collective Actions," that "only a separate and 'selective' incentive will stimulate a rational individual in a latent group to act in a group-oriented way." In other words, those who participate in a group action might openly advocate public and national interests but are, in fact, strictly pursuing personal interests.

The bigger the interest, the tighter the group will stick together, and the more intense the collective action will become. The problem is that the resistance of the general public to a collective action by a certain interest group is surprisingly insignificant. Why is the public so indifferent? The benefits are concentrated on a certain group, but the social cost is widely distributed, so each individual suffers minor damage. In this case, the group benefiting will ignore the damage on the general public based on the reasoning that its members will gain maximum benefits at a minimum cost. It is referred to as "rational ignorance." The flip side of the tendency is that even an important national interest can be ignored in order to minimize the individual damage on each interest group.

1. What can be inferred from the passage?
(a) Candle light should be cheaper than sunlight.
(b) Collective groups have little or no power to change economic laws.
(c) A collective group is only concerned with the needs of those within the group.
(d) Rational ignorance is the regular policy people follow in business practice.

2. Which of the following is incorrect according to the passage?
(a) Members of a group will accept more than minimal cost if they receive maximum benefit.
(b) French candle makers made a petition against the sun.
(c) Collective action generally causes benefits with minimal damage to the individual.
(d) People will act as a group effort when it is in their own interest to do so.

3. What would be the best title for this passage?
(a) Candle makers collective
(b) Maximum benefit versus minimum cost
(c) Collective bargaining and individual benefits
(d) The collective and rational ignorance

4. What was meant by the word 'artificial' in the phrase "to prevent 'artificial' competition and boost demand"?
(a) Other candle makers that were importing their cheaper product
(b) Sunlight, because it was seen as a source of light that was not from a candle
(c) Fake, unreal competition that causes a lower demand for quality product
(d) Competitors that does not take the concerns of the consumer into account

---

| WORDS & PHRASES |

lampoon *v.* 풍자하다   protectionism *n.* 보호무역주의   Chamber of Deputies (프랑스) 국민의회   ruinous *a.* 감당할 수 없는
wage *v.* 전쟁을 벌이다   mercilessly *ad.* 무자비하게   artificial *a.* 인위적인   boost *v.* 신장시키다   stimulate *v.* 자극하다
latent *a.* 잠재하는   strictly *ad.* 엄격하게   insignificant *a.* 대수롭지 않은, 사소한   flip side *n.* 이면

| 문장분석 |

■ The bigger the interest, the tighter the group will stick together, and the more intense the collective action will become. → 〈the + 비교급, the + 비교급〉 용법으로 '~할 수록 더 …하다'라는 뜻이다. the bigger the interest에서는 be동사가 생략되었다.

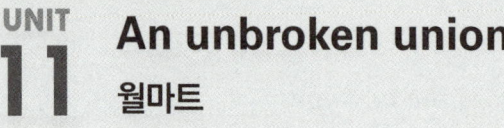

UNIT 11 An unbroken union
월마트

| 경영 |

You can find everything you can think of at Wal-Mart except a labor union. The retail giant is notorious for its policies against labor unions. The company is known to filter out candidates who could be potential union leaders at the time they are recruited. An internal memo written in 1991 gave managers a list of 24 signs that employees were interested in organizing a union. If employees increasingly talked to one another on the phone, became interested in the profits of the company or in its corporate policies, asked radical questions at meetings, mentioned union-related terms such as mediation, an ombudsman and longevity pay, or suddenly met with other employees they weren't normally friendly with, the manager was required to report the behavior to the union avoidance team at headquarters. The task force would immediately fly to the store in question on a chartered flight. That is how the company prevented the unionization of its workers for more than 40 years. There has been only one successful case of unionization, in a store in Quebec, Canada in 2004, but Wal-Mart closed the store the following year.

The no-union policy of Wal-Mart goes back to the customer-service philosophy of founder Sam Walton. Mr. Walton's Rule No. 1: The customer is always right. Rule No. 2: "If the customer happens to be wrong, refer back to Rule No. 1." No matter how unreasonable a customer's demand might be, the Wal-Mart employees must not express anger. Once a customer files a complaint, the staff in question will be rebuked or be required to write a letter explaining the circumstances. The "Ten Foot Rule" is also a must. Whenever a customer is within 10 feet of an associate, he should look into that person's eyes, greet the customer, and offer help. The unconditional return policy is also a part of the founder's philosophy. The customer does not need to explain why he wants to return a product. "I changed my mind" is reason enough. Some customers abuse the policy and return a tent after a camping trip or costumes after Halloween. Taking all the returns incurs enormous costs, which should be set off somewhere else. It is easiest for the company to save on wages, and it is part of the reason for the anti-union policy.

1. *What can be inferred from the passage?*
    (a) Wal-Mart uses unfair business practices.
    (b) Wal-Mart values the customer above all else.
    (c) Wal-Mart is difficult to compete with.
    (d) All the Wal-Mart employees are unhappy with their work conditions.

2. *What is the difference between the two rules Mr. Walton believed in?*
    (a) One rule was more important than the other.
    (b) There was one rule for women and one for men.
    (c) There is no actual difference between the two. They are both the first rule.
    (d) One rule saved money the other caused a loss of money.

3. *Which of the following is untrue according to the passage?*
    (a) Mr. Walton didn't have a high opinion of his workers and their ability.
    (b) Wal-Mart has an unconditional return policy.
    (c) Wal-Mart tries to prevent unions.
    (d) There are 24 signs to look for when preventing unions from forming.

4. *What would be the most likely topic of the next paragraph?*
    (a) The cost of the return policy on Wal-Marts profits
    (b) The other reasons for the anti-union policy
    (c) Why Mr. Walton believed in his rules
    (d) How to return items to Wal-Mart

| WORDS & PHRASES |

retail *n.* 소매   notorious *a.* 악명높은   filter out 걸러내다   radical *a.* 급진적인, 과격한   mediation *n.* 조정, 중재
ombudsman *n.* 고충 처리 담당자   immediately *ad.* 즉시, 즉각   chartered *a.* 공인된, 전세 낸   complaint *n.* 불평, 항의
rebuke *v.* 질책하다, 꾸짖다   associate *n.* (직장) 동료   unconditional *a.* 무조건적인   abuse *v.* 오용하다, 남용하다   incur *v.* 초래하다

| 문장분석 |

■ It is easiest for the company to save on wages, and it is part of the reason for the anti-union policy.
→ 첫 번째 it은 가주어이고 진주어는 to save ~, for the company가 의미상 주어이다. 두 번째 it은 대명사로 앞 문장 전체를 가리킨다.

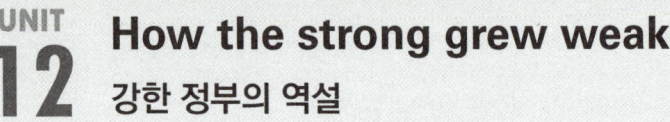

UNIT 12 How the strong grew weak
강한 정부의 역설

| 행정 |

When the oil shock of the 1970s hit, countries that imported oil responded in two ways: The majority of advanced nations immediately permitted a price increase in oil while many developing nations started to regulate domestic oil prices. The former allowed the market to adjust to the oil crisis; the latter directly manipulated the market. Which is the "strong government?" It might appear at first glance that governments that allow oil prices to float exude an anaemic influence on the market and governments that regulate oil prices are stronger. But the opposite holds true.

In countries where the price of oil increased according to market principles, consumers took it upon themselves to start conserving energy. Technology to reduce energy and replace oil naturally burgeoned. In countries that forcibly suppressed oil prices to soften the blow of booming oil prices, oil consumption did not decrease. Rather, this practice triggered speculative demand and cornering and hoarding practices, as well as the creation of black markets. While advanced nations decreased their dependence on oil, developing nations remained highly dependent.

A so-called "strong government" disregards the will of the market or the people when establishing national objectives and they enact policies to achieve these objectives. If an oil crisis occurs, the government establishes an objective of stabilizing domestic oil prices, and it jumps into the market to regulate prices. The problem remains that the more it throws itself into the market, the weaker the market function becomes, and the effectiveness of the policy drops dramatically. A vicious cycle ensues. The so-called "strong government" employs stronger policies and harsher restrictions to compensate for its previous policy failures.

As the government failures accumulate, it grows distant from the market and the people. The effectiveness and influence of the government shrivels and the government ultimately leads the country to an economic collapse or loses power. The American theorist of international relations and American foreign policy John Ikenberry referred to this as the "irony of state strength". Strong governments that enact strong policies end up becoming feckless — the people turn their backs on such governments.

1. What can be inferred from this passage?
   (a) States that control the markets in their countries will succeed while countries like America fall deeper into financial peril.
   (b) A truly strong government is not afraid to allow markets that influence their country run freely since the power to control these markets is not actually within their grasp.
   (c) John Ikenberry was actually incorrect in his assumptions about strong governments, as can be seen from the discussion on the oil crisis in this passage.
   (d) Failures by governments during times of crisis lead to the development of stronger future policies.

2. What is the main idea of the passage?
   (a) State strength exists not in the ability to control markets but rather to allow them to operate without undue influence, trusting society to maintain the balance of supply and demand.
   (b) How strong governments set an example for weaker ones to follow in times of crisis.
   (c) The control of the economic market over weak countries and their acceptance of this control through their failures.
   (d) How the American government was able to stabilize the domestic oil market and further influence the global market to help weaker countries.

3. Which of the following would be a good title for the passage?
   (a) The American government's global influence in the wake of the worldwide oil crisis
   (b) The irony of state strength, how seemingly anaemic governments are in fact not
   (c) How to control the economic markets in your country, a basic guide
   (d) The economic perils of government action during times of crisis

| WORDS & PHRASES |

manipulate *v.* 조종하다, 다루다   exude *v.* 물씬 풍기다   anaemic *a.* 활기 없는   conserve *v.* 아껴 쓰다   burgeon *v.* 급성장하다
forcibly *ad.* 강제로, 강력히   cornering and hoarding 매점 매석   disregard *v.* 무시하다   vicious *v.* 잔인한, 포악한
ensue *v.* 뒤따르다   accumulate *v.* 쌓이다, 늘다   shrivel *v.* 위축되다   collapse *v.* 붕괴되다, 무너지다   feckless *a.* 무기력한, 나약한
in the wake of ~에 뒤이어

| 문장분석 |

■ The problem remains that the more it throws itself into the market, the weaker the market function becomes, and the effectiveness of the policy drops dramatically. ➡ '~할수록 …하다'라는 ⟨the + 비교급, the + 비교급⟩ 구문이다.

UNIT 13 A crime of passion
'제2의 스위스' 된다는 영국의 망상

| 정치 |

Many psychologists analyze "Brexit" as a "crime of passion," or an illegal act committed out of a sudden fury rather than premeditation. They considered Brexit a short-sighted and irrational decision based on the outrage of the neglected class. Supporters of Brexit believe their withdrawal from the European Union will bring prosperity. And they like to cite the example of Switzerland. The U.K. Independence Party's Nigel Farage likes to say Switzerland set its own direction, and the Swiss are happy.

In a 1992 referendum, Switzerland voted against joining the European Communities, the predecessor of the European Union, but is still one of the wealthiest countries. Last year, Switzerland's per capita national income was $80,675, the second-highest in the world only after Luxembourg, and far higher than the United Kingdom's $43,771 or the United States' $55,805. And proponents of Brexit argue that Switzerland's prosperity is based on its independence from the European Union, as it does not pay the astronomical contribution required and makes its own trade policies.

However, experts disagree. They say that Switzerland's success owes to the unique work ethic of the Swiss people and not its separation from the European Union. In fact, on June 5, Switzerland conducted a national referendum on a very unique issue. It was about to introduce a basic income of 2,500 Swiss francs ($2,556) every month to boost consumption. Getting money for free sounds too good to be true, but Swiss voters rejected the proposal, mainly because it would lower the motivation to work. In 2014, a bill to extend the four weeks of paid holiday to six weeks was rejected.

The Brits don't share this sense of ethics, so leaving the European Union won't be like it was for Switzerland. <u>It is regrettable that Brexit, a spur-of-the-moment reaction, seems to anyone at all like scoring a goal for the United Kingdom.</u>

| 문장분석 |

■ Many psychologists analyze "Brexit" as a "crime of passion," or an illegal act committed out of sudden fury rather than premeditation. → analyze A as B 구문이며, 등위 접속사 or은 a crime of passion에 대한 동급 표현이다. committed은 분사로 명사 an illegal act를 수식한다. "A rather than B" B라기보다 오히려 A라는 의미로, out of sudden fury와 premeditation을 연결하고 있다.

1. *What's the passage mainly about?*
   (a) What the UK needs to do to make sure it doesn't make any of the same mistakes as Switzerland.
   (b) The reasons why leaving the EU may not be as bad for the UK as has been forecast.
   (c) The example of Switzerland that the UK should follow now it has quit the EU.
   (d) The difference between the UK and Switzerland in terms of not being a part of the EU.

2. *Which of the following can you infer?*
   (a) If the UK changes the way it feels about the EU, it will prosper.
   (b) The European Union's future is in jeopardy if the UK convinces more nations to withdraw.
   (c) Brexit will not happen if the people of the UK get their way.
   (d) The people of the United Kingdom have a different attitude to work than the Swiss do.

3. *What was surprising about the Swiss referendums?*
   (a) Swiss voters were nonchalant about participating in the referendums since they didn't care.
   (b) What the government was offering up to a vote was more than the people expected.
   (c) The voters chose to reject bonuses that many others would have eagerly accepted.
   (d) Despite expectations, the outcome of the vote did not make any difference to the lives of the Swiss.

4. *Which best paraphrases the underlined?*
   (a) That anyone would see the knee-jerk decision of Brexit as a good thing is unfortunate.
   (b) After Brexit, the decision made by UK voters has been regretted by a large number of them.
   (c) The fact that Brexit was decided by those who thought they were doing the best for the UK is a pity.
   (d) The immediate reaction to Brexit was that the right decision was made, but this isn't true.

| WORDS & PHRASES |

irrational *a.* 불합리한; 이성적이지 못한   outrage *n.* 분노   withdrawal *n.* 탈퇴; 철수   referendum *n.* 국민투표
proponent *n.* 제의자; 옹호자   astronomical *a.* 천문학의; 천문학적인, 엄청난   boost *v.* 밀어 올리다, 끌어 올리다
spur-of-the-moment 충동적인   regrettable *a.* 유감스런

UNIT 14 A rational vote
투표의 경제학

| 정치 |

In a democratic society, voting is an essential tool to express political opinion. To vote is regarded as a duty, but not everybody votes out of responsibility. The public choice theory is based on the hypothesis that political behavior is decided by economic interest. Voters calculate benefits and costs in voting and act in a way that maximizes their interest.

But if economic gains and losses are the sole consideration, abstaining is the best choice that voters can make. That is because the chance of one person's vote having an influence on an election result is almost zero, while one needs to go through a lot of trouble to cast a vote. However, this theory does not fully explain why people vote. Economists have come up with a supplementary idea. They decided that not only material gain but also non-economic gain come into play when people vote. For instance, participating in an election, an important political process, can give pride and pleasure to voters, instead of inconvenience. Voters' evaluation and judgment about current political situations affect turnout rates too. If people's self-interest changes a great deal depending on who wins an election, people will be more motivated to vote.

Some maintain that the motivation for voting must be studied from a long-term perspective. Abstention can be interpreted as wanting an alternative political system to democracy. Voting can be seen as a way of supporting democracy. If people realize that abstention and political disinterest might tear down the foundation of democracy, they will come up with an utterly different conclusion about the possible costs and benefits from voting. Voting is thus an act to protect the democratic system.

The problem is that voting does not always bring the best results. Kenneth Arrow, a winner of the Nobel Prize in economics, demonstrated that no voting system guarantees consistent results and a democratic voting process does not guarantee that the best person is elected. Nevertheless, voting is still regarded as the best democratic process because there is no better alternative. A voting system is imperfect but made legitimate through a fair voting process and acceptance of the results.

1. According to the passage, which of the following is NOT a motivation for voting?
   (a) Wanting to get prestige from your neighbors by voting for the government
   (b) A desire to uphold and protect the political system of democracy
   (c) A feeling of being involved in something important
   (d) Choosing a candidate who will provide the best economic situation for you

2. What's the main topic of the passage?
   (a) The reasons why people vote and what is gained by this participation
   (b) The people who want to see the end of democracy
   (c) How to improve your personal finances by voting
   (d) The most perfect voting process in the world

3. What can you infer about people who don't vote?
   (a) They are very busy and usually can't find the time to get to the voting booth.
   (b) Those who abstain from voting do so to show their dissatisfaction with democracy.
   (c) They are interested in politics and care greatly about who gets into government.
   (d) They hope to improve their economic situation.

4. Which of the following best summarizes economic-motivated voting?
   (a) Bringing money into voting is causing the downward spiral of politics.
   (b) Voters who vote based on economics feel they are supporting democracy.
   (c) The voter votes based on career; if he/she has a high-powered job, they vote in a particular way and vice versa.
   (d) The voter judges how his/her economic situation will be improved or hindered by each candidate.

| WORDS & PHRASES |

esessential *a.* 필수적인   hypothesis *n.* 가설   abstain *v.* 기권하다   supplementary *a.* 보충의, 추가의
inconvenience *n.* 불편, 애로   tear down 파괴하다   utterly *ad.* 완전히   consistent *a.* 한결같은, 일관된   alternative *n.* 대안, 선택
legitimate *a.* 타당한

| 문장분석 |

■ They decided that not only material gain but also non-economic gain come into play when people vote.   ➔ decide가 목적어로 절을 취하고, 목적절 안의 주어는 〈not only A but also B〉의 병렬구조이다.

UNIT 15 In the interest of whom?
수쿠크

| 경제 |

Greek philosopher Aristotle was against the idea of lending money at an interest rate, because he thought that money simply breeding more money without any exchange or trade involved was unnatural. The popes in medieval times thought the same way. They followed teachings from the Bible that said no one should charge a rate of interest in return for lending money, grain or any other thing that might accrue a greater value. Clergymen who demanded the payment of a usury had their titles taken away. Usurers who did not repent before death were not allowed a Christian burial. Even in those times, however, moneylenders still managed to charge and pay interest; the borrower would be charged a fee for remitting or exchanging money.

Some religious reformists who were active some 500 years ago also spoke out against charging interest on loans. Martin Luther, the German reformer, said in indignation that taking back more than the principal was stealing. He also said that moneylenders were thieves tainted with vice, and that they should be executed by having their legs torn apart. As the monetary economy gradually took root and a growing number of people started to live on income from usury, however, the church had no other choice but to recognize interest as a legitimate source of income.

The teachings of Islam still prohibit charging riba, or interest, on loans. But Muslims have also devised a way by which they could evade these religious regulations. Sukuk, the Islamic equivalent of a bond, is a typical example. Sukuk is not a loan but a financial product that is traded to evade the Islamic law that prohibits riba. For example, if someone wants to borrow money to buy a machine, the bank can buy the machine itself and collect rent on it, instead of charging interest for a loan. Since a rental fee is not technically interest, it is not in violation of Islamic law. There are similarities between sukuk and the asset-backed security (ABS), which is said to help achieve financial reform, because the asset-backed security is structured as a bond backed by underlying assets, and returns the profits from the assets to the bond holders.

1. What is the passage mainly about?
(a) Islamic people who are moneylenders
(b) The immoral practice of moneylending
(c) The punishments for those charging too much interest
(d) The practice of sukuk

2. How do Muslims get around the problem that interest on loans is prohibited?
(a) They just ignore the practice and nobody talks about it.
(b) They changed the wording of the law that prohibited moneylending.
(c) Rental fees are charged on a product rather than just giving money to buy the product.
(d) The banks became official moneylenders and a special law was devised to allow it.

3. Which of the following is true?
(a) Initially, the church did not allow usury but as times changed, the church had to change its opinion.
(b) The Bible states that only certain people can act as moneylenders.
(c) Martin Luther was sympathetic to the plight of the moneylenders.
(d) Clergymen frequently lost their titles after getting caught up with usuries.

4. What can you infer about the very first moneylenders?
(a) They were rich men when they died.
(b) They were very violent men who used physical threats to get money back.
(c) They were looked down and were outcasts from society.
(d) They were held in awe.

| WORDS & PHRASES |

pope *n.* 교황　**accrue** *v.* 누적되다, 축적하다　**clergymen** *n.* 성직자　**usury** *n.* 고리 (대금)　**repent** *v.* 회개하다　**burial** *n.* 매장
remit *v.* 송금하다　**indignation** *n.* 분노　**principal** *n.* 원금　**taint** *v.* 더럽히다　**monetary** *a.* 화폐의, 금융의　**legitimate** *a.* 합법적인
evade *v.* 피하다　**technically** *ad.* 엄밀히 말하면　**get around** 성공적으로 처리하다　**wording** *n.* 자구 선택, 단어 표현
outcast *n.* 따돌림을 당하는 사람

| 문장분석 |

■ As the monetary economy gradually took root and a growing number of people started to live on income from usury, however, the church had no other choice but to recognize interest as a legitimate source of income.

➡ 문두의 접속사 as는 여러 가지 의미로 쓰일 수 있는데, 본문에서는 '~함에 따라'로 해석하면 적절하다. however 뒤에 나오는 주절의 〈had no other choice but to R〉 구문 중 but은 예외를 나타내는 except의 의미로 쓰인 것이다. 따라서 위 구문은 '~외에 다른 대안이 없다', '~할 수밖에 없었다'로 해석하면 된다.

UNIT 16 NGO: A dearth of humility
인본주의가 결여된 NGO

| 정치 |

Legendary investor and co-founder of the Quantum Fund Jim Rogers is an eccentric figure in many ways. He travelled around the world on his motorcycle and in his car and wrote two books, "Investment Biker: Around the World with Jim Rogers" and "Adventure Capitalist: The Ultimate Road Trip." It is not common to see travel journals that point out the factors affecting the economic efficiency of the places visited.

The impediments include developed countries and NGOs. Their "soulless aid" weakens the industrial competitiveness of Africa and hinders economic development. He added that a considerable part of the aid was taken by dictators and intermediaries. He was especially harsh on NGOs.

Rogers wrote that people ride air-conditioned four-by-fours with windows up and live a posh life, residing in luxury housing complexes with security guards at the entrance and watching satellite television. And they explain to poor locals how foolish they are. If aid is canceled, NGOs would no longer get a job in Africa. NGOs have become a big business. Created by corrupt governments and equipped with enormous financial means, NGOs produced many brokers going between foreign aid and corrupt governments. So wrote Rogers.

Rogers exposed the hypocritical conduct of a German NGO that held a luxury meeting at a resort in Malawi and blocked the entry of local people. He claimed that local people felt mortified rather than grateful to NGOs and even called them neo-colonialists.

When the book was published in the early 2000s, the story belonged elsewhere in the world. In Korea, NGOs were praised for criticizing politics and businesses without sanctuary, using "freedom from money and power" as their weapon. But the contemporary mainstream NGOs in Korea _____, as they are characterized by ambiguous money management, an egoistic nature, flattery towards power and an absence of critical spirit.

166 Part 4 사회과학

1. What's the main idea of the passage?

   a) The relationship between Jim Rogers and NGOs.
   b) Jim Rogers' negative opinion of NGOs.
   c) The reaction of NGOs to Jim Rogers.
   d) Jim Rogers' exposure of the corruption of NGOs.

2. What can you infer from the passage?

   a) NGOs were well-meaning in the beginning, but their behavior and actions have changed.
   b) NGOs actively perpetuate the plight of many countries that they purport to help.
   c) Rogers used to work for an NGO and, therefore, knows firsthand what kind of work they do.
   d) Corrupt governments use NGOs to get the particular kind of aid that they want or need.

3. According to the passage, why does Rogers dislike aid from NGOs?

   a) He believes that NGOs like handing out aid to poor people because it makes them feel good.
   b) He heard that they do not even like interacting with the poor people they have gone to help.
   c) He says that aid demotivates people and prevents them from developing by themselves.
   d) He saw them give aid meant for the poor directly to the rich for their own purposes.

4. Which best completes the sentence?

   a) have always attracted criticisms and suspicion
   b) are not seen as corrupt but as vital to helping the needy
   c) have fought long and hard to stay clear of such criticisms
   d) don't seem to be far from what Rogers had criticized

| WORDS & PHRASES |

eccentric *a.* 특이한, 이상한 impediment *n.* 방해물, 장애물 posh *a.* 호화로운, 멋진 hypocritical *a.* 위선적인 mortify *v.* 굴욕(모멸)감을 느끼게 하다, (정욕을)극복하다 sanctuary *n.* 성소, 성역 flattery *n.* 아첨, 빌붙음 perpetuate *v.* 영속화하다

| 문장분석 |

■ It is not common to see travel journals that point out the factors affecting the economic efficiency of the places visited..

➡ It은 가주어, to 이하는 진주어로 '~ 한 여행기를 보는 것'은 일반적이지 않다(not common) 즉 독특하다는 뜻이다. that은 관계대명사 주격이고, affecting 이하는 factors를 꾸미는 형용사구이다.

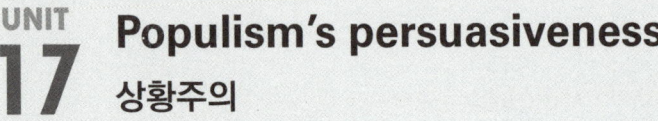

UNIT 17 Populism's persuasiveness
상황주의

| 정치 |

Chile is the first country to give birth to a socialist regime through a free election. In 1970, Salvador Allende was elected president on a promise to nationalize the copper mining industry, which was monopolized by a multinational giant at the time, and to return the profits to the society. Though Augusto Pinochet's military coup toppled the regime after only three years, the Allende administration ended the long argument among political scientists over whether it was possible to implement socialism through an election. Chile's military authorities might have been similar to those of other Latin American nations, but its social structure was very distinct. A community that could be called a civil society had already been established by the early 19th century. Political party mechanisms, which can moderate social discord, were functioning. That's why the chronic Latin American aliment of populism was an exception in Chile.

Despite its reputation, populism is not an exclusive property of the progressives and the left. In fact, the United States is the most sophisticated exploiter of populism. The word was even created in the United States. In opposition to the two-party system of the Republicans and the Democrats, the People's Party was founded in 1891 and advocated policies that were economically irrational, such as the unlimited coinage of silver. Populism originated from this ideology. American historian Michael Kazin wrote in "The Populist Persuasion" that American politics was being adopted to cultural populism based on the cultural values of the social mainstream, away from economic populism like farmers' issues.

The Democratic Party has triumphed in the decades since President Franklin Roosevelt through economic populism, which encouraged the middle class and working class to stand against the wealthy Republican supporters. The Republicans also learned how to deal with economic populism. Ronald Reagan effectively used cultural populism to distinguish himself from established politicians in Washington and various interest groups. Bill Clinton successfully came into power by representing the cultural values of the white working class. The New York Times columnist Maureen Dowd explains the characteristics of neo-populism as "situationalism." Populism is exploited to one's advantage instead of pursuing the truth.

1. *Which of the following is a good description of populism according to the passage?*
    (a) Becoming the popular person in a political party so that you can run the country.
    (b) Using popular culture to deceive people.
    (c) Adopting a false image that is pleasing to the voting public.
    (d) Learning what people want and using it to gain support even if it is completely irrational.

2. *What can be inferred from the passage?*
    (a) Bill Clinton lied to gain votes to become President.
    (b) Chile is the only country to ever become a Socialist state.
    (c) Political parties will continue to use populism to their own ends in the future.
    (d) American history is filled with people who use populism.

3. *Which of the following is the most likely topic of the next paragraph?*
    (a) How neo-populism is used in current U.S. politics
    (b) How Ronald Regan became President
    (c) Why the New York Times discredits populism
    (d) How countries can use populism as Chile did

4. *Which of the following is correct according to the passage?*
    (a) Parties that use populism well have had success in being elected.
    (b) Chile is now a Socialist state again.
    (c) The current Democratic President of the U.S. used cultural populism as well.
    (d) Maureen Dowd dislikes the use of such tactics in politics.

| WORDS & PHRASES |

nationalize *v.* 국영화하다   monopolize *v.* 독점하다   topple *v.* 뒤집다, 전복시키다   moderate *v.* 완화하다, 누그러뜨리다
discord *n.* 부조화, 불일치   exclusive propercy 전유물   sophisticated *a.* 세련된; 정교한   coinage *n.* 화폐 주조
triumph *v.* 승리하다, 개선하다   deal with ~을 다루다, 대처하다   exploit *v.* 이용하다, 활용하다

| 문장분석 |

■ Though Augusto Pinochet's military coup toppled the regime after only three years, the Allende administration ended the long argument among political scientists over whether it was possible to implement socialism through an election. ➡ 양보를 나타내는 종속절 뒤에, 주절의 주어는 the Allende administration이고, ended가 동사다. the argument over 이하가 목적어가 된다. 전치사 뒤에 wh-절은 동반될 수 있으므로, over whether ~가 쓰인 것이다.

UNIT 18 Korea lacks basic values
스마트 기업 50

| 경영 |

"Intelligence, Innovation, Change, Creation." These are the values that startup companies, large enterprises, the government and just about any organization aspire to embody. So we are always interested to see who is succeeding at this. Since 2010, the MIT Technology Review has published its "50 Smartest Companies" list. The list includes companies that are "overturning technology markets," based on analyses and observations of at least 12 months. Companies that created new business models or introduced new, attractive technologies to the market are selected, and quantitative indicators like revenue, net profit or patents are not considered.

Of course, this is not an absolute list. Nevertheless, the list is meaningful. This year, many of the companies that were ranked high last year were replaced. The absence of China's Xiaomi, which came second last year, is notable. Last year, Xiomi was described as "maturing beyond the original 'cut-price Apple' model with ideas like flash sales over its mobile messaging platform". But it was not included in this year's list as it did not bring any new ideas to the smartphone market. Xiomi's competitors are also not on the list. Apple was ranked 16th last year but is not included in this year's list. Samsung was fourth in 2014 but didn't make either last year's or this year's lists.

This year, Amazon topped the list. "Call out a request and AI-powered Alexa will play your favorite song or order you a pizza," it said. "And Amazon web services just keep growing." Baidu is ranked second as "China's leading search engine is now developing autonomous cars". Baidu has launched a research team in Silicon Valley in 2014 and plans to employ more than 100 autonomous-car researchers and engineers this year. Chinese companies like Huawei (10th), Tencent (20th), Didi Chuxing (21st) and Alibaba (24th) are highly ranked on the list. Coupang is the only Korean company on the list.

1. What is the passage about?

(a) The connection between success and inclusion on the "50 Smartest Companies" list.
(b) Why the "50 Smartest Companies" list matters in the tech world.
(c) The best way to get on the "50 Smartest Companies" list.
(d) The changing names on the "50 Smartest Companies" list.

2. What does the underlined mean?

(a) Growing out of its original nickname of being a cheaper version of Apple.
(b) Doing more than what Apple could possibly hope to do on a smaller budget.
(c) Finding a way to undercut the price of Apple while delivering the same quality.
(d) Demonstrating that Apple was not original in the first place, and it could do better.

3. What can be inferred from the passage?

(a) Xiaomi is on the brink of collapse as it has been unable to generate enough revenues.
(b) No company ever manages to retain its position at the top end of the list.
(c) Every company on the list was expected to turn a profit in the previous 12 months but didn't.
(d) There are probably other companies that could have made the list but for some reason were left of.

4. What is true about the list of companies?

(a) They are judged on qualitative criteria rather than quantitative information.
(b) Only those companies that have managed to turn a profit are eligible for inclusion.
(c) Every company included on the list aspires to be just like a much larger company above them.
(d) To be considered, the companies must be less than one year old at the time of judging.

| WORDS & PHRASES |

innovation *n.* 혁신   startup *n.* 신설기업   aspire *v.* 열망하다, 갈망하다   overturn *v.* 뒤집다   quantitative *a.* 양적
indicator *n.* 지표   absolute *a.* 절대적인, 완전한   notable *a.* 두드러진, 유명한   autonomous *a.* 자율의

| 문장분석 |

■ Last year, Xiaomi was described as "maturing beyond the original 'cut-price Apple' model with ideas like flash sales over its mobile messaging platform".

➡ Last year는 명백한 과거 시점 부사구로, 과거 동사 was described가 온다. describe A as B "A를 B로 묘사하다"의 수동형으로 as 뒤 "maturing beyond the original 'cut-price Apple' model with ideas like flash sales over its mobile messaging platform."는 Xiaomi와 동격을 이룬다. like는 전치사로 목적어 flash sales가 ideas에 대한 예를 제시하는 표현이다.

UNIT 19 Like Robin Hood, tax up to no good
부유세

| 경제 |

In the 17th century, King William III of England imposed an additional tax on the wealthy to help fund the cost of war. The tax, strangely enough, was tied to the number of windows on each home. At the time, having a fireplace in the house was a symbol of wealth, as most people opted for relatively sealed structures to keep in heat during the cold winters. Homes with fireplaces, however, typically had plenty of windows. The owners could afford the luxury because the fireplaces heated their homes in the winter, even though cold air seeped in through the window areas. Although the fireplace signified wealth, it was difficult for the government to confirm whether homes had a fireplace or not, as it would take a tremendous amount of energy and time to check each dwelling. Therefore, King William III decided to impose a tax based on the number of windows on each home — the so-called "window tax." After the window tax was introduced, some people sealed off their windows to avoid having to fork over extra money.

It reminds me of the type of taxes on the wealthy we see today. In a modern state, the purpose of imposing taxes specifically on the rich is to ease inequalities in the distribution of wealth. But these types of taxes can create unintended side effects. France, which levies relatively high taxes on wealthy people, is a prime example. In 2008, Alain Ducasse — regarded as one of the best chefs in France — fled his homeland and became an exile in Monaco to escape these taxes. Two years earlier, French singer Johnny Hallyday, who sold more than 100 million albums, fled his homeland to become an exile in Switzerland for the same reason. And then there's the case of Swedish businessman Ingvar Kamprad, chairman of IKEA, the world largest furniture retailer. Fed up with Sweden's taxes on the wealthy, he siphoned a chunk of his wealth to an overseas fund.

This type of tax creates what's called the "Robin Hood effect," named after the famous outlaw of British folklore. Robin Hood robbed rich people and then distributed the spoils to the poor. But, according to some modern-day economic scholars, Robin Hood would have actually made the poor worse off, because the well-heeled merchants would have moved to other places to protect their wealth. That would have driven up prices, as there would be fewer people who could afford to open and operate stores.

1. What is the purpose of taxing the rich according to the passage?
    (a) To get more money for the government
    (b) To create more equality between the upper and lower class in society
    (c) To give the poor a break from paying taxes
    (d) To pay for the extra expenditures of the government at times of war

2. Which of the following is incorrect according to the passage?
    (a) Hallyday, Kamprad, and Ducasse all fled France to escape high taxes.
    (b) Window tax was a tax aimed at the wealthy.
    (c) Both Sweden and France have high tax rates for the wealthy.
    (d) High taxes on the wealthy ease inequality with the poor.

3. What would be a likely topic of the previous paragraph?
    (a) How taxes were collected from people
    (b) How the idea of taxation originated
    (c) The other taxes imposed by King William II
    (d) The implementation of standardized taxation in a kingdom or country

4. What can be inferred from the passage?
    (a) People generally do not like to pay taxes.
    (b) Wealthy people should never have to pay taxes.
    (c) The poor will have to pay more to compensate for rich people leaving.
    (d) There is no proof that Robin Hood ever existed.

| WORDS & PHRASES |

fireplace *n.* 벽난로   opt for ~을 선택하다   seep in 스며들다   fork over 지불하다, (돈을) 내다   fed up with ~에 질리다
siphon *v.* (돈을) 빼돌리다   outlaw *n.* 범법자, 범죄자   spoil *n.* 전리품   well-heeled *a.* 부유한

| 문장분석 |

■ It reminds me of the type of taxes on the wealthy we see today. ➡ 〈remind A of B〉는 'A에게 B를 상기시킨다'는 의미이다.

UNIT 20 America's risky pot experiment
아슬아슬한 미국의 마리화나 실험

| 사회 |

On March 13, 2014, a career fair related to the marijuana industry was held in Denver, Colorado. A dozen businesses that grow and distribute cannabis-related products showcased the industry's prospects, and more than 500 jobseekers visited the event. This year, Colorado became the first state to legalize recreational marijuana. Considering the general direction of society, the legalization of marijuana is only a matter of time. Twenty states currently approve of the use of medical marijuana. While cannabis is classified as a controlled substance under federal law, the Obama administration has advised law enforcement not to target marijuana users in those states. A more significant change is the approval of recreational marijuana, as in Colorado. It has already been approved in Washington State, and Arizona and Alaska are likely to follow.

The latest research appears to support marijuana legalization. President Barack Obama said that he believes marijuana is less harmful than alcohol. A recent Wall Street Journal survey asked which of the four substances – tobacco, alcohol, sugar and marijuana – is most harmful, and Americans responded that tobacco is the most harmful, then alcohol, sugar and finally marijuana. Sugar received 15 percent of the vote, compared to only 8 percent for marijuana. Statistics released this week showed that the state of Colorado has collected $2 million in taxes from recreational marijuana. When cities like Detroit go bankrupt, many state governments find marijuana a tempting revenue source. Another study said that the legalization of marijuana would reduce alcohol consumption, which would be a net positive for public health. Attorney General Eric Holder said Friday that he supports reducing sentences _____.

Of course, most supporters of marijuana legalization agree with a few restrictions. The use of drugs should not be encouraged for young people, and safety-related issues, such as driving under the influence, should be restricted. However, it is doubtful whether American society has the capability to regulate itself very meticulously. Gun-related violence continues despite gun control. Many experts worry that the legalization of marijuana could create drug addicts and encourage the use of other, harder drugs. When drugs are combined with gun-related issues, terrible tragedies can happen. In January, Colorado State Patrol troopers found that 31 of 61 drivers stopped for impaired driving were under the influence of marijuana. However, Americans do not seem to be concerned about that correlation.

1. Which of the following statements is true?
   (a) Most impaired drivers stopped in Colorado were under the influence of alcohol as opposed to drugs.
   (b) Many Americans believe that alcohol is just as dangerous to health and society as marijuana.
   (c) The marijuana careers fair put a dampener on the industry in Colorado.
   (d) The number of states that has legalized marijuana for recreational use is rising.

2. Which of the following fits the blank best?
   (a) for non-violent drug crimes to reduce the prison population
   (b) for drug trafficking as it is more important to get the producers
   (c) if it would mean that people would stop taking drugs
   (d) as a last resort in the fight against drugs in America

3. What can be inferred from the passage?
   (a) Legalizing marijuana will improve the economy almost immediately.
   (b) Marijuana for medical use is the norm already throughout the whole of America.
   (c) As people become educated about the medicinal uses of marijuana, recreational use will decrease.
   (d) In due course, marijuana may receive full legalization in the U.S.

4. What is the argument in the passage against marijuana legalization?
   (a) America is not very able to control its dangerous practices as gun violence has shown.
   (b) Marijuana has been shown to be a gateway drug to harder substances.
   (c) When somebody ingests marijuana, they are less able to function in society.
   (d) Drugs and driving is already prevalent and legalization will make the rate skyrocket.

| WORDS & PHRASES |

howcase v. 소개하다, 전시하다   recreational marijuana 오락용 마리화나   controlled substance 마약류   restriction n. 제한
meticulously ad. 꼼꼼하게   impaired driving (각종 약물 포함) 음주운전   as opposed to ~와는 대조적으로   dampen v. 축축하게 하다,
풀 죽게 하다   in due course 적절한 때에   ingest v. 빨아들이다

| 문장분석 |

■ Another study said that the legalization of marijuana would reduce alcohol consumption, which would be a net positive for public health.

➡ which의 용법 가운데 앞문장의 전체나 일부를 받는 경우로, 여기에서 which는 the legalization of marijuana would reduce alcohol consumption을 받는다.

홍준기

전) 시설관리공단 영어과 출제위원
전) KBS 굿모닝팝스 독해 연재
현) 중앙일보(Korea JoongAng Daily) 객원해설위원
현) 중앙일보(Korea JoongAng Daily) 독해 연재 (2013~)
현) 박문각편입학원 총괄 디럭터 겸 대표교수

저서
The Best 리딩스펙트럼 (1,2,3,4)
The Best 리딩스펙트럼 컴팩트
오바마영어 직독직해/영작연습, 동의어 엑스퍼트
패러프레이즈 버스터 〈이상 종합출판 Eng〉
박문각편입 영어시리즈 〈㈜ 박문각출판〉
스타 영문법 사전 〈챔프스터디〉
프리미어 시사독해 실렉션 〈종합출판 Eng〉

The Best 리딩스펙트럼 컴팩트

발 행 일	2022년 5월 25일(초판 3쇄)
저 자	홍준기
발 행 인	문정구
발 행 처	종합출판 ǀ En G
출판등록	1988. 6. 17 제 9-175호
주 소	10387 경기도 고양시 일산서구 중앙로 1456, 603-1호
홈페이지	www.jonghapbooks.com
전자메일	jonghap@jonghapbooks.com
대표전화	02-365-1246
팩 스	02-365-1248

이 도서의 국립중앙도서관 출판예정도서목록(CIP)은 서지정보유통지원시스템 홈페이지 (http://seoji.nl.go.kr)와 국가자료공동목록시스템(http://www.nl.go.kr/kolisnet)에서 이용하실 수 있습니다. (CIP제어번호 : CIP2020031327)

ISBN 978-89-8099-722-0   13740

※ 낙장 및 파본은 바꾸어 드립니다.

|Summary & Paraphrase 코너|

본문(지문)활용 요약·패러프레이즈 이해·연습

부록 본문(지문)해석 / 문제해설·정답

SPECTRUM

KOREA JOONGANG DAILY
in association with
The New York Times

The Best
리딩스펙트럼 **컴팩트**

홍준기 지음

| Summary & Paraphrase 코너 | .... *p. 3* |

본문(지문)활용 요약·패러프레이즈 이해·연습

부록 본문(지문)해석 / 문제해설·정답 .... *p. 93*

Summary & Paraphrase

본문(지문) 순서와 동일(각 파트별 Unit 1~20)

Humanities

Part 1 인문

UNIT 01 Rumors: society's cancerous tumors
사람 잡는 루머

" Practice

▶▶ Example

Rumors are dangerous and cause problems. The decisions we make oftentimes rely on what others think. The more people who believe something to be true, the more likely you are to believe it. Moreover, people become more extreme in their opinions when talking with others who hold similar views. For example, after reports went out about the Pearl Harbor attack, rumors arose among Americans that the U.S. had incurred massive losses. Roosevelt refused to reveal exact data, but asked people not to believe the rumors since he knew negative rumors could lead to problems.

incur *v.* (좋지 못한 상황을) 초래하다; (비용을) 발생시키다

▶ 소문은 위험하며 문제를 일으킨다. 우리가 만드는 결정은 종종 다른 사람들이 무엇을 생각하는지에 의존한다. 무엇인가가 사실이라고 믿는 사람이 많아질수록 당신이 그것을 믿을 확률 역시 높아진다. 게다가 비슷한 생각을 가지고 있는 사람들과 이야기할 때 사람들의 의견은 더욱 극단적으로 변한다. 예를 들어 진주만 공격에 대한 보도가 나온 이후부터 미국인들 사이에서 미국이 큰 손실을 입었다는 소문이 생겨났다. 루스벨트 대통령은 정확한 수치를 밝히길 거부했지만 사람들에게 소문을 믿지 말 것을 요청했다. 왜냐하면 그는 부정적인 소문이 문제를 야기한다는 것을 알고 있었기 때문이다.

UNIT 02 'Social proofs' on the Web
인기 검색어

SUMMARY & PARAPHRASE

66 Practice

▶▶ Example

People copying or following what others are doing in order to fit in and not to make mistakes is a kind of social proof. This can be seen when people laugh along with laughter tracks or donate because others can be seen doing so. Social proofs, however, are anything but that. It is a way to influence consumers and direct behavior. Search keywords appear on our screens and adjust in the moment, making us think it is true. But, actually, a keyword that stands out may be clicked on even more than it would be otherwise, leading to skewed data. A keyword looks like it is popular when it was, in actual fact, simply an anomaly.

laughter track(laugh track) 웃음소리가 녹음된 테이프
otherwise *adv.* 그렇지 않으면; 그 외에는; (~와는) 다르게   **anomaly** *n.* 변칙

▶ 사람들이 어울리기 위해 그리고 실수를 하지 않기 위해 다른 사람들이 하는 것을 따라 하거나 따른다는 것은 일종의 사회적 검증이다. 이것은 사람들이 녹음된 웃음소리를 따라 웃거나 다른 사람들이 기부한 것을 보았기 때문에 기부하는 행동에서 보인다. 그러나 사회적 검증은 그런 것이 아니다. 이것은 소비자들에게 영향을 주고 행동을 조정하기 위한 방법이다. 검색 키워드가 화면에 나타나고 순간적으로 조정해 우리로 하여금 그것이 사실이라고 생각하게 만든다. 하지만 실제로 눈에 띄는 키워드는 눈에 띄지 않았을 때보다 더 많이 클릭 될 수 있고 이는 왜곡된 데이터를 야기할 수 있다. 키워드는 사실 단순한 변칙이었을 때 일반적인 것처럼 보인다.

UNIT 03 Give us hope!
피그말리온

SUMMARY & PARAPHRASE

66 Practice

▶▶ Example

The Pygmalion effect originates from the Greek myth of Pygmalion. He was fearful and critical of women while lacking self-esteem, so he sculpted his ideal woman. Loving it passionately and praying intensely, it came to life, and ultimately his views on women began to change. This demonstrates how one's life can change by having dreams. The Burne-Jones painting "Pygmalion and the Image" echoes this intent from the painter.

originate v. 유래되다; 발명하다 **self-esteem** n. 자존심
demonstrate v. 입증하다, 보여주다 **echo** v. 울리다; 공명하다

▶ 피그말리온 효과는 그리스 신화에 등장하는 피그말리온에서 유래한 것이다. 그는 여성을 두려워하고 여성에 대해 비판적이었던 반면 자존심이 부족했다. 따라서 그는 그의 이상적인 여성을 조각했다. 그것을 열정적으로 사랑하고 열심히 기도하자 그것이 살아났고 마침내 여성에 대한 그의 시각이 변화하기 시작했다. 이것은 꿈을 가짐으로써 누군가의 삶이 변화할 수 있다는 점을 시사한다. 번 존스의 작품 "Pygmalion and the Image"는 화가로부터 이러한 의도를 반영한다.

UNIT 04 Waiting for the cargo
카고 컬트(Cargo-Cult)

SUMMARY & PARAPHRASE

66 Practice

▶▶ Example

  The Ratchet Effect, aka the Cargo Cult, explains how once one has become accustomed to a certain standard of living, it is hard to return to earlier levels regardless of current economic status. For example, after the end of World War II, Pacific Islanders that had experienced the luxury of U.S. military supply boxes tried to attract more by imitating the U.S. army. However, they were misguided in thinking that those two events would always occur together. The phrase Cargo Cult has metamorphosed into to mean things that look the same but are different.

standard of living 소득수준　**metamorphose** v. 변하다; 변화시키다

▶ 카고 컬트라고 불리기도 하는 톱니바퀴 효과는 사람이 어떤 생활수준에 익숙해지고 난 뒤에는 현재 경제적 상황과 무관하게 이전 수준으로 돌아가는 것이 왜 어려운지를 설명한다. 예를 들어 제2차 세계대전이 끝난 뒤 미국 군수보급함이라는 사치품을 경험한 태평양 제도의 주민들은 미군인 척하면서 그것을 더 많이 얻고자 하였다. 그러나 그들은 그 두 사건이 언제나 동시에 일어날 것이라고 잘못 생각했다. 카고 컬트라는 구절은 같아 보이지만 다른 것들을 의미하는 단어로 변화했다.

UNIT 05 Lost in translation
오역

SUMMARY & PARAPHRASE

66 Practice

▶▶ Example

Mistranslations can have dire consequences or they can sometimes bring nice surprises. On the one hand, a mistranslation may have been a factor in the dropping of the atomic bomb in Japan as the erroneous translation led to the U.S. believing Japan was ignoring the Potsdam Declaration instead of Japan actually trying to delay negotiations. On the other hand, the incorrect translation of a word in the Bible actually improved on the original and led to a better saying in English.

negotiation n. 협상

▶ 오역은 심각한 결과를 초래하거나 뜻밖의 기쁜 소식을 가져다줄 수 있다. 한편 오역은 잘못된 번역이 미국으로 하여금 일본이 사실상 협상을 미루려 한다는 것 대신 포츠담 선언을 무시하는 것이라고 믿게 함으로써 일본에 원자폭탄을 투하하는 요인이 되었다. 다른 한편으로 성경 속 단어에 대한 오역은 오히려 원문의 의미를 향상시키고 영어로 더 잘 번역되도록 만들었다.

UNIT 06 Surviving stress
스트레스

SUMMARY & PARAPHRASE

66 Practice

▶▶ Example

Stress is everywhere, but this is not always a bad thing. Our bodies improve when under stress in terms of sight, hearing and muscle mass. We are more able to handle life's problems. Conversely, lowly-stressed people are less likely to be successful when under stress. Modern life reduced the kind of stress that our ancestors experienced, but introduced a new kind of stress: the media always makes us aware of global problems.

in terms of ~면에서   **introduce** v. 소개하다; 진행하다; 도입하다

▶ 스트레스는 어디에나 있지만 이것이 늘 나쁜 것만은 아니다. 우리의 몸은 스트레스를 받을 때 시각, 청각 그리고 근육량에 있어서 향상된다. 우리는 삶의 문제를 더 잘 통제할 수 있게 된다. 반대로 스트레스를 적게 받는 사람들은 스트레스를 받을 때 성공할 확률이 낮아진다. 현대의 삶은 우리의 조상이 경험한 스트레스의 가짓수를 줄였지만 새로운 종류의 스트레스를 만들어냈다. 즉, 미디어는 우리로 하여금 늘 세계 문제에 대해 경각심을 가지게 만든다.

UNIT 07 Fanning fears
도시의 전설

SUMMARY & PARAPHRASE

66 Practice

▶▶ Example

Rumors and superstitions abound everywhere. In America, there is the story warning people not to flick their lights at another car lest they be followed and killed by gang members. In South Korea, the fan death idea warns people not to sleep with their fans on at night or they may die from a drop in body temperature. This is, of course, impossible. Both these stories have been proven false.

rumor *n.* 소문, 유언비어   **superstition** *n.* 미신   **abound** *v.* 풍부하다

▶ 소문과 미신은 어디에나 많이 존재한다. 미국에서는 갱단의 단원들이 따라와서 살해하는 경우가 있으니 운전자들에게 다른 차를 향해서 빛을 깜빡거리지 말라는 경고가 담긴 이야기가 있다. 한국의 선풍기 사망설은 사람들에게 밤에 선풍기를 켜놓고 잠들면 체온이 떨어져 사망할 수 있기 때문에 선풍기를 켜놓고 잠들지 말라고 경고한다. 이는 당연히 불가능하다. 이러한 두 이야기는 거짓으로 판명되었다.

UNIT 08 Diamonds are forever
다이아몬드

SUMMARY & PARAPHRASE

66 Practice

▶▶ Example

Diamonds may now be used solely as jewelry, often for weddings, thanks to the slogan "A diamond is forever" which was masterminded by De Beers, but it wasn't always this way. 4,500 years ago, it was used as an abrasive. In 7 B.C., it acted as a talisman, protecting the wearer from harm due to its strength. It was in the 15th century that its modern role arose when a young man won his love's heart by discovering the abrasive properties of diamonds.

mastermind *v.* 지휘하다, 조종하다   talisman *n.* 부적

▶ 현재 다이아몬드는 드 비어에 의해 만들어진 "다이아몬드는 영원하다"라는 슬로건 때문에 특히 결혼을 위한 보석으로 자주 사용되지만 늘 이런 용도로 사용되지는 않았다. 4,500년 전 다이아몬드는 연마재로 사용되었다. 기원전 7세기에는 다이아몬드의 힘을 통해 해로움으로부터 그것을 지닌 사람을 보호하는 부적으로 사용되었다. 다이아몬드의 연마 특성을 밝힘으로써 젊은 남성이 그의 연인의 마음을 얻었던 15세기에 다이아몬드의 현대적 역할이 생겨나게 되었다.

UNIT 09 Straw-man logic
허수아비 논법

SUMMARY & PARAPHRASE

🙶 Practice

▶▶ Example

Straw-man arguments misrepresent the issue being discussed and reduce the quality of a debate. They present situations that do not accurately portray the original point and seek to discredit the opponent's opinion; thus, are disregarded by logical minds. President George W. Bush was an avid proponent of straw-man arguments, famously using one to support U.S. troops in Iraq by branding anyone who sought to debate the issue as unpatriotic and harmful to America.

discredit *v.* 신임을 떨어뜨리다; 신빙성을 없애다   **disregard** *v.* 무시하다
avid *adj.* 열렬한   **unpatriotic** *adj.* 비애국적인

▶ 허수아비 논법은 현재 논의되고 있는 사안을 잘못 보여주고 논쟁의 질을 낮춘다. 그것은 원점을 정확하게 묘사하지 않은 상황을 보여주고 상대 의견의 신빙성을 잃게 하려고 한다. 따라서 이는 논리적인 사람들에 의해 무시된다. 조지 워싱턴 부시 대통령은 허수아비 논증의 열렬한 지지자였고 미군의 이라크 파병에 대해 논쟁하고자 하는 사람을 미국에 대해 비애국적이고 해로운 사람이라고 낙인찍으며 허수아비 논법을 사용한 것으로 유명하다.

UNIT 10 When 'smaller is better' is not
'축소 지향' 일본의 그릇된 역사 인식

SUMMARY & PARAPHRASE

66 Practice

▶▶ Example

　The Japanese "smaller is better" mentality can be seen in everyday life, but it is also present in politically sensitive situations. UNESCO's recognition of the large numbers of innocent victims killed in the Nanjing Massacre drew the ire of the country, which sought to drastically reduce the number. Even now, the Japanese government is asking for a smaller official number. In regards to the "comfort women" of South Korea, Japan's lack of acknowledgement and attempts to ignore the issue show the Japanese mentality once again.

mentality *n.* 사고방식　**comfort women** 위안부 여성
acknowledgement *n.* 인정; 감사; 답신

▶ 일본의 "작을수록 좋다"라는 사고방식은 일상생활 어디에서나 볼 수 있지만 이 사고방식은 또한 정치적으로 민감한 상황에서도 보인다. 유네스코가 난징대학살에서 무고하게 죽은 피해자들의 수가 많다는 것을 인지한 것이 이 수를 급격하게 낮추려던 일본의 화를 불러일으켰다. 심지어 지금도 일본 정부는 더 적은 공식적 숫자를 요구하고 있다. 한국의 위안부 여성에 대해 일본이 인정하지 않는 것과 이 사안을 무시하려는 시도는 일본의 사고방식을 다시 한 번 보여준다.

UNIT 11 The Republic of Complex
콤플렉스

SUMMARY & PARAPHRASE

66 Practice

▶▶ Example

Originally, the term 'complex' was used by Freud and Jung to refer to the effect our unconscious thoughts have on our behavior; for example, Freud famously talked about the link between taboo and desire and Jung said that complex guides us psychologically. The term has also been used by Adler to talk of an inferiority complex, whereby humans develop by trying to overcome feelings of inferiority and become superior. This can be seen in the behavior of Demosthenes and Roosevelt who overcame their own obstacles.

unconscious *adj.* 의식을 잃은; 무의식적인; 의식하지 못하는   **obstacle** *n.* 장애

▶ 원래 콤플렉스라는 단어는 프로이트와 융에 의해 사용되었으며 우리의 무의식적 생각이 우리의 행동에 끼치는 영향을 지칭하는 데 사용되었다. 예를 들어 프로이트는 잘 알려졌듯이 금기와 욕망 사이의 관계에 대해 말했고 융은 콤플렉스가 우리를 심리적으로 인도한다고 말했다. 이 용어는 또한 아들러가 인간이 열등감을 극복하고 더 우월해지기 위해 시도함으로써 발전하게 된다는 열등감에 대해 말하기 위해 사용됐다. 이것은 장애를 극복한 데모스테네스와 루스벨트의 행동에서 볼 수 있다.

UNIT 12 Irrational minds
선택적 지각

SUMMARY & PARAPHRASE

❝ Practice

▶▶ Example

Selective perception and, as an extension of this, cognitive dissonance show the irrationality of humans. Our levels of self-esteem influence how we perceive the actions of others. We choose what to perceive in order to align them with our behavior. It is now used a lot in determining marketing campaigns, so that one company's brand will stand out among the hundreds of others we are exposed to daily. When our behavior does not match our attitudes, we are more likely to change our attitudes than our behavior.

irrationality *n.* 불합리성   **self-esteem** *n.* 자존감

▶ 선택적 지각과 이것이 확장된 개념인 인지 부조화는 인간의 불합리성을 보여준다. 우리의 자존감 수준은 우리가 다른 사람의 행동을 어떻게 인지하는지에 영향을 끼친다. 우리는 다른 사람의 행동을 우리의 행동과 맞추기 위해 무엇을 인지할지를 선택한다. 이것은 현재 마케팅 캠페인을 결정하기 위해 많이 사용되는데, 이를 통해 한 회사의 브랜드가 우리가 매일 노출되는 수백 개의 다른 회사 브랜드 사이에서 도드라질 수 있도록 만든다. 우리의 행동이 태도와 일치하지 않을 때에는 행동을 바꾸는 것보다 태도를 바꿀 확률이 더 높다.

UNIT 13 How accidents shape history
우연과 필연

SUMMARY & PARAPHRASE

💬 Practice

▶▶ Example

> Historical accidents can affect the course of history and in an interesting way. Although some believe that accidents have no effect, many including Blaise Pascal think it does. If Cleopatra's nose had been less attractive, Mark Anthony might never have fallen in love. The Roman Empire may have followed a different path. If Ottoman Sultan Bajazet had been healthy, he would have continued into central Europe. If one man hadn't said the wrong thing at the wrong time, the Berlin Wall would have taken much longer to come down.
>
> **historical** *adj.* 역사상의; 역사와 관련된   **come down** *v.* 무너져 내리다; (비나 눈 등이) 내리다

▶ 역사적 사건은 역사의 흐름에 영향을 줄 수 있고 이는 흥미로운 방향으로 갈 수 있다. 비록 몇몇 사람들은 사건들이 아무 영향을 끼치지 못한다고 믿지만, 블레즈 파스칼을 포함한 다수의 사람들은 사건이 영향을 끼친다고 생각한다. 만약 클레오파트라의 코가 덜 매력적이었다면 마크 앤소니는 절대 사랑에 빠지지 않았을 것이다. 로마제국은 다른 길을 가게 되었을 수도 있다. 만약 오스만 제국의 술탄 바자제트가 건강했다면 그는 유럽 중심부까지 계속 진격했을 것이다. 만약 한 사람이 잘못된 시기에 잘못된 것을 말하지 않았다면, 베를린 장벽은 무너지는 데 더 많은 시간이 걸렸을 것이다.

UNIT 14 No pain, no gain on literary road
작가의 각오

SUMMARY & PARAPHRASE

❝ Practice

▶▶ Example

> Two writers absorb themselves totally in the writing process, eschewing the frivolous lifestyle that fame can bring. Cormac McCarthy had a harsh early childhood, but instead of talking about it, he wrote. "The Road" details the journey life of a father and son who suffer greatly and live in abject poverty. Kenji Maruyama is a recluse absorbed in his work. He even refuses to have children with his wife lest it upset his writing schedule. Both wish to be left alone to simply write.
>
> **eschew** *v.* 피하다, 삼가다   **recluse** *n.* 은둔자   **lest** *conj.* ~하지 않도록; ~할까 봐

▶ 두 작가는 명성이 가져다줄 수 있는 경박한 생활 방식을 삼가고 집필에 완전히 몰두했다. 코맥 매카시는 힘든 어린 시절을 보냈지만 그것에 대해 말하는 것 대신 글을 썼다. "The Road"는 매우 고통받고 극심한 빈곤 속에 살고 있는 아버지와 아들의 삶을 상세히 서술한다. 겐지 마루야마는 그의 작품에 몰두한 은둔자이다. 그는 심지어 집필 계획에 차질이 생길까 봐 그의 아내와 더불어 아이를 낳길 거부했다. 이 두 사람은 단지 글을 쓰기 위해 혼자 남기를 바랐다.

UNIT 15 When the masses silent the wise
집단사고

SUMMARY & PARAPHRASE

66 Practice

▶▶ Example

> Groupthink is the situation in which people will agree simply for the sake of agreement. Stepping away from the group mentality and protesting is very difficult. Therefore, even smart people can make the wrong decisions as they don't want to listen to anyone outside the group or hear anything that goes against them. The Vietnam War and the Bay of Pigs invasion exemplify this. In the latter, Kennedy wanted everyone to agree with his idea to invade, so even though Arthur Schlesinger disagreed he was reluctant to do so and remained silent, which he later regretted.
>
> **group mentality** *n.* 공동체 의식   **exemplify** *v.* 전형적인 예가 되다   **regret** *n.* 후회 *v.* 후회하다

▶ 집단사고는 사람들이 동의를 위해 동의하는 상황을 의미한다. 공동체 의식에서 벗어나는 것과 항의하는 것은 매우 어렵다. 따라서 사람들은 아무리 똑똑할지라도 그룹 외의 누군가의 말을 듣고 싶지 않아서 혹은 그들에게 반대하는 의견을 듣고 싶지 않아서 잘못된 결정을 내릴 수 있다. 베트남전과 피그스만 침공은 이것의 전형적인 예가 된다. 후자의 경우 케네디 대통령은 침공하고자 하는 자신의 생각에 모든 사람들이 동의하길 바랐고, 아서 슐레신저가 반대했음에도 불구하고, 그는 그렇게 하기를 꺼려했고 침묵했으며 나중에 이를 후회했다.

UNIT 16 Moving to the left
사회주의에 빠진 20/30대

SUMMARY & PARAPHRASE

66 Practice

▶▶ Example

Socialism is on the rise in the West. It rose from the ashes of Germany and the Soviet Union three decades ago and now considered favorably by many young people as capitalism has not handed them comfortable lives. Young people are now facing up to being poorer than their parents. It is also worth noting that the true meaning of socialism is not understood by those claiming to be supporting it. We are now seeing the era of the democratic socialist, led by Alexandria Ocasio-Cortez, whereby the rich should be highly taxed, and the government should take care of everyone equally. This, however, is a rather simplistic view and will have a negative effect on the economy.

note v. 주목하다　**whereby** ad. 그것에 의해서　**simplistic** a. 지나치게 단순한

▶ 사회주의가 서방 세계에서 떠오르고 있다. 사회주의는 30년 전 독일과 소련의 잿더미에서 부활해 이제는 자본주의로부터 편안한 삶을 받지 못한 많은 젊은이들이 선호하는 것이 되었다. 젊은 사람들은 이제 그들의 부모보다 더 가난해질 지경에 처해 있다. 또한, 주목해볼 만한 것은 사회주의를 지지한다는 사람들이 진정한 의미의 사회주의를 이해하지 못하고 있다는 것이다. 우리는 지금 Alexandria Ocasio-Cortez가 이끄는 민주주의적 사회주의의 시대를 목격하고 있는데, 그것에 의하면 부자들은 세금을 많이 내야하고, 정부는 모든 사람들을 똑같이 대우해야 한다. 그러나 이것은 오히려 너무 단순하게 바라본 것이며, 오히려 경제에 부정적인 영향을 끼치게 될 것이다.

UNIT 17 Is the law the problem?
법이 문제인가?

SUMMARY & PARAPHRASE

66 Practice

▶▶ Example

> Modern law sees its origins in Roman law according to Cicero's work putting the universal principles together. He gave us the modern enlightenment and the philosophy of natural law that stated the rights of humans were above all else although he himself did not practice what he preached. Post-Renaissance, Roman law was invoked to protect the rich and by the Spanish to legitimize their colonial expeditions and oppression of native communities. Nowadays, a civic society works together to have natural consensus.
>
> **enlightenment** n. 계몽 **preach** v. 설교하다, 전파하다 **invoke** v. 적용하다, 들먹이다
> **legitimize** v. 정당화하다 **expedition** n. 탐험 **oppression** n. 억압, 압제

▶ 근대법은 보편적인 원리들을 한데 모은 키케로의 말에 따르면 그 기원이 로마법에 있다고 한다. 그는 우리에게 근대적 계몽을 선사했으며, 비록 자신이 전파한 것을 실제로 하지는 않았지만, 그 무엇보다 인간의 권리가 우선시된다는 자연법사상을 주었다. 후기 르네상스 시대의 로마법은 부유한 사람들을 보호하기 위한 목적으로 사용되었으며, 스페인 사람들에 의해서는 그들의 식민 원정과 원주민 사회에 대한 압제를 정당화하기 위한 목적으로 사용되었다. 오늘날, 시민 사회는 자연 발생적 의견일치를 위해 서로 합심한다.

UNIT 18 Not a curse, but still weighty issue
비만 할증료

SUMMARY & PARAPHRASE

66 Practice

▶▶ Example

The insatiable appetite of Erysichthon in Greek mythology is seen in reality in those suffering from Prader-Willi syndrome: a rare brain condition whereby the sufferer has an appetite that is never satisfied. A myriad of health problems come hand in hand with this syndrome. Films like Bridget Jones's Diary may put a comedic slant on being overweight, but it is actually very damaging to both one's health and bank account. Airline and ambulance companies are beginning to charge overweight customers more.

Prader-Willi syndrome 프래더윌리 증후군

▶ 그리스 신화의 에리직톤의 달랠 수 없는 식욕은 현실에서도 프래더윌리 증후군을 앓고 있는 사람들에 의해 볼 수 있다. 프래더윌리 증후군은 환자가 채워지지 않는 식욕을 지니게 되는 희귀한 뇌질환이다. 이 증후군에서는 무수한 건강 문제들이 연달아 생기게 된다. 브리짓 존스의 일기와 같은 영화는 비만이 되는 것에 대한 희극적인 견해를 주입할 수 있지만 이것은 사실상 한 사람의 건강과 은행계좌에 매우 큰 해를 줄 수 있다. 항공사와 앰뷸런스 회사는 과체중인 고객들에게 더 많은 요금을 지불하기 시작했다.

UNIT 19 Maternal instincts
부계 불확실성

SUMMARY & PARAPHRASE

66 Practice

▶▶ Example

Research has shown that paternity uncertainty makes people feel closer to their mothers and their maternal relatives. An extreme example of this can be seen in the maternal society of the Mosuo tribe, in which females take multiple sexual partners and fathers do not exist in the way we think of them. Men remain with their mothers throughout their lives. It also had an effect on how patriarchal societies evolved. Men wanted to give their assets to their real sons, so their wives became their property and were shielded from engaging with other men. Patriarchies, thus, go against our natural instincts for maternal rights.

patriarchy *n.* 가부장제 **maternal right** *n.* 모권

▶ 연구 결과에 따르면 친부 불확실성은 사람들이 어머니와 외척들에게 더 친밀한 감정이 생기게 만든다. 극단적인 예시로 모계 사회인 모수오(Mosuo) 부족에서 찾아볼 수 있는데 모수오 부족에서는 여성들에게 많은 성적 파트너가 있고 아버지들은 우리가 생각하는 방식으로 존재하지 않는다. 남성들은 그들이 사는 동안 어머니와 함께 지낸다. 이것은 또한 부계사회가 어떻게 발달되었는지에 영향을 주었다. 남성들은 그들의 진짜 자식에게 재산을 물려주길 원했고 따라서 그들의 부인들은 그들의 자산이 되어 다른 남성들과 관련되는 것으로부터 보호되었다. 따라서 가부장제는 모권에 대한 우리의 자연적 본능과 어긋난다.

UNIT 20 The return of Machiavelli?
마키아벨리

66 Practice

▶▶ Example

> Machiavelli's "The Prince" details his ideas on how to gain and handle power in a monarchy. A prince should be powerful, sly, manipulative, and ready to do whatever it takes. He helped Florence remain strong in the face of threats from states around it. This cold-hearted man honed his ideas and theories while living near the Basilica di Santa Maria del Fiore in exile. A true patriot, he would do anything to protect his fatherland.
>
> **sly** *adj.* 교활한, 음흉한   **cold-hearted** *adj.* 냉담한, 인정 없는
> **in exile** 망명 중인   **fatherland** *n.* 조국

▶ 마키아벨리의 "The Prince"는 군주제에서 어떻게 힘을 얻고 통제하는지에 대한 그의 생각을 상세히 보여준다. 군주는 힘 있고 교활하며 교묘하고 무엇을 수반하든 실행할 준비가 되어있어야 한다. 그는 피렌체가 주위 국가의 위협에 강력하게 남아 있을 수 있도록 도왔다. 이 냉혈한 남성은 망명 중 산타 마리아 델 피오레 성당 근처에 살며 그의 생각과 이론을 다듬었다. 진정한 애국자로서 그는 그의 조국을 지키기 위해 무엇이든 했을 것이다.

Culture & Arts

Part 2 문화·예술

UNIT 01 Mansplaining
잘난 척하는 남자들

SUMMARY & PARAPHRASE

🙶 Practice

▶▶ Example

The term "mansplaining" describes the situation where a man feels the need to explain something to a woman because he thinks she knows little about it. Rebecca Solnit coined the phrase after her experience at a party when a man tried to explain her own book to her, not realizing who she was. It has since become widely used both on social media and officially in dictionaries. Solnit hoped both men and women would start to consider the other point of view.

mansplain 남성이 여성보다 우위에 있다고 생각하며 여성에게 모든 것을 가르치려 드는 행위
coin v. 만들다; 주조하다

▶ "맨스플레인"이란 단어는 여성이 무엇인가에 대해 조금밖에 알지 못한다고 생각해 남성이 여성에게 이를 설명할 필요성을 느끼는 상황을 의미한다. 레베카 솔닛은 한 남성이 파티에서 그녀가 누구인지 알지 못한 채 그녀의 책에 대해 설명하려고 했던 경험을 한 뒤 이 단어를 만들어냈다. 그 뒤로 이 단어는 소셜 미디어와 공식적으로 사전에서 널리 사용되어왔다. 솔닛은 남성과 여성이 다른 관점을 고려하기를 바랐다.

UNIT 02 Battling it out on the football pitch
전쟁과 축구

SUMMARY & PARAPHRASE

❝ Practice

▶▶ Example

> Sports can be used as a diplomatic answer to aggressions between nations, such as the Ping Pong diplomacy that eased tensions between the U.S. and China in the 1970s. Maybe if this had been realized back in the late 19th century, the War of the Triple alliance could have had a much less tragic outcome. Paraguay ended up losing over half its population and the majority of its adult men as a result of its aggression against Uruguay, Brazil and Argentina.
>
> **aggression** *n.* 공격성; 침략   **the War of Triple alliance** 삼국동맹 전쟁

▶ 스포츠는 1970년대 미국과 중국 사이의 긴장을 완화시킨 핑퐁외교와 같은 국가 간의 침략에 대한 외교적 대안으로써 사용될 수 있다. 만약 19세기 후반에 이를 인지했다면 삼국 동맹 전쟁은 훨씬 덜 비극적인 결과를 가져왔을 것이다. 파라과이는 우루과이, 브라질 그리고 아르헨티나와의 전쟁의 결과로 인해 인구의 절반과 성인 남성의 대부분을 잃었다.

UNIT 03 An addiction we can't afford
명품 프렌들리

SUMMARY & PARAPHRASE

❝ Practice

▶▶ Example

> Objects that appear at iconic moments often overshadow the moment itself. One instance of this is the clamor for Parker pens after Gen. Douglas MacArthur used one to sign the end of the Pacific War. Then, the shoes Marilyn Monroe wore in the subway grate scene in "The Seven Year Itch" were more in demand than the movie. Finally, sales of trench coats from the luxury brand Burberry soared after World War I. Korea is now taking over from Japan as a main consumer of luxury items.
>
> **iconic** *adj.* ~의 상징이 되는, 우상의   **clamor** *n.* 시끄러운 외침, 아우성, 소란
> **take over from** ~에게서 이어받다

▶ 상징적인 순간에 보이는 물건들은 종종 그 순간 자체를 무색하게 만든다. 맥아더 장군이 태평양 전쟁의 종결을 나타내기 위해 사용한 뒤 파커 펜의 인기가 늘어난 것이 하나의 예이다. 그 다음에는 영화 "The Seven Year Itch"의 지하철 환풍구 철망 덮개 장면에서 마릴린 먼로가 신고 있던 신발이 영화보다 더 잘 팔렸다. 마지막으로 명품 브랜드인 버버리의 트렌치코트 판매가 1차 세계대전 이후 급증했다. 한국은 현재 일본으로부터 명품의 주요 소비국으로서의 지위를 물려받고 있다.

UNIT 04 Growing old peacefully
100세의 실종

SUMMARY & PARAPHRASE

❝ Practice

▶▶ Example

There are clean and fresh areas in the world, such as Pakistan's beautiful Hunza Valley, Aphasia in the Russian Caucasus, and Ecuador's Vilcabamba, that are known for their powers of longevity. Additionally, Okinawa is well-known for the ability of its residents to routinely live to over 100 through their consumption of healthy natural food. Another way to live a long time is to embrace life and relax, enjoying the process of life. You can prevent aging before it hits you.

routinely adv. 일상적으로

▶ 세계에는 파키스탄의 아름다운 훈자계곡, 러시아 카프카스 산맥의 알파샤, 에콰도르의 빌카밤바와 같은 깨끗하고 생기 넘치는 장소들이 있고 이러한 장소들은 장수의 힘으로 알려져 있다. 덧붙여 오키나와는 주민들이 건강한 자연식을 통해 일상적으로 100세가 넘게 장수할 수 있는 것으로 잘 알려져 있다. 장수할 수 있는 다른 방법은 삶을 포용하고 긴장을 풀면서 삶의 과정을 즐기는 것이다. 당신은 노화가 당신에게 닥치기 전에 이를 예방할 수 있다.

UNIT 05 The text generation
텍스트 세대

SUMMARY & PARAPHRASE

66 Practice

▶▶ Example

Even though high school students are getting smarter and should be getting higher grades, they are not because their literacy rate in understanding text is slipping. They have problems understanding what they are being asked to do, not how to answer. Dubbed the "text generation", they have been raised on abbreviations and short texts, finding problems when it comes to longer ones. They have the ability to decipher longer, more complex texts, but without practice they become rusty at doing so.

literacy rate 식자율, 문자해독률 **slip** v. 떨어지다; 악화되다 **dub** v. ~라고 부르다
abbreviation n. 축약형, 약자 **decipher** v. 해독하다 **rusty** a. 서투른, 둔한

▶ 고등학생들이 더 똑똑해지고 있어서 더 높은 성적을 얻게 될 수 있다고 하더라도, 실제로 그들은 그렇게 되지 못하는데, 그 이유는 학생들의 글 이해력이 계속 떨어지고 있기 때문이다. 학생들은 어떻게 답을 해야 하는지가 아니라, 무엇을 하도록 주문받았는지를 이해하지 못한다. "문자 세대"라고 불리는 고등학생들은 약자와 단문을 접하면서 자라왔기 때문에 글이 길어지면 어려움을 겪는다. 학생들은 더 길고 더 복잡한 글을 이해할 능력이 있지만, 그 능력을 활용하지 않는다면 아이들은 길고 복잡한 글을 잘 읽지 못하게 될 것이다.

UNIT 06 Memories of Mozart
모차르트

SUMMARY & PARAPHRASE

66 Practice

▶▶ Example

Although Mozart was poor and practically destitute while he lived and unable to take care of his family, if he were alive today, he would be one of the richest men in the world thanks to the public's thirst for his music. His legacy, moreover, keeps the whole of his hometown, Salzburg, in business with his face adorning an array of souvenirs from mugs and t-shirts to chocolate and beer. Mozart's music is more popular than that of other composers due to its joyfulness and lightness, which appeals to listeners.

thirst *n.* 갈증　**souvenir** *n.* 기념품(선물)　**joyfulness** *n.* 즐거움

▶ 비록 모차르트가 살면서 가난했고 사실상 생활이 곤란했으며 그의 가족을 부양하는 것이 불가능했지만, 만약 그가 오늘날 살아있었다면 그의 음악에 대한 대중의 갈증으로 인해 세상에서 가장 부유한 사람 중 한 명이었을 것이다. 게다가 그의 유산은 그의 얼굴이 장식된 머그잔과 티셔츠에서 초콜릿과 맥주에 이르는 다양한 기념품 사업을 통해 그의 고향인 잘츠부르크 전체를 먹여살린다. 모차르트의 음악은 청취자에게 매력이 될 수 있는 즐거움과 밝음으로 인해 다른 작곡가들의 음악보다 인기가 많다.

UNIT 07 Leaping tall buildings
수퍼맨

SUMMARY & PARAPHRASE

66 Practice

▶▶ Example

Since his creation in 1934, Superman has gone appeared in nearly every type of media, and set the trend for a whole host of superheroes that came after him. Superman was the original American hero, bringing peace not only to America but to the world. After all this time, Americans still adore Superman, although now Americans are looking to him to save them: the new Superman movie sees him save America, not the world. It has even been said that he is America's attempt to regain the morality they feel was lost after Sept. 11. Americans want to be the most powerful, but they also want to be benevolent.

adore v. 사모하다; 아주 좋아하다   **morality** n. 도덕성   **benevolent** adj. 인자한

▶ 수퍼맨은 1934년 처음 생겨난 뒤 거의 모든 유형의 미디어에 나왔고 이후에 나오는 무수한 영웅들에 대한 추세를 설정했다. 수퍼맨은 미국뿐만 아니라 전 세계에 평화를 가져다준 미국 최초의 영웅이다. 비록 지금 미국인들은 그에게 그들을 구해줄 것을 바라지만 지금까지도 미국은 수퍼맨을 좋아한다. 새로운 수퍼맨 영화는 수퍼맨이 세계가 아닌 미국을 구하는 것을 보여준다. 그는 9·11 테러 이후 그들이 느끼기에 사라진 도덕성을 다시 되찾고자 하는 미국의 시도라고 말해져 왔다. 미국인들은 가장 강력해지고 싶지만 또한 인자해지고 싶어 한다.

UNIT 08 Epicurean bean paste
칙릿

66 Practice

▶▶ Example

> Chick-lit, that appeals to modern twenty- and thirtysomething women with its focus on sex, love and work, is big business, spawning bestsellers, movies, and television series; for example, note the standout success of Bridget Jones's Diary, Sex and the City, and Confessions of a Shopaholic. Surprisingly, feminists approve of this seemingly lightweight genre as they steer away from traditional feminist issues and push the freedom and consumption of the modern feminist woman. On the other side, lad-lit shows men as the opposite of these women – weak and clueless.
>
> **chick-lit** (여성 독자를 겨냥한) 여자들 소설   **lightweight** *adj.* 가벼운
> **lad-lit** 주로 어수룩하며 결혼을 두려워하고 이기적인 젊은 남성 캐릭터들이 등장하는 남성 작가가 쓴 문학
> **clueless** *adj.* 어수룩한; ~을 할 줄 모르는

▶ 성, 사랑, 그리고 일에 집중하는 현대의 20대-30대 여성들의 흥미를 일으키는 칙릿은 대형 사업이며 베스트셀러, 영화 그리고 TV 시리즈를 양산해내고 있다. 예를 들어서 브리짓 존스의 일기, 섹스 앤 더 시티 그리고 쇼퍼홀릭의 눈에 띄는 성공을 보자. 놀랍게도 페미니스트들은 겉보기에 가벼운 장르에 우호적이다. 왜냐하면 이러한 작품들은 기존의 페미니스트적 이슈에서 벗어났고 현대 페미니스트 여성의 자유와 소비를 장려하기 때문이다. 반대로 래드릿은 남성을 이러한 여성의 반대로서 약하고 어수룩하게 표현한다.

UNIT 09 The essence of consumption
반소비

SUMMARY & PARAPHRASE

　　Practice

▶▶ Example

In the modern world, showing how much money you spend is a way to show that you belong in the upper class. Anxious to be as lucky as movie, rock and sports stars, people try to emulate their lavish spending, by displaying items with high brand value. Fake products show how eagerly people will try to imitate ostentation. The backlash from the truly rich is to underconsume, that is to spend very little, whether it be buying a small car or a cheap lunch. In this way, the original upper class stay distinct from the nouveau riche.

ostentation *n.* 과시　　nouveau riche *n.* 벼락부자

▶ 현대 사회에서 당신이 얼마큼 돈을 쓰는지 보여주는 것은 당신이 상류층에 속해있다는 것을 보여주는 한 방법이다. 사람들은 영화, 락 그리고 스포츠 스타만큼 운이 좋기를 갈망해서 높은 브랜드 가치를 지닌 물건들을 내보임으로써 그들의 사치스러운 소비를 모방하려고 한다. 모조품은 사람들이 얼마나 과시를 모방하려고 열심인지를 보여준다. 진정으로 부유한 사람들의 반발은 적게 소비하는 것, 즉 작은 차를 사든 싼 점심을 먹든 매우 적게 소비하는 것이다. 이러한 방식으로 원래의 상류층은 벼락부자들로부터 구분된다.

UNIT 10 When the internet splits
인터넷 분열화

SUMMARY & PARAPHRASE

66 Practice

▶▶ Example

  There is a worrying trend towards the creation of national internet networks that cut citizens off from the international internet, and it is no longer limited to totalitarian countries such as Russia, China, Iran, and North Korea that seek to control the flow of information to their citizens. The US and Europe are also looking into their own versions of the internet for their own reasons. If the internet is different in every country, it will have an effect on finance, trade, and information exchange worldwide.

worrying *a.* 걱정스러운 **totalitarian** *a.* 전체주의의

▶ 시민들을 국제 인터넷망으로부터 차단하는 국내 인터넷망을 구축하려는 걱정스러운 움직임이 있으며, 이는 더 이상 시민들이 접할 수 있는 정보의 흐름을 통제하려는 전체주의 국가들인 러시아, 중국, 이란, 북한에만 국한되어 있지 않다. 미국과 유럽 또한 자신들만의 이유로 자체적인 인터넷망을 구축하려고 하고 있다. 만약 인터넷망이 모든 국가에서 다 다르다면, 그것은 금융, 무역 그리고 정보 교환의 측면에 있어서 전 세계에 영향을 끼칠 것이다.

UNIT 11 Barbie does Freud
키덜트

SUMMARY & PARAPHRASE

66 Practice

_____
_____
_____
_____
_____
_____
_____

▶▶ Example

When Barbie launched, the adult form doll was in instant success and has been relaunched multiple times in different races and nationalities and situations as well as the trademark being used to sell other items. These days, however, school-age kids want electronic games and objects rather than dolls, leaving the toys to pre-school kids. With the declining birth rate, toy sales are in the doldrums. Then came the emergence of the kidult – an adult who embraces kids' products. Barbie, and other dolls created specifically for adults, are popular once again.

school-age *a.* 학령기의   **be in doldrums** 침체되다
kidult 어른이 되었음에도 계속해서 아이들의 물건이나 문화를 즐기려는 사람

▶ 바비가 처음 출시되었을 때, 이 성인 형태의 인형은 즉시 성공을 거두었고 다른 인종, 국적 그리고 상황에서뿐만 아니라 다른 상품을 판매하기 위해 사용되는 트레이드마크로서 여러 번 재출시되었다. 하지만 요즘 학령아동들은 장난감들을 미취학 아동들에게 남겨두고 인형보다는 전자게임과 전자기기를 선호한다. 출산율이 감소하면서 장난감 판매는 침체되었다. 이후, 아이들의 물건을 포용하는 성인이라는 뜻의 키덜트가 생겨났다. 성인들을 위해 특별히 만들어진 바비와 다른 인형들이 다시 한 번 유명해졌다.

UNIT 12 Is a college degree necessary?
대학 졸업장이 꼭 필요한가?

SUMMARY & PARAPHRASE

66 Practice

▶▶ Example

Despite having the need for a college degree drummed into them, young people are unable to find work with one. They watch while others enter the entertainment business without a degree and succeed. Replacing high school graduates, college graduates can now be found in large numbers working in factories – almost half of the workers there. This is because the skills of a college graduate are in greater demand in factories for automation than those of a high school graduate. Educated workers are going to become more essential in the future and simple workers become useless.

drum *v.* 되풀이하여 ~ 하게 하다, 주입하다 **automation** *n.* 자동화 **essential** *a.* 필수적인, 매우 중요한

▶ 대학 졸업장이 필요하다는 이야기를 귀에 못이 박히도록 듣지만, 젊은 사람들은 그것 하나만으로는 취직을 할 수가 없다. 그들은 다른 이들이 대학 졸업장도 없이 연예계에 뛰어들어 성공하는 모습을 본다. 고등학교 졸업생들을 대체하고 있는 공장에서 일하는 수많은 대학 졸업생들을 찾아볼 수 있으며, 그들은 공장 노동자의 대략 절반을 차지한다. 이는 대학 졸업생들의 기술을 고등학교 졸업생들의 것보다 자동화 공장에서 훨씬 더 필요로 하기 때문이다. 교육받은 노동자들은 미래에 훨씬 더 필수적인 존재들이 될 것이며, 평범한 노동자들은 쓸모없는 존재로 전락할 것이다.

UNIT 13 Sheep astray
학위 효과와 학력 검증

66 Practice

▶▶ Example

  Higher education usually gets more compensation in employment, but this does not always guarantee higher competence, and therein lies the problem. Many employers look to educational background, but when higher payment does not mean higher quality of work, the sheepskin effect appears, and pushes up demand for higher education. There are not many other ways to separate prospective employees, and higher education can guarantee some knowledge. A professor must show academic background to attain that position or he is deceiving and cheating others.

higher education 고등교육   **sheepskin effect** 졸업장 효과, 학위 효과

▶ 고등교육은 대개 고용되었을 때 더 많은 보상을 주지만 더 높은 능력을 보장하지 않으며 거기에 문제가 있다. 많은 고용주들은 학벌을 보지만 더 많은 급여가 더 높은 일의 질을 가져다주지 못할 때면 학위 효과가 발생하며 고등교육에 대한 요구를 높이게 된다. 예비 직원을 구분하기 위한 다른 방법은 많지 않고 고등교육은 어느 정도의 지식을 보장해준다. 교수는 그 자리를 얻기 위해 학문적 배경을 반드시 보여주어야 하고 그렇지 않으면 그는 다른 사람을 기만하고 속이는 것이다.

UNIT 14 Get fathers involved

'출산 보이콧'을 막으려면

SUMMARY & PARAPHRASE

66 Practice

▶▶ Example

> Birth inequality is happening right now as wealthier women have freedom over the size of their family while poorer women limit their family size due to expenses, such as childcare and education. On the bright side, a lower birthrate points to the greater wealth of a country overall and in some Northern European countries, as the national income grows even more, the birthrate is rebounding. It is a different story in Southern Europe where gender roles remain fixed and without the support of the father, women remain reluctant to have more children.
>
> *childcare* n. 보육

▶ 가난한 여성들이 양육비와 교육비와 같은 비용에 의해 가족의 크기를 제한하는 반면 부유한 여성들은 가족의 크기에 대해 자유를 가지게 되며 출생 불평등이 발생하고 있다. 긍정적인 측면으로 낮은 출산율은 대개 국가의 부가 더 늘어났음을 암시하고 몇몇의 북유럽 국가에서는 국민 소득이 더 증가하면서 출산율이 반등하고 있다. 성 역할이 고정되어 있고 아버지의 부양이 없으면 여성들이 더 많은 아이를 갖기를 꺼려하는 서유럽에게는 다른 이야기이다.

UNIT 15 The right to be forgotten online
잊혀질 권리

SUMMARY & PARAPHRASE

❝ Practice

▶▶ Example

　After a legal battle by a Spanish attorney to remove embarrassing but irrelevant information about him on Google, the European Court of Justice has ruled in his favor. Privacy in Europe is a big deal and "the right to be forgotten" is popular. However, it can be abused: one doctor wanted to prevent prospective patients from accessing details of his poor treatment, and a musician sought to remove bad reviews of his performance. Both ultimately failed.

attorney *n.* 변호사, 대리인　　**irrelevant** *adj.* 무관한, 상관없는
abuse *v.* 오용하다　　**prospective** *adj.* 유망한, 가망이 있는

▶ 구글에 올라온 자신에 대한 당혹스럽고 관련 없는 정보를 삭제해줄 것을 요구하는 스페인 변호사의 법정투쟁 이후, 유럽 사법 재판소는 그의 편을 들었다. 유럽에서 프라이버시는 중대한 일이며 잊혀질 권리는 대중적이다. 그러나 이는 오남용 될 수 있다. 한 의사는 예비 환자들이 그의 질 낮은 치료에 대한 세부사항을 보는 것을 막길 바랐고 한 음악가는 그의 연주에 대한 안 좋은 리뷰를 삭제하려고 했다. 이 둘은 결국 실패했다.

UNIT 16 No such thing as a free bribe
스폰서

SUMMARY & PARAPHRASE

❝ Practice

▶▶ Example

   Artists have, on many occasions, had to seek out a rich patron to fund their lifestyle and allow them the freedom to spend their time creatively. Haydn enjoyed the patronage of the Hungarian aristocratic Esterhazy family, but had to give back by creating some trios for a now-unknown instrument. Wagner, who spent his life in poverty because of his taste for living and working in luxury, could actually have benefitted from a patron. Some artists, such as Christo and Jeanne-Claude refuse patronage and are financed in other, less limiting, ways.

patronage *n.* 후원; 지원; 애용   **aristocratic** *adj.* 귀족적인, 귀족의   **trio** *n.* 3인조; 3중주
now-unknown *adj.* 지금은 알 수 없는   **in luxury** 사치스럽게

▶ 예술가들은 종종 자신의 라이프스타일에 자금을 대줄 부유한 후원자를 찾아야만 했고 그들의 시간을 창조적으로 사용할 자유를 주었다. 하이든은 헝가리 귀족인 에스테르하지 가의 후원을 받았지만 지금은 알 수 없는 악기를 위한 몇 개의 3중주를 작곡하는 것으로 갚아야만 했다. 사치스러운 삶과 일을 선호해 가난한 삶을 살았던 바그너는 사실상 후원자로부터 혜택을 받을 수 있었다. 크리스토와 잔 클로드와 같은 몇몇의 예술가는 후원을 거절하고 덜 제약을 받는 다른 방식으로 자금을 얻었다.

UNIT 17 A different perspective on love
진정한 사랑에 대하여

66 Practice

▶▶ Example

"My Love, Don't Cross That River" is loved by old and young alike and shows an elderly couple who have been together and in love for 76 years. The documentary details their life together and the respect and care they feel for one another. True love doesn't spring from who the other person is, but from simple acts of care. Thinking of the other and not of oneself is a key theme in the film. The fact that the husband never complains about his wife's cooking regardless of quality shows the depth of his love.

old and young (alike) 남녀노소

▶ "님아 그 강을 건너지 마오"는 남녀노소 모두에게 사랑받았고 76년간 함께 살며 사랑했던 노부부를 보여준다. 다큐멘터리는 노부부의 함께하는 삶과 서로에게 느끼는 존중과 보살핌을 자세히 보여준다. 진정한 사랑은 상대방이 누군지에서 나오는 것이 아니라 보살핌이라는 간단한 행동에서 싹트는 것이다. 자신이 아닌 상대방을 생각하는 것이 이 영화의 주요 테마이다. 남편이 부인의 요리 수준에 상관없이 불평하지 않았다는 사실은 그의 사랑의 깊이를 보여준다.

UNIT 18 Playing with blocks
테트리스

SUMMARY & PARAPHRASE

66 Practice

▶▶ Example

   The appearance of Tetris in 1988 transformed the video game market. Created by a Russian, Alexey Pajitov, it was simple and addictive, and anyone could play it. All you had to do was turn 7 shapes of blocks to fit together, kind of like pentominoes. However, due to the lack of copyright protection from Moscow, Pajitov never saw much from the massive global sales. Even today, it is popular on modern mobile devices, and has been shown to boost brain function and power.

transform *v.* 변형시키다; 완전히 바꿔 놓다   **addictive** *adj.* 중독성의, 중독성이 있는
pentomino *n.* 펜토미노

▶ 1998년 테트리스의 등장은 비디오 게임 시장을 완전히 바꿔놓았다. 러시아 사람인 알렉세이 파지토브에 의해 만들어진 테트리스는 간단하고 중독성 있으며 누구나 즐길 수 있다. 당신이 해야 할 것은 일종의 펜토미노처럼 7가지 모양의 블록이 서로 맞도록 회전시키는 것이다. 그러나 모스크바로부터 저작권 보호를 받지 못했기 때문에 파지토브는 막대한 세계적 판매로부터 많은 수익을 얻을 수 없었다. 심지어 오늘날까지 테트리스는 현대의 휴대폰 기기에서도 대중적으로 실행되며 뇌기능과 지능을 향상시키는 것으로 알려졌다.

UNIT 19 Cyberbullying is a crime
악플은 범죄다

SUMMARY & PARAPHRASE

" Practice

▶▶ Example

Attacking someone online is a global problem these days with those who have engaged in it citing anger, jealousy and envy, stress, and joking as reasons for doing it. With more celebrity deaths in Korea occurring, it is really out of hand. Recently, various global leaders have gotten behind drives to end cyberbullying and online trolling, yet it continues. Journalists are particular targets of trolls' ire. While internet trolls claim not to consider the consequences of their actions, the clear loss of life is evidently a result of this crime.

cite v. (이유나 예를) 들다 **out of hand** 통제 불능인 **ire** n. 분노, 노여움

▶ 온라인에서 누군가를 공격하는 것은 전 세계적인 문제이며, 그러한 행위를 하는 사람들은 분노, 질투, 부러움, 스트레스, 농담 등을 행위의 이유로 댄다. 점점 더 많은 유명인들이 사망하는 일이 한국에서 발생하면서, 온라인 폭행은 통제 범위를 벗어나고 있다. 최근, 여러 세계 지도자들은 사이버 폭력과 온라인 악플 및 선동 행위를 끝내려는 움직임에 힘을 실어주고 있지만, 여전히 그와 같은 일들은 계속되고 있다. 기자들이 특히 악플러와 선동꾼들의 분노 대상이 된다. 인터넷 악플러들은 그들의 행위로 인한 결과를 고려할 필요가 없다고 주장하지만, 그들의 범죄로 인해 명백히 누군가는 삶을 잃게 된다.

UNIT 20 A war over religious rights
부르카 전쟁 인권과 종교의 자유

SUMMARY & PARAPHRASE

❝ Practice

▶▶ Example

France, and more recently Europe, are debating the issue of whether Muslim women should be allowed to wear burqas in public or whether it goes against human rights to have women communicated with behind a veil. France abides by the separation of church and state when it comes to the cross, so expects Muslim to also adhere to it. Muslims, however, are calling it religious persecution and took their argument to the EU Court, albeit unsuccessfully. This may have an adverse effect on Muslim tourism to those European countries that choose to enact similar laws.

abide by *v.* 준수하다, 따르다   **when it comes to** ~에 관한 한, ~라면   **albeit** *conj.* 비록 ~일지라도

▶ 프랑스 그리고 최근 유럽에서는 무슬림 여성이 공공장소에서 브루카를 착용하는 것을 허용해야 하는지 혹은 이것이 여성들이 브루카를 착용한 채 대화를 나눌 수 있는 인권을 침해하는 것인지에 대한 토론이 벌어지고 있다. 프랑스는 십자가에 대해 정교분리 원칙을 따르며 무슬림들도 이를 따라주길 바란다. 하지만 무슬림들은 이것을 종교적 박해라고 주장하고 비록 성공적이진 않았지만 유럽 연합 법원에 자신들의 의견을 호소했다. 이것은 비슷한 법의 제정을 선택한 유럽 국가들의 무슬림 관광사업에 부정적인 영향을 가져올 수 있을 것이다.

Science & Technology

Part 3 과학·기술

UNIT 01 Racing toward a dissonant drive
전기자동차와 소음

66 Practice

▶▶ Example

Some engines have distinctive sounds such as the roar of a Harley-Davidson motorcycle which imitates human heartbeats, and Ferrari's deep growl. Lovers of such vehicles adore the sound of their engine. On the other hand, some engines make no sounds at all such as electric vehicles, whose lack of sounds increases accidents as others cannot hear them coming, and Jaguar who added a sound that is heard upon turning the engine on. The danger of silent engines is causing problems and will face legal regulation.

roar *n.* 포효 *v.* 으르렁거리다   **upon –ing** ~하자마자

▶ 일부 엔진은 인간의 심장박동을 모방한 할리 데이비슨 오토바이의 포효와 페라리의 낮은 으르렁거리는 소리와 같은 독특한 소리를 낸다. 이러한 차량의 애호가들은 이들의 엔진 소리를 좋아한다. 다른 한편으로는 소리가 나지 않아 다른 사람들이 차가 다가오는 것을 듣지 못해서 사고를 증가시키는 전기자동차와 엔진을 켜면 들리는 사운드를 추가한 재규어와 같이 일부 엔진은 아예 소리를 내지 않는다. 조용한 엔진의 위험성은 문제를 유발하고 법적 규제에 직면하게 될 것이다.

UNIT 02 Written in wrinkles
보톡스

SUMMARY & PARAPHRASE

❝ Practice

▶▶ Example

Botox is a very popular method to get rid of wrinkles. Although it lasts only a few months and can cause facial expression problems, it is cheap and works. Botox is 100 times more poisonous than the most poisonous artificial toxin known to man and can cause death. During its commercial history, 16 people have died from using it; however, they were cerebral palsy patients taking many times the regular dosage in order to ease muscle spasms. What's wrong with having wrinkles anyway? They show our life, our experiences and our maturity.

maturity n. 성숙

▶ 보톡스는 주름을 제거하는 매우 보편적인 방법이다. 비록 몇 달밖에 지속되지 않으며 표정 문제를 유발할 수 있지만 저렴하고 효과가 있다. 보톡스는 인간에게 알려진 인공 독소보다 100배나 독성이 강하고 죽음을 유발할 수 있다. 보톡스의 상업사 동안 16명의 사람이 사망했다. 그러나 그들은 근경련 완화를 위한 정량의 몇 배를 사용한 뇌성마비 환자였다. 그런데 주름을 갖게 되는 것이 무슨 잘못인 것일까? 주름살은 우리의 삶과 경험, 그리고 성숙함을 보여준다.

UNIT 03 Always polite, never complaining
밤새 일하고도 불평 없는 그 직원

SUMMARY & PARAPHRASE

❝ Practice

_____
_____
_____
_____
_____
_____
_____

▶▶ Example

> The fourth industrial revolution is necessary to replace the production line jobs that have already or will be lost to automation with new industries for human employees. All around the world, millions of jobs are being lost to robots and the high-quality production of said robots is rapidly increasing. Companies are full steam ahead with this new type of employee who never complains about hours or conditions and never stops working, takes breaks or takes vacations. Humans need different jobs that utilize skills that robots do not have.
>
> **The fourth industrial revolution** 4차 산업 혁명 **full steam ahead** 전력을 기울여
> **utilize** v. 활용하다

▶ 4차 산업 혁명은 이미 혹은 앞으로 자동화에 일자리를 내어줄 생산직들을 인간 노동자들을 위한 새로운 산업으로 대체하기 위해 필요할 것이다. 전 세계적으로 수백만 개의 일자리가 로봇에게 넘어가고 있으며, 시키는 대로 일하는 로봇들의 고품질 생산이 급속도로 늘어나고 있다. 기업들은 열을 올리며 노동시간과 조건에 절대 불평하지 않고, 끊임없이 일하며, 쉬지도 않고 휴가를 가지도 않는 이 신종 직원들을 확보하려 하고 있다. 인간들에게는 로봇이 가지고 있지 않은 기술을 활용할 수 있는 다른 직업들이 필요하다.

UNIT 04 Flying pandemics
조류 인플루엔자

SUMMARY & PARAPHRASE

66 Practice

▶▶ Example

The origins of the 1918 influenza epidemic have been pinpointed as coming from birds, according to Dr. Jeffrey Taubenberger, who extracted samples of the virus from a preserved corpse and sequenced its genome. This virus, called the Spanish flu or the French flu, was more feared than World War I which was taking place at the same time and quickly ran amok throughout the globe and across continents. Yet, for some reason, people remember the black plague from a much earlier time more than they do the influenza of 1918.

for some reason 무슨 이유로, 어떤 까닭인지   **the black plague** n. 페스트

▶ 보존된 시체에서 바이러스 샘플을 추출하고 유전체를 시퀀스(sequence)한 제프리 토벤버거 박사에 따르면 1918년 발병한 유행성 독감은 새로부터 유발된 것이다. 사람들은 동시에 발생했으며 재빠르게 세계와 대륙을 미친 듯이 들쑤시고 다녔던 제1차 세계대전보다 스페인 독감 혹은 프랑스 독감이라고 불리는 이 바이러스를 더 두려워했다. 하지만 무슨 이유에선지 사람들은 1918년 발병한 인플루엔자보다 더 일찍 발생했던 페스트를 더 많이 기억한다.

UNIT 05 Unfounded fears
공포의 문화

SUMMARY & PARAPHRASE

" Practice

▶▶ Example

> As a result of a 1982 NBC program that questioned whether the whooping cough vaccine could be harmful to children, the public became worried about the safety of vaccinating their children. The FDA attempted to alleviate this fear by compiling and issuing a very long and detailed document defending the DPT vaccine which showed complications were very rare. The damage was already done, though. Parents stopped vaccinating their children and whooping cough numbers rose. The blame has been put on the shoulders of the media, politicians, and others who use fear to their own advantage.
>
> **vaccinate** v. 예방접종하다, 예방주사를 맞히다   **alleviate** v. 완화하다, 누그러뜨리다

▶ 1982년 백일해 예방 백신이 아이들에게 유해한지에 대해 의문을 제기한 NBC 프로그램으로 인해 대중은 자녀에게 예방접종하는 것의 안전성에 대해 걱정하게 되었다. FDA는 합병증이 매우 드물다는 DPT 백신을 옹호하는 매우 길고 상세한 문서를 작성하고 배포함으로써 이러한 두려움을 완화하려고 했다. 그러나 이미 막대한 손해를 입은 뒤였다. 부모들은 아이들의 예방접종을 중단했고 백일해의 발병이 증가하게 되었다. 미디어와 정치인, 그리고 자신의 이익을 위해 두려움을 사용한 다른 사람들에게 비난이 향하게 되었다.

UNIT 06 Insane or sane?
정신분석 요법의 귀환

SUMMARY & PARAPHRASE

❝ Practice

▶▶ Example

Psychoanalytic therapy was questioned in 1970 when a group of researchers falsely declared they experienced symptoms of mental illness. All were diagnosed with a problem while in hospital which they didn't actually have. The furor that followed caused one psychiatric hospital to demand they be allowed to redeem themselves by trying to find more fake patients – they found 41, but no fake patients had been sent. But now, psychoanalytic therapy is making a comeback after decades of using drug treatments instead, and it must have improved if it is becoming popular again.

psychoanalytic *adj.* 정신분석의 **furor** *n.* 격렬한 감격; 열광; 열광적 유행; 분노
redeem oneself 속전을 내어 목숨을 건지다

▶ 한 연구인 단체가 정신질환 증상을 경험했다고 거짓으로 이야기한 1970년 정신분석 치료에 대한 의문이 제기되었다. 모든 이들은 병원에 있을 당시 문제가 있다고 진찰받았지만 사실 그들에게는 병이 없었다. 그 이후의 분노는 정신병원으로 하여금 더 많은 가짜 환자들을 찾음으로써 속전을 내어 목숨을 건지도록 요구하게 만들었다. 그들은 41명의 환자를 찾았지만 가짜 환자들은 받지 못했다. 하지만 현재 정신분석 치료는 수십 년이 지난 뒤 약물치료를 대신해 다시 돌아오고 있으며 다시 대중화되기 위해서는 반드시 개선되어야 한다.

UNIT 07 The silent organ
간

🙶 Practice

▶▶ Example

> The largest internal organ in humans – the liver – breaks down alcohol and expels the poison from the body, but it cannot get rid of all the toxins. When one eats, the food is broken down into things the body needs and is sent out to the cells. When there is a problem, it suffers through and doesn't complain until it is almost three-quarters harmed, so if your liver is complaining, you know there is a serious problem. The amazing thing about the liver is that even with only 15% still functioning, if help is administered immediately, it can regenerate fully.
>
> **internal organ** *n.* 장기   **complain** *v.* 불평하다; 고통을 호소하다
> **administer** *v.* 관리하다; 집행하다; 부여하다; 투여하다   **regenerate** *v.* 재건하다

▶ 인체에서 가장 큰 장기는 간이며 이것은 알코올을 분해하고 몸으로부터 독소를 배출한다. 하지만 간이 모든 독소를 배출해내진 못한다. 사람이 음식을 섭취할 때 음식은 신체가 필요한 것으로 분해되며 세포로 보내진다. 문제가 생겼을 때에는 3/4가 피해를 입을 때까지 고통을 겪지만 통증을 유발하지 않는다. 따라서 당신의 간에 통증이 있다면 당신은 심각한 문제가 발생한 것임을 알게 되는 것이다. 간에 대한 놀라운 사실은 단지 15%만이 기능을 해도 즉시 도움을 받는다면 다시 완전히 회복될 수 있다는 것이다.

UNIT 08 History in color
피부색

SUMMARY & PARAPHRASE

66 Practice

▶▶ Example

Skin color depends on carotene, which can turn skin yellow, and hemoglobin, which has a reddening effect, but most of all, it depends on melanin – a dark brown pigment. It is believed that ultraviolet radiation can change skin color since our ancestors who lived near the equator had darker skin to reflect heat, and cool the body. But not receiving those ultraviolet rays puts black people at risk of problems associated with less vitamin D. When our ancestors left Africa, their skin color lightened. The original inhabitants of Alaska were different, however, and didn't need to lighten their skin since their diet was high in vitamin D already.

ultraviolet ray n. 자외선   **original inhabitant** n. 원주민

▶ 피부색은 당신의 피부를 노랗게 바꿀 수 있는 카로틴과 붉게 만드는 효과가 있는 헤모글로빈에 따라 다르지만 대부분 어두운 갈색 색소인 멜라닌에 따라 달라진다. 적도 근처에 살았던 우리의 조상들은 열을 반사하고 체온을 내리기 위해 어두운 피부색을 가지고 있었다고 전해진다. 하지만 자외선을 받지 않는 것은 흑인들이 비타민 D와 관련된 문제를 겪게 만든다. 우리의 선조들이 아프리카에서 떠나고 그들의 피부색은 옅어졌다. 그러나 알래스카의 원주민들은 이미 비타민 D가 풍부한 식사를 하고 있었기 때문에 다른 선조들과 달랐으며 그들의 피부색은 옅어질 필요가 없었다.

UNIT 09 Addicted to speed
속도

SUMMARY & PARAPHRASE

❝ Practice

▶▶ Example

> Speed dominates the 21st century as it is correlated with power through history. Genghis Khan used horseback riders and Rommel used tanks to amass power. These days, the desire for speed is alive and well on rail, on roads and in the air. Alstom's TGV Est train travels at 300km/h, Acabion's GTBO car can do 480km in 30 seconds, and Lockheed's SR-71 reaches 4,000km/h! Those who cannot, or do not want to, keep up with the speed of society are being left behind. Moreover, the planet is suffering from global warming as speed eats up oil and coal.
>
> **dominate** v. 지배하다, 장악하다   **horseback rider** n. 기마인   **amass** v. 모으다

▶ 속도는 역사에 있어서 힘과 관련이 있기 때문에 21세기를 장악한다. 징기스칸은 기마인을 사용했고 롬멜은 힘을 모으기 위해 탱크를 사용했다. 요즘에도 속도에 대한 열망은 살아있으며 철도, 차, 그리고 비행기까지 나아가게 되었다. 알스톰사의 TBV Est 열차는 300km/h로 달리고, 아카비온사의 GTBO 자동차는 30초 안에 480km를 달릴 수 있으며, 록히드사의 SR-71의 속력은 4000km/h에 달한다. 사회의 속도에 맞출 수 없거나 맞추길 원치 않는 사람들은 뒤처지게 되었다. 게다가 지구는 속도가 석유와 석탄을 사용하게 되면서 지구온난화로 고통받고 있다.

UNIT 10 Under the microscope
다이옥신

SUMMARY & PARAPHRASE

❝ Practice

▶▶ Example

The human need to find ever smaller things is satisfied by science. First, it was micro, then nano, and now pico. The food industry is being affected as toxins that couldn't be seen before can now be identified. Take dioxin, a very poisonous substance, that has been found in food, most recently Irish pork. Dioxin levels increase up the food chain, bringing the safety of breast milk into the spotlight. However, the health benefits of breast milk should not be forgotten and breastfeeding should not be discarded.

dioxin n. 다이옥신   **bring something into the spotlight** 대중의 관심을 받게 하다   **breast milk** n. 모유

▶ 더 작은 것을 찾고자 하는 인간의 욕구는 과학에 의해 충족되었다. 처음에는 마이크로였고 그다음은 나노, 그리고 지금은 피코이다. 식품 공업은 이전에는 볼 수 없었던 독소들이 확인될 수 있게 되면서 영향을 받고 있다. 음식에서 발견되어왔고 가장 최근에는 아일랜드 돼지고기에서 발견된 독성이 매우 강한 물질인 다이옥신을 예로 들어보자. 다이옥신 수치는 영양 단계를 증가시키고 이러한 사실은 모유의 안정성이 대중의 관심을 받게 했다. 그러나 모유의 건강상 이점은 잊혀선 안되고 모유 수유를 없애서는 안 된다.

UNIT 11 Weather not an exact science
수치예보

SUMMARY & PARAPHRASE

66 Practice

_____
_____
_____
_____
_____
_____
_____

▶▶ Example

Humans have tried to forecast the weather for a long time, starting with listening to their senses and experiences. Then, thermometers were created, and other meteorological developments followed. High-tech equipment to gather and process massive amounts of data came in the 20th century. Weather forecasting can never be totally accurate due to the butterfly effect, which states that a small condition change can produce big changes in weather. So, ever more developments will not make weather forecasting any more accurate.

high-tech *adj.* 최첨단의
butterfly effect *n.* 나비 효과 (한 체제의 아주 작은 부분에 대한 변화가 다른 부분에 큰 영향을 가져오는 것)

▶ 인간은 그들의 감각과 경험에 귀 기울이는 것에서 시작해 오랜 시간 날씨를 예측하려고 시도해왔다. 그다음 온도계가 발명되었고 다른 기상학적 발달이 뒤따랐다. 20세기에는 엄청난 양의 데이터를 모으고 처리하기 위한 첨단 장비가 개발되었다. 기상 예측은 날씨에 있어서 작은 조건의 변화가 큰 변화를 유발할 수 있다는 나비효과로 인해 완전히 정확할 수는 없다. 따라서 앞으로의 개발에도 기상 예측은 더 정확해지지 않을 것이다.

UNIT 12 A different side to drones
드론

66 Practice

▶▶ Example

The optimism surrounding unmanned drones cannot be ignored: while their military use was frowned upon, their other positive uses are highlighted. We should, however, retain a level of skepticism about their use and their regulations. Drones on suspected terrorists in the Middle East have brought over 1,000 civilian deaths, drones have almost caused air accidents 25 times, and passenger jet pilots have reported drones near them 193 times. Hacking, breakdowns and terrorism are very real threats, too. Tight regulations are needed now to avoid drones ending up the same way as guns.

optimism *n.* 낙관론   **frown** *v.* 얼굴을 찌푸리다

▶ 무인 드론을 둘러싼 낙관론은 무시될 수 없다. 군사적 사용에는 얼굴이 찌푸려지지만 다른 긍정적인 사용은 강조되었다. 그러나 우리는 드론의 사용과 규제에 대한 일정 수준의 비관론을 유지해야 한다. 중동의 테러 용의자들에 대한 드론의 사용은 1,000명의 민간인의 죽음을 가져왔고, 거의 25배에 달하는 항공기 사고를 유발했으며, 여객기의 파일럿들은 드론이 가까이 있다는 보고를 한 횟수는 193회에 달한다. 해킹, 고장, 그리고 테러 역시 매우 실제적인 위협이다. 드론이 총기와 같은 방식으로 끝나지 않으려면 지금 엄격한 규제가 필요하다.

UNIT 13 Wrangling with nuclear risk
핵실험

66 Practice

▶▶ Example

America first tested an atomic bomb in 1945, then shortly after used them on Hiroshima and Nagasaki. In the 1950s, the Cold War and the threat of the Soviet Union saw more tests conducted. It is even said that John Wayne, and many others, died from cancer that resulted from exposure to radiation as they were filming a movie in the desert where tests were done. Even those outside the safety lines were affected, such as at Bikini Atoll, so ground and water nuclear tests were banned. Underground tests were exempt, but it seems they, too, were dangerous.

atomic bomb n. 원자 폭탄   **radiation** n. 방사선

▶ 미국은 1945년 처음으로 원자 폭탄을 실험했고 곧 히로시마와 나가사키에 투하했다. 1950년대에는 냉전과 소비에트 연합으로 인해 더 많은 실험이 실시되었다. 심지어 존 웨인을 비롯한 많은 사람들이 실험이 실시되었던 사막에서 영화 촬영을 하다가 방사선에 노출돼 암으로 사망했다고 전해진다. 심지어는 비키니 환초처럼 안전선 밖에 있던 사람들도 영향을 받았기 때문에 지상 및 수중 핵 실험이 금지되었다. 지하 실험은 면제되었지만 이러한 실험들 역시 위험해 보인다.

UNIT 14 A high-tech, brain-shrinking future
진화하는 인간

SUMMARY & PARAPHRASE

66 Practice

▶▶ Example

It's common to see somebody walking and talking on a cellphone, and doctors warn that overuse may cause cellphone elbow syndrome as well as health problems from electromagnetic waves. Despite this, we can't just give up cellphones as they are needed personally and professionally. Brain-machine interface has been developed to give humans brain control over tech and AI. If this progress continues, humans as we know them may evolve and change dramatically. Technology also deprives us of freedom, rest and mental stimulation; in fact, our skulls are now decreasing in size. Can naturally born humans survive this?

electromagnetic waves *n.* 전자파   **brain-machine interface** 두뇌 컴퓨터 인터페이스
deprive of *v.* ~을 빼앗다

▶ 통화를 하면서 걸어 다니는 사람을 보는 것은 흔한 일이며 의사들은 휴대폰의 과도한 사용은 팔꿈치 터널 증후군뿐만 아니라 전자파로 인한 건강상의 문제를 유발할 수 있다고 경고한다. 이러한 사실에도 불구하고 우리는 개인적으로도 사무적으로도 휴대폰이 필요하기 때문에 이것을 포기할 수 없다. 두뇌 컴퓨터 인터페이스는 인간에게 기술과 AI에 대한 뇌 통제권을 주기 위해 개발되었다. 만약 이러한 흐름이 계속된다면 인간은 우리가 알고 있듯 진화하고 극적으로 변화할 것이다. 기술은 또한 우리에게서 자유와 휴식 그리고 정신적 자극을 빼앗아갈 것이다. 사실 우리의 두개골은 크기가 줄어들고 있다. 자연적으로 태어난 인간들은 이것에서 살아남을 수 있을까?

UNIT 15 Painful patent protection
특허의 역설

SUMMARY & PARAPHRASE

66 Practice

▶▶ Example

   Patent rights can prevent much needed drugs and foodstuffs from reaching those who need them. Marketing a new drug is a minefield of patent negotiations, and many fail to reach the public due to this. For example, both a SARS vaccine and genetically engineered golden rice to feed starving children in Africa almost failed to see the light of day. Greed can ruin things. In history, merchant ships traveling the Rhine were destroyed by greedy barons demanding tolls. The ships stopped coming and the barons were also ruined. Everyone can come off worse when greed plays a part.

patent rights *n.* 특허권   **minefield** *n.* 지뢰밭
golden rice 황금의 쌀(유전공학으로 개발된 신품종 쌀; 비타민 A 생성 물질인 베타카로텐이 다량 함유)
see the light of day 출생하다; 널리 알려지다   **come off worse** (싸움, 경쟁 등에서) 더 크게 당하다

▶ 특허권은 많은 약과 식량이 이를 필요로 하는 사람들에게 전해지는 것을 막을 수 있다. 새로운 약을 시장에 내놓는 것은 특허권 협상의 지뢰밭이며 이로 인해 많은 약들은 대중에게 전해지는 데 실패하게 된다. 예를 들어서 사스 백신과 아프리카의 굶주린 아이들에게 먹이기 위한 유전공학으로 개발된 황금의 쌀은 거의 한 번도 빛을 보지 못했다. 탐욕은 일을 망칠 수 있다. 과거 라인강을 떠다니던 상선들은 요금을 요구하는 탐욕스러운 남작에 의해 파괴되었다. 배들은 그곳에 가는 것을 멈췄고 남작 역시 망해버렸다. 모든 사람은 마음속에 탐욕이 자리할 때 더 크게 당할 수 있다.

UNIT 16 Statistics use and misuse
통계의 사용과 오용

SUMMARY & PARAPHRASE

" Practice

▶▶ Example

> Although Gregor Mendel has earned the title "the father of modern genetics" for his work on pea plants that led to his discovery of the laws of inheritance, he was also guilty of altering his experiment results to present the findings he desired. This is one of the worst things a scientist can do, but fraud is not limited to scientists. The Nixon government modified data to present a more favorable image of the government's economic progress. Also, teachers have been found to improve students' test scores to get personal benefits.
>
> modify *v.* 수정하다   economic progress 경제 발전

▶ 비록 그레고르 멘델이 유전의 법칙의 발견으로 이끈 콩에 대한 연구로 현대 유전학의 아버지라는 칭호를 얻었지만 그는 또한 그가 원하는 결과를 보여주기 위해 실험 결과를 바꾼 죄가 있다. 이것은 과학자가 할 수 있는 가장 나쁜 행동 중 하나이지만 사기는 과학자들에게만 국한된 것이 아니다. 닉슨 정부는 정부의 경제 발전에 대한 더 좋은 이미지를 보여주기 위해 데이터를 조작했다. 또한 교사들은 개인적인 이득을 얻기 위해 학생들의 성적을 높여준 것으로 밝혀졌다.

UNIT 17 Autonomous driving dreams
자율주행차의 꿈

SUMMARY & PARAPHRASE

66 Practice

▶▶ Example

> When autonomous vehicles become part of our everyday lives in the not-too-distant future, there will be significant changes. Certainly, car sales will be affected as people share vehicles more, but on the other hand, the demand for car parts will increase. As accidents decrease, car insurance will become less necessary. Drivers - both public and private - will face a conundrum about what to do. In Korea, while plans are in place to start introducing autonomous vehicles, the chaotic nature of some roads and small streets may be an obstacle.
>
> **autonomous vehicle** 자율주행차량 **conundrum** *n.* 수수께끼, 난제

▶ 자율주행차량이 머지않은 미래에 일상생활의 일부가 된다면, 상당한 변화가 일어날 것이다. 사람들이 차를 더 많이 공유하면서 차량 판매 수치는 확실히 영향을 받겠지만, 자동차 부품에 대한 수요는 증가할 것이다. 차 사고가 줄어들면서, 자동차 보험도 덜 필요하게 될 것이다. 대중교통이든 자가용이든, 운전자들은 무엇을 해야 하는지에 대한 난제를 마주할 것이다. 한국에서는 자율주행차량의 도입을 시작하려는 계획이 진행 중이지만, 몇몇 도로와 좁은 거리의 혼란을 일으키는 특징이 하나의 걸림돌이 될지도 모른다.

UNIT 18 Repent, ye carbon emitters
환경 면죄부

66 Practice

▶▶ Example

To counter-attack carbon dioxide emissions, the carbon-offset system was introduced, which asks those who contribute more to emissions to pay to build trees or hydroelectric power plants and eases their guilty conscience. The problem with this is that people do not change their harmful travel habits, but simply try to pay their way out of any wrongdoing. Emissions trading also allows people to use more carbon than they would otherwise, and has little effect on overall emissions. Buying unused carbon emissions from poorer countries indulges the rich's behavior.

counter-attack v. 반격하다　**emission** n. 배출　**contribute** v. 기여하다; 기부하다
hydroelectric power plant n. 수력발전소　**guilty conscience** n. 죄책감
pay one's way 빚지지 않고 해나가다; 자기 몫을 내다; 수지가 맞다　**wrongdoing** n. 범법행위　**indulge in** v. ~에 탐닉하다

▶ 이산화탄소 배출에 반격하기 위해 탄소 상쇄 제도가 도입되었으며 이 제도는 이산화탄소 배출에 더 많이 기여하는 사람들에게 나무를 심거나 수력발전소를 건설하고 죄책감을 낮추도록 요청하는 것이다. 이것의 문제는 사람들이 그들의 해로운 여행 습관을 바꾸지 않고 단지 잘못된 행동에 대해 돈을 지불한다는 것이다. 배출권 거래 역시 사람들이 더 많은 탄소를 사용할 수 있게 만들며 전체 배출량에 큰 영향을 주지 못한다. 더 가난한 국가들로부터 사용되지 않은 탄소 배출량을 구입하는 것은 부자 국가의 행동을 탐닉하는 것이다.

UNIT 19 Turn off the lights
빛 공해

SUMMARY & PARAPHRASE

📝 Practice

▶▶ Example

The 24-hour biorhythm cycle is strong in our bodies and cannot be changed even if we try. Removing sunlight and attempting to reset to a new clock does not work. Sunlight, and by extension a lack of it, has such an influence on plants and animals that much natural behavior, from reproduction to hunting, is based on it. When our light cycles are interrupted, we become confused and do not act normally. Artificial light is affecting nature and our health.

biorhythm n. 바이오리듬 **by extension** 더 나아가 **artificial light** n. 인공조명

▶ 우리 몸의 24시간의 바이오리듬 주기는 강력하고 우리가 노력한다고 해도 바뀔 수 없다. 햇빛을 차단하고 새로운 시계를 다시 맞추는 것은 효과가 없다. 햇빛, 그리고 더 나아가 햇빛의 부재는 번식에서 사냥에 이르기까지 많은 자연적 행동이 해를 기반으로 하는 식물과 동물에게 많은 영향을 끼친다. 빛 주기가 방해를 받게 되면 우리는 혼란스러워지고 평소처럼 행동하지 않는다. 인공조명은 자연과 우리의 건강에 영향을 끼치고 있다.

UNIT 20 Kimchi in space
우주식품

SUMMARY & PARAPHRASE

66 Practice

▶▶ Example

> The problem of providing food to astronauts on space missions has greatly contributed to the developments in that field. Making food light to keep the vehicle light and hygienic enough to be on board a spaceship with no refrigerator was the primary goal, and both Russian and the U.S. carry pretty much the same foods. Furthermore, both have been instrumental in the advances in container and packaging technologies with Americans favoring foil-like material and airtight containers while the Russians choose transparent materials.
>
> **space mission** *n.* 우주 비행 임무   **hygienic** *adj.* 청결한

▶ 우주 비행 임무 중인 우주 비행사에게 음식을 제공하는 문제점은 이 분야의 발전에 크게 기여한다. 우주선을 가볍게 유지할 만큼 가볍고 냉장고가 없는 우주선에 실을 수 있을 만큼 위생적인 음식을 만드는 것이 주목적이었고 러시아와 미국 우주선은 거의 같은 음식을 싣는다. 뿐만 아니라 호일 같은 소재 밀폐용기를 선호하는 미국과 반대로 투명한 소재를 선호하는 러시아는 컨테이너와 포장기술의 발전에 큰 영향을 주었다.

Social Science

Part 4 사회과학

UNIT 01 At Google, there is no manual
"구글에는 매뉴얼이 없습니다"

SUMMARY & PARAPHRASE

66 Practice

▶▶ Example

The Googleplex has been designed to promote satisfaction and concentration which will in turn raise productivity. The theory goes that if employees are happy and relaxed – spending 20% of their working time on personal fulfillment – their best ideas will come to them. Anyone is allowed to take ideas straight to management, nobody is controlled and watched, and meetings are meant to be conducted with openness and boldness. No-one can argue against the success of Gmail and Adsense. Eating great food, exercising, and relaxing have taken Google to the top.

satisfaction *n.* 만족감　　**fulfillment** *n.* 이행; 실천

▶ 구글플렉스는 만족과 집중을 향상시킬 수 있도록 설계되었고 이것은 결국 생산성을 높일 것이다. 이것은 만약 직원들이 20%의 업무 시간을 개인의 만족을 위해 사용하며 행복하고 편해진다면 최선의 아이디어가 나올 것이라는 이론이다. 누구든 자신의 아이디어를 경영진에게 전달할 수 있고 그 누구도 통제받거나 감시받지 않으며 회의는 개방성과 대담함과 함께 진행된다. 그 누구도 G메일과 애드센스의 성공에 대해 이의를 제기할 수 없다. 훌륭한 음식을 먹고 운동하고 휴식하는 것은 구글을 최고의 자리에 오르게 만들었다.

UNIT 02 Candidate games
딜레마

SUMMARY & PARAPHRASE

🙶 Practice

▶▶ Example

> Dilemmas are situations where a decision between two difficult choices has to be made. "The Prisoner's Dilemma" whereby two prisoners are given different, difficult, options to incriminate themselves, the other or remain silent for varying punishments, is one example. The kids' game of chicken was seen in the car scenes in the movie "Rebel Without a Cause" and on a global scale with the Cold War. Both Russia and the U.S. knew the situation was brought on by fear of what the other was doing, and that backing down would prompt the other to do so, too, but neither was willing to back down first.
>
> dilemma *n.* 딜레마

▶ 딜레마는 두 가지의 어려운 결정 가운데 하나를 반드시 선택해야 하는 상황을 의미한다. 두 명의 죄수가 다양한 형벌에 대해 복죄하거나 다른 사람에게 죄를 돌리거나 침묵할 수 있는 서로 다르고 어려운 선택권이 주어지는 "죄수의 딜레마"가 한 예이다. 아이들의 치킨게임은 영화 "이유 없는 반항"의 자동차 장면에서 볼 수 있고 냉전에서는 세계적 규모로 보인다. 러시아와 미국은 상대방이 무엇을 하고 있는지에 대한 두려움으로 인해 그러한 상황이 발생했고 자신이 물러서면 상대방도 그렇게 할 것임을 알고 있었다. 하지만 이 두 국가는 먼저 물러서려고 하지 않았다.

UNIT 03 Progress over product
GDP

SUMMARY & PARAPHRASE

❝ Practice

_____
_____
_____
_____
_____
_____
_____

▶▶ Example

GDP simply evaluates total production volume of a country regardless of what kind of product it is and other damaging factors like sustainability, pollution, living standards, etc. Created during the 1930s Great Depression, its creator warned against reliance on it because it does not measure welfare. One example of this is how the GDP of Alaska increased as volunteers flooded in to help with a huge oil spill that threatened its natural habitat. The environment was harmed, but GDP increased. There are now calls for GDP to be replaced by GPI(Genuine Progress Indicator), which measures negative factors, too.

GPI(Genuine Progress Indicator) 세계평화지수(국민총생산이나 국내총생산의 대안으로 등장한 경제지표)

▶ GDP는 제품의 종류가 무엇인지, 그리고 지속 가능성, 오염, 생활수준 등의 손상 계수와 상관없이 한 국가의 총 생산량을 평가한다. 1930년대 대공황 기간에 고안된 GDP의 창안자는 GDP에 대한 의존에 대해 경고했다. 왜냐하면 GDP는 복지를 고려하지 않기 때문이다. 이것의 한 예로 알래스카의 자연 서식지를 위협하는 대규모의 기름 유출을 돕기 위해 자원봉사자들이 모여들면서 알래스카의 GDP가 늘어난 것을 들 수 있다. 환경은 피해를 입었지만 GDP는 증가했다. 현재 GDP를 부정적 요인들도 고려하는 GPI(세계평화지수)로 대체하자는 요구가 있다.

UNIT 04 Respecting privacy v. Public interests
사생활 보호 v. 공익

SUMMARY & PARAPHRASE

66 Practice

▶▶ Example

Japan does not enforce mandatory disclosure of the movements and information of Covid-19 patients on a national scale, so many citizens have no idea what's going on or where to avoid. Only limited information is relayed to citizens, and companies can choose whether to disclose more by themselves. On the other hand, Korea has enforced a disclosure system to protect its citizens. Cases are on the decline due to its successful tracing of infections. The more control we have, the safer we can make it for everyone. It is imperative to take back control of our information and distribute it ourselves rather than have it taken from us.

disclosure *n.* 폭로; 밝혀진 내용 **relay** *v.* 전달하다 **imperative** *a.* 반드시 해야 하는, 긴요한

▶ 일본은 코로나 바이러스 환자에 관한 정보와 동선을 전국적으로 의무 공개하는 법률을 실시하지 않았고, 그로 인해 많은 시민들은 무슨 일이 벌어지고 있는지 또는 어떤 곳을 꺼려야 하는지를 전혀 모르고 있다. 시민들은 오직 제한된 정보만을 제공 받지만, 기업은 스스로 정보를 더 공개할 것인지 말 것인지를 선택할 수 있다. 반면에, 한국은 자국민 보호를 목적으로 의무 정보 공개 시스템을 시행 중이다. 성공적인 감염 경로의 추적으로 인해 확진 판정을 받는 경우는 감소세에 있다. 우리가 더 많은 통제력을 지니면 지닐수록, 우리 모두가 더 안전해질 수 있다. 정보를 빼앗기는 것이 아니라 정보에 대한 통제력을 다시 되찾고 그것을 널리 전달하는 것이 매우 필요하다.

UNIT 05 Just give them some fish
물고기를 줘라

SUMMARY & PARAPHRASE

66 Practice

_____
_____
_____
_____
_____
_____
_____

▶▶ Example

Vocational skills are no longer necessary in the modern world that is experiencing globalization and digitization, and poor people are bearing the brunt of this change. In order to help them, a basic universal income has been suggested although this goes against what many, especially politically leftist people, think is right. It is seen as promoting laziness and a reliance on handouts.

vocational *a.* 직업과 관련된 digitization *n.* 디지털화
bear the brunt of ~을 정면으로 맞서다 basic universal income 기본소득
handout *n.* 지원금

▶ 세계화와 디지털화를 겪고 있는 현대 세계에서는 더 이상 직업 기술이 필요하지 않으며, 가난한 사람들은 이러한 변화를 정면으로 맞서고 있다. 그들을 도와주기 위해서 기본 소득제도가 계속해서 제안되어왔다. 비록 이것이 많은, 특히 정치적 좌파들이 생각하기에 옳은 것과는 거리가 멂에도 말이다. 기본소득제도는 게으름과 지원금에 대한 의존성을 조장하는 것으로 여겨진다.

UNIT 06 Dollar envy
시뇨리지

SUMMARY & PARAPHRASE

　　Practice

▶▶ Example

> Seigniorage is the profit that is earned on minting money and putting it into circulation. When coins are collected, such as with commemorative coins, and do not enter circulation, the difference between minting cost and face value becomes seigniorage. Total annual seigniorage comes from multiplying this difference by how much money is in circulation. However, when there is too much money in circulation, its value drops. The problem is that the U.S. dollar is the international currency and any inflation is felt globally. The U.S. Federal Reserve is going to start issuing more money and will earn lots in seigniorage.
>
> **seigniorage** *n.* 화폐주조세　　**mint** *v.* (화폐를) 주조하다

▶ 화폐주조세는 화폐를 주조하고 유통하는 데서 얻는 수익을 의미한다. 기념주화 같은 동전이 수집되고 유통되지 않으면 주화 비용과 액면가의 차이가 화폐주조세가 되는 것이다. 연간 총 화폐주조세는 이 차이에 얼마큼의 돈이 유통되고 있는지를 곱함으로써 구할 수 있다. 그러나 너무 많은 돈이 유통되게 되면 가치가 떨어지게 된다. 문제는 미국 달러가 국제 통화이며 모든 인플레이션이 국제적으로 체감될 수 있다는 것이다. 미국 연방준비제도 이사회는 더 많은 화폐를 발행하고 더 많은 화폐주조세를 걷어들일 예정이다.

UNIT 07 More Sea Story blame game
정보의 비대칭성

SUMMARY & PARAPHRASE

66 Practice

▶▶ Example

One example of information asymmetry is used car sales.: the seller knows more than the buyer, so may overcharge for personal gain. This situation can only happen a few times, however, before the seller gets a bad reputation and can no longer sell anymore. Furthermore, information asymmetry can harm owner-agent relationships, where the owner entrusts the agent to work for his interest, but without the necessary knowledge, cannot supervise. The agent then may be tempted to work for his own interests to cheat the owner.

cheat *v.* 속이다, 사기치다

▶ 정보 비대칭성의 한 예로 중고차 판매가 있다. 판매자는 구매자보다 더 많이 알고 있기 때문에 개인의 이득을 위해 바가지를 씌울 수 있다. 그러나 이 상황은 판매자가 나쁜 평판을 받고 더 이상 한 대도 팔지 못하기 전까지만 몇 차례 발생한다. 더 나아가 정보 불균형은 주인이 자신의 이익을 위해 일하는 대리인을 믿지만 필요한 지식이 없으면 대리인을 감독할 수 없는 주인과 대리인의 관계를 악화시킬 수 있다. 그렇게 되면 대리인은 주인을 속여 자신의 이익을 위해 일하려고 할 수 있다.

UNIT 08 Hierarchical incompetence?
피터원리

SUMMARY & PARAPHRASE

66 Practice

_____
_____
_____
_____
_____
_____
_____

▶▶ Example

It is true that when promotions are being considered, there are always incapable people in the waiting line. This is because of the Peter Principle where everyone moves up the chain until they reach their limit of competence. Everybody knows when they reach that stage, but do everything they can to hide it, from keeping up the appearance of being busy and capable to communicating endlessly in an attempt to appear knowledgeable. The rest of the organization has to suffer through this situation.

the Peter Principle 피터의 법칙(계층 사회 구성원은 각자의 능력 이상까지 출세하는데 이로써 상층부가 무능력자 집단이 된다는 것)

▶ 승진을 고려할 때가 오면 늘 무능한 사람들이 대기줄에 서있다. 이것은 모든 사람들이 자신의 능력의 한계에 다다를 때까지 승진을 한다는 피터의 법칙 때문이다. 모든 사람들은 자신이 이 단계에 도달한 것을 알지만 지적으로 보이기 위해 바쁜 척을 하고 끊임없이 의사소통할 수 있는 척을 하는 등, 이를 숨기려 필사적인 노력을 한다. 나머지 조직원들은 이 상황을 겪어야만 한다.

UNIT 09 Broken items
깨진 유리창

SUMMARY & PARAPHRASE

❝ Practice

▶▶ Example

The Broken Windows Theory surmises that if a company ignores small things, bigger problems will occur down the road. For instance, if a store's window is broken and the owner doesn't fix it properly, it looks like the owner doesn't care and vandals and crime will congregate in the area as a result. The store owner should replace the window correctly not only to keep further crime away, but to increase business. Alternately, that money would have been used for another service, so the window damage wasn't necessary for increased profit.

The broken windows theory 깨진 유리창 이론 **down the road** 장래에
congregate v. 모여들다 **alternately** adv. 번갈아; 엇갈리게

▶ 깨진 유리창 이론은 만약 회사가 사소한 것들을 무시한다면, 장래에 더 큰 문제가 발생할 것이라고 말한다. 예를 들어서 상점의 창문이 깨졌는데도 주인이 이것을 제대로 고치지 않으면, 주인이 신경을 쓰지 않는 것처럼 보여서 결과적으로 기물 파괴자와 범죄자가 그 지역으로 모여들게 될 것이다. 가게 주인은 범죄를 막는 것뿐만 아니라 사업을 확장하기 위해서도 창문을 올바르게 교체해야 한다. 그렇지 않더라도 그 돈은 다른 서비스에 사용됐을 것이므로 창문 파손이 수익 증가를 위해 필수적인 것은 아니다.

UNIT 10 Demonstrators in the dark
합리적 무시

SUMMARY & PARAPHRASE

❝ Practice

▶▶ Example

When people come together to demand the same thing, it might look like they are acting for others, but actually they are acting on their own behalf. When those personal interests are very important, the group will work even harder together, even if the aim of the group will have a negative effect on society at large. For example, Bastiat wrote a parody that depicted candlemakers seeking to ban the sun to further their own businesses. Rational ignorance can push people to pursue personal interest over that of the general public.

personal interest *n.* 개인적 관심, 개인적 이득   **rational ignorance** 합리적 무시

▶ 사람들이 같은 것을 요구하기 위해 모일 때, 그들이 다른 사람들을 위해 행동하는 것처럼 보일 수 있지만 사실 그들은 스스로를 위해 행동하고 있는 것이다. 개인의 이익이 매우 중요할 때에는 집단의 목표가 사회 전반에 부정적인 영향을 미칠지라도 집단은 더 열심히 일할 것이다. 예를 들어서 바스티아는 자신들의 사업을 더 번창시키기 위해 햇볕을 차단하고자 했던 양초 제조업자들에 대해 묘사하는 패러디를 썼다. 합리적 무시는 사람들로 하여금 대중이 아닌 개인의 이익을 추구하도록 독려할 수 있다.

UNIT 11 An unbroken union
월마트

SUMMARY & PARAPHRASE

66 Practice

▶▶ Example

Wal-mart prevented unions amongst its employees for four decades by following specific policies. When recruiting, there is a list of signs that implicate someone as being sympathetic to unions. Further, certain behavior can highlight someone as becoming dangerously interested in union activities. If a store were to create a union, chances are it would be closed immediately. It is a part of Wal-mart's policy to always put the customer first, whether it be never showing anger, always greeting a customer warmly, or always accepting returns. This all costs money that Wal-Mart then cannot afford to spend on employees' wages.

union *n.* 노조; 연방; 미국; 통합   decade *n.* 10년

▶ 월마트는 40년간 특정 정책을 따르게 함으로써 노조 설립을 방해해왔다. 채용을 할 때에는 노조에 동조하는 사람을 암시하는 징후의 목록이 존재한다. 더 나아가 특정 행동은 한 사람이 위험할 만큼 노조 활동에 관심을 가지게 되었음을 강조할 수 있다. 만약 상점이 노조를 설립한다면, 즉시 폐점할 가능성이 있다. 이것은 고객에게 절대 화난 기색을 보이지 않는 것이든, 늘 고객을 따뜻하게 맞이하는 것이든, 늘 반품을 해주는 것이든 간에 고객을 최우선으로 생각하는 월마트 정책의 일부이다. 이는 돈을 필요로 하는데, 이로 인해 월마트는 직원들의 월급을 충분히 지불할 수 없게 된다.

UNIT 12 How the strong grew weak
강한 정부의 역설

66 Practice

▶▶ Example

The 1970s oil crisis saw governments split into two camps: those that allowed price increases which meant people consumed less oil and became less dependent on it, and those who stepped in to control the oil prices maintaining the dependence of the nation on oil. However, the more a government intervenes and fails, the more the government has to enact new stronger policies to solve this new problem. This can only lead to the collapse of the economy and the country.

oil crisis *n.* 석유위기   **camp** *n.* 야영지; 수용소; 막사; 진영   **step in** *v.* 개입하다

▶ 1970년대 발생한 석유위기로 인해 정부는 두 진영으로 갈라지게 되었다. 한 진영은 석유값을 올려서 사람들이 석유를 적게 사용하고 덜 의존하게 만들고자 했고, 다른 진영은 석유에 대한 국가의 의존을 유지하며 유가를 통제하기 위해서 개입했다. 하지만 성부가 개입해 실패를 거듭할수록 성부는 새로운 문제를 해결하기 위해 더욱 강력한 법안을 제정해야만 한다. 이것은 경제와 국가의 붕괴로 이끌 것이다.

UNIT 13 A crime of passion
'제2의 스위스' 된다는 영국의 망상

❝ Practice

▶▶ Example

> The UK's quick decision to leave the European Union has done the country no favors. Brexit supporters were led to believe that they could become like Switzerland, who had never joined the EU and maintained a high level of prosperity because they don't have to pay the EU's fees or follow its trade rules. However, Swiss people are very different to Brits. Swiss voters rejected both a free basic income proposal as they felt motivation to work would drop, and an extension of paid holidays by 50%. The Brits would never do the same thing.
>
> **do somebody no favours** ~에게 득이 안 될(~에 대해 안 좋은 인상을 주는) 일을 하다   **prosperity** *n.* 번창

▶ EU 탈퇴에 대한 영국의 빠른 결정은 나라에 아무런 도움을 주지 못했다. 브렉시트 지지자들은 영국이 EU에 가입한 적이 없고 EU에 돈을 지불하거나 무역 규칙을 지키지 않아도 돼 높은 수준의 번영을 유지하는 스위스와 같이 될 것이라고 믿었다. 스위스 사람들은 영국 사람들과 매우 다르다. 스위스의 유권자들은 일에 대한 동기가 저하될 것이라고 생각해 기본소득 지급 정책과 유급 휴가를 50%까지 늘리는 것에 반대했다. 영국인들은 절대 똑같이 행동하지 않을 것이다.

UNIT 14　A rational vote
투표의 경제학

SUMMARY & PARAPHRASE

66 Practice

_____
_____
_____
_____
_____
_____
_____

▶▶ Example

Democracy is built upon the assumption that people will vote, but this doesn't always happen. Voting happens because of economic interest, but abstention would have a bigger effect as the inconvenience of voting is larger than the effect of one vote. There must then be other, more personal, reasons why people take the time to vote. Abstention might be used as a tool for showing dissatisfaction with democracy, but in the absence of an alternative system democracy is the best one we have although it doesn't always give the best results.

democracy *n.* 민주주의　　**assumption** *n.* 가정　　**abstention** *n.* 절제; 기권

▶ 민주주의는 사람들이 투표할 것이라는 가정을 기반으로 하지만 늘 그렇지만은 않다. 경제적 이익을 위해 투표를 하지만 투표의 불편함이 한 표의 영향력보다 더 크기 때문에 기권은 더 큰 힘을 가질 수 있게 된다. 그렇다면 사람들이 시간을 내 투표하는 데에는 더 개인적인 이유가 반드시 존재할 것이다. 기권은 민주주의에 대한 불만족을 보여주는 도구로써 사용될 수 있다. 하지만 대안이 되는 체제가 없는 상황에서는 늘 최고의 결과를 보여주지는 않지만 우리가 가진 것들 중 최선의 체제는 민주주의 체제이다.

UNIT 15 In the interest of whom?
수쿠크

SUMMARY & PARAPHRASE

❝ Practice

▶▶ Example

Both Aristotle and medieval popes disagreed strongly with the idea of interest rates when something has been lent with harsh punishments threatened, but usurers still found a way to extract money from the transaction. Religious reformists, such as Martin Luther, also disagreed calling it akin to stealing. As it didn't disappear and became common, the church had to finally accept it. Islam, however, still prohibits it although legitimate ways have been found around this, too, based on technicalities. Asset-backed security system is based on the Islamic method that treats assets as guarantees for loans.

usurer *n.* 고리대금업자   **technicality** *n.* 세부사항

▶ 아리스토텔레스와 중세 교황들은 가혹한 처벌이 사라지면서 무언가를 빌려줬을 때 이자를 받는 것에 대해 매우 강하게 처벌을 가하겠다며 반대했지만 고리대금업자들은 거래에서 돈을 얻어내기 위한 방법을 찾아냈다. 마틴 루터와 같은 종교개혁자들은 이것이 절도와 같은 것이라 말하며 반대했다. 이자를 받는 것이 사라지지 않고 대중화되면서 교회는 결국 이를 받아들여야만 했다. 하지만 이슬람은 이자와 관련해 적법한 방법이 있음에도 불구하고 세부 규칙을 근거로 여전히 금지하고 있다. 자산담보부증권 시스템은 자산을 대출에 대한 담보로 취급하는 이슬람적 방식을 기반으로 한다.

UNIT 16 NGO: A dearth of humility
인본주의가 결여된 NGO

SUMMARY & PARAPHRASE

66 Practice

▶▶ Example

  Jim Rogers wrote extensively on what he saw as the ills affecting the places he visited, singling out NGOs specifically for his ire. Not only does the aid from NGOs prevent industrialization and economic development, but the NGOs themselves act more like their governmental oppressors than their helpers as they use expensive cars and buildings for their work. In Korea, NGOs traditionally had a good reputation but that has changed in modern-day Korea as they are accused of acting as Rogers described others as doing in Africa.

extensively *ad.* 광범위하게, 폭넓게   **single out** 선발하다, 선별하다
oppressor *n.* 압제자   **reputation** *n.* 명성

▶ Jim Rogers는 그가 방문한 지역을 덮친 질병에 대한 그의 사견을 광범위하게 글로 풀어냈으며, 특히 그의 분노의 대상으로 비정부기구들을 택했다. 비정부기구들의 원조가 산업화와 경제적 발달을 저해했을 뿐만 아니라, 비정부기구 자체도 일을 한답시고 값비싼 차와 건물을 사용하면서, 조력자라기보다는 압제자와 비슷한 역할을 했다. 한국에서 비정부기구들은 전통적으로 평판이 좋았다. 그러나 현대 한국에서 명성은 차차 바뀌기 시작했는데, 비정부기구들이 Rogers가 이야기한 바와 같이 다른 비정부기구들이 아프리카에서 하는 것과 같은 (부패한) 행위를 한다고 비난을 받기 때문이다.

UNIT 17 Populism's persuasiveness
상황주의

SUMMARY & PARAPHRASE

66 Practice

▶▶ Example

The election of Salvador Allende in Chile, a country quite different from its Latin American neighbors, showed it was possible for a socialist party to win a free election; populism didn't win out this time. The idea of populism was invented in the U.S. in 1891 to provide a rival to the two-party system and the People's Party ran with often illogical but popular policies. Populism since then evolved to be cultural rather than economic. Both parties have used versions of populism to win elections, but it is the truth that loses out in the end.

election *n.* 선거   socialist party *n.* 사회주의 정당   populism *n.* 포퓰리즘

▶ 주위 라틴아메리카 국가들과 매우 다른 국가인 칠레에서 살바도르 아옌데의 선거는 사회주의 정당이 자유선거에서 이기는 것이 가능한 일임을 보여줬다. 이번에는 포퓰리즘이 먹히지 않았다. 포퓰리즘은 1891년 미국에서 야당에게 양당 체제를 제공하기 위한 목적으로 고안된 것이고 민주당은 비논리적이지만 대중들에게 인기 있는 정책을 이용했다. 포퓰리즘은 그때부터 경제적이기보단 문화적으로 발전했다. 양당은 선거에서 이기기 위해 다양한 포퓰리즘을 사용하지만 결국 지는 것이 현실이다.

UNIT 18 Korea lacks basic values
스마트 기업 50

SUMMARY & PARAPHRASE

66 Practice

▶▶ Example

All companies, big and small, aim to be smart, but not all succeed. The MIT Technology Review focuses on companies that are doing new and creative things in technology irrespective of profit. Year by year, companies rise and fall: this year, highly-ranked Xiomi, Samsung and Apple have all gone because they have brought nothing new to the table over the past 12 months. Amazon has taken the top spot with Alexa – its AI helper. Baidu is next with its own automobile AI technology. Other Chinese companies are also ranked highly while Korea has only Coupang to represent the nation.

The MIT Technology Review 테크놀로지 리뷰   rank *v.* 순위를 매기다; 순위를 차지하다

▶ 규모가 크든 작든 모든 기업은 스마트해지려고 하지만 모두가 성공하는 것은 아니다. 테크놀로지 리뷰는 수익에 상관없이 새롭고 독창적인 기술을 사용하고 있는 기업을 조명한다. 매년 기업의 순위는 변화한다. 올해는 상위권이었던 샤오미와 삼성 그리고 애플의 순위가 모두 내려갔다. 왜냐하면 그들 모두 지난 12개월간 새로운 것을 내놓지 않았기 때문이다. 아마존은 AI 헬퍼인 Alexa로 1위에 올랐다. 바이두는 자동차 AI 기술로 그다음 순위에 올랐다. 한국에서는 쿠팡 만이 순위에 오른 반면, 다른 중국 기업들 역시 높은 순위를 차지했다.

UNIT 19 Like Robin Hood, tax up to no good
부유세

❝ Practice

▶▶ Example

Taxes on the wealthy are not a new thing. Since wealthy people in England had lots of windows in their home because they had fireplaces, King William III imposed a window tax. Tax dodgers hid their windows to avoid higher taxes. Taxing the rich should ease the burden on the poor in society, but often does not because of the Robin Hood effect. Wealthy citizens leave their country when faced with high taxes to settle in places with low taxes. In the end, the poor are in a worse situation than before.

tax on the wealthy *n.* 부유세 **window tax** *n.* 창문세 **tax dodger** *n.* 탈세자
Robin Hood effect *n.* 로빈후드 효과
('가진 자'의 것을 빼앗아 '없는 자'에게 나눠주면 일하는 사람이 갈수록 줄어들어 결국 없는 자만 남는다는 뜻)

▶ 부유세는 새로운 것이 아니다. 영국의 부유한 사람들의 집에는 벽난로가 있어 창문이 많았기 때문에 윌리엄 3세는 창문세를 부과했다. 탈세자들은 높은 세금을 피하기 위해 창문을 숨겼다. 부자들에게 세금을 부과하는 것이 사회의 빈곤층에 대한 부담을 완화해주어야 하지만 로빈후드 효과 때문에 그렇지 않을 때가 많았다. 세금을 많이 내게 되면, 부유한 시민들은 세금이 낮은 곳에서 정착하기 위해 나라를 떠난다. 결국 가난한 사람들은 이전보다 더 안 좋은 상황에 처하게 되는 것이다.

UNIT 20 America's risky pot experiment
아슬아슬한 미국의 마리화나 실험

SUMMARY & PARAPHRASE

66 Practice

▶▶ Example

Legalization of marijuana cannot be far off. Twenty states approve its use medically, users will not be targeted by authorities, and recreational marijuana has been approved in two states with two more considering it. Not only does government but also most people think that marijuana is not a harmful substance. Marijuana use reduces alcohol consumption and raises revenues for states through taxation. There does need to be some control, though, when it comes to young people and activities under the influence. How effective this may be considering the situation with gun control remains to be seen.

legalization *n.* 합법화　**marijuana** *n.* 마리화나, 대마초
state *n.* 국가; 상태; 주　**remain to be seen** 아직 두고 볼 일이다

▶ 대마초의 합법화는 먼 훗날의 일이 아니다. 20개의 국가가 대마초의 의료적 사용을 허가하고 사용자들은 당국의 표적이 되지 않으며 두 국가는 오락용 마리화나를 허가했고 다른 두 국가는 이를 고려 중이다. 정부뿐만 아니라 대부분의 사람들은 마리화나가 해로운 물질이 아니라고 생각한다. 마리화나의 사용은 알코올의 섭취를 줄이고 조세를 통해 국가의 세입을 증가시킬 수 있다. 그러나 젊은이들과 약에 취해 하는 행동들에 대해서는 어느 정도의 규제가 필요하다. 총기 규제를 고려해봤을 때, 이것이 얼마나 효과가 있을지는 아직 두고 볼 일이다.

 **Break Time**

A lion from Savanna charged a chaplain. Then, the chaplain on his knees with his eyes closed started to pray to God.

"Dear God, please transform this beast into a devout Christian."

After a while, the chaplain opens his eyes and sees the lion kneeling down and praying: "Dear God, may you bless this meal which I'am about to take."

사바나에서 사자와 딱 마주친 목사는 무릎을 꿇고, 그리고 눈을 감고 전지전능하신 하나님에게 기도를 드립니다.

"하나님, 어떻게든 이 야수를 신성한 크리스찬으로 변하게 해주세요."

잠시 시간이 지나고, 목사가 눈을 떠보니 그 사자는 무릎을 꿇고 신에게 기도를 드리고 있습니다. "하나님, 지금부터 먹게 될 식사에 부디 축복을 내려주시길."

transform A into B	A를 B로 바꾸다
devout	독실한, 믿음이 깊은
chaplain	목사
pray	기도하다
bless the meal	식사에 축복을 주다

본문(지문)해석 & 문제해설·정답

본문(지문) 순서와 동일(각 파트별 Unit 1~20)

Part 1

UNIT 01

Rumors: society's cancerous tumors
사람 잡는 루머

1941년 12월 7일 항공기와 잠수함을 앞세운 일본군이 진주만을 공격했다. 일본이 공격했다는 소식이 전해지자 미 국민 사이에는 흉흉한 소문이 파다했다. 그러자, 프랭클린 루스벨트 대통령이 진화에 나섰다. 진주만 공격으로 미군 2,340명이 사망했고, 1,100명이 부상당했다. 진주만에 배치된 군함 중 사용 불가능할 정도로 파괴된 건 단 세 척이다. 미군이 1,000대가 넘는 군용기를 잃었다는 이야기는 사실무근이다. 일본은 자신들이 항공기를 얼마나 파괴했는지 모르며, 루스벨트도 그에 대한 정보를 알려주지 않았다. 다만, 그는 국민들에게 지금까지 미군이 파괴한 일본 군용기 수가 그보다 훨씬 많다는 것만큼은 확실하며, 그들이 듣거나 읽는 모든 정보를 무조건 믿지 말고 먼저 확인하라고도 당부했다. 소문이 조직 구성원들의 사기를 꺾고 조직을 좀먹는 암적 존재가 될 수 있음을 잘 알고 있었던 까닭이다. 국가 위기상황에서 리더가 루머와 어떻게 맞서야 하는지 본보기가 될 만하다.

루머는 도마뱀 꼬리와 같다. 자르면 또 생겨난다. 종종 무고한 사람을 잡기도 한다. 우리는 왜 루머를 받아들일까. 캐스 선스타인 하버드대 교수는 자신의 저서인 '루머: 어떻게 거짓이 확산되고, 우리는 왜 소문을 믿는지, 무엇을 할 수 있는지'에서 이를 '사회적 폭포 효과'라고 설명했다. 우리는 판단을 내릴 때 타인의 생각과 행동에 의존하려는 경향을 보인다. 그래서 자기가 아는 대부분의 사람이 어떤 루머를 믿으면 어느새 따라 믿게 된다. 두 번째 요인은 '집단 극단화'다. 같은 생각을 가진 사람들이 모여 대화하다 보면 이전보다 훨씬 더 극단적인 생각을 갖게 된다. 그러면서도 자신이 나름 합리적이라고 생각한다.

해설

1. repudiate는 '공식적으로 부인한다'는 뜻의 동사로 보기에서는 deny가 가장 근접한 단어이다.

2. '우리는 판단을 내릴 때 타인의 생각과 행동에 의존하려는 경향'을 보이는 것이 사회적 폭포효과에 대하여 본문에서 서술한 내용이므로, (a)처럼 단지 멀리만 퍼지는 것이 아니고, (c)처럼 사회적으로 더 높이 올라갈수록 더 많이 믿게 된다는 것도 아니다. 사람들이 많이 믿고 더 많이 퍼져갈수록 그 소문은 더 강력해진다는 (b)가 정답이다.

3. 두 번째 단락에서 사회적 폭포효과와 집단 극단화에 대한 용어의 정의를 내리고 글이 끝났으므로, 이 뒤에는 그 두 가지 원리에 대한 상세한 설명이 나오는 것이 글의 흐름상 타당하다. 참고로 (b)와 (c)는 첫 번째 단락과 관계되는 내용으로 두 번째 단락과는 관계가 없으며, (d)는 본문의 내용과 무관한 설명이다.

4. 소문은 사회에 암적인 존재이며, 너무나 많은 사람들이 믿으면 굉장히 위험해질 수 있고, 첫 번째 단락에 언급한 사태에 대해서는 미국과 일본의 생각이 달랐던 것도 사실이다. 하지만 (d)의 경우 루스벨트가 미국인들에게 거짓말을 하였다는 얘기는 근거없는 진술이다.

정답 1.(c) 2.(b) 3.(a) 4.(d)

UNIT 02
'Social proofs' on the Web
인기 검색어

뉴욕시 대로 한복판에서 한 남자가 하늘을 쳐다봤다. 행인 대부분이 그냥 지나쳤다. 그런데 4% 정도가 따라서 하늘을 쳐다봤다. 쳐다보는 사람의 수가 늘어나자, 따라 쳐다보는 사람의 수도 늘었다. 5명이 하늘을 쳐다보면 행인의 8%, 15명이 쳐다보면 길 가던 사람 중 40%가 멈춰서서 뭘 그렇게 보나 보려고 쳐다봤다. '사회적 증거(social proof) 현상'에 대한 유명한 심리학 실험이다. 사람들은 다수의 행동인 '사회적 증거'를 따라 하면 실수를 줄일 수 있다고 생각해 남을 좇아한다는 것이다. TV 코미디에 삽입되는 가짜웃음과 베스트셀러임을 강조하는 상품광고가 이에 속한다. 코미디 프로의 가짜웃음은 바보스럽고 어색하지만, 시청자들은 다른 사람들의 웃음소리를 듣고 더 자주 오래 웃으며 그 프로를 더 재미있게 느끼는 것으로 조사됐다. 자선바자회 성금을 모금하면서 성금 낸 명사의 명단을 보도한다든지, 교회에서 헌금 바구니를 돌리는 것도 이 효과를 노린 것이다.

그러나 사회적 증거들이 언제나 진실은 아니다. 오히려 진실에 반할 때가 많다. 현대 미디어나 광고에서 행해지는 여론조작의 심리적 기제(機制)가 바로 사회적 증거라고 할 수 있다. 인터넷 포털사이트에서도 사회적 증거들을 찾아볼 수 있다. 의제 설정이나 여론몰이에 크게 기여하는 인기 검색어가 그중 하나다. 인기 검색어는 눈에 잘 띄는 위치에 배치되며 긴박감과 극적 효과를 더하며 실시간 순위를 바꾼다. 부정확하고 편향된 정보이거나 자극적인 이슈들도 많지만 인기 검색어라는 이름으로 선보이는 즉시 강력한 사회적 증거 효과를 낸다. 낯선 이름이나 단어가 인기 검색어에 올라 있으면, 사람들은 이게 왜 인기 검색어인지 궁금해 하면서 클릭한다. 비록 내 관심은 아니지만 타인들의, 혹은 사회적인 관심사라는 전제다. 다시 검색 순위가 올라간다. 과연 정보로서 가치가 있는지는 중요치 않다. 심지어 애초부터 많은 사람들이 진짜 궁금해 한 사안인지도 중요치 않아진다.

해설

1. (a)의 남과 똑같아지고 싶다는 것은 사회적 증거의 올바른 정의가 아니며, (b)의 호기심을 불러일으키면서 이를 연구하게 된다는 것 역시 사회적 증거의 현상을 드러낸 정확한 표현이 아니다. (c)처럼 한 사람이 좋아한다고 해서 모두가 좋아한다는 것 역시 근거가 없다. 이에 반해 사회적 증거의 현상에 대해서는 본문에서 '사람들은 다수의 행동인 '사회적 증거'를 따라 하면 실수를 줄일 수 있다고 생각해 남을 좇아한다는 것'이라 정의를 내리고 규범이라 생각하기 때문에 다른 사람의 행동을 따라한다는 (d)가 정답이다.

2. '현대 미디어나 광고에서 행해지는 여론조작의 심리적 기제(機制)가 바로 사회적 증거'라고 하면서 '의제 설정이나 여론몰이에 크게 기여하는 인기 검색어'를 그 예로 들고 있다. 그러므로 검색 엔진은 사람들이 찾는 것에 대해서 통제가 가능하도록 조작할 수 있다는 (a)가 정답이다.

3. 사회적 증거 현상의 예로 TV 코미디에 삽입되는 가짜웃음과 베스트셀러임을 강조하는 상품광고를 들고 있으므로, (a)는 본문의 내용과 배치되는 진술이다.

4. '쳐다보는 사람의 수가 늘어나자, 이를 따라 쳐다보는 사람의 수도 늘었다'는 진술로 볼 때 정답은 (c)가 된다. 참고로 (a)는 '사람들이 흉내를 내는지 아닌지는 지도자의 외모에 달려있다.' (b)는 '대규모의 군중이 모이면 사람들은 시위가 발생한 것이라 생각한다.' (d)는 '소집단은 비웃음의 대상이 되지만, 대규모 집단의 (행동이나 의견은) 진지하게 받아들여진다'는 뜻이다.

정답 1.(d) 2.(a) 3.(a) 4.(c)

UNIT 03

Give us hope!
피그말리온

그리스 신화에 나오는 키프로스 왕 피그말리온에게는 여성 기피증이 있었다. 외모에 자신이 없었고, 여성에겐 결점이 많다는 선입관을 갖고 있었기 때문이다. 그는 속세의 여성과는 사랑을 할 수 없다고 생각했다. 그래서 상아로 이상형을 조각하는 일에 몰두했다. 사랑을 단념하는 대신 대리만족을 추구한 것이다.

탁월한 조각가였던 그가 창조한 여인상은 아름다웠다. 그걸 그는 끔찍이 아꼈다. 날마다 조상(彫像)에 꽃을 바쳤고, 보듬고 어루만졌다. 그러는 사이 소망이 생겼다. 조각이 사람이었으면 하는 꿈을 꾸게 된 것이다. 그는 소원을 비는 축제일에 미(美)의 여신 아프로디테 신전을 찾았다. 그리고 조각상의 여인을 아내로 맞이하게 해달라고 간절히 기도했다. 그러자 기적이 일어났다. 여인상이 숨을 쉬기 시작한 것이다. 그는 이 여인과 결혼했고, 딸 파포스를 낳았다. 그의 여성관도 달라졌다.

여기서 '피그말리온 효과'라는 말이 나왔다. 꿈과 소망을 가지면 현실이 달라진다는 얘기다. 19세기 영국 화가 에드워드 번 존스는 이 신화를 그림으로 그렸다. 영국 버밍엄 미술관엔 그의 '피그말리온 조상' 4부작이 걸려 있다. 그는 그림을 그리기 전 "사람들이 '와!' 하고 감탄하는, 그저 그 말밖에 할 수 없는, 그런 대작을 남기고 싶다"고 했다 한다. 많은 이들이 그의 작품을 경탄의 눈으로 감상하는 걸 보면 그의 소망도 피그말리온처럼 성취된 셈이다.

해설

1. 이 글에서 그리스 신화에 나오는 피그말리온도, 이를 그림으로 그린 에드워드 번 존스도 역시 소망을 가지고 열심히 노력하여 뜻을 이루었다는 것을 추론할 수 있다. 신화에 나오는 이야기를 가지고 (a)처럼 때로는 동상에 생명력을 불어넣을 수 있다고 할 수 없으며, (c)처럼 그림은 사람들에게 경외감을 준다는 추론을 본문에서 끌어내도록 구체화하기에는 부족한 감이 있다.

2. 피그말리온은 '속세의 여성과는 사랑을 할 수 없다고 생각'했다는 내용으로부터 미래에 사랑을 찾을 것을 알았다는 진술을 끌어낼 수 없다. 그러므로 (a)는 본문과 일치하지 않는 진술로, 이 문제의 정답이 된다. 참고로 (d)의 동상은 절대로 생명력을 부여할 수 없다는 진술은 피그말리온이라는 예외가 있으므로 역시 틀린 보기라고 착각할 수 있는데, 그리스 신화에 나오는 얘기로부터 동상에 생명력을 부여할 수 있다는 일반 진술을 구성할 수는 없으므로, 올바른 진술이라고 해야 한다.

3. 단어의 정의를 이해하고 있는가를 묻는 문제로 공포증에 빠진 사람이란 무언가에 대해 두려워하는 사람을 의미한다.

4. 이 글은 소망을 가지고 열심히 노력하여 뜻을 이룬 두 가지 사례를 들어, 인생을 살면서 무언가를 성취하기 원하는 것이 그 뜻을 이루는 데 얼마나 소중한지에 대하여 보여주고 있다.

정답 1.(b) 2.(a) 3.(d) 4.(c)

UNIT 04

Waiting for the cargo
카고 컬트(Cargo-Cult)

2차 세계대전이 끝난 후 태평양 여러 섬의 원시부족들 사이에서 기이한 풍습이 나타났다. 미군이 건설했던 보급기지를 본떠 어설프게 활주로를 만들고 얼기설기 큰 관제탑도 세웠다. 야자열매 헬멧을 쓰고 나무 막대기 소총을 든 채 활주로를 따라 순찰을 돌기도 했다. 그들의 특이한 관습에 인류학자와 종교학자들이 큰 관심을 가졌다.

원주민들은 미군처럼 활주로를 만들면 보급품을 가득 실은 비행기들이 돌아올 것이라고 생각한 것이다. 전쟁 중에 미군 수송기가 잘못 투하했거나 해변에 떠밀려온 군수 보급품들로 갑자기 유복해졌던 생활수준을 원래 상태로 되돌리기는 원주민들로서도 견디기 어려웠을 것이다. 한번 높아진 소비수준은 소득이 떨어져도 낮추기 어렵다는 경제학의 '톱니바퀴 효과(Rachet Effect)'는 원시부족에서도 예외는 아니었다.

그러나 이들의 간절한 기원에도 불구하고 보급품 상자는 더 이상 하늘에서 떨어지지 않았다. 논리학에서 말하는 선후 관계를 인과 관계로 혼동하는 오류(after this, therefore because of it)를 범했기 때문이다. 그들은 단순한 사건의 순서를 혼동했다. 즉 어떤 사건이 시간적으로 다른 사건보다 먼저 일어났다는 이유만으로 앞에 일어난 사건을 뒤에 일어난 사건의 원인으로 잘못 간주해버린 것이다.

1945년 말 호주의 시사잡지 '월간 태평양군도(Pacific Islands Monthly)'는 파푸아뉴기니 원주민들의 이 새로운 풍습을 '카고 컬트(Cargo-Cult)'라고 명명했다. 그 후 카고 컬트란 신조어는 외부에서 온 제도나 물건들을 이유도 모른 채 무작정 모방하는 원시부족의 의식(儀式)과 행태를 일컫는 학술용어로 정착됐다. 카고 컬트는 나중에 '사이비 과학'이나 '모조품'을 지칭하는 용어로까지 진화했다. 외견상 비슷하게 형식은 갖췄으나 알맹이가 없는 연구나 기능이 떨어지는 제품을 빗댄 말이다.

해설

1. '논리학에서 말하는 선후 관계를 인과 관계로 혼동하는 오류(after this, therefore because of it)를 범했기 때문이다. 그들은 단순한 사건의 순서를 혼동했다. 즉 어떤 사건이 시간적으로 다른 사건보다 먼저 일어났다는 이유만으로 앞에 일어난 사건을 뒤에 일어난 사건의 원인으로 잘못 간주해버린 것'이란 진술을 바탕으로 일어난 모든 일이 필연적인 관련을 맺고 있는 것은 아니라는 추론을 할 수 있다. 하지만 우연히 일어난 사건들이 서로 관련되어 있다는 것은 결국 정답인 (b)의 내용과 배치되는 것이므로 틀렸고, (a)는 '갑자기 유복해졌던 생활수준을 원래 상태로 되돌리기'가 어렵다는 것에서 나온 것이지, 카고 컬트가 현실을 받아들이는 데 문제가 있는 사람들로 구성되어 있다는 것은 아니므로 역시 올바르지 않다.

2. 카고 컬트란 개념이 어떠한 것이며, 어떻게 유래하였는가에 대하여 서술하고 있는 글이다.

3. '카고 컬트는 나중에 '사이비 과학'이나 '모조품'을 지칭하는 용어로까지 진화'했다고 언급한 후 구체적인 진술이 따라오지 않았기 때문에, 이 글의 뒤에는 이와 관련된 내용들이 나오는 것이 논리적으로 타당하다. 참고로 (b)의 미국 정부의 보급품에 대한 얘기는 이미 나온 내용이며, (c)에서는 기다리던 보급품 없이 떠난 이유에 대하여 설명한다고 하였는데, 그 일화의 후일담이 중요한 것이 아니라 그것을 어떠한 현상으로 볼 수 있는가의 논의로 이어졌기 때문에 역시 글 뒤에 이어서 나올 수 있는 내용은 아니다. (d)에서는 톱니바퀴 효과에 대한 상세한 설명이 이어져야 한다고 하지만, 톱니바퀴 효과 즉 '한번 높아진 소비수준은 소득이 떨어져도 낮추기 어렵다'는 경제학적 개념은 원시부족에도 적용된다는 것을 밝히기 위해서 사용된 개념으로 더 이상 나올 필요는 없는 내용이다.

4. 파푸아뉴기니의 원주민들이 결국 보급품을 받았다는 것은 사실과 다르다. 그러므로 정답은 (a)이다. 참고로 호주의 한 잡지가 카고 컬트란 용어를 만들었다는 것은 올바른 진술이며, 섬의 원주민들은 계속해서 보급품을 받을 수 있을 것이라고 생각했다는 것 역시 본문의 내용과 일치한다.

정답 1.(b) 2.(d) 3.(a) 4.(a)

UNIT 05

Lost in translation
오역

> 오역은 어디에나 있다. 성경도 예외가 아니다. "내가 다시 너희에게 이르노니, 낙타가 바늘귀를 통과하는 것이 부자가 하늘나라에 들어가는 것보다 쉽다"는 구절을 보자. 아랍어 원어는 '밧줄'(gamta)이었는데 번역자가 이를 '낙타'(gamla)로 잘못 옮긴 것으로 드러났다. 다행인 것은 이 오역이 원문의 뜻을 훼손하기는커녕 더 뛰어나게 표현한 것으로 평가된다는 점이다.
>
> 오역은 한 언어를 다른 언어로 번역할 때 생길 수 있다. 그 비극적인 예가 1945년 7월 일본 수상 칸타로 스즈키의 기자회견이다. 당시 일본은 연합국에 항복할 준비를 하고 있었다. 다만 공식적인 발표는 연합국 측이 공식 채널을 통해 최후통첩을 할 때까지 미루기로 결정했다. 그때까지 시간을 벌어 항복조건을 협상하려 했던 것이다. 그러나 스즈키 수상은 기자회견에서 실수를 저지르고 만다. 무조건 항복을 요구하는 포츠담 선언에 대해 "일본 내각은 모쿠사츠(默殺 : 묵살)의 입장을 견지한다"고 모호하게 답변한 것이다. 취지는 "답변을 당분간 보류한다"는 것이었다고 한다. 하지만 '모쿠사츠'란 표현은 "무시한다(ignore)"와 "언급을 삼간다(no comment)"의 어느 쪽으로도 해석될 수 있는 상황이었다. 일본 언론과 라디오 도쿄의 영어방송은 이를 전자, 즉 포츠담 선언의 거부로 보도해버렸다. 그로부터 사흘 만에 트루먼 대통령은 일본에 원폭 투하를 지시하는 문서에 서명했다. 원폭 투하는 이와 같은 오해와 오역이 없었으면 생기지 않을 수 있었을지도 모른다.

해설

1. 이 글은 오역으로 인하여 일어나는 문제에 대해 적당한 사례를 들어 설명한 글이다.

2. 일본 수상의 답변에 대한 오역으로 인하여 문제가 초래된 것이므로 (a)는 옳은 진술이고, 성경에 나온 낙타의 비유에 대한 오역을 소개하므로 (c)도 타당하다. 오역은 때때로 발생할 수밖에 없는 것이므로 (d)도 올바르다. 하지만 (B)의 경우 원자폭탄의 투하가 단지 오역만이라는 것은, 하나의 동인이긴 하지만, 이것 때문이라고 단정하는 것은 논리의 비약으로 볼 수밖에 없다.

3. '낙타가 바늘귀를 통과하는 것이 부자가 하늘나라에 들어가는 것보다 쉽다'는 성경 구절의 의미는 부자가 하늘나라에 가기가 그만큼 어렵다는 뜻이다. 이에 해당하는 적당한 보기로는 (c)의 '이런 일이 일어나기는 불가능하다'란 것이 유사한 의미를 지닌 것으로 볼 수 있다.

4. 언어의 차이를 인식하지 못하면, 상황에 따라서 오역을 할 수 있고, 이러한 오역으로 인해 매우 다른 결과를 초래할 수 있다. 그러므로 (b)라는 추론은 가능하다. 하지만 (c)처럼 성경에 오역의 예가 많다는 것은 본문만으로는 알 수 없다. 글에서는 낙타의 비유에 대해서만 언급했기 때문이다.

정답 1.(a) 2.(b) 3.(c) 4.(b)

UNIT 06

Surviving stress
스트레스

"스트레스는 피할 수 없을 뿐만 아니라 반드시 나쁜 것만은 아니다." 스트레스 연구의 권위자인 미국 록펠러 대학교 브루스 맥웬의 주장이다. 스트레스를 받을 때 분비되는 호르몬은 주위 환경에 대한 인식을 강화하고, 시력과 청력을 향상시키며 근육을 더 잘 움직이게 만든다. 우리가 복잡한 도로에서 사고를 내지 않고 운전을 할 수 있는 것은 이 호르몬 덕분이다. 뿐만 아니라 스트레스는 삶의 요구를 처리하는 메커니즘으로 기능한다. 성공해서 지위가 높은 사람들은 그렇지 못한 사람들에 비해 코르티솔 같은 스트레스 호르몬 수치가 높다고 한다.

맥웬은 "스트레스는 신체를 보호한다. 스트레스를 받은 사람은 주변 환경을 경계하고 위험을 피하기 위해 계획을 세운다. 반면 즐겁고 태평한 사람은 함정 속으로 걸어 들어가고 있음을 알아차리지 못한다."라고 말한다. 진화심리학은 스트레스를 더 잘 받는 사람이 생존경쟁에 더 잘 대처해서 우리 인류의 조상이 되었다고 추정한다. 초기 인류시대에 불안하고 의심이 많고 (삶과 타인에 관하여) 최악을 가정하는 사람이 자연선택되었다는 것이다.

그렇다면 여기서 의문이 생긴다. 원시인들은 생존 환경이 혹독해서 그랬다고 하더라도 평균 수명이 늘고 물질적으로 풍요로워진 현대사회에서 사람들이 여전히 스트레스를 많이 받는 이유는 무엇인가? 스트레스는 기본적으로 불안과 공포에 대한 인체의 반응이지 않은가? 현대사회에서 스트레스가 늘어난 주요한 원인은 미디어라고 한다. 미국 뉴욕 대학의 스트레스 연구자 조지프 르두는 불안이 과장된 헤드라인 때문이라고 한다. "옛날 사람들은 직접 접촉하는 것들 때문에 스트레스를 받았다. 하지만 오늘날은 다르다. 모든 사람이 전 세계에서 발생하는 끔찍한 사건과 미래의 위험 요소를 알고 있다. 걱정할 필요가 있을 듯한 사항의 목록이 엄청나게 길어진 것이다."

해설

1. '스트레스는 피할 수 없을 뿐만 아니라 반드시 나쁜 것만은 아니다'라는 표현에서 스트레스는 우리 삶의 한 부분이라는 것을 알 수 있다. 참고로 (c)를 혼동하면 안 되는데, 진화심리학에서 '스트레스를 더 잘 받는 사람이 생존경쟁에 더 잘 대처해서 우리 인류의 조상이 되었다고 추정'한 것이지 스트레스를 받지 않은 사람은 역사적으로 생존할 수 없었다는 것은 논리의 비약이다. 또한 '현대사회에서 스트레스가 늘어난 주요한 원인은 미디어'라는 진술로부터 미디어가 모든 스트레스의 원인이라 하는 것 역시 과장이며 논리 비약이다. 그러므로 (d)도 오답이다.

2. '스트레스를 받을 때 분비되는 호르몬은 주위 환경에 대한 인식을 강화하고, 시력과 청력을 향상시키며 근육을 더 잘 움직이게 만든다. 뿐만 아니라 스트레스는 삶의 요구를 처리하는 메커니즘으로 기능한다.'는 것이 맥웬 교수가 주장하는 스트레스의 긍정적 기능이다. 그러므로 인식이 강화되고 환경에 대한 대처 능력이 생긴다는 (d)가 정답이다. (a)의 불안정성은 부정적인 측면이고, (b)의 공격 성향이 증대하는 것도 장점일 수 없고, (c)의 걱정이 증대되는 것 역시 단점이다.

3. 과거에 대한 스트레스 분석에 있어서, '진화심리학은 스트레스를 더 잘 받는 사람이 생존경쟁에 더 잘 대처해서 우리 인류의 조상이 되었다고 추정한다.' 그러므로 (a)가 올바른 진술이다.

4. 이 글에서는 현대적인 스트레스 유발 요인에 관하여 미디어를 꼽고 있으며, 이 뒤에는 자연스럽게 어떻게 그러한 결론에 도달하고 이를 어떻게 대처해야 하는가에 대한 이야기로 이어져야 논리의 흐름상 적당하다.

정답 1.(b) 2.(d) 3.(a) 4.(c)

UNIT 07

Fanning fears
도시의 전설

> "갱단의 새로운 신고식에 대한 보고: 신참 갱단이 살인을 저지르기 시작했다. 그들은 야간에 자동차의 전조등을 끈 채 도로를 주행하면서 범행 대상을 노린다. 불이 꺼져 있음을 알려주기 위해 맞은편에서 전조등을 깜빡이는 차량이 있으면 따라가서 살해하는 것이다. 이미 두 가족이 희생되었다. 절대로 다른 차량을 향해 전조등을 깜빡이지 않도록 하라." 위의 글은 1993년 미국인들을 불안에 떨게 했던 일리노이 주 경찰국에서 제공되었다는 팩스 전단을 요약한 것이다. 일리노이 주 경찰국이 '사실 무근'이라고 부인해도 불안은 쉽게 가라앉지 않았다. 이 루머는 2006년 이메일 버전으로 약간 변형된 형태로 다시 유행했다. 루머·전설 전문 사이트 snopes.com은 이를 소개하고 'Urban Legend(도시의 전설)'로 규정했다. "많은 사람이 믿는 이상하거나 놀라운 이야기로서 진실이 아닌 것"이라는 뜻이다. 우리말로는 '대중적 미신'이라고 할 수 있겠다.
>
> 국제적으로 유명해져서 좀 망신스러운 현상이 있다. 온라인 백과사전 위키피디아는 '선풍기 사망(Fan Death)'을 '대한민국의 대중적 미신(South Korean Urban Legend)'으로 규정하고 있다. 내용은 이렇다. "한국 정부와 언론은 선풍기 사망을 사실로 믿고 있다. 하지만 선풍기 바람 때문에 죽었다는 사람은 다른 나라에는 전혀 없다. 사망 원인으로 거론되는 것은 저체온증, 호흡 곤란 등이다. 하지만 선풍기 바람으로 한여름 실내에서 체온이 28도 이하로 떨어질 수는 없다. 공기 흐름으로 질식한다면 오토바이를 타는 사람은 왜 죽지 않는가. 진짜 사망 원인은 심장·뇌혈관 질환, 알코올 중독인데 우연히 선풍기가 켜져 있었던 것뿐이다."

해설

1. 도시 괴담이 진실인지 아닌지의 여부에 대하여 여러 사례를 들어 설명하고 있다. 선풍기로 인한 사망에 대한 언급은 두 번째 단락의 소재이지, 글의 전체적인 화제는 아니다.

2. 선풍기로 인한 사망은 아니라는 글이지 일부 의사가 인정한다는 것은 근거가 없으므로 (a)는 틀렸고, (b)처럼 선풍기로 인한 사망이 여러 나라에서 보고되었고 점점 확산된다는 것도 역시 틀린 진술이며, (c)의 경우 오토바이를 빠르게 타면 죽는다는 이야기 역시 틀린 진술이다. 글에서는 선풍기로 인한 사망은 말도 안 된다며 든 예로 '공기흐름으로 질식한다면 오토바이를 타는 사람은 왜 죽지 않는지'에 대해 묻는 것뿐이다. 그러므로 정답은 (d)로 그간 선풍기로 인한 사망에 대한 설명은 진정한 사망 원인을 가리는 효과가 있었던 셈이다.

3. 갱단의 새로운 신고식에 대한 도시 괴담은 너무나 충격적이어서, 당국에서 그 내용은 거짓임을 밝혀도 쉽게 가라앉지 않았다는 (d)가 정답이다. snopes.com은 이 내용이 사실이라거나 주범이 누구인지 밝혔다거나 하는 등의 행위를 한 것이 아니라, 단지 루머나 전설을 전문으로 다루는 사이트에 불과하다.

4. 앞의 빈칸은 일리노이경찰이 거짓경보라고 알렸다는 내용과 두려움은 가라앉지 않았다는 내용 사이의 관계를 살펴봐야 한다. 일부의 사실(일리노이경찰이 거짓경보라고 알렸다)은 인정하면서 새로운 사실(두려움은 가라앉지 않았다)을 제시하는 것이므로 양보의 구조가 필요하다. 그러므로 even though가 들어가야 한다. 뒤의 빈칸은 사망의 원인을 체온 저하라고 한 뒤에, 체온은 그렇게 떨어지지 않는다는 문장이 뒤이어 온다. 그러므로 반대의 구조가 성립하여 However가 나와야 한다. 정답은 c)이다.

정답 1.(b) 2.(d) 3.(d) 4.(c)

UNIT 08

Diamonds are forever
다이아몬드

인류가 다이아몬드에서 찾아낸 첫 용도는 연마재였다. 4,500년 전의 중국 신석기 시대 돌도끼에서 그 흔적이 발견됐다. 루비와 사파이어 성분이 포함된 돌도끼의 표면이 거울처럼 매끄럽게 갈려있는 것이다. 2005년 이를 조사한 하버드 대학 연구팀은 "다이아몬드를 연마재로 사용하지 않고서는 있을 수 없는 결과"라고 결론지었다. 두 번째 용도는 주술적 장신구였다. 기원전 7세기 경 인도 드라비다 족의 왕과 전사들은 '세상에서 가장 단단한 돌이 착용자를 보호해주는 마법을 지닌 것'으로 믿었다. 이것은 다이아몬드의 어원과 정확히 일치한다. 이 말은 그리스어의 '아다마스'에서 유래하였는데 그 의미는 '정복할 수 없는'이란 뜻이다. 서양 중세와 르네상스 시대에도 왕가와 귀족이 '질병을 예방하고 재앙을 막기 위해' 다이아몬드를 지니고 있었다.

보석으로 대접받기 시작한 것은 15세기 경 연마법이 발견된 이후의 일이다. 베네치아에서 금속 세공을 하던 가난한 청년이 주인집 딸을 사랑하여 그녀에게 청혼했다. 그녀의 아버지는 불가능한 조건을 내건다. "다이아몬드를 연마할 방법을 찾아오면 딸을 주겠다." 오랜 고심 끝에 청년은 기어이 답을 찾아낸다. 다이아몬드끼리 서로 비빌 때 떨어지는 미세한 가루를 연마제로 사용하는 것이다. 오늘날 보석용 다이아몬드의 주된 용도는 결혼 예물이다. "다이아몬드는 영원하다(diamond is forever)"라는 광고 문구 덕분에 '영원한 사랑의 상징'으로 자리 잡았다. 드비어스사의 이 광고는 세계 다이아몬드 시장을 휩쓸었고 역사상 가장 성공적인 것으로 꼽힌다.

해설

1. 다이아몬드는 주술적 장신구로 이용되었으므로 부적으로 사용되었다는 (a)는 올바른 진술이고, (c)의 연마재로 사용되었다는 것은 첫 문장의 '인류가 다이아몬드에서 찾아낸 첫 용도는 연마재'라는 것에서 찾아낼 수 있다. (d) 역시 '보석용 다이아몬드의 주된 용도는 결혼 예물'이라는 진술에서 쉽게 찾아낼 수 있다. 하지만 (b)의 경우 영원한 생명의 상징이라는 것은 틀린 표현으로, '영원한 사랑의 상징'이어야 한다. 그러므로 정답은 (b)이다.

2. '다이아몬드끼리 서로 비빌 때 떨어지는 미세한 가루를 연마제로 사용'하는 방법을 찾아냄으로써 청년은 사랑하는 주인집 외동딸을 아내로 맞이할 수 있었다.

3. 다이아몬드로 된 결혼반지를 교환한다고 부유한 삶을 보장하는 것은 근거없는 진술이며, 다이아몬드의 기원은 '그리스어의 '아다마스'에서 유래하였는데 그 의미는 '정복할 수 없는'이란 뜻'이라 본문에 언급되어 있으므로 (c)는 틀린 진술이다. (d)는 인간온 처음에는 다이아몬드의 용도를 몰랐다고 하였는데, 본문에서는 처음부터 연마재로 사용하였으므로 본문의 내용과 배치된다. 반면 (b)의 경우 다이아몬드의 용도는 처음에는 장신구가 아니라 도구였다는 것은 본문의 내용과 일치되는 것으로 타당한 추론이다.

4. 본문의 내용에 따르면, 왕과 귀족들은 부정적인 측면을 제거하고자 다이아몬드를 소지했다. 즉 질병을 막고 재난을 피하기 위함이다. 그러므로 빈칸에는 질병을 막는다는 의미의 숙어인 ward off가 들어가야 한다. 참고로 call off는 '취소하다', put off는 '연기하다', kick off는 '시작하다'라는 의미이다.

정답 1.(b) 2.(d) 3.(b) 4.(b)

UNIT 09
Straw-man logic
허수아비 논법

'허수아비 논법(straw-man argument)'이란 무너지기 쉬운 허상을 만들어내 재빠른 한 방으로 그것을 완전히 날려 버리는 것을 말한다. 상대방의 가상 주장을 설정한 다음, 일방적인 공격을 퍼붓는 것이다. 그리고는 흡사 상대방의 주장이 무너진 것처럼 기정사실화한다.

예컨대 "어린이가 혼잡한 길가에 나다니게 하면 안 된다"는 주장에 대해 "그렇다면 아이를 하루 종일 집 안에 가둬 두란 말이냐"고 받아치는 식이다. 이를 반박하려면 허수아비 주장이 원래의 주장과 다르다는 점을 해명해야 하는데 왠지 구차하고, 변명처럼 들린다. 이 때문에 이 고도의 말싸움 기술에 걸려들면 웬만해서는 빠져나오기 힘들다.

조지 W. 부시 미국대통령은 허수아비 논법을 자주 구사하는 것으로 유명하다. 2005년 말 '이라크에서 철군을 고려해야 한다'는 주장이 제기되자, 그는 즉각 "지금 당장 미군을 철수해야 한다고 주장하는 사람들이 있다"며 "그러면 크게 실수하는 것"이라고 결론지었다. '철군 고려'가 '무조건 즉시 철수로 둔갑한 뒤 '중대한 실수'로 낙인찍힌 것이다. 이 판에 철군 얘기를 잘못 꺼냈다간 '테러와의 전쟁'에 반대하는 비애국자로 몰리거나, 미군의 안전을 도외시하는 무책임한 인사가 되기 십상이다.

허수아비 논법의 문제는 애초부터 상대방의 주장을 왜곡함으로서 공정한 논의 자체를 막는 데 있다. 잘못된 논거를 바탕으로 대중을 호도해 그릇된 결론으로 유도하는 것이다. 그래서 논리학은 이런 논법을 부도덕한 논리적 오류의 하나로 지목한다. 당장 눈앞의 말싸움에서는 이길 수 있을지 모르지만 결과적으론 모두에게 손해를 끼치기 때문이다.

해설

1. 마지막 단락에서 '허수아비 논법의 문제는 애초부터 상대방의 주장을 왜곡함으로서 공정한 논의 자체를 막는 데 있다'라고 언급한 것처럼, 이 글은 허수아비 논법이 무엇인지를 밝히고 이의 문제점을 언급한 글이다. 그러므로 이 글의 목적은 합리적인 논의의 기회를 차단하는 허수아비 논법을 비난하는 것이다.

2. (a)의 경우 문제의 핵심에 대하여 이의를 제기하기 때문에 논란을 불러일으키는 것이 아니라, '애초부터 상대방의 주장을 왜곡함으로서 공정한 논의 자체를 막는 것'이 문제이다. (b)의 스캔들에 대하여는 본문에 언급이 없고, '조지 W. 부시 미국대통령은 허수아비 논법을 자주 구사하는 것으로 유명'하다고 하였는데 (d)의 경우는 정반대로 언급하므로 틀린 진술이다. 그러므로 허수아비 논법은 고도의 말싸움 기술로 이에 말려들면 빠져 나오기 힘들기 때문에 (c)가 정답이다.

3. (a)의 진술은 부시 대통령이 이라크에서의 철군 주장에 대해 비난하는 입장이므로 틀렸고, (b)의 토론 기술 여부에 대한 논의는 본문의 논점이 아니므로 역시 추론할 수 없는 진술이다. 허수아비 논법은 공정한 논의 자체가 불가능하므로 (c)도 역시 틀린 진술이다. 이에 반해 (d)는 '철군 얘기를 잘못 꺼냈다간 '테러와의 전쟁'에 반대하는 비애국자로 몰리거나, 미군의 안전을 도외시하는 무책임한 인사가 되기 십상'이므로 올바른 추론이 된다.

4. 허수아비 논법은 '상대방의 가상 주장을 설정한 다음, 일방적인 공격을 퍼붓는 것'이므로 정답은 (c)이다.

정답 1.(b) 2.(c) 3.(d) 4.(c)

UNIT 10
When 'smaller is better' is not
'축소 지향' 일본의 그릇된 역사 인식

이어령 전 문화부 장관은 『축소지향의 일본인』에서 문화 깊숙이 박혀있는 일본인의 속성을 '축소지향'이란 키워드로 명쾌하게 풀어냈다. 쥘부채와 분재, 꽃꽂이, 도시락, 휴대용 라디오 등 일상의 사물에서 일본을 발견했다. 최근 (『축소지향의 일본인』이 담고 있는) 예리한 분석에 새삼 감탄한 일이 생겼다. 과거사, 특히 침략전쟁과 식민지 지배 등 가해 역사에 대한 일본의 인식이 놀라울 정도로 '축소지향'이란 사실을 깨달았다.

중국 난징(南京)대학살 자료가 유네스코 세계기록 유산으로 등재되자 일본은 발끈했다. 그러면서 중·일 전쟁 때인 1937년 12월 난징을 점령한 일본군이 6주간 저지른 대학살의 사망자 수를 문제 삼았다. 30만 명 이상이라는 1947년 난징시 군사법정 판결문을 인정할 수 없다고 했다. 중국의 일방적인 주장일 뿐이라며 유네스코가 정치적으로 이용당했다고 질타했다. 일본 내에선 10년 전까지만 해도 난징 희생자가 최소 20만 명에 이른다는 게 정설로 통했다. 2005년 일본 고등학교 교과서 검정에서 "20만 명 이상이라는 설이 유력하다"는 내용이 심의를 통과했다. 지금 일본은 사망자 수를 엄청나게 줄여서 희생자가 2만~4만 명이라고 한다. 일본 정부의 공식적인 입장은 그 당시 민간인의 사망이 있었던 것은 부인할 수는 없다고 하지만, 역사적인 책임과는 거리를 두고자 하는, 심지어는 부인하고자 하는, 일본인들의 수정 요구가 거세다.

일본의 '축소지향' 본능은 위안부 문제에서도 일관되게 나타난다. 아베 신조(安倍晋三) 정권은 강제로 연행되어 위안부 시설로 끌려갔다는 사실도 계속 부정한다. (위안부 문제가 한·일 관계 개선을 가로막고 있다며) 한·일 관계의 '미래지향'을 옹호하고 나선다. 증인과 증거가 모두 사라지길 기다리는 '시간 끌기' 속셈이다. 어두운 과거는 축소한다고 없어지지 않는다. 숨긴 것은 언젠가 반드시 드러난다. 일본은 진정한 반성과 사죄를 해야 한다. 그래야 미래가 있다.

해설

1. 현재 일본은 기록되어 있는 난징대학살의 사망자 수를 대폭 축소하고 한국의 위안부 문제를 부정하며 현실을 부정하고 있다. 하지만 이러한 방식으로 그들의 어두운 과거는 지워지지 않으며 언젠가는 다시 드러날 것이다. 그러므로 글의 핵심은 과거를 인정하고 정부는 이를 공개적으로 밝혀야 한다는 것이다.

2. 과거를 부정하고 왜곡하는 일본의 행위는 잘못된 것이며 진심으로 반성하고 사죄해야 미래가 있을 것이라는 (b)가 적합하다. (c)와 (d)는 작가가 의도하는 메시지와 반대되는 내용이다.

3. "Tokyo's tactic is to waste time, to wait until the witnesses and the evidence have disappeared" 이 문장에서 일본은 그들이 과거에 한 잘못이 시간으로 해결되길 원한다는 점을 알 수 있다.

4. 일본은 중국 난징대학살 자료가 유네스코 세계기록 유산으로 등재되자 희생자가 30만 명 이상이라는 1947년 난징시 군사법정 판결문을 부정했다. play는 '가지고 놀다/장난치다'라는 의미로 중국이 유네스코를 속였다는 (d)가 올바르다.

정답 1.(a) 2.(b) 3.(d) 4.(d)

UNIT 11
The Republic of Complex
콤플렉스

'콤플렉스'라는 단어는 심리학과 관련되어 쓰일 때는 인간 행동의 원천이 되는 무의식이나 감정을 지칭한다. 지그문트 프로이트나 카를 융 같은 분석 심리학자들이 만든 용어이기는 하나 이는 라틴어 'com(함께)'과 'ple ctere(짜기)'를 합성해 생긴 말로 '짜진 것', '엉켜서 복잡한 것'을 뜻한다. 프로이트에게 콤플렉스는 금지와 갈망 사이의 복잡한 갈등을 의미한다. 도덕·윤리·양심이 허용하지 않은 내용을 억눌러 생긴 '억압적인 감정의 복합체'다. '이드 – 자아 – 초자아'와 함께 심리학적 인간관의 근간을 이룬다. 콤플렉스의 변형에는 유아가 이성 부모에게 느끼는 오이디푸스 콤플렉스, 엘렉트라 콤플렉스 등이 있다. 융은 나아가 "콤플렉스는 심리적인 생명의 핵이자 인간의 감정·지각·욕망의 원형"이라고 썼다.

보다 대중적인 의미의 콤플렉스는 열등감이다. 알프레드 아들러가 '열등 콤플렉스(inferiority complex)'라는 용어를 내놓은 것이 일반에까지 퍼졌다. 프로이트의 제자였던 아들러는 성과 쾌락의 결정력에 집착하는 스승에 반발해, 열등감을 극복하는 건강한 인간관을 제시했다. 아들러에 따르면 "인간 존재가 된다는 것은 자신이 열등하다고 느끼는 것을 의미한다." 그러나 이 열등감은, 곧 인간 행동의 동기이자 추진력이 된다. 인간에게는 열등감과 함께 우월 추구의 욕구 또한 있기 때문에 그것은 강력한 동력이 된다. 가령 어린이는 성인에 비해 약하고, 무력하며, 의존적인 존재인데, 이에 대한 열등감이 성인으로 성장해가는 심적 동력이 된다는 설명이다. 아들러는 열등 콤플렉스의 승화를 중시했다. 말더듬이를 극복한 고대 그리스의 웅변가 데모스테네스, 허약한 체질을 극복한 미국 루스벨트 대통령 등을 예로 들었다. 열등감을 생산적으로 극복하지 못하면 신경증을 앓거나 범죄자가 된다고도 강조했다.

> **해설**
>
> 1. 첫 번째 단락에서는 '프로이트에게 콤플렉스는 금지와 갈망 사이의 복잡한 갈등을 의미'하였고, 두 번째 단락에서는 아들러가 '열등 콤플렉스(inferiority complex)'라는 용어를 바탕으로 '열등감을 극복하는 건강한 인간관을 제시'한 것이 글의 중심축이다. 참고로 (d)의 경우는 어원상의 기원이 본문의 첫 단락에 나오긴 하지만 그것이 글의 요지는 아니다.
>
> 2. '아들러는 열등 콤플렉스의 승화를 중시'하였다. 이를 근거로 하면 (c)의 열등감을 극복하지 못하면 심리적인 문제가 발생할 수 있다는 부정적인 언급보다는 (d)의 열등감을 인식하고 이를 극복하려는 노력이 더 나은 삶으로 인도한다는 것은 훨씬 더 '열등감을 극복하는 건강한 인간관'에 적합하다.
>
> 3. 아들러에 따르면 모든 인간이 가진 열등감은 곧 모든 행동의 동기이자 추진력이 된다. 인간에게는 열등감과 함께 우월 추구의 욕구 또한 있기 때문이다. 그러므로 열등감 콤플렉스에 대하여, 이는 인간에게 자신을 개선할 수 있도록 하고 남보다 우월하게 될 수 있는 긍정적인 기능을 한다는 것을 끌어낼 수 있다. 그러므로 정답은 (b)이다.
>
> 4. 유아가 이성 부모에게 느끼는 오이디푸스 콤플렉스, 엘렉트라 콤플렉스 등이 자연스럽지 못한 태도임은 타당하고, 프로이트는 '성과 쾌락의 결정력에 집착'했고, '대중적인 의미의 콤플렉스는 열등감'이라는 것도 타당하다. 프로이트의 제자였던 아들러는 성과 쾌락의 결정력에 집착하는 스승에 반발해, 열등감을 극복하는 건강한 인간관을 제시'하였다는 진술에서 아들러와 프로이트는 서로 의견이 일치하지 않는다는 것을 알 수 있다.

정답 1.(a) 2.(d) 3.(b) 4.(c)

UNIT 12
Irrational minds
선택적 지각

심리학자들은 인간의 합리성을 믿지 않는다. 심리학자들은 왜 사람들이 외부 정보를 있는 그대로 받아들이지 못하는지를 설명하기 위하여 '선택적 지각(Selective Perception)'이라는 용어를 사용한다. 대신에 자신의 믿음과 일치하거나 자기에게 유리한 것만 선택적으로 받아들인다는 것이다. 비슷한 개념으로 '칵테일 파티 효과(Cocktail Party Effect)'가 있다. 소리가 식별되지 않는 파티장에서도 자기 이름을 부르는 소리는 잘 들린다는 개념이다.

선택적 지각은 선택적 노출 → 주의 → 이해의 과정을 거친다. 원래 인지심리학 용어지만 광고·마케팅의 주요 개념이 됐다. 돈을 많이 들인 광고라도 소비자의 선택적 지각을 끌지 못하면 소용없기 때문이다. 소비자가 하루 1,500개 광고를 본다면 70여 개를 지각하고 10여 개 정도만 기억한다는 연구가 있을 정도다. 선택적 지각은 일상 생활에서도 많이 경험된다. 열등감이 많은 사람은 타인의 무심한 행동도 자신에 대한 위협으로 오해하는 경향이 있다. 망상증 환자들은 선택적 지각의 완벽한 예가 된다.

광고주들은 선택적 지각 이론에 근거해서 잘 결합된 광고 캠페인을 만드는 경향이 있으며, 사람들이 진실이라고 믿는 것이 무관한 경우가 존재한다. 또 이에 더해 '인지 부조화(Cognitive Dissonance)'라는 것도 있다. 자기 태도와 행동 사이에 불일치가 생기면 그 불편함을 해소하기 위해 둘을 일치시키려 한다는 것이다. 그런 불일치가 생기면 사람들은 보통 행동에 맞게 태도를 바꾼다.

해설

1. 자기 태도와 행동 사이에 불일치가 생기면 그 불편함을 해소하기 위해 둘을 일치시키려 한다는 인지 부조화에 대하여 이야기를 이어가는 부분이므로, 이에 대하여 상세한 설명이 나오는 것이 글의 흐름으로 적당하다.

2. '자기 태도와 행동 사이에 불일치가 생기면 그 불편함을 해소하기 위해 둘을 일치시키려 한다는 것이다. 그런 불일치가 생기면 사람들은 보통 행동에 맞게 태도를 바꾼다'에서 사람들은 자신의 현실을 기꺼이 바꿔간다는 것을 추론할 수 있다.

3. 자존감이 낮은 사람이 폭력적이란 얘기는 글의 어느 부분에서도 언급되지 않은 틀린 진술이다. 반면 선택적 지각은 '인지심리학 용어지만 광고·마케팅의 주요 개념'이 되었고, 이는 또한 '기존 자신의 믿음과 일치하거나 자기에게 유리한 것만 선택적으로 받아들인다는 것'이며, 인지 부조화에 따르면 '자기 태도와 행동 사이에 불일치가 생기면 그 불편함을 해소하기 위해 둘을 일치시키려 한다는 것'이다.

4. 선택적 지각과 인지 부조화 이론 등을 통하여 어떻게 사람들이 사회에서 합리성을 유지해 나가는가에 대해 설명하고 있다.

정답 1.(a) 2.(b) 3.(a) 4.(c)

UNIT 13
How accidents shape history
우연과 필연

프랑스의 철학자 파스칼은 자신의 명저인 『팡세』에서 겉으로는 우리가 인식하지 못하는 사소한 일이 지정학적인 사건에 영향을 끼친다고 썼다. 그는 또 "클레오파트라의 코, 그것이 조금만 낮았더라면, 지구의 모든 표면은 변했을 것이다."라는 유명한 말을 했다. 역사를 이성보다는 인과 관계에 입각한 우연적 사건의 연속으로 보는 우연사관(偶然史觀)의 신봉자들도 파스칼과 같은 편에 선다. 만약 그랬더라면(코가 낮았더라면), 안토니우스가 클레오파트라의 치맛폭에 빠져 가족을 버릴 일도 없었을 것이고, 따라서 처남 옥타비아누스와 격돌한 악티움 해전도 일어나지 않았을 것이고, 여기서 승리한 옥타비아누스가 로마제국의 초대황제로 등극하는 일도 없었을 것이란 가정이다. 그러니 한 남성이 이집트 여왕에 매혹당한 우연적 사건이 역사의 향방을 바꿨다는 설명이다.

물론 우연만으로 역사를 설명할 수는 없다. 우연도 따지고 보면 필연의 산물이었기 십상이다. 그래서 '역사는 과거와 현재의 끊임없는 대화'라는 명제를 남긴 E. H. 카는 명저 『역사란 무엇인가』에서 역사적 사건들의 역할을 강조하는 관점을 배격했다. 하지만 역사에는 분명히 우연의 역할이 존재한다. 예를 들어 14세기의 터키 황제 바자제트는 통풍이 발병해 중앙 유럽으로의 진격을 중단했다. 역사가 에드워드 기번은 이 사건을 들어 "한 사람의 한 가닥 근육에 생긴 종기가 많은 국민들의 비참함을 방지하거나 연기시키는 수가 있다"고 기술했다.

또한 베를린 장벽의 붕괴 역시 동독 공산당 대변인의 말실수에서 촉발되었다. 동독 주민의 여행 자유화 조치를 발표한 동독 공산당 대변인에게 기자들이 득달같이 발효시점을 묻자 얼떨결에 "지금 당장"이라고 대답해 버린 게, 뜻하지 않게도 동독 주민들로 하여금 망치와 도끼를 들고 달려가 장벽을 무너뜨리는 결과로 이어졌다는 것이다. 물론 베를린 장벽의 붕괴는 필연이겠지만, 하필이면 그날 그렇게 극적인 방식으로 무너진 것은 분명 우연의 힘이다. 그래서 역사는 재미있다. 우연 없는 필연만으로 돌아가는 역사의 수레바퀴란 그 얼마나 따분하고 답답하겠는가.

해설

1. 베를린 장벽이 그날 그렇게 극적인 방식으로 무너진 것은 분명 우연이겠지만, 이 사건은 시기의 문제이지 결국은 필연일 수밖에 없는 역사의 흐름이 존재했던 것이다. 그러므로 (c)는 틀린 진술이다.
2. 역사적인 사건들이 어떻게 우연과 필연을 통하여 전개되는가에 관한 논의이다.
3. (a)에 나온 얘기는 전혀 본문에 근거가 없는 틀린 진술이다.
4. 우연과 필연의 여러 사건들로 인해 역사가 어떻게 형성되어 가는가에 관한 이야기이다.

정답　1.(c)　2.(c)　3.(a)　4.(a)

UNIT 14
No pain, no gain on literary road
작가의 각오

　도시와 시골이 대재앙으로 초토화된다. 살아남은 인간들은 서로 공격하고, 약간의 음식이라도 남아있으면 훔칠 수밖에 없는 상황에 내몰린다. 새 출발을 위해 길을 떠나는 아버지와 어린 아들에겐 이런 냉혹한 환경에서의 하루하루의 삶이 견딜 수 없는 고문이다. 2007년 퓰리처상을 받은 소설 『로드』의 배경은 묵시록에 가깝다. 겨울의 암흑이 짙게 드리운 속에서의 굶주림과 혹한의 고통에 관한 세밀한 묘사가 현실감을 높이는데, 소실을 쓴 코맥 매카시가 젊은 시절 겪었던 가난의 흔적들이다. 8년간 헛간에서 살기도 했던 그는 한때 치약 살 돈마저 없었다고 한다. 그런 비참한 상황을 벗어난 후에도 매카시는 거액의 사례비를 주겠다는 강연이나 인터뷰 제의를 거절했다. 대신 다른 작가들과 어울리지 않은 채 글쓰기에 몰입했다. 그를 보기 힘든 TV 토크쇼로 끌어낸 것은 오프라 윈프리의 끈질긴 설득이었다. 그는 그간 인터뷰를 거절해 온 이유에 대해 "내 방식대로 살고 싶었을 뿐"이라고 했다.

　일본의 대표적인 '은둔 작가'로는 마루야마 겐지를 꼽을 수 있다. 그는 22세 때 일본 최고 권위의 문학상인 아쿠타가와상을 탄 뒤 도쿄를 떠났다. 아내와 함께 고향에 살면서 소설 창작에 전념했다. 글 쓰는 데 필요한 절제된 삶에 장애가 될 수 있다는 생각에 아이도 갖지 않았다. 지금도 그런 결단력과 절제력으로 수도승처럼 삭발하며 살고 있다. 그는 "창작이란 고(孤·외로움)의 자세로 정신의 깊은 곳을 비집고 들어가는 것"이라며 "문단에 종속되고 대중의 취향에 영합하는 순간 소설은 엉망이 된다."고 말한다.

해설

1. 부와 명예를 가져다주는 것을 멀리하고 오직 자신의 글에만 몰두하는 은둔 작가들의 얘기이다.

2. 매카시가 자신의 소설 The road에 나오는 그런 여정을 경험했다는 것은 근거 없는 진술이고, 매카시가 그간 인터뷰를 거절해 온 이유에 대해 "내 방식대로 살고 싶었을 뿐"이라고 했으므로 역시 (b)도 올바른 진술이 아니다. 하지만 (c)의 경우 코맥 매카시가 젊은 시절 겪었던 가난의 흔적들에 대해서 언급하며 일례로 8년간 헛간에서 살기도 했던 그는 한때 치약 살 돈마저 없었다는 진술로부터 올바른 진술임을 알 수 있다. (d)의 경우 문학을 위하여 아기를 낳지 않았다고 하였지 불임수술에 대한 언급은 전혀 나오지 않는 이야기이다.

3. 이 글 전반에 나오는 사상의 흐름을 보면 문학 자체를 위함이지 부나 명성을 위하여 글을 쓰는 것이 아님을 알 수 있다. 하지만 문학상에 대한 언급이나, 수도승의 삶을 따를 것이란 얘기는 어디에도 나오지 않는다.

4. 특정 정보를 묻는 문제로 마루야마 겐지는 "창작이란 고(孤·외로움)의 자세로 정신의 깊은 곳을 비집고 들어가는 것"이라며 "문단에 종속되고 대중의 취향에 영합하는 순간 소설은 엉망이 된다."고 말한 것에서 (b)를 끌어낼 수 있다.

정답　1.(d)　2.(c)　3.(a)　4.(b)

UNIT 15
When the masses silent the wise
집단사고

피그스만(灣) 침공 작전의 실패는 존 F. 케네디 대통령의 명성에 지울 수 없는 오점을 남겼다. 대통령으로서의 경험이 없던 케네디는 CIA가 주도한 피델 카스트로가 세운 사회주의 정권을 무너뜨리는 작전계획을 승인했다. CIA는 순진하게도 카스트로에 대한 반군의 행위인 것처럼 꾸밀 수 있을 거라 생각했다. 그러나 1,400명의 망명자들은 피그스만에 상륙하기 무섭게 중무장한 쿠바 전투 부대에 의해 섬멸되었다. 이런 연유로 케네디 행정부는 국내외에서 미묘한 냉전시기에 벌인 이러한 미숙한 군사작전에 대해 집중포화를 받았다.

당시 백악관 특보를 지낸 역사학자 아서 슐레진저는 훗날 회고록에서 그 자신은 수많은 사람들에게 신정부에 대한 부정적인 이미지를 남길까 봐 이러한 계획에 반대했음에도 불구하고, 만장일치를 원하는 대통령의 뜻을 거스르지 않으려고 자신의 의견을 드러내지는 않았다고 했다. 무모한 계획이 실패로 돌아간 후에 "나는 이러한 말도 안 되는 것에 대해 알리려는 충동이 회의의 분위기에 눌려 단지 몇 가지 의문사항을 제시한 것에 그쳤을 뿐 그 이상은 하지 못했다."고 탄식했다.

모두가 '예'라고 할 때 혼자서 '아니오'를 외치는 것은 엄청난 용기와 책임을 필요로 한다. 이처럼 성급하고, 비판적 사고 없는 논리로 잘못된 의사 결정을 하는 현상을 '집단사고(groupthink)'라 한다. 미 심리학자 어빙 재니스는 1972년 저서 『집단사고의 희생자들』에서 베트남전 개입, 피그스만 침공 작전을 똑똑한 사람들의 집단사고로 얼마나 멍청한 결정을 내리게 되는지에 관한 주목할만한 사례로 꼽았다. 결속을 강요하는 집단 분위기, 외부 의견의 철저한 차단, 긴급 사태로 인한 공황 상태 등이 잘못된 집단사고를 부추기는 원인이라 보았다. 이런 상황에 처하면 대개 심도 있는 토론은 물 건너가고 목소리 큰 다수의 주장에 이성의 목소리가 묻힌다는 거다.

해설

1. '성급하고, 비판적 사고 없는 논리로 잘못된 의사 결정을 하는 현상'은 집단이 자신이 처한 문제의 장단점에 대해 토론을 벌이지 않고 성급하게 결정을 내리는 것을 뜻한다.

2. 당시 백악관 특보를 지낸 역사학자 아서 슐레진저는 훗날 회고록에서 "말도 안 되는 작전을 당장 그만두라고 경고하고 싶었지만 회의 분위기에 눌려 감히 입을 열지 못했다"고 자책했다는 진술로부터 (d)가 틀린 보기임을 알 수 있다.

3. 집단사고는 문제가 있다는 것을 지적하는 글이다.

4. (a)처럼 집단사고가 여전히 오늘날에도 사용되는지에 대해서는 언급한 바 없으며, 피그스만 침공사건은 케네디의 외교상의 오점이므로 (c)도 틀렸다. (d) 역시 집단사고에 빠져든 사람들이 권력을 얻는다는 것까지는 알 수 없다. 그러므로 정답은 집단사고의 문제는 집단으로부터 개인의 고립이 문제라고 하는 (b)이다.

정답 1.(b) 2.(d) 3.(d) 4.(b)

UNIT 16
Moving to the left
사회주의에 빠진 20/30대

영국 남부 도시 브라이턴에 사는 대학생 알렉스 매킨타이어(19)는 학교 앞 허름한 방 임대료를 감당할 수 없다는 것을 깨달은 뒤 사회주의자가 됐다. 졸업 후 갚아야 할 융자금이 4만6500파운드(약 6800만원)나 된다는 걸 깨닫기도 했다. 매일 자정부터 오전 8시까지 주방 보조 아르바이트를 했더니 몸이 상했다. 동료 대부분이 대졸인 걸 알고 나서는 졸업장을 따도 좋은 일자리를 구할 자신이 없어졌다. 최저임금 인상 시위와 반(反)자본주의 워크숍, 마르크스 독서 모임에 참가하게 됐다. 최근 뉴욕타임스가 소개한 한 젊은이가 어떻게 사회주의자가 되었는지에 관한 이야기이다.

밀레니얼 세대로 불리는 이들이 사회주의에 빠져드는 현상에 영국과 미국 등 서구 사회가 주목하고 있다. 베를린 장벽이 무너지고 소련이 해체된 지 30년, 자본주의가 사회주의에 완승하며 이데올로기 논쟁이 끝났다고 생각했다. 그런데 다시 사회주의가 유행이라니. 2018년 미국 갤럽 여론조사(복수응답)에서 18~29세 미국인 중 '사회주의를 긍정적으로 본다'는 답변이 51%를 차지했다. '자본주의를 긍정적으로 본다'는 응답보다 처음으로 더 많았다.

이에 대한 여러 가지 이유가 있다. 반세기 만에 가장 낮은 실업률을 기록할 정도로 미국 경제가 호황인데도 젊은이의 삶은 힘겹다. 경제 불평등에 대한 사회의 불만이 사회주의 선호 현상으로 나타난 것으로 보인다. 그런 불만은 처음으로 부모 세대보다 못 사는 세대라는 청년층에서 뚜렷할 수밖에 없다. 사회주의나 냉전을 겪지 않아 무지하다는 의견도 있다. 호주 설문조사에서 사회주의를 선호한다는 응답자(58%) 가운데 레닌·스탈린·마오쩌둥을 아는 비율은 각각 26%, 34%, 21%에 그쳤다.

미국 역사상 최연소로 하원의원에 당선된 알렉산드리아 오카시오 코르테즈(29) 민주당 의원은 자칭 '민주주의적 사회주의자'다. 소득세 최고세율을 현재 37%에서 70%까지 올리고 국가가 모두에게 일자리와 복지 혜택을 제공해야 한다고 주장한다. 달콤한 얘기지만 부자에게 더 많은 세금을 걷는 것으로는 막대한 복지 서비스를 유지할 수 없다. 국가의 시장 통제 강화는 민주주의 후퇴와 경쟁 쇠퇴를 불러온다. 경제는 활력을 잃을 것이다. 마거릿 대처 전 영국 총리는 "저소득층이 임대로 거주하는 공공주택을 살 수 있게 될 때 자본주의 참여자가 된다"고 말했다. 평생 집 장만을 못 할 것으로 예상하는 젊은이가 많으면 자본주의는 힘을 잃게 된다.

해설

1. 사회주의는 사라진 것으로 생각되었지만, 자본주의의 속성상 빈부의 격차가 발생하고, 젊은이들이 불투명한 미래를 접하게 되면서, 사회주의 본질을 모른 채 환상에 빠지게 되는 경우가 많다. 그래서 사회주의적 개념이 전면에 다시 등장하여 관심을 끌고 있다는 (b)가 정답이다.

2. 청년들의 삶이 팍팍한 것일 뿐. 반세기 만에 가장 낮은 실업률을 기록할 정도로 미국 경제가 호황(Even as the U.S. economy is thriving with its lowest unemployment rate in a half century)이다. 그러므로 (a)는 올바른 진술이다. 참고로 (b)의 경우는 사회주의에 대한 선호가 민주주의에 대한 선호를 넘어섰다고 나오므로 틀린 진술이다.

3. 젊은이들이 사회주의를 선호하게 된 이유에 대한 분석이 3번째 단락에 자세히 소개되어 있다. 미국 사회는 호황이지만 청년층의 삶은 힘겹고, 부모보다 못 사는 첫 세대이기도 하다고 본문에 언급하고 있다. 그러므로 정답은 (c)가 된다.

4. 첫 단락은 알렉스 매킨타이어가 사회주의자가 된 과정에 대한 이야기이다. 고된 삶의 여정을 거치면서 점차 사회주의에 눈을 뜨고 결국은 사회주의자가 되었다. 그러므로 빈칸에 들어갈 부분은 '어떻게 사회주의자가 되었는지'가 타당하다. 정답은 (a)이다.

정답 1(b) 2(a) 3(c) 4(a)

UNIT 17
Is the law the problem?
법이 문제인가?

마르쿠스 툴리우스 키케로(B.C 106~B.C 43)는 서양 근대법의 모태인 로마법의 보편 원리를 집대성했다. 그는 『법률론』(De Legibus)에서 "인민의 행복이 최고의 법률이다(Salus populi suprema lex esto)"고 했다.

(단순히 성문법을 해석하는 데 그쳤던) 로마법은 키케로에 의해 '정의'의 정신을 얻었다. 근대 계몽주의와 자연법 사상 역시 그의 유산이다. 인간 본성이 옳다고 믿는 원칙이 인간이 만든 법보다 상위에 있으며, 법은 정의로워야 한다는 의미이기도 하다.

하지만 키케로조차 자신의 철학을 실천하진 못했다. 로마법을 한 단계 끌어올린 법률가이자 철학자로 칭송받지만, (정파(政派)적 이익을 위해 집정관 후보로 나선) 카틸리나를 '초법적' 방법으로 탄핵했다. 4년 뒤엔 이 행동 때문에 고발당했고, (로마 시민이 참여한 재판을 거치지 않고서는 처벌되지 않는다는) 법의 흠결을 이용해 도주했다.

르네상스 이후 서양 사회의 부가 축적되면서 로마법은 다시 조명을 받았는데, 주로 교회와 왕, 귀족의 재산권을 규정하기 위해서였다. '법의 정신'은 시민의 권리를 보호하기 위한 것이었지만 때때로 악용됐다. 16세기 스페인이 아메리카 대륙을 식민지로 만들 때 원주민의 재산권 침해에 대한 논쟁이 생겼다. 당시 교회와 왕실은 '자유로운 왕래를 거부하는 것은 자연법에 위배된다'거나 '재산은 시민공동체와 사회에 기초하는데 이를 형성하지 못한 원주민 사회는 재산권을 주장할 수 없다'는 논리를 만들어냈다.

수백 년의 시행착오를 거쳐 근대법이 완성됐다. 여전히 자연법의 정의와 거리가 멀 때가 있지만, 민주주의 역사가 긴 나라의 법은 대체로 그 간극이 크지 않다. 법체계가 다를지언정 판례와 시민사회의 합의로 자연법에 가까운 공감대를 형성한다.

해설

1. 키케로에 의해 정의의 정신이 법에 반영되고, 계몽주의와 자연법사상이 동반되어 오랜 시행착오를 거쳐서 근대법이 완성되었다. 즉 윗글은 로마 시대 이후 법의 발전과정을 설명한 글이다. 이런 내용이 들어있는 a)가 정답이다.

2. 키케로는 로마법을 근대법의 토대로 만든 장본인이지만, 자신의 이익을 위해 법의 흠결을 이용하였다. 그러므로 그는 자신이 설파한 정의의 정신에 부합되지 않게 행동한 것이다. 그러므로 정답은 a)이다.

3. 로마법은 "주로 교회와 왕, 귀족의 재산권을 규정하기 위해서(mostly to define the property rights of the church, kings and aristocrats)라고 하였으므로 a)는 옳은 진술이다. 16세기 스페인이 아메리카 대륙을 식민지로 만들 때 "원주민의 재산권 침해에 대한 논쟁이 생겼다(the infringement of native people's property rights became controversial)"고 하였으므로 c)도 옳은 진술이다. 이를 바탕으로 한 d) 역시 옳은 진술이다. 반면에 키케로가 카틸리나의 몰락을 가져오기 위해 내부에서 일했다는 것은 근거 없는 진술이므로 b)는 틀린 보기이다.

4. 오랜 시행착오를 거쳐 완성된 근대법은 자연법의 정의에 비하면 완벽하진 않겠지만, 그래도 오랜 세월을 거쳐 세상의 정의를 반영하는 법이다. far from~ (~와 거리는 멀지만)을 써서, 자연법의 정의와는 거리가 멀다고 하였다. 그 뒤에 바로 but을 써서 반대 구조로 그렇지만 그래도 심하지 않다는 내용으로 이어져야 한다. 그러므로 정답은 d)가 된다.

정답 1(b) 2(a) 3(b) 4(d)

UNIT 18
Not a curse, but still weighty issue
비만 할증료

그리스 신화에는 '굶주림의 저주'를 받은 에리직톤(Erysichton) 얘기가 나온다. 에리직톤은 여신(女神) 데메테르의 신성한 정원에 있는 나무를 도끼로 쓰러뜨리고, 그녀가 총애하는 요정을 죽였다. 진노한 여신은 그에게 아무리 먹어도 허기를 느끼는 저주를 내렸다. 그는 눈에 띄는 것은 닥치는 대로 먹어댔고, 급기야 애지중지하던 딸까지 노예로 팔아 음식을 구했다. 모든 걸 먹어 치우고도 성에 차지 않았던 에리직톤은 팔다리부터 시작해 제 몸을 모두 뜯어먹었다. 죽어서야 끔찍한 저주에서 벗어날 수 있었던 것이다.

억제할 수 없는 '식욕의 고통'은 신화 속 얘기만은 아니다. '에리직톤 증후군'이라고 해도 됨 직한 '프래더윌리(Prader-Willi) 증후군'을 앓는 환자에겐 현실이다. 유전 질환이나 대뇌의 특정 부분 기능 장애로 생기는 희귀병인데, 한없이 먹어도 배부른 줄 모른다. 당연히 비만을 초래하고 심장병과 고혈압 등의 합병증을 얻는다. 식사량 조절이 절대적이지만 그게 여의치 않아 합병증으로 고통이 이만저만 아니란다.

저주나 질병까진 아니더라도 비만이 만인(萬人)의 고민거리인 건 분명하다. 2001년 영화 '브리짓 존스의 일기'에서 브리짓이 데이트를 앞두고 섹시한 팬티를 입을지, 아니면 아랫배를 감추기 위해 체형 보정용 속옷을 입을지 고민하는 건 그나마 애교로 봐줄 수 있지만, 비만 때문에 건강을 해치거나 돈이 들어가는 지경에 이르면 문제가 심각하다. 에어프랑스가 4월 1일 출발분부터 뚱뚱한 승객에게 '비만 할증료'를 부과했다고 한다. 비슷하게 지난해 10월 미국에선 구급차 업체들이 비만 환자에게 정상요금의 최고 두 배나 되는 할증료를 부과해 논란이 됐다.

해설

1. 세 문단으로 나눠진 지문이다. 각 문단별 주제를 파악한 후 공통점으로 다루는 전체 주제를 파악해야 한다. 첫 번째 문단에선 '굶주림의 저주'를 받은 에리직톤을 통해 '끊이지 않은 굶주림'에 대한 비극적인 이야기를 다루고 있다. 두 번째 문단은 '프래더윌리 증후군'의 이야기를 언급하면서 아무리 먹어도 배부르지 않는 환자를 이야기하고 있다. 세 번째 문단에서 '브리짓 존스의 일기'와 유럽과 미국의 비행사와 구급차 회사를 통해 동일한 주제인 비만을 다루고 있다. 즉, 각 문단의 공통된 주제는 바로 비만이다.

2. 본문에서 언급되는 '프래더윌리 증후군'은 바로 아무리 먹어도 배부르지 않는 현상을 말한다. 두 번째 문단 전체에서 이에 대한 언급이 등장하지만 문단 초반부인 'It is a reality for the patients who suffer from Prader-Willi syndrome, which recalls the hunger Erysichthon was stricken with'에서도 바로 내용을 이끌어 낼 수 있다. 즉, 에리직톤과 유사한 현상을 겪는 환자를 일컫는 병명이다.

3. '비만 때문에 건강을 해치거나 돈이 들어가는 지경에 이르면 문제가 심각하다.'의 본문에서 (a)는 옳음을 알 수 있고, 첫 번째 문단에서 에리직톤은 자신의 배고픔을 달래기 위해 딸과 음식을 바꾸고, 나아가 자신의 몸을 먹는 지경에 이르렀다고 언급되어 있다. 비만인 사람들이 항상 불행하다는 일반화를 이끌어 내는 것은 옳지 못하다. 본문에서 언급된 특정 사례를 통해 일반화를 이끌어 낼 경우엔 본문에 그것이 명시되어 있는지를 반드시 확인해야 한다.

4. (b)의 경우 에어프랑스가 비만인 사람을 차별하려는 의도로 가격을 올리는 것이 아니라 차량 운영비, 특히 기름 값과 관련해 가격을 올린 것이다. '브리짓 존스의 일기'를 보는 관중은 그녀의 모습을 애교로 봐 줄 수 있다고 언급되어 있다. 이러한 점과 같은 맥락에서 (d)가 옳음을 알 수 있다.

정답 1.(d) 2.(a) 3.(c) 4.(d)

UNIT 19

Maternal instincts
부계 불확실성

'부계 불확실성'이란 말은 자신이 아이의 아버지인지 확신하지 못하는 남자를 가리킨다. 최근 영국과학원 회보 '프로시딩스'에 나온 흥미로운 연구에서 사람들은 친가보다 외가에 친밀감을 더 느끼며, 그 이유는 부계 불확실성 때문이라는 것이다. 연구에 따르면 사촌 집에 불이 났을 때 뛰어들어 구하겠느냐는 질문에 외가 쪽이 높은 순위를 차지했다. 부계 불확실성이 모계 쪽 친척에 대한 이타적 행동을 차별적으로 조절하는 심리 기제를 발전시켰다는 것이 연구진의 설명이다.

중국 원난성(雲南城)부근의 '모수오(摩梭)족'은 세계에서 보기 드문 여인국이다. 해발 2,700m 첩첩산중에 살고 있는 이들은 '주혼' 또는 '걸어 다니는 결혼'이라는 독특한 풍습으로 1,500여 년간 모계 사회를 유지해 왔다. 여자가 13살이 돼 성인식을 치르면 자유롭게 복수의 성적 파트너를 택하는 풍습이다. 남자들은 어머니와 함께 살면서 성관계를 맺을 때만 여자 집을 찾는다. 당연히 아버지가 분명하지 않다. 태어난 아이들은 여자들이 기른다. '아버지', '남편', '시집간다'는 단어 자체가 없다. 필요에 따라, 외삼촌이 최소한의 아버지 역할을 대신한다. 가장은 여자다. 역시 부계 불확실성이 낳은 일이다.

자세히 살펴보면, 지금의 가부장적 가족관계의 뿌리도 부계 불확실성이다. 농경사회 부의 축적이 시작되면서, 재산을 진짜 자기 아들에게 물려주려는 남성들의 보존 욕망이 낳은 제도가 바로 가부장제이기 때문이다. 시집 온 여자는 남편에게 귀속되며 재산과 혈통은 아들들에게 물려지고 정조의 의무는 여성들에게만 주어지는, 부권 중심 제도다. 위의 연구는 부계 불확실성이 부권 사회를 확립시켰지만 사람들의 심리 속에는 아마도 '모계 확실성'과 모권에 대한 반사적 그리움이 오랫동안 쌓여 있었음을 보여준다고 말한다.

해설

1. 문제에서 요구하는 사항은 옳은 진술을 고르는 것이다. (a)에서 'the tribe returns to a lower location'에 대한 진술은 없다. (b)의 경우 'paternal-centric'이 아니라 'maternal-centric'이라 말해야 옳다. 두 번째 문단 마지막의 진술로 보아 (d)만이 옳다.

2. 첫 번째 문단에 나오는 '프로시딩스'의 연구에 대한 내용을 묻고 있다. 연구에서 밝혀낸 사실은 '사람들은 친가보다 외가에 친밀감을 더 느끼며, 그 이유는 부계 불확실성 때문이라는 것'이다. 따라서 (b)가 가장 적절한 진술이다.

3. 남자들은 오직 성관계를 맺을 때에만 자신의 파트너를 찾으므로 (b)는 옳은 진술이다. 참고로 (a)의 경우 13세에 달한 여성들이 복수의 남성과 결혼하는 것이 아니며 단지 선택권이 있을 뿐이므로 틀린 진술이다. (c)의 경우 남자는 자신의 파트너가 된 여성과 관계를 맺은 이후에도 자신의 어머니와 계속 살기 때문에 틀린 진술이다. (d)의 경우 "아버지가 분명하지 않다"고 하였지, 어느 누구도 모른다는 것은 올바른 진술이 아니다.

4. 글쓴이가 궁극적으로 전달하려는 사항은 마지막 문단이다. 즉, 현대 사회의 가부장적 가족관계의 뿌리는 바로 부계 불확실성의 영향일 수 있다는 것이다.

정답 1.(d) 2.(b) 3.(b) 4.(c)

UNIT 20

The return of Machiavelli?
마키아벨리

이탈리아 피렌체의 한복판에 우뚝 솟은 두오모(산타 마리아 델 피오레 성당)는 팔각형의 석재 돔으로는 서유럽 최초의 건축물이다. '꽃의 도시' 피렌체의 자랑이자 상징이다. 소설과 영화『냉정과 열정 사이』에서 두 남녀가 10년 전의 약속을 지켜 재회하는 그곳이다. 두오모는 니콜로 마키아벨리(1469~1527)에게도 각별한 의미가 있다. 『로마인 이야기』의 저자 시오노 나나미는 "이유 없이 관직에서 쫓겨난 마키아벨리가 피렌체 인근 산장에서 두오모를 바라보며 자기 자신에게 쏟아 부었을 들끓는 분노를 생각하며 그의 생애를 쓰리라 마음먹었다"고 적었다. 피렌체 출신의 마키아벨리는 두오모를 보며 출세하고, 추락하며 두오모와 영욕(榮辱)을 함께했다고 한다. '자신의 영혼보다 조국을 더 사랑한' 마키아벨리는 역작『군주론』을 집필하면서 외부의 침략으로부터 두오모를 온전히 지켜내는 게 군주의 사명이라고 봤다.

마키아벨리만큼 사후(死後) 500년이 지나도록 논란의 대상이 된 인물도 드물다. 전제군주를 옹호하는 냉혹한 이론가로 평가돼 왔다. 권모술수(權謀術數)의 화신이기도 했다. '여우와 사자론(論)'이 대표적이다. 그는 "군주는 사자의 힘과 여우의 교활함"을 동시에 갖춰야 한다고 주장한다. 또한 "군주는 필요한 경우 악(惡)을 행할 줄 알아야 한다"며 인간의 나약한 심리를 역이용하라고 권고한다. 당시 피렌체 공화국은 주변 강대국의 위협 속에서 생존을 고민하는 작은 도시국가에 불과했다. 그래서 '근대국가'를 위해 강력한 리더십이 필요하다고 마키아벨리는 생각했다. 그는 전제군주정치 찬양을 의도한 것이 아니었다. 군주론(The Prince)은 군주정 아래서 권력을 어떻게 획득·유지하는지에 관한 방법과 수단을 논한 책이다.

해설

1. 이 글은 마키아벨리에 관하여 서술하고 있으므로 정답은 (d)이다. 마키아벨리가 쓴 군주론은 그의 사상을 총체적으로 담은 것일 뿐 이 글의 핵심은 마키아벨리 자신에 관한 것이다.

2. '이유 없이 관직에서 쫓겨난 마키아벨리'라는 표현만 나올 뿐, 본문에서는 부연설명이 없기 때문에 자세한 이유를 알 수 없다. 그러므로 정답은 (a)이다.

3. '전제군주를 옹호하는 냉혹한 이론가로 평가'되고 있다.

4. 마키아벨리는 "군주는 사자의 힘과 여우의 교활함"을 동시에 갖춰야 한다고 하며, 군주는 필요한 경우 악(惡)을 행할 줄 알아야 한다고 말하였다. 당시 피렌체 공화국은 주변 강대국의 위협 속에서 생존을 고민하는 작은 도시국가에 불과했기에 마키아벨리는 '근대국가'를 위해 강력한 리더십이 필요하다고 생각했다. 이러한 그의 사상에서 (d)를 끌어낼 수 있다.

정답 1.(d) 2.(a) 3.(a) 4.(d)

Part 2

UNIT 01

Mansplaining
잘난 척하는 남자들

세계 여성의 날을 전후해 소셜네트워크서비스(SNS)상에서 '맨스플레인(mansplain)'이라는 단어가 화제에 올랐다. '남자(man)'와 '설명하다(explain)'를 결합한 것으로, 2014년 Macquarie 사전에 '올해의 단어'로 뽑혔다. 그런데 이게 무슨 뜻일까? 옥스포드 영어사전에 따르면 '맨스플레인(mansplain)'은 '(남자가) 대체적으로 여자에게 잘난 체하며 아랫사람 대하듯 설명하는 것'을 말한다. 보다 쉽게 풀어 쓰자면 "여자인 네가 알아봐야 얼마나 알겠니, 이 오빠가 설명해줄게" 정도이다.

맨스플레인이라는 단어의 시작은 문화비평가 레베카 솔닛이 2008년 LA타임스의 블로그 포스트에 '남자들은 자꾸 날 가르치려 든다. 사실은 그들에게 문제가 되지 않았다.'라는 제목으로 게재한 글에서부터 비롯됐다. 솔닛은 몇 년 전 자신이 한 남성과 나눈 대화에 관한 이야기를 했다. 솔닛이 "(움직이는 말 사진으로 유명한) 에드워드 머이브릿지에 관한 책을 썼다"고 자신을 소개하자, 그 남자는 솔닛의 말을 뚝 끊고는 "올해 머이브릿지에 관한 중요한 책이 출간된 걸 아느냐"며 떠들었다. 솔닛 친구가 "바로 그 책을 얘(솔닛)가 썼다니까요"라고 서너 차례 말하고 나서야 그 남자는 비로소 상황을 파악했다. 알고 보니 그는 그 책은 읽지도 않고 두어 달 전 이 책에 관한 뉴욕타임스 서평을 읽은 게 전부였다.

솔닛이 든 이 사례가 극적이기는 하지만 그다지 드문 일도 아니다. 정도의 차이만 있을 뿐 많은 여성이 일상생활 속에서 비슷한 상황과 맞닥뜨린다. 오죽하면 솔닛이 "일부 남성, 그리고 모든 여성은 내가 무슨 말을 하는지 알 것"이라고 했을까. 이건 단지 개인에게 일어난 해프닝으로 끝나는 게 아니라 여성인권 문제까지 이어진다. 어디에 서서 바라보느냐에 따라 보이는 세상은 달라진다. 성차별 같은 얘기까지 굳이 할 필요도 없다. 남성은 여성의 자리, 여성은 남성의 자리에서 세상을 바라보는 건 어떨까?

해설

1. '맨스플레인(mansplain)'이라는 단어가 뜻하는 것이 무엇인지를 유래에서부터 의미까지 자세히 살펴보고 있는 글이다. 그러므로 정답은 (c)이다.

2. 솔닛이 사례로 든 남성은 사실 머이브릿지에 관해 아는 것이 별로 없으며, 단지 두어 달 전 이 책에 관한 뉴욕타임스 서평을 읽은 게 전부였다. 그러므로 그가 머이브릿지의 전문가라는 (c)는 틀린 진술이다.

3. 솔닛이 접한 사례는 정도의 차이만 있을 뿐 많은 여성이 일상생활 속에서 이런 상황과 자주 맞닥뜨린다. 그러므로 거의 모든 여성들이 계속해서 맨스플레인을 접하고 있다는 것을 추론해낼 수 있다. 참고로 (b)나 (c)처럼 여성들이 다른 여성들에게 그렇게 대한다거나, 모든 남성들이 다 그렇다는 것을 끌어낼 수 있는 근거는 없다.

4. 단지 가끔씩 남성은 여성의 자리, 여성은 남성의 자리에서 세상을 바라보는 건 어떨까? 라는 의미는 남녀 모두 반대의 입장에서 생각해 볼 필요가 있다는 것이다. 그러므로 정답은 (a)이다.

정답 1.(c) 2.(c) 3.(d) 4.(a)

UNIT 02
Battling it out on the football pitch
전쟁과 축구

'남미의 나폴레옹'을 자처하던 파라과이의 야심찬 독재자 프란시스코 솔라노 로페스로 인해 1864년에서 1870년 사이에 삼국동맹 전쟁이 시작됐다. 브라질의 군대가 우루과이를 침공한 후, 로페스는 브라질과 아르헨티나 모두에 선전포고를 하기로 결심한다. 잘 준비돼 있었던 파라과이군은 개전 초 두 나라에 대항해 잘 싸웠지만, 로페스 정권의 외교 부재로 우루과이가 등을 돌리게 되었다. 두 나라와 싸우는 대신, 파라과이는 브라질, 아르헨티나 그리고 우루과이의 삼국동맹에 맞서야만 했다.

1869년 파라과이의 수도 아순시온이 동맹군에 의해 함락되고, 1870년 파라과이 북부 국경 지역에서 군대 잔당들과 함께 싸우던 로페스가 사살되면서 전쟁은 막을 내렸다. 무모한 전쟁의 결과는 참혹했다. 약 9만에서 10만의 군인과 시민이 동맹국 편에서 죽음을 당하고, 파라과이는 전쟁 전 52만 명이던 인구가 22만 명으로 감소했다. 대부분의 파라과이 남성 인구가 죽임을 당했다. 역사가들은 살아남은 남성 인구가 총 2만8,000여 명뿐이었다고 추정한다. 남미 지역 국가들이 월드컵에서 경기하는 것을 보면 그 삼국동맹 전쟁을 떠올리지 않을 수 없다. 경기 전반에 흐르는 공격적인 경쟁과 민족주의로 인해 나는 축구선수들이 경기장에서 역사적 투쟁을 다시 재현하는 듯 느껴졌다. 미국의 인류학자 리처드 사이프스는 1973년 "축구와 같은 스포츠는 갈등 주체 간의 공격적 긴장을 해소시켜 전쟁의 대안으로 기능한다"고 주장한 바 있다. 1970년대 미국과 중국은 이러한 생각에서 득을 얻었다. 미국 정부의 전략인 중국에서 경합을 벌이는 탁구 선수와 관련된 '핑퐁 외교정책'은 냉전시대에 미국과 중국의 차가운 관계를 녹이는 결과를 가져왔다. 우리는 또 다시 긴장감이 고조될 때, 말도 안 되는 투쟁으로 죽은 이들을 생각하고, 경기장에서 이것을 표출하는 이득을 고려해 볼 필요가 있다.

해설

1. 본문 마지막 문장에서 글쓴이의 주장이 드러난다. 글의 초반부에서 드러나는 독재자 프란시스코 솔라노 로페스로 인해 많은 이들이 죽게 되는 전쟁의 무용성을 주장하면서, 이러한 충돌을 경기장에서 푸는 지혜를 발휘할 필요가 있는 내용이 골자이다. 이러한 내용을 가장 잘 드러내는 보기는 (b)이다.

2. '핑퐁 외교전략'이 구체적으로 언급된 본문을 찾고, 그것의 의미와 역할을 먼저 파악해야 한다. 본문 마지막 문단에서 미국은 중국에서 자국의 탁수선수가 경합을 벌이게 하면서 자연스레 양국 간의 정치적 긴장감을 완화시키려 했다는 내용을 확인할 수 있다.

3. 두 번째 문단에서 구체적 수치를 들었듯이, 많은 군인과 민간인이 목숨을 잃었는데 파라과이의 경우 남자 인구의 대부분을 잃을 정도로 심각하다고 언급하고 있다.

4. 본문 초반에 (a)에 대한 내용이 언급되어 있고, 파라과이는 초기에 전쟁에서 상황이 좋았다('잘 준비돼 있었던 파라과이군은 개전 초 두 나라에 대항해 잘 싸웠지만'). '로페스 정권의 외교 부재로'라는 내용에서 보기 (c)는 옳지 못함을 알 수 있다.

정답 1.(b) 2.(a) 3.(b) 4.(c)

UNIT 03
An addiction we can't afford
명품 프렌들리

1945년 9월 2일 일본의 동경만에서 미국의 전함 미주리호에 탄 맥아더가 일본의 항복문서에 서명하는데, 이는 동맹국을 대표해 일본의 파견단에 의해 처음 동의된 것이다. 태평양 전쟁이 막을 내리는 역사적인 장면이었다. 그런데 사람들의 관심은 다른 데 쏠렸다. "저 만년필 어디 것이지?"라고 사람들은 물었다. 이에, 파커 펜 회사는 그가 사용한 도구(펜)가 자사의 것이라고 인정했다.

몇 년 후, 마릴린 먼로가 지하철 통풍구에 서서 자신의 무릎 위로 드레스가 날리자 자신의 드레스를 내리는 장면은 영화 '7년 만의 외출'을 그 이야기 자체보다 이런 상징적 이미지로 더 유명하게 만들었다. 그러나 영화가 나왔을 때, 여성 관중의 관심은 다른 곳에 쏠렸다. 이들 모두는 마릴린 먼로가 어떤 브랜드의 신발을 신고 있었는지 알고 싶어했다. 이것은 페라가모였는데, 먼로의 섹시한 자세는 이 회사가 바로 디자이너 상표가 되게 만들었다.

일본에선 버버리는 여전히 럭셔리 아이콘이다. 옷 장수가 만든 트렌치 코트는 세계 1차 대전 이후 민간인들 사이에서 인기를 끌었다. 한때 그 회사 공장 라인의 절반 이상이 일본에서 팔렸는데, 여기서 일본 주부들이 경제난에 허덕이던 버버리 회사를 살리는 데 도움을 줄 정도였다고 한다. 월스트리트 저널은 최근 한국이 '세계에서 가장 명품에 호의적(luxury friendly)'이라고 보도했다. 이 신문은 조사 응답자의 46%가 지난 1년간 전보다 명품 소비가 늘었다고 답했으며, 또한 응답자 중에 고가의 명품을 구입하고 죄의식을 느낀 적이 있다는 사람은 5%에 불과했다고 했다.

해설

1. 첫 번째 문단에선 맥아더 장군의 이야기를 통해 '파커'라는 명품이 탄생한 이야기, 두 번째 문단은 마릴린 먼로를 통해 명품의 자리에 오르게 된 페라가모 그리고 마지막 문단에선 일본과 한국의 명품 열기를 살펴보고 있다. 세 문단의 공통된 주제는 바로 명품이며 역사적 사건을 중심으로 기록하고 있다. 딱 떨어지는 답은 없지만, 단락마다 명품 종류들이 나왔으므로 (b)가 가장 근접한 답이 된다.

2. 세 번째 문단 초반부에서 답을 찾을 수 있다. '일본 주부들이 경제난에 허덕이던 버버리 회사를 살리는 데 도움을 줄 정도였다고 한다.'라는 진술에서 알 수 있듯이, 버버리 코트에 열광하는 일본 주부로 인해 회사가 경제난을 해결할 정도였다고 말하고 있다.

3. 본문 마지막 두 문장에 답이 명시되어 있다.

4. 본문에서 마릴린 먼로가 페라가모를 신음으로 디자이너 상표가 되었다고 언급되어 있기에, (a)는 틀린 진술이다. 맥아더가 배에 승선한 채 일본의 항복 문서에 서명했고, '7년 만의 외출'은 마릴린 먼로의 특정 장면으로 인해 유명세를 탔으며, 일본에서 버버리가 누구나 추구하는 명품으로 여겨진다고 본문에 모두 언급이 되어 있다.

정답 1.(b) 2.(a) 3.(d) 4.(a)

UNIT 04
Growing old peacefully
100세의 실종

파키스탄의 북쪽에 있는 '훈자'계곡은 태곳적 신비의 아름다운 풍광으로 유명하다. 이 계곡은 샹그릴라를 그린 제임스 힐튼의 소설 『잃어버린 지평선』에 영감을 주었다. 또한 미야자키 하야오의 만화 시리즈이자 애니메이션인 '바람계곡의 나우시카'의 배경이 된 곳이기도 하다. 그러나 훈자가 유명한 것은 자연 풍광뿐 아니라 장수하는 주민 때문이기도 하다. 코카서스의 압하지아와 에콰도르의 빌카밤바와 더불어 세계 3대 장수마을이다. 공통점은 모두가 거대한 산맥에 자리 잡고 있고, 공기와 물이 맑다는 것이다.

일본의 오키나와는 섬인데도 장수촌이다. 인구 130만 명 가운데 100세 이상 노인이 700명이 넘는다. 여기선 '70세 어린이, 80세 젊은이'라고 한다. '나이 90에 조상들이 천국으로 부르거든 기다리시라 하라. 100세가 되면 생각해 보겠노라고'란 속담이 있을 정도다. 그러자 이들의 생활방식을 따라 하자는 '오키나와 프로그램'까지 나왔다. 오키나와 주민들은 18가지 음식을 먹는데, 이 중 78%가 채소류라고 한다. 주로 곡물과 채소류와 해조류를 먹는다. 고기도 굽지 않고 먹는다.

불로장생(不老長生)은 예부터 뭇 인간들의 희원이지만, 도끼 들고 막아서도 백발(白髮)이 제 먼저 알고 지름길로 온다. 결국, 우리가 할 수 있는 것이란 우아하게 늙는 것이 답이다. 우리는 장수촌 노인들에게서 힌트를 얻을 수 있다. 이들 모두 여유롭게 산다는 점이다. 세월에 저항하기보다 거기에 익숙해지라고 우리에게 충고한다. 그래서일까. 근래 들어 화장품도 안티 에이징(Anti aging)보다 웰 에이징(Well aging)을 내세운다.

해설

1. 문단이 나눠진 경우 각 문단에서 중점으로 다루는 공통분모를 찾으면 된다. 각 문단이 모두 '장수'와 '건강한 삶'에 관한 이야기를 다루고 있다.

2. 구체적 내용파악 문제이다. 훈자는 미야자키 하야오의 애니메이션 '바람계곡의 나우시카'의 배경이 된 곳이며, 장수하는 마을인 동시에 샹그릴라를 그린 제임스 힐튼의 소설 『잃어버린 지평선』에 영감을 준 곳이라 했다. (b)에 대한 언급은 없다.

3. 100세나 되서야 하늘에 계신 조상들에게 돌아갈 생각을 한다는 것은 그 때까지 장수할 수 있다는 말이다.

4. 다음에 이어질 내용을 추론하는 문제는 일반적으로 본문 마지막에서 힌트를 얻을 수 있다. '웰 에이징'에 관한 내용이 등장해야 한다.

정답 1.(c) 2.(b) 3.(a) 4.(b)

UNIT 05

The text generation
텍스트 세대

"10년 된 영어교재인데 요즘 들어 좀 더 쉽게 만들어달라는 고교 영어교사들의 요청이 이어지고 있어. 학생들이 너무 어려워한대." 영어 독해 교재를 만드는 출판사에 다니는 A가 모임에서 이야기했다. 다들 그의 얘기에 귀를 기울였다. 고등학생 영어실력이 예전보다 좋아졌을 텐데. 왜 영어교재를 이해하는 데 어려움이 있지?

그가 의외의 답을 내놨다. "영어실력 문제가 아니었어. 긴 지문을 읽고 이해하는 능력이 떨어진 거야. 그게 영어이든, 한국어이든." 고교 국어교사 B가 전혀 놀랍지 않다는 표정으로 이렇게 말한다. "국어시험을 보면 지문을 이해하지 못하는 애들이 수두룩해. 심지어 지문이 아니라 문제를 이해 못해서 틀려. '가장 거리가 먼 것'을 고르라고 했는데, 도대체 가장 거리가 먼 것이 무슨 뜻인지를 모르겠다는 거야."

C가 고개를 갸웃거리며 묻는다. "요즘 애들이 그렇게 읽기를 못한다면, 도대체 왜 유튜브에는 온통 자막을 달아놓는 거지? 맞춤법 엉망인 자막, 읽기도 괴로워." 다시 B가 나서서 정리해준다. "어려서부터 카카오톡으로 소통해 온 텍스트 세대니까." 긴 글은 읽을 수 없고 추상적 표현은 이해 못하는 새로운 텍스트 세대가 탄생한 것이다.

미국 인지신경학자 매리언 울프는 저서 『다시, 책으로』에서 놀라운 연구결과를 소개했다. "길고 난해한 문장을 받아들일 수 있는 '깊이 읽기 회로'는 지속되지 않는다. 상당한 지적 수준의 독자라고 해도 책에 몰입하는 경험을 잃으면 '초보자 수준의 읽는 뇌'로 회귀한다." 몰입하는 독서의 경험, 당신은 얼마나 하고 있는지?

해설

1. 학생들 사이에서 글을 읽고 이해하는 능력이 과거에 비해 떨어졌음을 얘기하는 글이다. 그 이유로는 카카오톡 등으로 소통하는 텍스트세대의 문제점을 들고 있다. 그러므로 읽기 능력의 하락을 얘기한 c)가 정답이다.

2. 책에 몰입하는 경험이 많으면 많을수록 글을 이해하는 능력이 발달하고, 그러한 경험을 잃으면 다시 초보자 수준으로 회귀한다 하였으므로, 글에 몰입할수록 글을 더 능숙하게 잘 읽어낼 수 있다는 d)가 정답이다.

3. 길고 복잡한 문장을 읽어낼 수 있는 능력이 예전에 비해 떨어지고 있다. 그것이 영어로 된 글이건 한국어로 된 글이건 마찬가지(The ability to read and understand long texts has diminished, whether it is English or Korean)라고 앞부분에도 언급하고 있다. 그러므로 정답은 b)이다. a)의 경우, 영어와 한국어의 이해능력을 비교한 것이 아니므로 틀린 진술이며, c)의 경우 자막은 10대들의 독서능력과 무관하므로 역시 틀리다.

4. 길고 복잡한 문장을 이해할 수 있는 상당한 지식수준의 독자도 결국 초보독자로 돌아갈 수도 있다고 하였는데, '깊이 읽기 회로'는 지속되지 않는다(it doesn't last long)을 근거로 한 번 독서를 해 놓으면 끝나는 것이 아니라는 것을 알 수 있다. 또 뒤의 문장에서 얼마나 몰입하고 있는지를 묻는 문장으로 연결되는 것을 보면, 몰입하는 것이 중요하고 몰입하지 못하면 읽기능력이 떨어진다는 것을 암시하는 것이다. 그러므로 빈칸에 들어갈 표현은 "독서에서 몰입하는 경험을 잃는다면"이 올바른 표현이다. 그러므로 정답은 a)이다.

정답 1(c) 2(d) 3(b) 4(a)

UNIT 06

Memories of Mozart
모차르트

필립 솔레르스는 『모차르트 평전』에서 "현대인은 누구나 모차르트 음악과 살고 있다"고 했다. 휴대전화에도, 엘리베이터에도, 쇼핑몰에도 모차르트의 음악이 있다. 극단적으로 표현하면 이 세상에 태어난 사람들은 어머니 뱃속에서 '마술피리'를 듣고 세상에 나와, '피가로의 결혼'을 테마곡으로 삼아 짝을 찾고 '레퀴엠'의 선율 아래 영면한다고 한다. 모차르트가 살아 있어서 저작료를 받는다면 오스트리아를 통째로 살 수 있을 것이란 말도 그리 과장이 아니다.

하지만 생전의 그는 늘 돈에 쪼들렸다. 1789년이 최악이었다. 그가 당시 프리메이슨 동료였던 푸흐베르크에게 쓴 구걸조 편지엔 이런 궁색함이 절절히 담겨있다. "절친한 친구이자 형제인 당신이 나를 버린다면, 나와 불쌍하고 병든 아내, 그리고 아이들까지 어찌할 도리가 없는 처지가 됩니다. 슬프게도 운이 너무 나빠서 아무리 해도 돈이 벌리지 않습니다. 14일간 연주회 (예약)명부를 돌렸지만 이름을 올린 사람은 슈비텐 한 사람뿐입니다."(로빈스 랜던 『모차르트의 마지막 나날』)

살아선 궁핍했지만 오늘날 그는 고향 잘츠부르크시를 먹여 살린다. 이 도시엔 티셔츠와 연필, 재떨이와 라이터는 물론 맥주와 골프공까지 웬만하면 다 모차르트 표다. 포장지에 그의 얼굴을 인쇄한 유명 초콜릿 브랜드 모차르트 쿠겔은 지난해 1억 개, 약 580억 원어치가 수출됐다고 한다. 잘츠부르크시는 모차르트의 브랜드 가치를 54억 유로(약 6조 4,000억원)로 평가했다. 필립스(49억 유로)나 폴크스바겐(46억 유로)보다 높다.

모차르트의 이런 브랜드 파워는 '친숙함'에서 나온다. 베토벤의 엄격함이나 바흐의 경건함과는 다르다. 모차르트는 밝고 쉽고 재미있고 감미롭다. 현대인의 브랜드 코드와 그대로 들어맞는다. 떼려야 뗄 수 없는 친구 같은, 연인 같은 모차르트를 그래서 앨버트 아인슈타인은 이렇게 표현했다. "죽는다는 것은 더 이상 모차르트를 들을 수 없게 된다는 의미이다."

> **해설**

1. 독해에서 특정 문장의 의미를 물을 땐, 문장 자체의 의미만을 살피는 것이 아니라 제시된 문맥 속 의미를 파악해야 한다. 바로 뒤에 이어지는 내용인 '휴대전화에도, 엘리베이터에도, 쇼핑몰에도 모차르트의 음악이 있다.'에서 알 수 있듯이 오늘날 사회에 어디를 가도 그의 음악이 흔하게 깔려 있다는 의미이다.

2. 두 번째 문단에서 그는 생전에 경제적으로 힘든 생활을 했다는 절실한 내용이 등장한다. (d)와 같은 경우 '14일간 연주회 (예약)명부를 돌렸지만 이름을 올린 사람은 슈비텐 한 사람뿐입니다.'에서 알 수 있듯이 옳지 못한 진술이다. (a)가 정답이다.

3. 모차르트는 생애 동안 자신의 진정한 가치를 인정받지 못해 경제적으로 힘든 삶을 살았지만, 그의 음악은 후대의 삶에 많은 것을 남겼다. 그의 고향인 잘츠부르크시는 그의 이름을 딴 다양한 제품으로 엄청난 경제적 득을 누리고, 현대인들에게는 그가 남긴 음악을 즐기면서 '떼려야 뗄 수 없는' 그런 친구와 연인 같은 음악을 남겼다. 이러한 내용을 잘 반영한 보기는 (c)이다.

4. (a)는 두 번째 문단의 내용처럼 그의 구설소의 편시에서 자세히 드러나 있다. 부유한 가정이 아닌 점과 그의 음악이 생후 진정한 평가를 받는 내용은 본문에서 이끌어 낼 수 있지만, (d)와 같이 그의 자손이 그의 음악으로부터 부자가 되었다는 내용은 없다. 그의 고향인 잘츠부르크의 사람들이 그의 이름을 건 상품을 통해 금전적 득을 얻는다는 내용만 등장할 뿐이다.

> **정답** 1.(d) 2.(a) 3.(c) 4.(d)

UNIT 07
Leaping tall buildings
수퍼맨

　수퍼맨의 탄생은 1934년 미국 만화였다. 경제 공황기 미국인에게 희망과 용기를 준 이 불멸의 영웅은 이후 라디오 드라마와 소설·애니메이션·두 개의 TV 시리즈·뮤지컬로 옮겨졌다. 우리가 흔히 기억하는 크리스토퍼 리브 주연의 영화는 1978년부터 1987년까지 총 네 편이 나왔다. 나중에 수퍼맨에 대한 어린 시절과 로맨스에 초점을 둔 두 번째 TV 시리즈가 방영되었다. 수퍼맨은 '배트맨', '스파이더맨' 등 슈퍼 히어로 캐릭터의 원조가 됐다. 움베르토 에코는 수퍼맨을 "산업사회 개인들이 가진 권력에 대한 꿈을 한 몸에 체현하면서, 관객이 쉽게 동일시할 수 있는 영웅"이라고 풀이했다. 특히 영화 속에서 수퍼맨은 미국인이 주도한 세계 평화를 이끄는, 아메리칸 영웅의 대표 아이콘이 됐다. 그만큼 인종주의와 미국 중심주의를 비판하는 사람도 많았다. 수퍼맨, 초영웅 자체는 새로운 것이 아니다. 수퍼맨의 여정은 조셉 캠벨이 숱한 신화와 종교, 전설 속에서 분석한 영웅담과 똑같다. "비정상적인 탄생, 어린 시절의 고난, 조력자와의 만남, 기적적인 권능의 획득, 귀환"의 여정이다.

　그렇다면 미국인들은 왜 그토록 수퍼맨에 열광할까. 최근의 분석에 따르면 미국은 200년 남짓으로 역사가 짧고 건국 신화가 없기에 미국인들에게는 수퍼맨이 자국 신화 속 영웅이 되어주기 때문이라고 한다. 수퍼맨은 크립톤 행성의 지도자인 아버지에 의해 지구에 보내지고 지구를 구한다. 외계에서 온 이방인이 불세출의 영웅이 되는 구도다. 세계 평화의 수호자를 자임하게 된 미국 사회의 이미지가 겹쳐진다. 새 영화 '수퍼맨 리턴즈'가 나왔다. 새 영화는 수퍼맨의 메시아적 성격을 더욱 강조했으며, 심지어 '구세주(saviour)'라는 호칭을 사용하고 있다. 악당이 미 대륙을 물에 잠기게 하려 할 때 수퍼맨의 힘에 저지당한다. 수퍼맨은 전 지구가 아닌 미국을 구한다. 이 '돌아온 수퍼맨'은 미국인들이 여전히 슈퍼 파워를 갈망하지만 그것은 정당하고, 심지어 성스러운 것이어야 함을 잘 보여준다. 그런 점에서 '수퍼맨 리턴즈'는 9·11 이후 그에 대한 반응에도 불구하고 도덕적 정당성을 찾고 싶어하는 미국인의 자기인식을 보여준다. 브라이언 싱어 감독도 수퍼맨을 "9·11 이후 혼란한 세상에 위로와 안식을 주는 존재"라고 말했다. 한 마디로 선하고 희생적인 강한 권력에 대한 소망이다.

해설

1. 수퍼맨은 미국적 이미지와 유사한데, 본문의 표현을 빌자면 "최근의 분석에 따르면 미국은 200년 남짓으로 역사가 짧고 건국 신화가 없기에 미국인들에게는 수퍼맨이 자국 신화 속 영웅이 되어주기 때문"이라고 한다. 이런 연유로 수퍼맨에 대해서 과도하게 열광하는 것으로 볼 수 있으므로 정답은 (a)이다. 반면 수퍼맨이 평화의 상징이라든지 창조된 인물 중 최고라는 등의 본문에 언급되지 않은 극단적 표현은 일반적으로 정답이 아니다.

2. 주제가 선명하게 드러나는 문제는 아니지만, 보기 중에서 하나를 고르는 것이 객관식의 룰이기 때문에, 이에 근거해 보면 미국인들은 '선하고 희생적인 강한 권력에 대한 소망'이 있고, 이것이 수퍼맨을 통하여 반영이 되었다는 것이다. 그러므로 미국사회의 영웅주의의 시각을 말하는 (d)가 정답이 된다.

3. '수퍼맨의 여정은 조셉 캠벨이 숱한 신화와 종교, 전설 속에서 분석한 영웅담과 똑같다.'에서 (b)가 옳음을 알 수 있다. 수퍼맨은 실존하는 인물이 아니다. (a)는 전혀 말이 되지 않는 내용이다. 더불어 (c)의 경우에도 본문에는 수퍼맨을 섬기는 다양한 종교가 있다는 언급은 없다.

4. 이어지는 문단에 관한 내용을 추론하는 문제다. 일반적으로 마지막에 전개된 내용에서 힌트를 얻을 수 있다. 본문 마지막에 언급된 '선하고 희생적인 강한 권력에 대한 소망'에 대한 구체적 이유를 언급하는 (a)가 가장 적절하다.

정답 1.(a)　2.(d)　3.(b)　4.(a)

UNIT 08
Epicurean bean paste
칙릿

'칙릿(chick-lit)'은 20-30대 여성독자들을 겨냥한 영미 대중소설의 한 장르이다. 90년대 중반 영국에서 등장한 후 미국과 아시아, 동유럽으로 급속하게 퍼졌다. 주인공은 보통 미디어나 패션업계에 종사하는 젊은 도시 여성들로서, 성과 사랑, 일을 수다 떨듯 가볍게 풀어간다. 칙릿은 전 세계 베스트셀러 상위 목록에 주요 장르로 자리를 굳혔다. 책을 바탕으로 하거나 영향을 받은 영화와 TV 시리즈도 빅히트했다. 『브리짓 존스의 일기』, 『섹스 앤 더 시티』, 『쇼퍼홀릭』이 대표적이다. 칙릿은 단순한 하위 문학장르가 아니라 금세기초 주요한 문화 현상이 되고 있다. 소설 『악마는 프라다를 입는다』와 미혼여성 처세서들이 인기다. 할리우드는 남성이 아닌 여성이 주연인 칙릿의 영화 버전인 '베이브버스터(babebuster·babe는 아가씨라는 뜻)'에 주목하고 있다.

칙릿은 뭔가 대단한 철학이 담기지 않은 가벼운 읽을거리로 여겨지지만, 페미니스트들은 인정하는 듯하다. 전통적인 여성적 주제들을 새로운 방식으로 다뤄 '포스트 페미니즘'의 가능성이 있다는 것이다. 한마디로 칙릿은 성과 소비, 욕망, 육체성 등에서 과거와는 전혀 다른 가치를 지닌 '요즘 여자들'을 전제로 한다는 것이다. 『칙릿-새로운 여성소설』의 말로리 영은 "페미니즘이 완전히 뿌리내리지 못한 사회에서 칙릿은 페미니즘적 자유와 포스트 페미니즘의 소비주의를 동시에 만족시킨다"고 썼다. 칙릿에 맞서는, '요즘 남자들'을 대상으로 한 소설들은 '래드릿(lad-lit)'이라고 불린다. 영화 『사랑도 리콜이 되나요』, 『어바웃 어 보이』의 원작자로 잘 알려진 닉 혼비가 대표주자다. 칙릿의 여자들이 세속적 욕망추구에 거침없다면, 래드릿의 남자들은 시류에 둔감하고 타인과 관계맺기에 서툰 일종의 사회부적응자로 그려진다.

해설

1. 첫 번째 문장에서 '칙릿'의 대표적 여성상이 잘 드러나 있다. '미디어나 패션업계에 종사하는 젊은 도시 여성들로서 성과 사랑, 일을 수다 떨듯 가볍게 풀어간다'

2. 두 번째 문단에서 '래드릿'은 '칙릿'에 맞서는, '요즘 남자들'을 대상으로 한 소설이며, 현대 사회에서 남성들이 가지는 문제점에 초점을 맞추고 있다고 드러나 있다.

3. '칙릿'에 등장하는 여성 주인공들은 성과 사랑 그리고 직업 모두에 관심을 보인다고 했기에 (a)는 틀린 표현이며, 현재 '칙릿'은 전 세계적으로 붐을 일으키고 있다는 점에서 (b) 또한 틀린 진술이다. (c)에서 '칙릿'이 페미니즘과 대치된다고 했지만, '페미니스트들은 인정하는 듯하다. 전통적인 여성적 주제들을 새로운 방식으로 다뤄 포스트 페미니즘의 가능성이 있다는 것이다.' 부분과 말로리 영의 언급('페미니즘의 자유와 포스트 페미니즘의 소비주의를 만족시킨다')으로 보아 틀린 진술임을 알 수 있다. (e)는 첫 번째 문단 마지막에 등장한다.

4. '칙릿'의 가벼운 내용에도 불구하고, 페미니스트들은 이 장르를 인정한다는 내용이다. 그 이유는 바로 뒤에 제시되고 있다.

정답 1.(b) 2.(c) 3.(e) 4.(c)

UNIT 09
The essence of consumption
반소비

과시와 낭비를 현대 소비의 특징으로 본 이는 장 보드리야르다. 그는 현대의 영웅을 '낭비가'로 불렀다. 오늘날 영웅의 기준은 낭비의 규모라는 것이다. 실제로 사람들은 연예·스포츠 스타들이 누리는 천문학적 수치의 호화생활을 부러움 반, 놀라움 반으로 지켜본다. 마르셀 모스 역시 "재화의 낭비가 낭비하는 사람에게 특권과 위세를 가져다 준다"고 썼다. 부르디외에 따르면 소비는 계층 간 구별짓기의 표시이기도 하다. 명품의 소비는 내가 상류층이라는 증표다. 귀족적 품위를 뜻하는 'distinction'의 원 뜻이 차이·구별이듯 말이다. 누구나 자신보다 한 단계 높은 계층의 소비 방식을 따르며 신분상승을 꾀하려 한다. 경제적 무리를 감수하며 명품을 사들이거나, 거침없는 상류층의 낭비벽을 흉내내기도 한다. 민망하지만 '짝퉁'도 있다. 모두 소비의 본질이 과시라는 증거다.

여기서 딜레마가 생긴다. 풍요사회로 진입하면서 대중이 대량소비로 상류층을 좇는데, 이로 인해 이른바 명품의 대중화 현상이 발생한다. 너도 나도 명품을 들며 소비의 계층 표식이 불투명해지자 최상류층이 택한 전략이 바로 '반(反)소비' 또는 '과소 소비'다. 최고 갑부들이 소형차를 타고 서민 식당을 찾는 것이다. 이에 대해 박정자 상명대 교수는 자신의 책 『로빈슨 크루소의 사치』에서 이를 냉소했다. "중간 계층 20대 여성에게 루이비통 핸드백이 지위를 높여주는 차이 표시 기호라면, 재벌 오너에게는 5,000원짜리 순두부 한 그릇이 차이 표시 기호다. 그러한 검약은 극단적 힘의 표출의 한 형태"이다. 리스먼도 비슷한 지적을 했다. "기존의 상류층은 과소 소비를 하면서 벼락부자와 자신을 구별한다."

해설

1. 본문에서 말한 과소 소비는 돈이 많은 상류층이 오히려 대중화된 과소비에서 자신을 구별하는 수단으로 작용하고 있다. (c)가 이런 점을 가장 잘 드러낸다.

2. 일반인과 자신을 구별하는 상류층에서 일고 있는 현상인 과소 소비를 설명하는 글이다.

3. 본문의 구체적 내용을 묻고 있다. '너도 나도 명품을 들며 소비의 계층 표식이 불투명해지자, 최상류층이 택한 전략이 바로 '반(反)소비' 또는 '과소 소비'다.'에서 (b)가 정답임을 알 수 있다.

4. fake product는 모조품, 즉 짝퉁을 뜻하므로 knock-off가 정답이다. 참고로 museum pieces는 진기한 물건, precious stone은 보석, flagship은 주력상품을 뜻한다.

정답 1.(c) 2.(a) 3.(b) 4.(d)

UNIT 10
When the internet splits
인터넷 분열화

지난달 말 러시아는 국제 인터넷망을 대체할 국내용 네트워크 테스트를 성공적으로 마쳤다고 발표했다. 러시아는 이에 앞서 작년 초에 자국만의 독자적인 인터넷망을 만드는 법안을 통과시킨 바 있다. 만약 계획대로 이행할 경우 러시아인들은 세계인이 사용하는 국제 인터넷망으로부터 완전히 단절되거나, 그렇지 않더라도 러시아 정부가 승인한 정보만을 접할 수 있게 된다. 즉, 국가의 정보통제가 용이해지는 것이다.

러시아뿐 아니다. 중국은 이미 오래전부터 유투브, 구글 검색, 페이스북, 인스타그램, 넷플릭스 같은 서비스는 물론 해외의 유명 언론매체도 차단하는 소위 만리방화벽(Great Firewall) 정책을 취하고 있다. 이를 통해 자국의 인터넷 산업을 육성하는 한편, 정부가 원하지 않는 정보의 유통을 차단하고 있다. 이란과 북한 등의 국가에서도 비슷한 방법을 사용 중이다.

전문가들은 과거에는 전체주의 국가들에 국한되었던 이런 시도가 이제 '인터넷 분열화(internet disintegration)' 혹은 '스플린터넷(Splinternet=splint+internet)'이라는 하나의 세계적인 추세로 발전하고 있다고 우려한다. 중국, 러시아 외에도 심지어 서방세계 국가들 사이에서도 인터넷을 어떻게 관리하느냐를 두고 의견이 갈리면서 미국 버전의 인터넷과 유럽 버전의 인터넷이 탄생 중이다. 전자의 경우 국가안보와 범죄예방에 초점을 맞추고 있다면, 후자의 경우 프라이버시와 개인의 보호를 강조하는 새로운 규칙을 만들고 있다.

이렇게 국가와 지역별로 서로 다른 기준과 접근성을 가진 인터넷이 탄생하게 되면 국제적인 정보의 교환은 물론, 국제금융과 무역에도 영향을 줄 수밖에 없다. 과거 누구나 접근 가능한 '정보의 바다'로 비유되던 하나의 글로벌 인터넷이 서로 분리된 크고 작은 연못처럼 변할지도 모른다.

해설

1. 자유로운 정보의 장소이던 인터넷 공간이 이제 각국의 이해관계에 따라 분열되고 있다는 내용이 큰 축이다. 그러므로 정답은 a)이다.

2. 중국, 러시아, 북한, 이란 등은 자국의 인터넷 산업을 육성하는 한편, 자국이 승인한 정보만을 접할 수 있게 하여 정부가 원하지 않는 정보의 유통을 차단하고 있다. 그러므로 정답은 b)이다. c)처럼 서양에서 자국을 전체주의 국가로 볼 것이라는 내용이나, d)에 나온 국가 안보나 온라인 공격에 대한 대비는 전혀 본문에 없는 내용이다.

3. 러시아나 중국 같은 국가들은 표면적으로는 정보의 바다라는 인터넷 환경을 지지하는 것처럼 보이지만, 실상은 자국이 승인한 정보만을 접할 수 있게 하여 정부가 원하지 않는 정보의 유통을 차단하고자 한다. 결국 인터넷을 통한 정보의 통제를 하고자 하는 것이 목적이다. 정답은 c)이다.

4. '정보의 바다'로 비유되던 하나의 글로벌 인터넷이 각국이 추구하는 바에 따라 각각의 인터넷 버전이 발생할 조짐을 보이고 있다. 그러므로 분리되고 나눠진다는 의미가 들어가야 한다. 정답은 d)가 된다.

정답 1(a) 2(b) 3(c) 4(d)

UNIT 11
Barbie does Freud
키덜트

바비는 1959년 3월 9일 미국 국제 완구박람회에 처음 선보였다. 수백만 개가 팔렸는데, 이런 초기 성공은 아이들 장난감 인형은 모두 유아용 인형이었던 당시에 바비는 성숙한 몸매의 인형이었기 때문이었다. 바비 인형을 생산한 회사인 마텔사는 엄청난 돈을 벌었다. 다양한 국적과 인종이 선보였고, 다양한 직업도 가졌다. 가족도 생겼다. 친구와 동생들도 있다. 사실 바비의 친구인 미지는 임신했다. 미지는 바비가 단지 섹스 심벌이란 비판을 상쇄하기 위해 고안되었다. 바비는 또한 옷과 가구와 같이 관련된 장난감 상품이 팔리게 했다. 바비의 세상은 의상, 출판, 완구, 전자 제품을 포함해 실질적으로 무한했다. 바비는 요즘 유행하는 '원 소스 멀티 유즈'의 원조격이다.

전통적 장난감 시장에 최근의 변화는 바비에게 고민을 안겨주고 있다. 아이들이 더 이상 바비를 거들떠 보지 않는다. 요즘 여자아이들은 초등학생만 되면, 컴퓨터 게임, 비디오, 휴대폰과 MP3를 원한다. 그에 따라 전통적 장난감의 주요 고객층이 미취학 유아로 좁혀졌다. 더구나 세계적인 출산률 저하라는 요소도 있다. 이러한 각각의 요소가 전통적 완구업계에게 근심을 안겨주었다. 실제로 세계적인 장난감 유통업체 토이즈 알 어스는 미국에서만 70여 개의 매장을 없앴다. 어떤 회사는 선물업체로 탈바꿈했다.

지그문트 프로이트는 "아이의 빛나는 지능과 평균적인 어른의 나약한 정신 사이에 비참한 대조가 존재한다"라고 말했다. 장난감 회사는 이러한 생각을 마음에 새겼다. 일본 최대의 완구회사인 반다이는 장난감이 더 이상 아이들만의 것이 아님을 인식했다. 이 회사는 은퇴한 사람과 성인 여성을 겨냥한 인형을 현재 개발했다. 이들의 새로운 패션 인형인 사쿠라나는 자신만의 커리어를 가진 도시 여성이다. 반다이의 홍보담당자는 성공적으로 보이는 인형과 동일시하려는 성인 여성의 욕망에 어필할 것이며, 자신을 돌보듯 인형을 돌볼 것이라고 기대하고 있다. 이것이 바로 아이와 같은 어른인 새로 출현하는 키덜트이다. 바비의 경우조차 어른 마니아 콜렉터들이 가장 중요한 소비자들이다. 이들은 아이들이 등을 돌린 장난감을 통해 자신의 유년기를 늘리고 있다.

해설

1. 본문에 따르면 아이들이 초등학교(primary school)에 다니게 되면, 이제는 장난감을 거들떠보지 않고 컴퓨터 게임 등에 빠져든다고 하였으므로, 초등학교에 입학하면서 관심이 변해간다고 할 수 있다. 그러므로 정답은 (d)이다.

2. 주로 장난감 시장의 변화를 다루고 있다. 난관을 걷고 있는 전통적 장난감 시장에서 새로운 상품과 시장을 통해 해결책을 찾는 내용이 특히 세 번째 문단에 잘 드러나 있다.

3. 사쿠라나는 세련된 외모의 커리어 우먼 인형이며, '아이들이 등을 돌린 장난감을 통해 자신의 유년기를 늘리고 있다'를 통해 (d)를 유추할 수 있다. (b)와 같은 비교는 본문에 정확히 언급이 되지 않았으며, 바비의 초기 전성기 시대를 뛰어 넘을 정도로 인기가 있다고 보기는 무리가 있다. 사쿠라나는 주로 일하는 여성을 대상으로 한 제품이므로 보기 (c)는 옳지 않다.

4. '미지는 바비가 단지 섹스 심벌이란 비판을 상쇄하기 위해 고안되었다.'에서 (a)가 옳다는 것을 알 수 있다. '실제로 세계적인 장난감 유통업체 토이즈 알 어스는 미국에서만 70여 개의 매장을 없앴다.'로 보아 (c)도 옳다. 바비가 초기 성숙한 몸매와 함께 이후 다양한 소비자의 욕구에 맞게 변화를 거듭했기에 성공할 수 있었다. 즉, 단순히 바비가 성적 매력을 상징하는 몸매를 갖추었기에 성공한 것은 아니다.

정답 1.(d) 2.(a) 3.(d) 4.(b)

UNIT 12

Is a college degree necessary?
대학 졸업장이 꼭 필요한가?

"대학 졸업장은 있어야 밥 벌어 먹고산다." 예나 지금이나 한국 부모들이 하는 말이지만 나는 그게 사실인지 궁금하다. 대졸 20대 실업자 수는 매년 20만 명 정도이다. '대학 졸업장을 갖고도' 밥을 못 벌어먹는 청년이 절대 적지 않은 게 현실이다. '크리에이터' '아이돌 가수' 같은 직업이 롤 모델이 되면서 대학에 가지 않아도 되는 시절이 온 것처럼 느껴지기도 한다.

최근 월스트리트저널(WSJ) 보도를 보면 또 다른 생각이 든다. WSJ는 지난 9일 '미국 제조업은 블루칼라 일자리에 화이트칼라를 원한다'는 기사를 게재했다. 연방정부 데이터를 분석해봤더니 미국 제조업 공장에서 일하는 직원 가운데 대졸자 비율이 사상 최고를 기록했다는 것이다. 2000년 29%였던 대졸자 비율은 올해 40.9%까지 올라갔다. 같은 기간 고졸자 비율은 53.9%에서 43.1%로 낮아졌다. 이는 자동화 설비와 로봇의 도입 때문이다. 2012~2018년 전체 고용은 3% 줄었지만, 복잡한 기계를 다룰 수 있는 직원의 고용은 10% 늘었다. 단순직 노동자는 일자리를 잃은 반면, 첨단 기계 관련 교육을 받은 '대졸' 노동자는 증가했다.

한국 상황도 다르지 않다. 제조업체들은 자동화 설비와 로봇으로 사람의 자리를 대신한다. 제조업 일자리가 줄어드는 것 같지만, 첨단 기계를 다루는 일자리는 증가한다. 앞으로도 새로운 산업변화에 따라 '교육받은' 노동력의 수요는 계속 늘어날 게 틀림없다. 다시 '대학 졸업장이 있어야 밥 벌어먹는' 세상이 될까. 그건 아닐 것 같다. 산업의 변화에 맞는 전문교육을 받은 사람이 경쟁력을 갖게 될 것이다.

해설

1. 대학 학위가 직업을 구하는 데 필요한지에 대해 일부 부정적인 의견도 있지만, 향후 기술의 발전을 볼 때 전문교육을 받은 사람들만이 구직시장에서 살아남을 수 있다. 그러므로 대학교육은 필수적이라는 주제의 내용이고 정답은 c)이다.

2. 설비의 자동화와 로봇의 도입(the facility automation and introduction of robots)으로 인해, 이런 시설들을 운용할 수 있는 전문적인 교육을 통해 능력을 갖춘 대졸자들에 대한 수요가 증가하였다. 그러므로 정답은 a)이다.

3. 점점 더 자동화되어 가면서, 고졸자 (고용)비율은 53.9%에서 43.1%로 낮아졌다. 즉 고졸자들이 일자리를 잃어가고 있다는 d)가 정답이다. 참고로 b)의 경우는 이전의 최고치까지 올라갔는지는 본문에 전혀 언급이 없다.

4. 글의 마지막에 그렇다면 대학교육은 여전히 필요한지의 의문에 대해 그렇다는 응답이 나와야 하며, 이를 비유적으로 표현하여 기술의 발전으로 향후 일자리를 얻기 위하여 전문교육을 받아야 한다고 하였다. 그러므로 b)가 들어가는 것이 타당하다. d)는 마지막 문장과 전혀 관련 없는 일반적인 이야기일 뿐이다.

정답 1(c) 2(a) 3(d) 4(b)

UNIT 13

Sheep astray
학위 효과와 학력 검증

어느 사회든(통계적으로) 학력(學歷)이 높을수록 더 많은 임금을 받는다. 높은 학력을 얻기 위해 남보다 시간과 에너지를 더 들인 사람들은 더 많은 보상을 기대한다. 이같은 상관관계가 유지되려면 많이 배운 사람이 일을 더 잘한다는 전제 또한 충족되어야 한다.

문제는 학력과 능력이 일치하지 않을 때다. 만일 고학력에도 불구하고 능력이 기대에 미치지 못한다면 기업은 학력에 따라 임금을 더 주지 않으려 할 것이다. 많은 분야에서 학력이 중요하지 않은 것으로 간주되고 있다. 어떤 직종에선 고용주가 채용 단계에서부터 아예 학력을 따지지 않는 경우도 많다.

문제가 되는 것은 학력의 차이에 비해 임금 격차가 지나치게 큰 경우다. 경제학에선 이를 '학위 효과(sheepskin effect)'라고 한다. 이 이론에 따르면, 학력에 비해 능력의 차이가 크지 않은데, 학위만 따면 임금을 훨씬 많이 받는다는 것이다. 이런 현상이 만연하면 자연히 고학력 수요가 늘어날 수밖에 없다.

학력이 능력을 보증할 수 없음에도 기업이 인재를 채용할 때는 여전히 학력을 따진다. 지원자들의 능력을 판별할 수 있는 다른 기준이 마땅치 않기 때문이다. 업무의 성격상 고도의 지식과 전문성을 필요로 할 경우에는 더 높은 학력이 요구된다.

연구직이나 대학교수에게 일정 수준 이상의 학위와 연구 실적을 요구하는 이유다. 이때의 학위는 학위 효과가 아니라 그 일을 할 수 있느냐 없느냐를 가르는 자격요건이다. 허위 학위로 대학교수가 됐다는 것은 가짜 운전면허증으로 자동차를 운전하는 것이나 마찬가지다. 단순한 거짓말이 아니라 범죄 행위다.

해설

1. 학력과 실제 능력 사이의 상관관계가 주로 다뤄지고 있다.

2. '어떤 직종에선 고용주가 채용 단계에서부터 아예 학력을 따지지 않는 경우도 많다.'에 따르면 (a)는 옳다. (b)의 경우도 '이런 현상이 만연하면 자연히 고학력 수요가 늘어날 수밖에 없다.'와 바로 앞에 진술로 보아 옳다. '학력이 능력을 보증할 수 없음에도 기업이 인재를 채용할 때는 여전히 학력을 따진다. 지원자들의 능력을 판별할 수 있는 다른 기준이 마땅치 않기 때문이다.'에서 (c)도 옳음을 알 수 있다. (d)의 경우 마지막 문단을 참조하면 본문과 정반대의 내용임을 알 수 있다.

3. 고학력을 조장할 가능성이 큰 '학위 효과'를 묻고 있다. '학력에 비해 능력의 차이가 크지 않은데, 학위만 따면 임금을 훨씬 많이 받는다는 것이다.'로 보아 (c)가 가장 적절하다.

4. 학력이 높으면 임금을 많이 받는다는 경향을 볼 때, (b)가 가장 적절하다.

정답 1.(c) 2.(d) 3.(c) 4.(b)

UNIT 14

Get fathers involved
'출산 보이콧'을 막으려면

국민건강보험공단에서는 보험납부액을 소득 수준을 기준으로 1~5분위로 나눠 연구를 하였다. 전체 출산 중 4·5분위 고소득층 산모 비율은 2006년 39.2%에서 지난해 51.0%로 증가하여 11.9%가 늘어났다. 반면 쪼들리는 1·2분위 산모는 33.7%에서 22.4%로 11.3%가 줄었다. 중간인 3분위는 26.2%에서 26.0%로 엇비슷했다. 부자들만 마음껏 아이를 낳는 출산 불평등 시대가 도래한 것이다.

지난 6월 공개된 한 연구 결과도 이를 뒷받침해준다. 첫아이 출산 후 단산(斷産)하겠다는 여성의 44.6%가 "양육비·교육비 부담 때문"이라고 답했다. 가치관(16.3%), 일·가정 양립 곤란(15.4%), 소득·고용불안정(10.1%) 등 다른 이유는 상대가 못 됐다.

출산율이 안 오른다고 낙담만 할 건 없다. 그간에는 "국민소득이 늘면 국가 전체의 출산율은 떨어진다"는 게 정설이었다. 여성의 사회 진출이 크게 늘어나게 되면 아이 하나 키우는 데 들어가는 돈은 물론 엄마들의 희생, 즉 개인적 기회비용이 급등하는 까닭이다.

하지만 최근 수년간 노르웨이 등 북유럽에서는 소득 증가에도 출산율이 줄어들기는커녕 완만하게 반응하는 유례없는 상황이 벌어졌다. 이러한 현상을 인구학자들은 (출산율 곡선이 끝에서 구부러지는 J와 닮았다 해서) 'J커브 현상'이라 부른다. 유럽 국가라고 다 그런 건 아니다. 스페인·이탈리아 등 남유럽에서는 소득이 늘어도 출산율은 제자리걸음이다.

영국 옥스퍼드대 연구 결과 이들 지역에서 J 커브가 나타나지 않는 건 남녀 간의 뚜렷한 역할 분담 탓에 남자들이 가사와 양육을 돕지 않기 때문인 것으로 조사됐다. 즉 남편이 집안일을 돕는 게 일상화돼야 소득이 늘면 출산율도 증가한다는 얘기다. 흥미로운 건 아내가 가사를 도맡는 사회일수록 첫 아이만 낳고 그만두는 경우가 허다하다는 사실이다. 육아에 나 몰라라 하는 남편으로 인해 부담감을 느낀 부인들이 둘째 낳기를 거부한 탓이다.

해설

1. 첫 번째 단락과 두 번째 단락에서는 소득분위에 따라서 출산율도 달라지는 경향이 있으며 소득이 많을수록 출산율 또한 높아진다고 한다. 하지만 세 번째 단락에서는 낮은 출산율은 무조건 낙담할 일이 아니라고 한다. 여성이 사회에 진출하며 국민소득이 늘어 전체 출산율이 떨어진다는 것이 정설이었는데, 노르웨이와 북유럽 국가들처럼 소득이 많아질수록 출산율은 낮아졌다가 다시 급등하는 사례도 있으며 이는 집안일을 하고 육아를 할 때 남녀 간의 뚜렷한 역할 분담이 없고 남편 또한 아내를 도울 때 가능하다고 주장한다. 그러므로 이 글의 핵심은 낮은 출산율은 다시 높일 수 있다는 (d)가 된다.

2. 빈칸에는 국민소득이 증가할수록 출산율이 낮아진다는 점을 뒷받침해줄 원인이 들어가야 한다. 그러므로 더 많은 여성들이 사회에 진출할수록 육아에 드는 비용은 물론 엄마들의 희생이 급등한다는 (a)가 적합하다.

3. (d)의 오로지 부자들만이 가족의 크기, 즉 가족 규모를 선택할 수 있는 시대가 왔다는 것은 그들만이 몇 명의 아이를 낳을지를 결정할 수 있다는 밑줄 친 문장과 일치한다.

4. 서유럽에서 소득이 높아질수록 출신율이 낮아졌다가 다시 올라가는 J커브 현상이 일어나지 않는 것은 집안일과 육아에 있어서 남녀 간의 역할을 뚜렷하게 구분 짓기 때문이라고 한다. 남편이 집안일과 육아를 돕는다면 출산율은 소득과 함께 증가할 것이다. 그러므로 이러한 의미의 (a)가 정답이다. 본문에서는 일부 지역에서 남녀 역할을 구분 짓는 여부에 따라 출산율이 달라진다는 점을 말하지만 남성이 육아를 돕지 않으려 한다는 경향성을 나타내지는 않는다. 그러므로 (b)는 정답이 될 수 없으며 (c)와 (d)는 추론할 수 없다.

정답 1.(d) 2.(a) 3.(d) 4.(a)

UNIT 15

The right to be forgotten online
잊혀질 권리

충치 하나둘은 다 있듯, 누구에게나 부끄러운 과거는 있기 마련이다. 예전엔 망각 속에 묻으면 됐지만 이젠 시대가 변했다. 인터넷 검색으로 치욕스런 과거가 다 뜨는 세상이다. 마리오 코스테자란 스페인 변호사가 그런 꼴을 당했다. 1998년 빚에 몰린 그는 집을 경매처분 당할 위기에 몰린다. 그리고 불운하게도 이런 사실이 지역 신문에 실렸다. 그는 얼마 후 빚을 갚아 집은 건졌지만 차압당했다는 기사는 없어지지 않았다. 그의 이름을 검색하면 주택 압류 기사는 계속 떴다. 참다못한 그는 신문사와 구글을 상대로 기사를 삭제해 달라는 소송을 내 2014년 5월 유럽사법재판소(ECJ)에서 이겼다. 전 세계에서 처음으로 '잊혀질 권리'가 인정받는 순간이었다.

이 판결 뒤 구글에는 자신과 관련된 내용을 지워달라는 요청이 10개월간 21만여 건이나 쏟아졌다. 잊혀지려는 이들이 이토록 많았던 것이다. 잊혀질 권리는 최근에야 도입됐지만 사생활 중시의 전통이 강한 유럽을 중심으로 빠르게 뿌리 내리고 있다. 지난 3월 24일에는 잊혀질 권리를 제대로 보장하지 못했다는 이유로 구글이 프랑스 당국에 의해 10만 유로(1억3000만 원)의 벌금을 맞았다. 최근에는 '오블리비언'이란 소프트웨어까지 개발돼 개인의 명예와 관련된 자료들을 순식간에 지워준다.

하지만 논란도 적지 않다. 잊혀질 권리만 챙기면 공익 차원의 알 권리가 침해당한다. 2014년 영국의 한 성형외과 의사가 자신의 수술 결과에 대한 글들을 지워달라고 요구해 관철시킨 적이 있다. 하지만 대중들의 비난이 빗발쳐 결국 그 일은 취소되었다. 의사의 형편없는 수술 실력에 관한 고발 글들이었기 때문이다. 따라서 이런 정보를 없애는 건 올바른 의료 선택권을 막는 일이 된다. 같은 해 크로아티아 출신의 데잔 라직이란 피아니스트가 비슷한 일을 꾸미려다 실패했다. 그는 자신의 연주에 대한 악평이 워싱턴 포스트에 실리자 "악의에 찬 비열하고 자기주장만 펼치는 일방적이며 중상모략의 글이고 예술과는 무관"하다며 기사 삭제를 요구했다. 이 역시 타인의 평가를 무시하려는 잘못된 태도라는 이유로 받아들여지지 않았다.

해설

1. 이 글은 사생활 중시의 전통이 강한 유럽을 배경으로 개인의 치욕스러운 과거가 사생활 보호 차원에서 잊혀야 할지 혹은 공익 차원에서 공개되어야 할지에 관한 논란을 다루고 있다.

2. (c)와 (d)처럼 this는 바로 전 문장의 내용과 이어져야 하기 때문에 새로운 단락의 첫 문장으로서는 적합하지 않으며, 만일 this를 사용하는 것이 무관하다 해도 '오블리비언'이라는 소프트웨어 개발은 '잊혀질 권리'를 전체적으로 받아주는 내용이 아니다. 빈칸 이후의 내용은 '잊혀질 권리'의 부정적인 면이기 때문에 현재 논란이 되고 있다는 (a)가 정답이다.

3. 영국의 한 성형외과 의사는 자신의 형편없는 수술 실력을 고발한 글을 삭제할 것을 요청했고 크로아티아 출신의 피아니스트 데잔 라직 또한 연주에 대한 악평이 실린 기사를 삭제할 것을 요구했다. 이는 모두 사람들이 올바른 선택을 하는 데 필요한 타당한 정보로 여겨진다.

4. 마치 모든 사람들이 충치 하나둘은 있듯, 부끄러운 과거는 누구에게나 있다는 의미와 동일한 것은 (d)이다. 밑줄 친 문장의 부끄러운 과거는 (d)에서 다른 사람들이 몰랐으면 하는 면으로 표현된 것이다.

정답 1.(b) 2.(a) 3.(d) 4.(d)

UNIT 16

No such thing as a free bribe
스폰서

독일의 작곡가 리차드 바그너는 극적인 새로운 경지까지 오페라를 이끈 음악의 신동으로 현재 찬사를 받는다. 하지만, 그의 당대 적에게는 그가 소문난 구걸꾼이기도 했다. 생애 대부분을 빚에 시달렸기에, 바그너는 지인들에게 손을 벌리는 편지를 보냈다. 그는 자비를 구걸하는 분야에서는 전문가였다. 그의 친구 프란즈 리스트는 그의 장인이기도 했는데, 바그너는 교묘하게 자신의 부인을 이용해 동정을 샀다. "아내가 행복해진다면 도둑질도 마다하지 않을걸세."라고 그는 말했다.

그러나 그의 돈 타령은 가난 탓이 아니라 실은 호사스런 습성 때문이었다. 그의 걸작 '니벨룽겐의 반지'를 쓰는 내내 작곡하는 데 완벽한 환경을 만든답시고 소음과 햇빛을 흡수하는 특별 제작된 커튼, 최고의 카펫 그리고 실크 옷을 사느라 돈을 물쓰듯 써댔다. 그는 예술은 값싼 술이나 딱딱한 침대에서 만들어질 수 없다고 믿었다. 폴 존슨은 자신의 책 '창조자들에서 바그너를 '쾌락의 술고래'라고 불렀다.

바그너처럼 사치를 부리진 않더라도 예술가는 일반적으로 자신의 재능만으로 최고를 추구할 수 없다. 그래서 많은 유명한 예술가들은 돈 많은 예술 후원자에 의해서 태어난다. '교향곡의 아버지' 하이든은 평생 부유한 헝가리 귀족 에스테르하지 가문으로부터 끊임없이 실험할 자유를 얻었다. 하이든과 같이 금전적인 걱정 없이 자신의 원하는 만큼의 음악가와 리허설을 자유롭게 선택할 수 있을 만큼의 사치와 지원을 누린 작곡가는 거의 없다. 그러나 세상에 공짜는 없다. 자신의 주된 후원가인 니콜라스 왕자를 만족시키기 위해, 그는 현재 거의 연주되지 않는 왕자가 가장 좋아하는 현악기인 바리톤 삼중주곡을 126개나 써야 했다.

때로 후원자가 예술의 자유를 침범하기에 예술가들은 후원을 받는 선을 엄격하게 정하게 되었다. 이름 난 부부 작가 크리스토-잔 클로드는 후원을 거부하는 대신 대형 건물과 자연경관을 천으로 덮는 거대한 환경작품의 자금을 위해 은행 대출에 의존한다. 이들에게, 공짜를 제공하도록 허용된 유일한 사람은 산타뿐이다.

해설

1. 예술가와 후원자의 관계를 주로 다루는 글이다. 예술가는 금전적 지원을 위해 후원자가 필요한 반면, 후원자로 인해 예술적 자유가 침해될 가능성도 있다는 것이 주된 내용이므로 (c)가 가장 적절한 답이다.

2. '하이든은 평생 부유한 헝가리 귀족 에스테르하지 가문으로부터 끊임없이 실험할 수 있는 자유를 얻었다.'라는 정보만 제시되어 있다. 하이든이 가난한 집에서 태어났는지 알 수 없다. '그의 걸작 '니벨룽겐의 반지'를 쓰는 내내 작곡하는 데 완벽한 환경을 만든답시고 소음과 햇빛을 흡수하는 특별 제작된 커튼, 최고의 카펫 그리고 실크 옷을 사느라 돈을 물 쓰듯 써댔다. 그는 예술은 값싼 술이나 딱딱한 침대에서 만들어질 수 없다고 믿었다.'에서 (b)는 옳은 진술임을 알 수 있다. 본문 마지막 단락에서 크리스토-잔 클로드는 후원을 거부했다고 했으므로 (c)는 옳지 않다. (d)에서 교향곡이 아니라 바리톤 삼중주곡이다.

3. 산타는 보상을 바라지 않고 선물을 주는 대상이다. 즉 본문에서 후원자를 통해 금전적 지원을 받을 경우 예술적 자유를 방해 받는다고 했다. 실현 가능성이 없는 산타를 언급하면서 예술 자유를 구속 받느니 후원을 받지 않는 것이 낫다고 억실하고 있다. 따라서 (d)가 가장 적절한 해석이다.

4. '바그너는 교묘하게 자신의 부인을 이용해 동정을 샀다.'에서 (a)는 옳은 진술임을 알 수 있다.

정답 1.(c) 2.(b) 3.(d) 4.(a)

UNIT 17
A different perspective on love
진정한 사랑에 대하여

다큐 '님아, 그 강을 건너지 마오'가 100만 명 이상의 관객을 모으며 독립영화로는 이례적인 성공을 거두고 있다. 영화는 76년을 함께 해 온 노부부의 사랑 얘기다. 노부부는 한복을 맞춰 입고 젊은 연인들처럼 서로 장난을 치고 농담을 주고받는다. 그들이 이별할 때 객석은 눈물바다가 된다. 이 영화는 상업 대작 영화들 사이에서 흥행해 영화사의 획기적인 사건이 되었으며, 중장년층 뿐 아니라 젊은 관객들에게서도 호응을 얻어 다큐멘터리의 영역을 확대했다.

혹자는 '불멸의 사랑이라는 노인판 로맨스 판타지'라고 일축하지만, 사실 그렇게 단순한 영화는 아니다. 영화는 그저 사랑의 위대함이 아니라, 사랑하는 자의 자세에 대해 말한다. 89세 할머니는 영화 내내 "예쁘다"란 말을 입에 달고 산다. 새를 보고 감탄하고, 들꽃을 보고 감탄하며, 그 꽃을 귀에 꽂은 98세 할아버지를 보고 감탄한다. 할머니는 "불쌍하다"라는 말도 곧잘 한다. 집 잃은 강아지를 보고 가엾게 여겨 데려다 기른다. 할아버지가 세상을 떠났을 때도 "할아버지 불쌍해서 어쩌누"라며 울먹인다. 그녀는 "날 두고 가다니 난 어떻게 살라고"라는 통상 할 법한 말을 하는 사람이 아니다.

사랑의 본질은 사랑의 대상이 아니라 사랑하는 자의 태도에 있음을, 이 다큐멘터리 영화는 보여준다. 우리는 종종 사랑할 만한 상대를 찾지 못해서 혹은 상대가 사랑할 만한 사람이 아니라서 라고 하지만, 진정한 사랑은 서로 아끼고 사랑하려는 마음, 혹은 사랑 그 자체에 대한 자세에 있다. 또 그 사랑하는 마음이란 세상 만물에 대한 연민과 애정에서 시작하는 것이다.

진모영 감독은 "76년간 습관처럼 상대를 배려했던 부부"라며 "서로의 행동이 서로의 사랑을 불러들였다"고 했다. 영화 속 할아버지는 "평생 아내가 해준 음식을 두고 맛없다는 얘기를 한 적 없다. 그저 맛있으면 많이 먹고, 맛없으면 조금 먹으면 된다."고 했다. 이런 배려 깊은 태도가 바로 사랑하는 데 있어 필수적인 것이다.

해설

1. 영화에서 노부부는 오랜 세월을 함께 했음에도 젊은 연인들처럼 옷을 맞춰 입고 장난을 치는 모습을 보여준다. 나이와는 상관없이 사랑에 빠진 사람의 태도를 보여주기 때문에 관객들은 노부부에 대해 애틋한 감정을 갖게 되는 것이다.

2. 이 영화는 진정한 사랑은 우리가 사랑할 수 있는 완벽한 사람을 찾는 것이 아니라 서로를 사랑하고 아껴주는 마음에서 생기는 것이라고 말하고 있다. 그러므로 진정한 사랑을 찾는 사람들에게 이 영화를 권하는 것이다.

3. 첫 문장에서 "님아 그 강을 건너지 마오"라는 다큐가 독립영화치고는 이상하리만큼 흥행에 성공했다고 말해주고 있기에 정답은 (d)이다.

4. 빈칸 앞 문장에서 남편은 아내의 음식에 대해 불평한 적이 없고 맛이 없으면 적게 먹고 맛있으면 많이 먹었다고 한다. 이러한 행동은 남을 배려하는 행동이므로 정답은 (a)이다.

정답 1.(b) 2.(d) 3.(d) 4.(a)

UNIT 18
Playing with blocks
테트리스

1988년 비디오 오락 세계가 버블버블과 슈퍼마리오의 양대 산맥으로 나뉘있을 때, 블록으로 이뤄진 전혀 새로운 오락이 폭발적인 인기를 얻으며 데뷔한다. 모든 사람의 사랑을 받은 테트리스는 퍼즐게임으로 7개 형태의 블록을 조립하는 것이다. 다양한 색상의 블록이 화면 아래로 내려와 수평선을 만들어 완성되면 없어진다. 한 판이 끝날 때마다 목각으로 된 병정이 튀어나와 슬라브 민요 '칼린카'에 맞춰 익살스런 춤을 춘다.

이 러시아 터치(탄주법)는 1985년 구소련 과학아카데미에서 일하면서 이 게임을 디자인하고 프로그램을 짰던, 퍼즐을 아주 좋아했던 수학자였던 이 게임의 창시자 알렉세이 파지토브에게 찬사를 바치는 것이다. 그의 아이디어는 고대 로마에 기원을 둔 블록형 퍼즐 '펜토미노스'에 기원한다. 펜토미노스는 정사각형 5개로 구성된 각기 다른 모양의 블록 12개를 상자에 맞춰 넣는 게임이다. 그는 지나친 복잡함을 피하려고 블록 하나를 구성하는 정사각형 수를 4개로 줄여 7개의 블록을 만들 수 있도록 했고 4를 의미하는 그리스어의 접두사 '테트라에서 따서 게임에 이름을 붙였다.

여가 시간을 때우기 위해 만들어진 이 게임은 IBM PC의 번들로 끼워팔리면서 소련 밖에서 돌풍을 일으켰다. 2년도 채 안 되어, 유럽 뿐 아니라 미국, 일본에서도 소프트웨어 블록버스터가 되었다. 하지만 공산주의 국가 소련으로 인해 개발자는 이런 엄청난 성공으로 돈을 가져가지 못했다. 구소련이 저작권을 주장하는 데 거의 한 것이 없어, 이 게임이 1993년까지 법정 싸움에 휘말렸기 때문이다. 러시아가 마침내 끼어들었지만, 파지토브에게 돌아온 것이라고는 IBM 컴퓨터 한 대였다. 닌텐도 게임보이용으로만 7,000만 장 넘게 팔린 걸 생각하면 파지노프가 아직도 부아가 치밀지 않을까 생각할 수도 있다.

놀라운 건 이 게임이 다양한 버전으로 여전히 게이머에게 인기가 있다는 점이다. 테트리스는 PDA와 휴대폰과 같은 오늘 날의 전자장비에서도 지속적으로 요구되는 기능으로 탑재된다. 온라인 게임으로도 진화해 우리나라에서만 50만 명의 동시접속자 수를 유지하고 있다. 테트리스는 또한 그것을 베낀 수없이 많은 아류작을 낳았다. 이 게임의 가장 매력적인 부분은 바로 단순함에 있다. 누구나 부담 없이 덤빌 수 있다. 한 컴퓨터 게임 잡지는 "믿지 못할 만큼 단순하지만 방심할 수 없을 정도로 중독성을 가진" 게임이라고 말했다. 이 게임은 뇌의 활동을 높이고, 기억 감퇴를 예방하며, 스트레스의 부정적인 효과를 줄여주는 것으로 연구에서 밝혀졌다.

해설

1. 본문의 중심 소재는 테트리스다. 중심 소재가 반영되지 않은 보기 항은 모두 오답이다. (a)와 (b)는 중심 소재 설정 자체가 빗나갔다. (c)의 경우 테트리스의 부정석인 측면에 중심을 둔 '데트리스의 중독'이라고 주제를 잡았는데, 본문과 거리가 멀다. 테트리스의 기원부터 현재까지 인기가 있다는 내용을 가장 잘 드러낸 (d)가 정답이다.

2. bombshell이란 '폭발적인 인기'라는 뜻이다. 이러한 의미를 가장 잘 드러낸 것은 (a)이다.

3. 파지토브가 저작권 싸움으로부터 받은 것은 고작 컴퓨터 한 대라고 언급이 되어 있다. 따라서 (a)는 옳은 진술이다. 테트리스의 아류작이 많다고 했으므로 (c)는 옳지 않다. '러시아가 마침내 끼어들었지만, 파지토브에게 돌아온 것이라고는 IBM 컴퓨터 한 대였다.'에서 (d)도 옳지 않음을 알 수 있다.

4. '유럽 뿐 아니라 미국, 일본에서도 소프트웨어 블록버스터가 되었다'에서 (a)가 틀린 진술임을 알 수 있다. 아프리카는 포함이 되지 않는다. '다양한 색상의 블록이 화면 아래로 내려와 수평선을 만들어 완성되면 없어진다.'와 'The Russian touch is a tribute to the game's creator'에서 (b), (c) 모두 옳다는 것을 알 수 있다. 두 번째 문단 마지막에서 (d)의 내용을 확인할 수 있다.

정답 1.(d) 2.(a) 3.(a) 4.(a)

UNIT 19

Cyberbullying is a crime
악플은 범죄다

뉴스 범람의 시대라 벌써 유명인들의 사망에 대한 울림이 사그라지고 있지만, 고(故) 최진리씨(설리)와 고(故) 구하라씨의 명복을 빈다. 얼마나 지났다고, 이들이 사망한 지 얼마 안 돼서, 이젠 심지어 펭귄 캐릭터 펭수까지 악플에 시달린다고 한다. 악플러 중 상당수가 별생각 없이 악플을 단다는 점이 어처구니없다. 최근 한 설문조사(인크루트·두잇서베이) 결과에 따르면 성인 3,162명 중 '악플을 단 경험이 있다'는 응답자가 전체의 5%였다. 악플을 단 이유는 분노(55%), 시기와 질투(16%), 스트레스 해소(15%), 단순 장난(9%)이었다. 악플러 다섯 중 한 명은 익명성 뒤에 숨어 스트레스를 풀거나 심심풀이를 했던 셈이다. 국가 운명에 대한 고매한 비전과 치밀한 분석, 노벨문학상급 표현을 악플에 기대하는 건 아니지만 좀 심하다.

악플은 국제사회에서도 골칫거리다. 버락 오바마 전 미국 대통령은 지난달 사이버 왕따 문화인 '캔슬 문화(cancel culture·비판 대상의 존재 자체를 '소멸'시킨다는 온라인 왕따)'에 대한 반대 목소리를 냈다. 영국 윌리엄 왕세손은 2017년부터 사이버 왕따(cyber bullying) 반대 캠페인을 이끌고 있다. 국경없는 기자회(RSF)도 지난해 악플의 폐해를 다룬 보고서를 펴냈는데, 스웨덴·핀란드에서도 약 3분의 1의 기자들이 악플에 시달리고 있다고 한다. 영국의 독립 언론인 존 론슨은 악플 등 인터넷 스캔들로 황폐해진 경우들을 추려서 『공개 망신을 당했다고? (So You've Been Publicly Shamed)』라는 제목의 책을 냈다. 악플 피해자뿐 아니라 악플러를 직접 찾아가 속내를 인터뷰하였다. 대다수 악플러는 "이렇게까지 일이 커질 줄은 몰랐다"거나 "실제 아는 사람이었으면 그렇게까지 공격하진 못했을 것"이라며 미안해한다. 하지만 사람 목숨까지 앗아갈 수 있는 악플은 범죄다.

해설

1. 악플로 인하여 목숨을 끊는 사람이 있을 정도로 심각하지만, 악플을 다는 사람들은 단지 스트레스 해소나 재미를 위해서 하는 사람들이 있을 정도로 경각심이 없는 현실을 알리고 있다. 그러므로 사이버 폭력인 악플의 문제점과 부작용에 대하여 언급한 c)가 정답이다.

2. 영국의 독립 언론인 존 론슨은 자신의 저서 『공개 망신을 당했다고? (So You've Been Publicly Shamed)』에서 악플러들을 상대로 인터뷰를 진행하였고, 그 결과 이들은 인터넷의 익명성을 이용하여 악플을 달고 있다는 것을 보여주었다. 그러므로 악플러는 키보드의 익명성 뒤에 숨고 있다는 b)가 정답이다.

3. 존 론슨이 사이버불링에 대하여 자신의 경험을 바탕으로 책을 냈다는 a)는 틀린 진술이다. 일부는 악플을 재미나 스트레스 해소로 달았다고 하였으므로 b)는 올바른 진술이고, d)처럼 유명인들의 잇따른 죽음으로 사람들이 점차 이러한 충격에 면역되어 간다는 것 역시 올바른 진술이다. 그러므로 정답은 a)이다.

4. 빈칸에는 고귀한 비전이나 노벨 문학상 수준의 표현에 상응하는 긍정적인 내용이어야 한다. 그래야만 그 정도로 대단한 것을 기대한 것은 아니지만, 너무 지나치다는 내용으로 이어질 수 있다. 그러므로 정답은 d)이다.

정답 1(c) 2(b) 3(a) 4(d)

UNIT 20

A war over religious rights
부르카 전쟁 인권과 종교의 자유

이슬람 여성들은 율법에 따라 부르카, 니캅, 히잡, 차도르를 입는다. 이 중 부르카는 전신을 감싸는 겉옷으로, 눈 주변은 베일로 가린다. 이슬람 여성들이 공공장소에서 부르카나 기타 얼굴을 가리는 복장의 착용을 금지하도록 한 것을 두고 유럽에서 논쟁이 한창이다.

이런 종교적 복장의 착용을 가장 먼저 금지한 나라가 프랑스다. 프랑스는 1789년 대혁명 이래 라이시테(국가의 비종교성)라고 하는 정종분리(政宗分離: 정치와 종교의 분리)의 원칙이 확고해 공공장소에서 종교적 상징물을 드러내는 것을 위헌으로 규정한다. 학교나 공공장소에 기독교의 상징인 십자가도 보이게 하지 못한다.

그러나 프랑스에서 종교적 복장인 히잡과 부르카 등의 착용을 금지하자, 이슬람교도들은 이것이 '종교탄압'에 가깝다며 격렬히 항의했다. 2009년에는 당시 대통령이었던 사르코지가 부르카를 두고 "이 나라에 사회 생활과 단절되고 자신의 정체성도 빼앗긴 채 옷감으로 된 감옥에 사는 여성이 있다는 사실을 용납할 수 없다"고 했다. 이후 부르카 금지법이 제정되고 2011년 4월 1일 발효되었다. 이를 어기고 온 몸을 감싸는 복장을 하는 여성은 150유로(약 20만원), 여성들에게 그러한 복장을 착용하도록 강요한 사람에게는 3만 유로(약 4,100만원)까지 벌금이 부과된다.

일부 이슬람교도들이 이 법안이 차별적이라고 주장하며 EU 법원에 고소했지만 EU 법원은 올해 7월 초 프랑스 법이 유효하다는 판결을 내렸다. 그 근거는 그런 옷이 여성의 인권을 침해한다는 것이었다. 이 판결이 나오자 독일과 오스트리아 등 EU 회원국들과, EU 회원국이 아닌 스위스까지 반 부르카법을 만들겠다고 준비 하고 있다.

이들 나라들에는 관광과 쇼핑에 거금을 쓰는 이슬람 부호들이 많이 온다. 따라서 이 법의 반대자들은 전국적으로 100여 명에 불과한 부르카 착용 여성들에게밖에 영향을 주지 못하는 이 법이 관광수입에 타격을 줄 수 있다고 주장한다. 반면 찬성론자들은 여성의 인권과 존엄을 지켜야 한다고 주장하고 있다. 찬성론자들은 사람이 사람과 얘기할 때는 복면이 아니라 얼굴을 마주보고 할 수 있어야 한다고 말한다.

해설

1. 프랑스는 1789년 프랑스 혁명 이후 종교적 복장을 금지했고 이슬람 여성들이 온몸을 가리는 것을 금지했다. 지문에서는 여성들의 인권을 내세워 이를 반대하는 프랑스와 이슬람교도의 항의에 대해 다루고 있다. 그러므로 정답은 (d)이다.

2. 네 번째 단락에서 EU 법원은 여성의 인권을 침해한다는 이유로 프랑스 법의 손을 들어주었다는 내용이 있다. 그러므로 정답은 여성을 보호하는 것이 가장 중요하다고 생각했다는 (a)이다.

3. 기독교를 기반으로 하고 인권을 중시하는 유럽에서 테러, 시리아와 이라크의 내전, 이슬람 세계의 불안정은 전체적으로 좋지 않은 인상을 주고 있다. 이로 인해 다른 유럽 국가들도 여성 인권을 침해한다고 여겨지는 이슬람교의 복장을 금지할 것으로 보인다.

4. 복장 착용을 금지하는 측의 주장은 이슬람 부호들이 이 법으로 인해 발길을 끊는다면 관광산업에 많은 영향을 미칠 것이라는 것이다.

정답 1.(d) 2.(a) 3.(d) 4.(c)

Part 3

UNIT 01

Racing toward a dissonant drive
전기자동차와 소음

모터사이클 '할리 데이비슨'의 특징은 무엇보다 우렁찬 배기음이다. 엔진의 연소 주기를 사람의 심장 박동수와 연계시켰다고 한다. 시동을 거는 순간 사랑에 빠진 젊은이의 심장이 고동치는 것처럼 둥둥거린다. 할리는 특유의 배기음에 대해 1944년 특허를 출원하기도 했지만, 복잡한 서류 절차에 결국 포기했다. 한국에 수입되는 할리는 현지 법규에 따라 배기음이 80데시벨(db) 이하로 조정돼 있다. 그래서, 따로 조작하지 않는 한 원래의 우렁찬 배기음을 감상하기 어렵다. 스포츠카의 대명사 페라리도 마무리에서 가장 신경 쓰는 것이 엔진 배기음이라고 한다. 낮은 금속성 박동 소리는 이탈리아 명차에 대한 스포츠카 매니어들의 탄성을 자아낸다. 자동차 경주 팬들에 따르면 F1의 묘미도 레이싱카가 내뱉는 찢어지는 듯한 굉음이라고 한다.

물론 엔진 소음은 로맨틱한 매력 말고도 실용적인 목적이 있다. 고급 세단은 너무 조용해서 시동이 꺼진 줄 알고 다시 키를 돌리는 경우가 있다. 그래서 재규어는 시동이 켜질 때 '테너 C' 높이로 조절된 엔진음을 차 내로 흘려보낸다고 한다. 이에 반해 전기자동차는 연소 기관이 아닌 전기 모터로 움직이니 소음이 없다. 시속 40㎞ 이하로 달리면 바퀴와 노면 사이에 마찰음도 없다. 이렇게 소음이 너무 없으니 탑승자와 보행자의 안전에 적신호가 켜진 것이다. 다른 차들이나 도로를 건너는 사람들이 차가 다가오는 소리를 듣지 못하기 때문에, 사고의 가능성도 크게 증가한다. 한때는 고급차 제조사들의 자부심이었던 이 무소음이 안전상의 문제로 대두된 것이다. 현재 미국 의회는 전기자동차에 안전 차원의 최소 소음을 강제하는 방안을 검토 중이다.

해설

1. 본문은 소음으로 치부될 수 있는 소리의 중요성에 관한 글이다. 할리 데이비슨의 심장이 고동치는 소리에서부터 페라리의 엔진 배기음, 재규어의 테너 C로 맞춰진 엔진음, 소리가 나지 않아 문제인 전기자동차에 최소 소음을 강제하려고 하는 움직임까지. 이 모두를 아우르는 것이 (a)이다.

2. (a)의 경우 재규어는 음악을 내보내는 것이 아니라 엔진음을 테너 C로 내보낸다고 했으며, (c)의 경우 전기자동차가 사고의 가능성이 큰 이유는 주행(driving)의 문제가 아니라 무소음이라고 했다. (d)의 경우 우렁찬 엔진 배기음을 강조한 것이므로 본문과 다르다. 정답은 (b)로 두 번째 문단의 'They do not even make noise from the friction ... at speeds less than 40 kilometers per hour' 부분을 다시 설명하고 있다.

3. 마지막 부분은 전기자동차에 최소 소음을 강제하는 방안을 검토하고 있다는 내용으로 끝나므로, 이와 이어지는 내용이 와야 한다. 따라서 정답은 새로운 법안에 관한 내용인 (d)가 정답이 된다.

4. 자동차 소음의 정도(level)가 중요하다는 내용은 할리 데이비슨, 페라리, 재규어 등에 해당하고 자동차 소음의 부족(lack)은 전기자동차에 해당하므로 정답은 (b)가 적합하다.

정답 1.(a) 2.(b) 3.(d) 4.(b)

UNIT 02
Written in wrinkles
보톡스

요즘 주름을 펴 주는 대표적인 약은 바로 보톡스(Botox)다. 보톡스는 상품명이지만 보툴리눔 독소를 이용한 여러 주름 개선제를 사실상 통칭한다. 이 약은 약효의 지속기간이 3~6개월에 그치고, 자연스러운 얼굴 표정을 짓기가 어렵다는 것이 약점이다. 그러나 주름 제거 수술에 비해 비용 부담이 적다는 점과 사람들이 실제 나이보다 젊어 보이고 싶어하기 때문에 인기가 있다. 보톡스는 의약품 분야에서 비아그라에 이어 No. 2의 브랜드 파워를 갖고 있다.

약 이름 끝에 붙은 'tox'는 '독소(toxin)에서 딴 것이다. 보툴리눔 독소는 자연 발생하며, 식중독을 일으킨다. 인공 유해물질 중 독성이 최고라는 다이옥신보다 최소 100배는 더 유독하다. 그래서 설사·복통에 그치는 일반 식중독과는 달리 보툴리눔 식중독의 치사율은 50%에 달한다. 한마디로 보툴리눔은 가장 치명적인 독소이다.

지난달 미국 식품의약청(FDA)이 보톡스의 안전성에 우려를 표명했다. 보톡스 시판 뒤 16명이 보톡스 치료를 받고 부작용으로 숨졌다고 지난달 말 미국의 시민단체인 '퍼블릭 시티즌'이 발표한 것이 계기였다. 우리 식약청도 조치를 취했다. 보톡스를 과량 주사하면 숨쉬기와 음식을 씹어 넘기기가 힘들어져 생명이 위태로워질 수 있다고 봐서다. 여기서도 문제는 용량 과다이다. 희생자는 대부분 근육 경련을 보톡스로 일시 해소하려 했던 뇌성마비 환자였다. 이들에겐 주름을 펼 때 쓰는 양의 28배가 주입됐다.

주름은 그 사람의 인생을 보여주는 자취이다. 20대 후반에 눈가부터 생기기 시작해 30대 후반엔 이마, 40대 후반엔 입가로 옮겨가면서 세월의 궤적(軌跡)을 남긴다. "눈가 주름은 이성(理性), 이마 주름은 인생, 입가 주름은 천리(天理)를 알만한 나이에 생긴다"는 속담이 있다.

해설

1. (a)는 마지막 문단만 설명할 수 있고, (b)는 첫 번째 문단에만 해당되므로 전체 주제가 되지 못한다. 본문에서는 보톡스의 독성과 위험성을 설명하고 있으므로 정답은 (c)가 된다. 마지막으로 (d)는 본문과 무관해서 답이 될 수 없다.

2. 보톡스를 맞고 사망한 이들은 대부분 근육 경련을 보톡스로 치료하려고 했던 뇌성마비 환자라고 세 번째 문단에서 설명하고 있다. 주름 개선을 위한 양보다 28배가 더 많았다고 한 부분을 통해 과다 주입(overdose)이 있었음을 알 수 있으므로 정답은 (a)가 된다. 식약청이 관심을 보이고 있기 때문에 (b)는 적절하지 않으며, 취급 주의로 보톡스의 독성이 줄어드는 것이 아니므로 (c)도 적절하지 않다. 보톡스의 위험을 모르고 구입한 사람들이 사망한 것도 있겠지만, 치료 중 목숨을 잃었다고 나오기 때문에 (d)는 이 전체를 설명하지 못한다.

3. 보톡스는 부작용이 있다고 했으며, 보톡스를 맞으면 표정 짓기가 어렵다고는 했지만 아픔을 참고 지내야 한다는 내용은 등장하지 않는다. 그리고 약효가 떨어질 때쯤 주름이 더 많아진다는 내용도 본문과는 무관하다. 정답은 (d)로 보톡스를 맞는 주요 목적은 주름 개선과 젊어 보이려는 갈망이라고 첫 번째 문단에서 설명하고 있다.

4. 보톡스를 맞는다고 대부분 사망하는 것은 아니므로 (a)는 어색하며, 얼굴 주름을 일시적이 아닌 영구적으로 제거해준다는 것은 본문과 다르므로 (c)도 답이 될 수 없다. 정답은 (b)로 일시적으로 주름이 사라진다는 점과 얼굴 표정을 짓기 어렵다는 점을 설명하고 있다.

정답 1.(c) 2.(a) 3.(d) 4.(b)

UNIT 03
Always polite, never complaining
밤새 일하고도 불평 없는 그 직원

"(그 모범적인 직원은) 지각하는 적이 없고, 휴가 간다고 자리를 비우지도 않고, 고객들에게 항상 예의 바르고 심지어 비싼 상품을 사도록 합니다." 미국 패스트푸드 체인 하디스의 모기업 CKE의 앤드류 퍼즈더 전 최고경영자는 2017년 미국 경제지와 인터뷰에서 한 직원을 이렇게 극찬했다. 이 직원은 바로 매장 입구에 비치된 키오스크였다. 퍼즈더는 한걸음 더 나아가 "(사람) 직원을 고용하지 않는(Employee-free) 매장을 시도해 볼 예정이라고 밝히기도 했다.

인간이 기계에 일자리를 내주는 곳은 하디스 같은 소규모 매장 뿐이 아니다. 산업용 로봇은 제조라인에서 대규모 노동력을 공장 밖으로 내몬다. 국제로봇연맹(IFR)의 '세계 로보틱스 보고서'에 따르면 2017년 한해에만 전세계에서 산업용 로봇이 38만1000대 팔렸다. 휴대폰 부품을 만드는 중국의 창잉 정밀기술은 최근 650명이 할 일을 로봇 60대로 대체했다. 그러자 연간 8000대의 생산량이 2만1000대로 늘었고 불량률은 25%에서 5%로 크게 줄었다. 창잉의 경우처럼 로봇 한대가 약 10명의 일을 대신한다고 가정하면 지난해에만 전세계에서 381만명의 일자리가 로봇으로 대체됐다는 결론이 나온다.

고용 유연성이 떨어져 힘겹게 투쟁하는 한국 CEO들은 어떤 선택을 하고 있을까? 노동자 1만명당 로봇 대수에서 한국은 631대로 압도적 세계 1위다. 세계 평균의 8배를 웃돈다. 제조 강국 독일(309대), 일본(303대)도 로봇 고용에선 한국에 상대가 안 된다. 초과근무에도 불평 없고, 파업하지도 않고, 휴식조차 없는 로봇직원을 CEO들은 사랑하지 않을 수 없다.

약 100년 전 2차 산업혁명은 대량 생산 혁명이었다. 대량 생산은 대량 고용으로 가능했다. 공채로 수 천, 수 만명을 뽑아 교육시킨 후 생산라인에 일제 투입하는 일은 그래서 그간 유효했다. 대규모로 일자리를 제공했던 제조업은 자동화 시대, 산업 전환의 시대를 맞아 더는 과거처럼 고용할 수 없다는 신호를 보내고 있다. 창의적인 젊은이들에게 새 일자리의 보고가 될 4차 산업혁명은 그래서 더 절실한 이유이다.

해설

1. 시간을 엄수하며, 자신의 일에 충실하고, 고객 응대도 잘 하는 사원이 최고의 사원이라고 적고 있다. 본문에서 'they never take a vacation'이라는 표현을 바꿔 써서 휴가를 요청하지도 않는다는 얘기한 d)가 정답이다.

2. 노동자 1만 명 당 로봇 대수에서 한국은 631대로 압도적 세계 1위(There are 631 robots per 10,000 workers in Korea, the highest in the world)라고 하였으므로, 한국 회사들이 다른 나라들보다 근로자 1인당 더 많은 로봇을 보유하고 있다는 b)가 올바른 정답이다.

3. 앞 문장에서 인간이 기계에 일자리를 내주는 곳은 하디스 같은 소규모 매장 뿐이 아니라고 적고 있다. 그러므로 산업용 로봇이 생산라인을 장악하는 대규모 공장에서도 인간이 기계에 일자리를 내준다는 표현이 나와야 한다. 결국 산업용 로봇이 장악하면서 인간 근로자들이 대규모로 일자리를 잃고 있다는 c)가 정답이다.

4. 현재의 경제구조로 보면 대규모로 일자리를 제공했던 제조업의 시대는 가고, 자동화 시대, 산업 전환의 시대를 맞아 더는 과거처럼 고용할 수 없다. 그러므로 창의적인 젊은이들에게 새 일자리의 보고가 될 4차 산업혁명은 더욱 절실한 것이다. a)가 정답이다.

정답 1.(d) 2.(b) 3.(c) 4.(a)

UNIT 04
Flying pandemics
조류 인플루엔자

1918년 3월 11일에 미국 캔자스 주 포트 라일리의 캠프 펀스턴 내 군병원은 하루 종일 비슷한 증상을 보이는 유난히 많은 군인들을 치료하느라 분주했다. '감기에 걸린 것 같다'는 병사가 수백 명 넘게 몰려왔기 때문이다. 이들 중 일부는 며칠 뒤 1차 대전에 참전하기 위해 유럽으로 향했다. 그해 5월 프랑스군의 참호에서 '감기'가 돌았다. 6월엔 스페인에서만 800만여 명의 '감기' 환자가 발생했다. 이 역병을 프랑스인은 '스페인 감기', 스페인인은 '프랑스 감기'라 불렀다. 인플루엔자는 프랑스군이 독일군을 향해 쏘아 올린 포탄보다 더 위력적이었다. 그해 여름이 끝날 무렵 인플루엔자는 독일군 막사를 덮쳤고 독일에서만 40만 명이 생명을 잃었다. 재앙은 아시아로 건너가 인도·중국을 휩쓸었다. 1918년 전 세계적으로 퍼진 유행성 전염병(pandemic)은 이듬해까지 지속되었고, 세계는 패닉 상태에 빠졌다. 더 놀라운 사실은 대재앙이 너무 빨리 잊혔다는 것이다. 지금도 가장 치명적인 유행병이었던 중세의 흑사병(黑死病)은 알아도 20세기의 '스페인 감기'는 모르는 사람이 더 많다. 그 대재앙의 주 원인은 감기 바이러스가 아니고, 인플루엔자(독감) 바이러스였다. 2005년 미 군사병리연구소 제프리 토벤버거 박사는 1918년 발생한 유행성 전염병의 바이러스 유전자 물질을 밝혀내는 데 성공한다. 그는 보존 조직에서 1918년의 바이러스 샘플을 추출해서 게놈 배열을 한 업적으로 잘 알려졌다. 그는 조류독감이 발생했던 해인 1918년에 사망한 후 80년 동안 알래스카의 얼음 속에 묻혀있던 원주민 남성의 사체에 대한 심층적인 연구를 수행했다. 그도 처음엔 '범인'이 돼지일 것으로 봤다. 돼지인플루엔자는 인수공통 전염병으로 사람에게 전염 가능하다. 그러나 시신에서 얻은 바이러스 유전자를 면밀히 검토한 뒤 조류에서 유래했다는 결론을 내린다.

해설

1. 1차 대전 당시 독감 바이러스는 유행성 전염병을 일으켰으므로 엄청난 파괴력을 지녔음을 짐작할 수 있다. 그리고 독감에 걸린 미군들이 유럽에 참전하러 가면서 프랑스와 스페인, 독일에서 바이러스가 퍼졌으므로 전쟁이 없었다면 그렇게까지 심각한 지경에 이르지 않았을지 모른다는 (c)는 일리가 있다. 중세의 흑사병은 알아도 당시의 독감은 금세 잊혔다고 했으므로 (d)도 바른 추론이다. 정답은 (b)로 치료약을 과학자들이 개발했다는 내용은 등장하지 않는다.

2. 스페인과 프랑스에서 서로 상대 국가의 독감이라고 부른 것은 바이러스 유입에 대한 책임을 떠넘기려 한 것이므로, 그리고 실제로 어디에서 유입됐는지 알지 못한 것이므로 정답은 (c)가 적합하다.

3. 처음에는 돼지일 것으로 의심했지만 알고 보니 조류에서 넘어온 것이라고 마지막 부분에 설명되어 있다.

4. 유행병이 있던 해 숨져 80년 간 알래스카의 얼음 속에 묻혀 있던 원주민의 시신에서 바이러스 샘플을 추출한 것이므로 (a)와 (b)는 적합하지 않다. 그리고 프랑스에 바이러스를 옮겨온 나라는 미국이었다. 정답은 (d)로 원래는 돼지에서 유래했을 것으로 생각했지만 사실은 조류에서 넘어온 것이었다고 나온다.

정답 1.(b) 2.(c) 3.(a) 4.(d)

UNIT 05

Unfounded fears
공포의 문화

1982년 4월 19일, 미국 NBC 방송은 'DPT: 백신 룰렛'이라는 한 시간짜리 프로그램을 방영했다. 백일해 백신 성분이 신경에 끔찍한 손상을 일으켜 죽음을 초래할 수 있다는 내용이었다. 심한 장애를 앓는 어린이의 영상과 가슴 저미는 부모들의 증언을 내보냈다. 이 내용은 그 후 몇 주에 걸쳐 NBC의 '투데이 쇼'와 여러 신문에서 다시 보도됐다. 그러자 전국의 모든 소아과 의사들에게 전화가 쇄도했다. (예방접종을 받은) 자기 자녀들이 곧 죽게 되느냐고 부모들이 문의했기 때문이다.

이에 대해 FDA(식품의약국)는 즉시 45쪽에 달하는 백신이 사망이나 심각한 합병증을 유발할 가능성은 극히 희박하다는 반박 자료를 배포했다. 그러나 대부분의 언론은 이 같은 해명을 축소 보도했다. 몇 주 만에 백신 피해자 단체가 결성돼 조직적으로 모금과 홍보 활동을 시작했다. 1984년에 이르자 항의 집회, 피해자 단체의 청문회 증언, 수많은 소송에 시달리다 못해 DPT 백신 제조업체 세 곳 가운데 두 곳이 문을 닫았다. 몇 년 후 100만 명에 가까운 어린이를 대상으로 한 조사연구 결과 백신의 위험은 터무니없이 과장된 것으로 밝혀졌다.

그렇다면 피해는 어떠했을까? 미국에선 부모들이 백신 접종을 꺼린 탓으로 백일해에 걸리는 아이들이 늘어났다. 백신이든 아니든 실질적인 위험이 그토록 작은데도 대중이 우려하는 이유는 무엇일까? 『공포의 문화(The Culture of Fear)』를 쓴 미국 사회학자 배리 글래스너는 '공포의 상인'들을 지목한다. 신문 판매 부수나 시청률을 높이기 위해 공포를 선전하는 언론매체, 공포 분위기를 조장해 표를 얻고 정작 중요한 사회 이슈들로부터 국민의 이목을 돌려놓는 정치인들, 사회의 공포를 자신의 마케팅에 동원하는 각종 단체들 모두가 주된 책임이 있다는 것이다.

해설

1. 세 번째 문단에서 말하는 '공포의 문화'가 무엇인지는 그 문단의 마지막 줄에 잘 나타나 있다. 한마디로 언론이나 정치인들, 각종 단체 등이 공포를 이용해 자신들에게 유리한 방향으로 이용한다는 것이다. 그리고 본문 전체로 보면 나중에 그다지 위험하지 않다고 판명된 DPT의 위험성에 대한 공포로 인해 일반인들이 오히려 피해를 보았다는 것이 본문의 요지이다. 따라서 (b)와 (c)보다 더 근원적 내용인 (d)가 정답이 된다.

2. 본문은 백신이나 백일해가 위험하거나 심각한 질병이라는 것을 말하고 있는 것이 아니다. 오히려 공포심에 질려 사람들이 사실이 아닌 것을 사실로 받아들일 수 있다는 내용이므로 (b)가 정답으로 적합하다.

3. 결국 DPT가 그다지 위험하지 않은 것으로 두 번째 문단의 마지막 줄에 나온다. 따라서 실상은 DPT가 위험하다고 했던 것만큼 실제로는 위험하지 않다는 내용의 (a)가 정답이 된다.

4. 다시 말하지만 이 글은 백신이나 백일해에 대한 내용이 아니다. 따라서 (a)와 (d)는 제목으로 적합하지 않다. 세 번째 문단의 내용이 글의 저자가 지적하고 싶은 본질적 내용으로, 공포를 하나의 도구로 사용한다는 (b)가 제목으로 가장 적합하다.

정답 1.(d) 2.(b) 3.(a) 4.(b)

UNIT 06

Insane or sane?
정신분석 요법의 귀환

정신과 의사들은 어떤 사람이 정신질환자인지 아닌지 제대로 가려낼 수 있을까? 1970년대 초반 미국의 무명 심리학자였던 데이비드 로젠한은 이를 시험해보는 실험을 진행했다. 로젠한과 그의 친구 7명은 전국의 정신 병원으로 흩어져 거짓 증상을 호소했다. "목소리가 들립니다. '쿵' 소리요". 이 증상을 말한 것만으로 모두 정신 병원에 입원이 되었다. 하지만 입원 후에는 정상인과 똑같이 행동했다. 그들은 의사에게 일상생활의 만족과 불만족에 관해 있는 그대로 털어놓았다. 실험이 끝날 무렵, 7명은 정신분열증, 1명은 조울증 진단을 받았다. 평균 19일 입원 치료 후 모두 '일시적 증세 회복'으로 퇴원했다. 실험 결과를 기초로 로젠한은 '정신 병원에서 제정신으로 지내기'란 논문을 발표했다. 부정적인 여론이 일자 한 정신 병원에서 "우리에게 앞으로 3개월간 가짜 환자를 보내보라. 찾아내겠다"라고 주장했다. 3개월 뒤 병원 측은 가짜 환자 41명을 찾아냈다고 발표했다. 그렇지만 실제로는 가짜 환자는 단 한 명도 보내지 않았었다.

그런데 이런 치료법이 다시 유행인 듯하다. 미국의 뉴욕타임스 10월 1일자 인터넷판은 '정신분석 요법, 지지를 얻다'란 새로운 소식을 전했다. "프로이트 이론에 바탕을 둔 집중적인 정신분석학적 '상담 치료(talking cure)는 투약 처방과 관리 요법에 밀려 존재가 희미해졌다. 그러나 불안 장애와 경계선 인격장애(감정을 조절하지 못하는 병) 같은 만성 정신질환 등에는 효과가 큰 것으로 드러났다"는 것이다. 1,000여 명 이상의 환자가 관련된 이 연구는 금요일 미국의학협회지에 실렸다. 정신분석 요법의 귀환은 정신 의학이 로젠한의 공격을 계기로 더욱 실질적이고 효과적인 방향으로 발전했다는 증거로 보아야 할 것이다. 문명과 마찬가지로 학문도 도전을 통해서 발전하는 것이 아니겠는가?

해설

1. 첫 번째 문단에 등장하는 로젠한 실험에서는 기존의 상담 치료에 문제가 상당하다는 내용을 내포하고 있다. 실제 정신병 환자를 제대로 가려내지 못한다는 것을 무명의 심리학자가 실험을 통해 제시했기 때문이다. 따라서 (a)와 반대의 내용인 (c)가 정답이 된다.

2. 병원 측에서는 (d)처럼 41명의 환자를 찾아냈다고 했지만 실제로는 한 명도 가짜 환자를 보내지 않았기 때문에 한 명도 제대로 찾아내지 못한 것이 되어서 (c)가 정답이 된다.

3. 두 번째 문단의 "Intensive psychoanalytic therapy, the 'talking cure' ... has all but disappeared in the age of drug treatments and managed care." 부분을 통해 상담 치료가 사라진 이유는 투약 처방과 관리 요법 때문이라는 것을 알 수 있다. 따라서 정답은 (d)가 된다.

4. 1970년대에는 상담 치료에 문제가 있다는 공격을 받았지만 최근에는 다시 각광을 받고 있다는 내용이므로 (a)가 정답이 된다.

정답 1.(c) 2.(c) 3.(d) 4.(a)

UNIT 07

The silent organ
간

　과학 전문지 『사이언스』 276호엔 프로메테우스 신화는 간은 일부를 절제하거나 손상돼도 바로 재생된다는 사실을 고대 그리스인도 알고 있었다는 것을 보여주는 것이라는 논문이 실렸다. 이처럼 간은 손상된 조직을 자연스럽게 재생할 수 있는 몇 안 되는 장기 중 하나이다. 15% 정도의 크기로도 두세 달 뒤면 원래 크기로 자란다. 과음이나 간염으로 손상돼도 며칠 술을 끊거나 간염이 완치되면 곧 원상회복된다.

　성인의 간은 보통 1.5kg이 나가며, 인체의 장기 중 가장 크고, 몇몇 중요한 기능을 수행한다. 알다시피 간은 알코올을 대사시키거나 분해하는 주요 장기다. 알코올 같은 독성 물질을 덜 위험한 형태로 변환해 몸 밖으로 배출한다. 하지만 간이라고 해서 모든 독성 물질을 해독하거나 제거할 수 있는 것은 아니다. 중성화시킬 수 없는 유독성 물질은 그대로 통과시킨다.

　인체 내 간의 역할을 축구 포지션으로 비유하자면 링크맨(미드필더) 같은 존재다. 우리가 먹는 음식은 포도당, 아미노산, 지방산 등 기본 성분으로 분해된 뒤 몸 안에서 완전히 소화가 된다. 이 물질들은 모두 (장과 간을 잇는) 간문맥을 거쳐 간에 들어와 각각 필요한 세포로 '볼 배합'이 된다. 음식의 양이 적어 식욕을 채워주지 못할 때 "간에 기별도 안 간다"고 하는 것은 과학적인 근거가 있는 말이다.

　바로바로 고장 신호를 보내는 다른 장기와는 달리 70%가 파괴될 때까지도 묵묵히 일만 하기 때문에 간은 '침묵의 장기'다. 따라서 간이 '신음 소리'를 내면 이미 돌이킬 수 없는 상황이기 십상이다. 경고 신호를 보내기 전에 간에 신경 쓸 필요가 있는 것이다.

해설

1. 본문은 간의 특징에 관한 대략적인 설명이므로 주제로는 (d)가 적합하다.

2. '침묵의 장기'라고 간이 불리는 것은 손상을 입어도 별다른 신호를 보내지 않기 때문이다. 따라서 정답은 (a)가 적합하다.

3. (a)의 경우 마지막 문단을 통해 추론이 가능하다. 간은 다른 장기와는 달리 70%가 파괴될 때까지도 묵묵히 일만 한다고 했기 때문이다. (b) 또한 마지막 문단의 '침묵의 장기'라는 부분을 통해 추론 가능하며, (d)는 첫 번째 문단에 나온 간의 재생력을 통해 추론할 수 있다. 정답은 (c)로 두 번째 문단에 보면 모든 독성 물질을 해독할 수 있는 것은 아니라고 했으므로 사실과 다르다.

4. 두 번째 문단에서 간은 몇몇 중요한 기능을 수행한다고 했으므로 하나의 기능만을 수행한다는 (a)는 올바르지 않다. (b)는 세 번째 문단에 "간에 기별도 안 간다"는 부분을 참고하면 되고, (c)는 첫 번째 문단에서 간이 최고의 재생력을 지녔다는 것을 통해 유추할 수 있다. 그리고 마지막 문단을 통해 간은 '침묵의 장기'라는 설명에서 (d)를 추론할 수 있다.

정답 1.(d) 2.(a) 3.(c) 4.(a)

UNIT 08

History in color
피부색

인간의 피부색에 대한 과학적 설명은 멜라닌, 헤모글로빈, 카로틴 등 주로 세 성분에 의해 결정된다는 것이다. 이 중 카로틴은 당근, 귤 등 카로틴이 풍부한 식품을 과다 섭취했을 때 피부색을 노랗게 바꾸는 등 일시적인 영향을 미친다. 헤모글로빈은 피부 표면에 많으면 피부가 불그스름해지는 정도다. 하지만 인종과 피부색을 가르는 핵심은 피부의 진갈색 멜라닌 색소의 양이다. 인종에 따라 멜라닌 세포의 수가 달라지는 것은 아니며 멜라닌 세포 속에 멜라닌 소체가 얼마나 조밀하게 들어있느냐에 따라 피부색이 결정된다.

피부색은 태양의 자외선에 대한 적응의 산물이란 이론도 설득력이 있다. 대부분 아프리카 적도 부근에서 살았던 현대 인류의 조상은 검은 피부였다. 열을 반사하고, (땀을 빨리 발산시켜) 체온을 낮추며, '유해한' 자외선을 막는 데 검은 피부가 더 효과적이어서이다. 같은 양의 햇볕을 받았을 때 백인이 흑인보다 피부암에 걸릴 위험은 10배나 높다. 그런데 신체가 자외선을 너무 적게 받아들이면 '선샤인 비타민'으로 통하는 비타민 D가 결핍된다. 흑인이 백인에 비해 비타민 D의 부족에 의한 구루병, 류머티즘 관절염, 심혈관 질환, 대장암, 폐암, 전립선암에 걸릴 위험이 높은 것은 이래서다.

인류가 아프리카를 떠나 유럽, 아시아 등에 정착한 뒤엔 비타민 D를 더 많이 받을 필요가 있었을 것이다. 이들은 생존을 위해 노랗거나 흰 피부를 갖게 됐다. 예외적으로 알래스카 원주민들은 햇볕 보기가 힘든 극 지역에 살면서도 피부가 검다. 전문가들은 이들이 평소 비타민 D가 풍부한 생선을 많이 먹어 굳이 피부가 밝을 필요가 없었을 것이라고 풀이한다.

해설

1. 햇볕과 비타민 D가 관련 있기 때문에 이를 충분히 받지 않으면 여러 질병에 걸릴 가능성이 커진다고 했다. 그리고 두 번째 문단에서 피부색은 자연의 적응에 의한 산물이라고 말하고 있다. (c)는 본문의 서두에 나오는 내용이다. 정답은 (d)로, 인종이 피부색에 미치는 영향이 아닌 환경이 피부색에 미치는 영향에 대해 진화론적 관점에서 설명하고 있다.

2. (a)는 알래스카 사람들의 예에서 알 수 있으며, (c)는 'Africa had darker skin because it was more effective at reflecting heat'에서 확인할 수 있다. (d)는 본문 초반의 'Excessive consumption of foods high in carotene … may turn one's skin yellow for a short time' 부분을 통해 알 수 있다. 정답은 (b)로 흑인이 백인에 비해 상대적으로 비타민 D 결핍과 관련된 질병에 더 많이 걸린다는 것이지, 백인은 이런 질병을 겪지 않는다는 뜻은 아니다.

3. 이 글은 피부색에 관한 내용이다 따라서 아프리카인들의 이주나 식단의 중요성은 관련이 없으며, 건강에 관한 내용도 아니다. 정답은 (c)로 피부색은 태양의 자외선에 대한 적응의 산물이라고 설명하고 있다.

4. 본문 후반부에 알래스카에 살고 있는 원주민들은 햇볕을 보기 힘든 극 지역에 살지만 피부가 검다고 나온다. 평소 비타민 D가 풍부한 생선을 많이 먹어서라고 했으므로 정답은 (a)가 된다. 피부암에 대한 내용은 두 번째 문단 중반에 나오는데 백인이 흑인보다 피부암에 걸릴 위험이 10배라고 했으므로 피부색과 관련이 있다는 것을 알 수 있다. (c)의 경우 적도에 가까울수록 피부색이 검은데, 예외적으로 알래스카 사람들을 들고 있다. (d)의 경우 첫 번째 문단 후반에 인종에 따라 멜라닌 세포 수가 달라지는 것은 아니라고 했다.

정답 1.(d) 2.(b) 3.(c) 4.(a)

UNIT 09

Addicted to speed
속도

세계에서 가장 빠른 여객 철도편인 알스톰사의 고속 열차 TGV는 파리~스트라스부르 사이를 최대 시속 575㎞로 달린다. 2007년 4월 성공적인 데뷔를 치른 업그레이드된 이 프랑스의 총알 열차는 경쟁 관계인 독일의 ICE나 일본 신칸센을 능가한다. 속도 면에서, 신칸센이 2003년 시속 581㎞로 달린 기록이 있으나 당시에는 자기부상 방식이었다. 이 방식은 엔진 과열과 무게 문제로 상용화되기 어렵다. 평상시 TGV는 시속 300㎞ 남짓으로 유럽을 관통한다.

세계에서 가장 빠른 차로 통하는 GTBO는 영국의 아카비온에서 디자인 제작되었다. 이 컨셉트 카는 올 2월 최고 시속 547㎞로 달리는 모습을 선보였다. 360㎏의 무게가 나가는 돌고래 모양의 이 2인용 자동차는 불과 30초 만에 시속 480㎞까지 도달할 수 있다. 물론 가격이 2백만 달러를 호가해서 일반인들이 넘보기는 어렵다. 하늘에서는, 록히드사의 SR-71 블랙버드 정찰기가 단연 발군이다. 이 장거리 전략정찰기는 시속 4,000㎞에 이르는 마하 3.3의 속도로, 한때 마하 2.23 속도를 자랑하던 콩코드기보다 훨씬 빠르다.

21세기는 '속도의 시대'다. 역사는 속도는 곧 힘이란 사실을 실증적으로 보여준다. 징기스칸은 기마군의 도움으로 몽골 제국을 세웠고, 독일의 영웅 롬멜 장군은 2차 세계대전 동안 북아프리카 사막에서 아프리카 콥스 탱크로 승리를 이끌었다. 속도를 높이면 더 높고, 먼 곳까지 갈 수 있고, 더 빠른 시간에 더 많은 정보를 얻을 수 있고, 더 많은 일을 할 수 있다. 속도는 성장을 부추기고, 성장이 다시 속도를 내도록 재촉한다. 어떤 이들은 '속도 바이러스'를 얘기한다. 현대 사회의 빠른 속도에 보조를 맞추지 못하는 사람은 도태되고 소외될 수밖에 없다며 비판한다. 인간의 더 빠른 속도에 대한 갈증으로 자연과 자원이 희생양이 된다. 인류가 일 년 동안 소모하는 에너지의 양은 거의 100만 년 동안 축적된 화석 연료의 양에 해당한다. 석유, 석탄 같은 화석 연료의 과소비는 지구 온난화를 더욱 부추기고 있다.

해설

1. '속도 바이러스가 무엇을 지칭하는지는 바로 앞부분(Speed can accelerate growth while growth presses on for more speed.)에 나온다. 빠르게 일을 처리해서 성장이 이뤄졌는데, 오히려 그 성장이 더 빠른 일처리를 요구하고 있는 상황이다. 마치 끊임없이 더 빠른 속도를 원하는 속도 바이러스가 사람들을 감염시키는 것 같다는 것이다. 그리고 이런 속도에 적응하지 못하는 사람들은 뒤처지고 소외된다는 것이다. 따라서 이 바이러스는 실제 바이러스가 아닌 비유적인 표현인데, 마치 이를 실제 바이러스처럼 묘사한 (a)는 적절하지 않다.

2. (a)는 본문 마지막 부분을 통해 알 수 있으며, (b)와 (d)는 1번 문제에서도 다루었던 부분이다. 정답은 (c)로 이는 본문을 통해서는 알 수 없는 내용이다.

3. 영국에서 제작된 '아카비온 GTBO'는 최고 시속 547㎞까지 달려 가장 빠른 자동차 자리에 올랐지만, 가격이 비싸 일반인들이 넘보기 어렵다고 했으므로 이를 승용차(passenger vehicle)라고 할 수 없으므로 (d)가 정답이 된다.

4. 마지막 부분이 화석 연료의 대량 소비와 지구 온난화로 끝났으므로 이에 대한 대체에너지가 나올 수 있을 것으로 예상할 수 있다.

정답 1.(a) 2.(c) 3.(d) 4.(c)

UNIT 10

Under the microscope
다이옥신

극미의 세계를 향한 인간의 지적 호기심은 끝이 없다. 과학의 발달이 탐구욕을 채워준다. 바이러스나 프리온은 전자현미경으로, 극소량의 화학 물질은 GC-MS나 HPLC-MS같은 분석 장비로 탐색한다. 현재 40대 이상은 '마이크로(micro, 100만분의 1)'라는 개념을 보고 신기해했다. 1990년대엔 나노(nano, 10억분의 1)라는 용어가 유행했다. 지금은 과학용어 앞에 붙는 피코(pico, 1조분의 1)까지 낯설지 않게 되었다.

요즘은 식품업계가 현미경하에 놓여있다. 과거엔 너무 작아 측정이 불가능해 보이지 않던 vCJD(변종크로이츠펠트야콥병)나 노로바이러스, 다이옥신, PCB 등까지 신경 써야 하기 때문이다. 이러한 맥락에서 "식품에서 발암 물질이 일체 검출돼선 안 된다"는 1958년의 '딜레이니 조항'(Delaney clause)을 미 식품의약국(FDA)이 슬그머니 없앤 것이다.

분석 화학의 발달로 검사 과정에서 실체가 드러난 대표 유해 물질은 최근 아일랜드산 돼지고기 파문의 주범인 다이옥신(dioxin)이다. 다이옥신 등 유해 물질은 먹이 사슬의 위쪽(최종 소비자 방향)으로 갈수록 누적된다. 그래서 최종 소비자의 다이옥신 수치가 1차 소비자의 수치보다 훨씬 높다. 이런 유독성 물질은 물보다는 플랑크톤과 같은 미생물에 더 고농도로 축적된다. 물고기가 플랑크톤을 먹게 되면 더 고농도로 물고기 몸에 쌓이게 되는 것이다.

사람 중에서도 엄마 젖을 먹는 아기가 먹이 사슬의 최정점에 있다. 1999년 벨기에서 있었던 다이옥신 오염사고 같은 인재(人災)가 아니라면 우유보다 모유에서 다이옥신이 더 많이 검출되는 것은 당연한 일이다. 그럼에도 모유 먹이기를 권장하는 것은 전반적인 아기의 건강과 성장에 모유의 득이 훨씬 크다는 신빙성 있는 증거 때문이다.

해설

1. 이 글은 기술을 이용해 먹거리에서 유독성 물질을 제거한다는 내용이 아니며, 또한 모유 수유를 권장하는 글도 아니다. 그리고 기술의 발달이 지금의 먹거리가 내포한 문제를 해결해 줄 수 있을 것으로 낙관한다는 내용도 아니다. 기술의 발달로 이전에는 알려지지 않았던 유독 물질들을 검출할 수 있게 되었으며, 그런 물질 중에서 다이옥신에 대해 상세한 설명을 하고 있으므로 정답으로는 (a)가 적합하다.

2. 본문 마지막 줄에서 모유 수유가 더 많은 다이옥신에 노출될 수 있지만 장점이 단점보다 많기 때문이라고 말한 것으로 봐서 저자가 모유 수유를 반대하는 것은 아니라는 사실을 알 수 있다. 따라서 정답은 (d)가 된다.

3. 첫 번째와 두 번째 문단을 통해 측정 및 분석 기술의 발달로 이전에는 발견할 수 없었던, 그래서 신경 쓰지 않아도 됐던 vCJD, 노로바이러스, 다이옥신 등까지 이제는 신경 써야 한다고 했으므로 정답은 (a)가 된다.

4. (a)에 대한 내용은 세 번째 문단에 등장하지만 아일랜드산 돼지고기의 판매량 여부는 본문에 등장하지 않는다. 그리고 다이옥신은 먹이 사슬 상단에 있는 생명체에 더 많이 검출된다고 했으므로 먹이 사슬의 가장 꼭대기에 있는 인간은 가장 많은 다이옥신이 검출되는 것은 당연하다. 이런 내용을 통해 어느 정도의 다이옥신은 몸에 쌓이는 것은 어쩔 수 없는 사실이란 것을 알 수 있으므로 (b)는 올바른 추론이 된다. (c)의 경우 물보다는 플랑크톤에 다이옥신과 같은 유독성 물질이 더 고농도로 축적된다는 내용이므로 (c)와는 무관하며, (d)의 경우 개연성은 있지만 본문에는 명시적으로 등장하지 않는다. 측정 및 분석 기술의 발달로 보다 다양한 미세 불실을 구별할 수는 있겠지만 현재도 잘 먹고 있는 음식에서 미래에 더 많은 위험 물질을 발견한다면 지금 당장 그 음식을 먹지 말아야 하기 때문에 논리적으로 맞지 않게 된다.

정답 1.(a) 2.(d) 3.(a) 4.(b)

UNIT 11

Weather not an exact science
수치예보

날씨 예측의 정확성을 높이는 일은 그리 간단치 않다. 기상 예보가 근본적으로 자주 틀릴 수밖에 없는 숙명을 안고 있기 때문이다. 사실 날씨를 과학적으로 예측하기 시작한 것은 비교적 최근의 일이다. 정확한 기상 관측기구가 없었던 시절에는 감각기관이나 경험에 의존해 날씨를 점칠 수밖에 없었다. 갈릴레오 갈릴레이가 온도계를 발명한 것이 1660년대 초였고, 벤자민 프랭클린이 기상현상이 지역별로 움직인다는 사실을 발견한 때가 1773년이었다. 무선전신이 발명된 19세기에 이르러서야 광범위한 지역의 날씨를 보여주는 일기도가 일기예보에 활용되기 시작했다. 20세기 중반에는 인공위성과 기상레이더 등 첨단 기상 관측 장비가 발명되고, 대규모 기상정보를 처리할 수 있는 슈퍼 컴퓨터가 등장했다. 현재의 날씨에 관한 정보를 바탕으로 미래의 날씨 정보를 수치로 계산해 내는 이른바 '수치예보'의 시대가 열린 것이다.

문제는 날씨에 영향을 미치는 엄청난 양의 정보를 슈퍼 컴퓨터를 사용해 분석해도 예보의 정확성을 높이는 데는 한계가 있다는 점이다. 1961년 미국의 기상학자 에드워드 로렌츠가 만든 용어인 이른바 '나비효과' 때문이다. '브라질에 있는 나비의 날갯짓이 텍사스에 토네이도를 불러올 수 있다'는 말처럼, 사소한 초기의 기상 현상이 엄청난 차이를 만들어낸다는 이론이다. 아무리 정교한 기상예측 모델을 만들어도 처음에 입력한 정보가 조금만 잘못되면 예측 결과가 판이하게 달라진다. 날씨에 대한 정보가 많아지고, 예측모델이 정교해진다고 해서 예보가 더 정확해진다는 보장은 없다. 숫자가 정확하다고 예보가 정확한 것은 아니란 얘기다. 컴퓨터가 계산해낸 수치를 분석해 날씨를 예보하는 것은 결국 사람의 몫이다.

해설

1. 나비효과는 두 번째 문단에 정의가 나오는데, "The flap of a butterfly's wing in Brazil can set off a tornado in Texas." 부분을 보면 알 수 있다. 한 곳에서 발생한 아주 사소한 현상이라도 다른 곳에서는 큰 영향을 미칠 수 있다는 말로, 기상현상이 초기 조건에 매우 민감해서 그만큼 예측이 어렵다는 것을 설명하고 있다. 따라서 정답은 (b)가 된다.

2. 첫 번째 문단 마지막 부분에 수치예보의 시대가 열린 것은 대규모 기상정보를 처리할 수 있는 슈퍼 컴퓨터가 등장한 이후라고 했으므로 정답은 (a)가 된다.

3. 슈퍼 컴퓨터는 두 번째 문단에 나오는 내용으로, (a)의 내용은 등장하지 않는다. (b)의 경우 정확한 예보를 하는 것은 '나비효과' 등의 이유로 어렵다고 했으므로 정확히 사용된다고 해서 나올 수 있는 결과는 아니다. (c)의 경우 수치는 컴퓨터가 해석하지만 결국 날씨를 예보하는 것은 사람이라고 마지막 줄에서 설명하고 있으므로 사람은 아무런 인풋도 제공하지 않는다는 내용은 본문과 일치하지 않는다. 정답은 (d)로 모든 데이터를 사용한다고 하더라도 정확한 날씨 예측은 예기치 않은 변수가 많아 어렵다는 것이므로 내용과 부합한다.

정답 1.(b) 2.(a) 3.(d)

UNIT 12
A different side to drones
드론

무인항공기 드론을 반대하는 건 시대에 역행하는 듯 보인다. 기술 발전에 둔감해 보일 수도 있고 회의론자로 여겨질 수도 있다. 드론을 가지고 철학적 논쟁을 벌이는 게 어쩌면 이미 의미 없을지도 모른다. 규제가 대거 풀릴 것으로 예상되면서 시장이 이미 움직이고 있기 때문이다. 드론이 긍정적인 목적으로 쓰이는 경우도 점차 늘고 있다. 네덜란드 같은 나라들에서 사용되는 '앰뷸런스 드론'은 (긴급) 현장에 가장 먼저 도착해 의료 장비를 제공한다. 군사적 용도만 강조됐을 때에 비하면 요즘 드론에 대한 거부감은 훨씬 줄어든 느낌이다.

하지만 최근 미국과 유럽에서 나온 보고서들은 우리가 드론의 사용이나 규제의 효용을 너무 믿고 있는 건 아닌가 하는 우려를 던져준다. 영국 (인권단체인) 리프리브(Reprieve)는 미국이 드론으로 중동의 테러 용의자들을 공격하는 과정에서 천 명이 넘는 민간인들이 숨졌다고 주장했다. 예멘에선 미국의 드론이 한 결혼식장을 공격해 하객과 신부를 포함해 12명이 숨졌다. 미국 언론들이 보도한 연방항공청 자료도 주목할 만하다. 지난 6개월간 드론과 대형 여객기가 충돌할 뻔한 사례가 25건이 된다는 것이었다. 여객기 조종사가 비행 중에 드론을 발견하고 신고한 경우도 193건에 달했다. 항공기 안전도 안전이지만 테러 위협도 생각할 필요가 있다.

미국 정부의 기본적인 입장은 정교한 규제가 가능하다는 쪽이다. 그러나 총기 규제의 현실을 보면 낙관론이 꼭 좋은 것만은 아니다. 총기 관련 폭력은 예방이 사실상 불가능하다. 사고 후 대처 능력만 키울 뿐이다. 이미 총기가 광범위하게 보급된 상황에서 규제의 실효성은 떨어지기 때문이다. 드론은 대량살상 무기로서 총보다 훨씬 더 위험하다. 총기 규제의 전철을 밟지 않으려면 지나칠 정도로 보수적인 사전 검토가 필요하다. 경제 논리에 휘둘려서도 안 되고 낙관론에 휩쓸려서도 안 된다. 해킹 가능성 등 그 외 기술적 논의도 필요하다. 시장이 먼저 움직이고 규제가 따라 가는 식이 된다면 재앙을 불러올 수도 있다. 당국이 완벽하게 규제할 자신이 없다면 철저히 준비가 될 때까지 엄격하게 규제하는 게 해결법이 될 수 있다.

해설

1. 이 글의 전반적인 어조에는 드론의 확산에 대하여 주의가 필요하다는 필자의 입장이 드러나 있다. 본문의 마지막 문장에서 '완벽하게 규제할 자신이 없으면, 철저히 준비가 될 때까지 엄격하게 규제하는 게 해결법'이라고 한 것에서도 역시 단서를 찾을 수 있다.

2. 본문의 첫머리에 '무인항공기 드론을 반대하는 건 시대에 역행하는 듯 보인다. 드론을 가지고 철학적 논쟁을 벌이는 게 어쩌면 이미 의미 없을지도 모른다.'라고 하였으므로 이미 실재하고 확산되는 과정에 있는 드론의 존재 유무에 대한 논의는 의미 없는 논쟁이라고 할 수 있다.

3. 드론의 부정적인 사례를 보여주는 두 번째 단락의 '예멘에선 미국의 드론이 한 결혼식장을 공격해 하객과 신부를 포함해 12명이 숨졌다.'는 내용에서 드론의 문제점을 적나라하게 드러내고 있다. 그러므로 정답은 (d)이다.

4. 드론을 규제해야 하지만, '총기 규제의 전철을 밟지 않으려면 지나칠 정도로 보수적인 사전 검토가 필요하다'는 필자의 입장을 고려하면 완벽하게 규제할 자신이 없는 경우에는 "철저히 준비가 될 때까지 엄격하게 규제하는 게 해결법"이라고 할 수 있다.

정답 1.(b) 2.(a) 3.(d) 4.(a)

UNIT 13

Wrangling with nuclear risk
핵실험

　1945년 7월 16일 오전 5시, 미국 뉴멕시코 주 알라모고도에서 인류 최초의 원폭 실험이 있었다. 암호명이 트리니티(trinity)인 이날 사용된 20kt짜리 핵폭탄은 사막 위에 거대한 버섯 모양의 구름을 남겼다. 이 폭탄의 위력은 바로 몇 주 후 실전에서 검증됐다. 히로시마와 나가사키에 떨어진 리틀 보이와 팻 맨은 20만 명의 목숨을 앗아갔다.

　미국의 핵무기 실험은 구소련과의 냉전이 한창이던 1950년대에 절정에 달했다. 실험은 주로 네바다 주 사막 한 가운데 있는 시험장에서 이뤄졌는데, 이 핵실험이 미국의 영화배우 존 웨인의 죽음에 한몫을 했다는 주장이 있다. 존 웨인은 1954년 핵 실험장에서 137km 거리인 유타 주의 평원에서 징기스칸을 소재로 한 영화 '정복자(Conqueror)'를 촬영하고 있었다. 일본 저널리스트 히로세 다카시의 저서 '존 웨인은 누가 죽였나'에 따르면, 향후 30년 동안 전체 출연진과 스태프 220명 중 90명이 암에 걸렸고 그중 46명이 사망했다. 방사능과의 상관관계를 부정하기 힘든 수치이다. 존 웨인은 1964년 발병한 폐암에선 살아남았지만 1979년 끝내 위암으로 죽음을 맞았다. 딕 파웰 감독과 여주인공 수전 헤이워드 역시 암으로 숨을 거뒀다.

　미국의 첫 수소폭탄 실험은 1954년 마샬 제도의 비키니 환초에서 이뤄졌다. 폭발 당시 근처 해역을 일본의 참치잡이 원양어선 다이고후쿠류마루(第五福龍丸) 즉 Lucky Dragon 5가 지나고 있었는데 낙진을 흠뻑 뒤집어썼다. 이 배는 미 해군이 설정한 안전선 밖에 있었는데도 선원 1명이 사망하고 다수가 두통과 잇몸 출혈 등을 호소했다. 일련의 사고가 핵실험 위험에 대한 주의를 환기한 결과 각국은 1963년 지상-수중 핵실험의 금지 협약에 사인했지만 지하 핵실험은 금지 대상에서 제외됐다. 대기나 해양의 오염과 무관하다는 이유였다. 하지만 지하수나 토양의 오염, 그리고 지진 유발 가능성에 대한 위험성은 여전히 열려 있다.

해설

1. 이 글은 핵폭탄의 부정적 측면을 서술하고 있다. 따라서 효용성에 대한 (a)는 정답과 거리가 멀고, (c)는 두 번째 문단에만 해당하는 지엽적인 내용이다. 그리고 (d)에서와 같이 핵폭탄의 역사를 말하려고 한 글이 아니므로 이 또한 적절하지 않다. 정답은 (b)로 실험 중 발생한 낙진에 부작용이 있다는 내용이 두 번째 문단과 세 번째 문단 모두를 설명할 수 있어서 주제로 적합하다.

2. (a)와 (b), (d)는 사실일 수도 있지만 이 글의 내용만으로는 추론하기 어렵다. 상세한 내용이 본문에 등장하지 않기 때문이다. 정답은 (c)로 핵실험으로 인해 배우 존 웨인이나 일본 원양어선 선원들이 피해를 본 것은 당시 과학자들이 방사능 영향에 대해 충분히 알지 못했음을 알 수 있다.

3. 유타 주의 평원에서 촬영하던 전체 스태프 220명 중 90명이 암에 걸렸다고 나오므로 모든 사람이 암으로 사망했다는 (d)는 본문과 다르다.

정답　1.(b)　2.(c)　3.(d)

UNIT 14

A high-tech, brain-shrinking future
진화하는 인간

요즘 휴대전화로 통화하며 걷는 사람을 거리에서 만나는 것은 너무도 흔한 일이다. 유인원과 같은 크로마뇽인에 이어 한 손을 귀에 대고 걷는 현대인의 모습을 '인류의 진화' 그림에 담아야 하지 않을까 하는 생각도 든다. 최근의 언론 보도에 따르면, 미국의 의사들이 이른바 '휴대전화 엘보' 증후군에 대해 경고하고 있다. 의사들이 이런 걸로 호들갑을 떠는 게 우스워 보이기도 한다. 테니스를 즐기다 테니스 엘보에 걸려 계속되는 통증에 시달리는 것처럼 휴대전화 통화를 오래 하면 손에 통증이 생기고 무감각해지는 게 휴대전화 엘보다. 넷째, 다섯째 손가락이 특히 그렇다.

팔꿈치 통증에 전자파 걱정도 있지만 멀리할 수 없는 게 휴대전화다. 인류에 공간의 한계를 뛰어넘는 능력을 제공하기 때문이다. 여기에다 랩톱 컴퓨터나 무선 인터넷, 자동차 내비게이션까지 가세한 요즘 인간의 능력은 10년 전과 비교해도 엄청나게 커졌다. 이들 휴대용 장치들은 사람의 뇌보다 훨씬 많은 정보를 저장하고, 더 정확하게 기억한다.

최근엔 '뇌-기계 인터페이스(BMI)'라는 새로운 기술이 주목받고 있다. 이 기술은 인간의 뇌에서 나오는 신호를 이용해 로봇이나 기계를 제어할 수 있도록 고안되었다. 유전공학·로봇공학·정보기술·나노기술의 진보가 인간 능력을 더 높은 단계로 끌어올릴지는 알 수 없다. 그렇게 발전된다면 인류는 더 건강하게, 더 오래 살 수 있고 문화적·언어적 장벽도 쉽게 뛰어넘을 수 있게 될 것이다. 자지 않고 먹지 않는 인간이 나타날지도 모른다.

하지만 시간과 장소를 가리지 않고 울려대는 휴대전화 벨소리에 진정한 휴식, 정신적인 자유를 박탈당하고 있는 것도 사실이다. 계산기·사전 덕분에 머리를 쓸 필요가 없다 보니 우리가 기억하는 전화번호 개수는 갈수록 줄어든다. 오스트랄로피테쿠스에서 호모 사피엔스로 진화할 때까지는 인류의 두개골 용량이 늘었지만, 최근 3만 년 동안에는 인간의 뇌 크기가 오히려 10~15% 줄었다는 분석도 있다. 도구나 사회 시스템에 더 많이 의존하면서 뇌 자체의 역할은 그만큼 줄어든 때문인지도 모른다.

인간은 서서히 '사이보그'를 향해 진화하고 있다. 하지만 첨단 디지털 휴대기기를 소유하지 못한 '자연인'은 경쟁에서 도태될 수도 있다. 미래에 대해 예상하는 바보다 상황이 심각해지지 않을까 걱정되기도 한다.

해설

1. 휴대전화 엘보는 본문에서 'cell phone gabbers complain of pain or numbness in the hand — especially the pinky and ring fingers'와 같이 설명하고 있다. 따라서 손가락 중 일부에 통증이나 무감각한 증상이 온다는 내용이므로 (d)가 정답이 된다.

2. (a)의 경우 인간의 두뇌가 완전히 쓸모없어진다는 내용이므로 극단적이며, (c)는 본문과 무관하다. (d)도 (a)와 마찬가지로 인간의 두뇌를 불필요하게 만든다고 말해 극단적인 내용이 된다. 본문에서는 뇌에서 나온 신호를 사용한다고 말하고 있다. 정답은 (b)로 마지막 문단의 내용을 통해 알 수 있다.

3. 기술의 진화와 더불어 인간의 두뇌는 더 줄어드는 현상에 대해 언급하고 있으므로 (a)가 제목으로 적합하다. 기술에 대한 내용을 짐작할 수 없으므로 (c)와 (d)는 적절하지 않다.

4. 마지막 문단에 등장하는 'Humans are slowly evolving toward becoming cyborgs.' 부분을 통해 기술적으로 진화해가는 인간을 언급하고 있고 이런 점에서 우려되는 부분도 언급하고 있으므로 (b)보다는 (c)가 더 적합하다.

정답 1.(d) 2.(b) 3.(a) 4.(c)

UNIT 15
Painful patent protection
특허의 역설

독일의 가장 긴 강인 라인강은 중세 유럽 무역의 젖줄이었다. 신성로마제국 황제의 보호 아래 안전하게 운항하는 대가로 상선들은 각 나라를 지날 때마다 통행료를 지불했다. 그런데 13세기 들어 제국의 권위가 약화하면서, 봉건 귀족들이 멋대로 라인 강변에 성을 짓고 제각기 통행료를 걷기 시작한 것이다. 수백 개나 되는 이들 요금소의 횡포에 지쳐 상선들은 아예 강을 지날 생각을 접게 됐다. 라인강 무역은 쇠퇴했고 덩달아 단물을 빨아먹는 귀족들의 수입도 줄어들었다.

이처럼 여럿이 공공의 자원을 조각조각 나눠 갖게 되면 결국 자원의 존재를 위태롭게 하고 모두가 망한다. 컬럼비아 법대 교수 마이클 헬러는 이에 따른 폐단을 이른바 '반(反)공유재의 비극'이라 일컫는다. 주인 없는 자원을 제대로 쓰지 못하고 낭비하는 것도 문제지만, 라인강 사례 같이 자기 잇속만 차리는 광범위한 소유권 다툼 역시 곤란하단 얘기다. 마이클 헬러는 자신의 저서 『소유의 역습, 그리드락』에서 지나치게 파편화되거나 광범위한 소유권은 결국 산업과 시장을 막다른 골목으로 내몰 수 있다고 주장한다.

현재 생명공학 분야는 특허가 넘쳐난다. 지난 30년간 승인된 DNA 관련 특허만 4만여 개다. 신약을 판매하려는 제약회사들은 보통 수십 개의 특허 보유자를 일일이 접촉해 협상하지 않으면 안 된다. 많은 실험이 특허 보유자들과의 소송 분쟁을 두려워해 실험실을 벗어나지 못하고 사장된다. 사스(SARS·중증급성호흡기증후군)가 맹위를 떨치던 당시 백신 개발이 지지부진했던 것도 그래서다.

비타민 A가 부족한 아프리카와 그 밖의 빈곤국들의 수백만의 아이들을 구하기 위한 유전자 변형 황금쌀(Golden Rice) 역시 인도적 지원 노력이 없었다면 하마터면 못 태어날 뻔했다. 1999년 과학자들이 (비타민 A를 강화한) 기적의 쌀 개발에 성공했지만 무려 70여 개의 특허 사용 허가를 받아야 하는 난관에 부닥친 것이다. '인도주의적 사용권'을 가진 것으로 재정립한 후에야 그들은 그 쌀을 나눠줄 수 있었다.

해설

1. 공공재의 비극과 반대되는 개념으로 반공유재의 비극을 예로 들면서, 주인이 너무 많아도 문제라고 말하고 있다. 대표적인 예로 특허를 들고 있다. 이런 특허를 탐욕이라고 보는 (a)는 지나치며, 특허 등의 권리를 두고 장단기적으로 따지고 있는 득실을 따지는 글이 아니므로 (b) 또한 어색하다. 이 글에서 말하고자 하는 것은 특허 같은 문제가 백신 개발이나 쌀 품종 개발에서 볼 수 있듯이 개발을 막는 역할을 할 수 있다는 (c)가 정답으로 적합하다.

2. 특허의 취득이 이전보다 더 빨라졌다는 내용은 등장하지 않으므로 정답은 (b)가 된다.

3. 각종 특허 분쟁으로 인해 실험실을 벗어나 상용화 단계에 이르지 못하는 경우가 많다는 것이 세 번째 문단의 내용이므로 정답은 (a)가 된다.

4. 주인이 너무 많아 문제가 되고 있다는 '반공유재의 비극'을 설명한 (d)가 정답이 된다.

정답 1.(c) 2.(b) 3.(a) 4.(d)

UNIT 16

Statistics use and misuse
통계의 사용과 오용

만일 오스트리아의 수사인 그레고르 멘델(1822~1884)이 자신이 몰두하던 정원 완두를 가지고 교배하는 실험을 중단했다면, 세계 유전학에 미친 그의 업적은 달랐을 것이다. 그는 이들 식물의 일부 특성이 특정한 유전법칙을 따른다는 자신의 가설을 증명하고자 무려 15년 동안 완두콩 연구에 매달렸다. 그는 연구 결과의 변화에 따라 번호 순서대로 기록하여 통계를 내 분석하였다. 당시 사람들이 통계에 어두웠기에 사람들은 별 반응이 없었다.

그러다 20세기 초가 되어 멘델이 구상한 개념을 과학자들이 알게 되면서 사후에 그에게 '현대 유전학의 아버지'라는 칭호를 붙인다. 그의 연구를 통해 유전 법칙만이 밝혀진 것은 아니었다. 이들은 실험 결과 비율에 차이가 있음을 발견하고는, 멘델이 자신의 가설을 입증하고자 실험 기록들을 검열하여 삭제했거나 자기 이론과 동떨어진 결과가 나오면 이를 통계에서 제외시켜 버렸을지도 모른다는 의혹을 제기했다.

영국 수학자 찰스 배비지는 자신의 1830년 저서 『영국 과학의 쇠퇴에 대하여』에서 과학자들이 저지를 수 있는 세 가지의 학술 사기를 언급하고 있다. 요리하기(cooking), 다듬기(trimming), 위조하기(forging)라고 표현했다. 여기서 '요리하기'란 자신이 세운 가설에 맞는 값만 취하고, 나머지는 버린다는 뜻이다. 배비지가 더 크게 문제 삼은 건 '다듬기'였다. 측정값이 아주 정확하게 보이게끔 불규칙한 면들을 매끈하게 다듬는 행동이다. 이렇게 위조를 하고 원하는 결과가 나올 때까지 숫자를 다듬는 행태는 사회 통계의 영역에서도 종종 발견된다.

닉슨 행정부의 경제보좌관이었던 케빈 필립스는 닉슨 정부가 경제 지표를 긍정적으로 보고하기 위해 식료품과 에너지 가격을 소비자물가지수 계산에서 제외시켰다고 폭로했다. 미국 경제학자 스티븐 래빗의 책 『괴짜경제학』에는 시카고 공립학교에서 있었던 부정행위 사건이 나온다. 시 당국이 학생 성적이 나쁘면 승진·연봉에 불이익을 주는 정책을 시행했기 때문에, 교사들이 학생들의 시험성적을 조작한 것이다.

> **해설**
>
> 1. 이 글은 과학적 사기에 대해 나열하고 있다. 따라서 주제는 (a)가 적합하다. 나머지 보기들은 모두 단편적인 일부의 내용만을 담고 있어서 주제로 적합하지 않다.
> 2. [3]의 'will contradict'가 'would contradict'로 수정되어야 한다. 과거 시제와 맞춰 글이 서술되고 있기 때문이다. 따라서 과거의 시점에서 '향후 모순될 수도 있는'의 의미를 부여하기 위해서 would를 사용한다.
> 3. 멘델은 현대 유전학의 아버지로 불린다는 내용이 두 번째 문단 서두에 등장한다. 마지막 문단에서 Kevin Phillips는 닉슨 행정부의 부정을 폭로했으므로 밀고자린 의미의 whistleblower는 적절한 단어라 할 수 있다. 그리고 본문의 마지막 부분에서 (d)에 관한 내용이 나온다. 본문과 맞지 않는 내용은 (b)로 세 가지의 학술 사기에 해당하는 요리하기(cooking), 다듬기(trimming), 위조하기(forging) 등을 소개하고 있는데, 이들 중 일부가 서로 유사하다는 내용은 등장하지 않는다.
> 4. rampant는 만연했다는 의미를 지니므로 '광범위한'에 해당하는 (a)가 가장 유사하다.
>
> **정답** 1.(a) 2.(c) 3.(b) 4.(a)

UNIT 17
Autonomous driving dreams
자율주행차의 꿈

"사람을 태우는 승용차와 짐만 싣는 화물차 중 어느 것이 운전자 없는 완전 자율주행을 더 쉽게 할까요?" 몇 해 전 한 인공지능 전문가가 강의에서 한 질문이다. 대부분의 청중들이 화물차라고 답했다. 사람이 차에 타지 않으면 설사 자율주행 중 사고가 발생하더라도 인명피해는 없을 테니 말이다. 하지만 답은 반대였다. 전문가의 설명에 따르면 "돌발 상황의 경우, 예를 들어 길 한가운데에 철재 같은 파편이 떨어져 있을 때 승객이 타고 있다면 그걸 치울 수 있지만 사람이 없으면 해결할 길이 없기 때문"이라고 했다.

11월부터 세종시의 일반도로에서도 고속 자율주행 버스가 시범 주행을 시작한다. 초기엔 운전자가 있는 '레벨3' 수준으로 주행하다 안전성이 검증되면 운전자가 필요 없는 '레벨4' 수준으로 높인다. 미래라고 여겼던 완전 자율주행차 시대가 거의 다가왔다.

자율주행차가 가져올 변화는 혁명 수준이다. 자동차 부품업체를 운영하는 한 기업인은 몇 해 전부터 이 거대한 물결에 맞설 방법을 고민 중이다. 가장 큰 과제는 신차 판매 급감이다. 개인이 소유하는 '자차'가 아닌 공유하는 '자율주행 택시' 형태로 차량의 개념이 바뀔 것이기 때문이다. 그는 "신차 판매대수가 절반 이하로 줄어들 것"이라며 "차량 1대당 주행거리는 늘어나서 부품 소모 주기가 지금보다 짧아질 거란 점이 그나마 다행"이라고 말했다.

보험업계도 곤경에 처했다. 완전 자율주행차 시대엔 교통사고가 급감한다. 단기적으로는 자동차보험 수익성엔 희소식이다. 하지만 사고위험이 없다는 건 결국 보험의 쓸모 역시 없다는 뜻. 자동차보험은 역사 속으로 사라지고 제조물책임보험만 남게 될 것이다.

운전석이 필요 없는 완전히 새로운 자동차 실내 디자인도 상상할 수 있다. 자동차를 타는 동안 승객들이 무엇을 하며 시간을 보낼지는 콘텐츠 업계의 화두가 될 것이다. 택시·버스기사가 사라질 거란 일자리 문제와 함께 윤리적 문제, 보안 문제도 제기된다. 이렇게 상상의 나래를 펴가도 냉정한 현실적 분석이 찬물을 끼얹는다. 한 자동차보험 전문가는 "우리나라는 인도와 차도 구분이 없는 골목이 많아서 완전 자율주행차 까지 가는 데 상당히 시간이 걸릴 것이고 어쩌면 불가능할 수도 있다"고 내다봤다.

해설

1. 자율주행차의 미래와 자율주행차로 인하여 생기는 문제점들에 대해 쓴 글이다. 그러므로 정답은 d)이다.

2. 본문의 내용에 따르면 초기엔 운전자가 있는 '레벨3' 수준으로 주행하다 안전성이 검증되면 운전자가 필요 없는 '레벨4' 수준으로 높일 예정이라 하였으므로, 이미 '레벨3'은 성공적이라는 a)는 틀린 진술이다. 그러므로 a)가 정답이다.

3. 자율주행차로 인하여 보험업계가 받는 영향에 대해서는 '자율주행차 시대엔 교통사고가 급감하기에, 단기적으로는 자동차보험 수익성엔 희소식이다. 하지만 사고위험이 없다는 건 결국 보험이 필요 없기 때문에 보험이 사라질 위험에 처하게 될 것'이라고 하였다. 그러므로 c)가 정답이다.

4. 이렇게 자율주행차의 미래에 대해 장밋빛으로 보고 있지만, 빈칸 뒤의 문장을 보면 부정적인 내용들이 이어지고 있다. 그러므로 빈칸에는 이러한 상상에 대해 '현실적인 분석은 이런 생각에 찬물을 끼얹었다'는 부정적인 언급이 오는 b)가 정답이다.

정답 1.(d) 2.(a) 3.(c) 4.(b)

UNIT 18

Repent, ye carbon emitters
환경 면죄부

지구 온난화 시대의 중죄라 할 탄소 배출에도 면죄부가 등장했다. 탄소를 많이 배출하는 대신 친환경적인 사업에 돈을 내도록 하는 이른바 '탄소 상쇄(carbon offset)' 제도이다. 교통수단 중 가장 많은 탄소를 내뿜는 비행기 여행자들이 주로 산다. 아프리카에 나무를 심고 브라질에 수력발전소를 짓는 데 쓰라며 항공료 외에 10~40달러를 더 지불한다. 죄책감을 덜려는 수요 덕분에 전 세계적으로 이 제도로 벌어들인 매출이 이백만 달러에 달한다.

하지만 탄소배출권이라고 알려진 이 시스템에 대한 비판이 만만치 않다. 중세 때 면죄부가 사람들이 맘 편히 죄를 짓도록 부추겼듯이 탄소 상쇄 제도도 더 많이 여행하고, 더 많이 소비하는 풍조만 조장한다는 것이다.

교토의정서에 따라 2005년 부분 조정된 탄소배출권 거래(cap and trade) 역시 온난화를 악화하고 있다고 환경 전문가들은 지적한다. 온실가스 배출한도를 넘긴 나라가 한도를 못 채운 나라로부터 배출권을 사들일 수 있게 한 이 제도도 과다 배출국들에 면죄부를 줄 뿐 감축 효과는 미미하다는 얘기다. 나사(NASA)의 기후과학자 제임스 한슨은 런던 타임스지를 통해 "그들은 면죄부를 팔고 있는 것이다. 선진국들은 평소대로 사업을 계속하고 싶어하고 개도국에 푼돈이나 쥐어주면서 면죄부를 살 수 있을 거라 기대하는 것이다. 상쇄와 적응 기금이라는 형태로 말이다."라고 개탄한다.

해설

1. 본문은 탄소배출권 제도를 부정적인 시각으로 바라보고 있다. 마치 중세의 면죄부를 발부하는 것처럼 실제로 탄소 배출이 줄어드는 것이 아니라 돈으로 자신의 잘못을 사면 해결된다는 인식이 더해져서 실제 감축 효과는 미미할 것이라고 설명하고 있다. 따라서 실효성이 없이 선진국에서 현재의 생활 방식을 계속 유지하게 할 것이라는 (c)가 정답이 된다.

2. 1번과 같은 이유에서 현재의 탄소배출권 제도는 개선되어야 한다는 (a)가 정답이 된다.

3. 탄소배출권 제도와 면죄부를 서로 비교한 이유는, 서로의 취지가 같다고 생각해서이다. 따라서 (b)가 정답이 된다.

4. 본문은 단순히 탄소배출권 제도를 설명하는 데 그치지 않는다. 이런 제도를 통해 중세 시대에 죄를 저지르고도 면죄부를 발부받아 자신의 죄를 탕감했듯이 오늘날의 탄소배출권 제도가 중세의 면죄부가 될 수 있다고 경고하고 있는 글이다. 따라서 정답은 (d)가 된다.

정답 1.(c) 2.(a) 3.(b) 4.(d)

UNIT 19

Turn off the lights
빛 공해

1938년 7월 미국 시카고 대학 생리학자인 너대니얼 클라이트먼은 수염으로 뒤덮인 얼굴을 하고 32일 동안의 지하 생활을 보낸 후 동굴에서 나왔다. 동굴 속에서 그는 하루를 28시간으로 정해놓고 생활했지만 새로운 리듬에 끝내 적응하지 못했다. 인체 내부에는 태양이 뜨고 지는 24시간에 맞춰진 강력한 시계가 존재하기 때문이다.

인간뿐만 아니라 동식물들도 태양빛의 영향을 강하게 받는다. 벼·들깨·코스모스 등은 가을철에 매일 햇빛을 받아야 꽃을 피우고 열매를 맺는다. 지난해 3월 영국 로슬린 연구소와 일본 나고야 대학 연구팀은 봄이 돼 새가 짝짓기를 위해 노래를 부르는 것도 태양빛의 영향임을 밝혀냈다. 수컷 메추라기들은 낮이 길어져 빛을 많이 쬐면 뇌 표면의 세포(뇌하수체)가 자극을 받아 호르몬 분비가 늘고, 정소(精巢)가 커져 짝을 찾는 노래를 부르게 된다는 설명이다.

태양에서 쏟아지는 빛 에너지 덕분에 지구 표면은 평균 15도의 기온을 유지할 수 있고, 식물은 광합성을 할 수 있다. 하지만, 생물에게는 태양빛이 없는 밤도 중요하다. 캄캄한 밤은 수컷 반딧불이 암컷에게 자신의 존재를 드러내는 시간이다. 작고 약한 동물이 포식자를 피해 먹이를 구하는 시간이기도 하다.

인간이 만들어낸 인공 빛은 이런 밤의 질서에 영향을 미쳤다. 인공위성에서 내려다 보면 지구의 밤에 새어 나오는 강력한 불빛에 눈부실 정도다. 오랜 지구의 역사를 통해 낮과 밤, 사계절 변화에 익숙해진 생물들이 엉뚱한 계절, 엉뚱한 시간에 밝은 빛을 만난다면 혼란을 겪을 수밖에 없다.

인공 빛은 인류 자신에게도 어두운 문제가 되고 있다. 세계 인구의 3분의 2가량이 별빛으로 가득 찬 밤하늘을 더이상 보지 못한다. 호주에서는 (자국의 상징인) 남십자성을 하나씩 잃어가고 있다. 국기에 그려진 별을 육안으로 볼 수 없게 된 것이다. 지난해 2월 이스라엘 연구팀은 밤중에 전등이나 TV화면 같이 인공 빛에 노출된 여성들이 가로등 없이 어두운 곳에 사는 여성들에 비해 유방암 발생률이 37%나 높다는 연구결과도 내놓기도 했다.

해설

1. 이 글은 빛이 사람과 동물 및 식물에 어떤 식으로 영향을 주는지에 관해 서술하고 있으므로 정답은 (a)가 된다.

2. 본문의 마지막 부분에 빛이 여성의 유방암 발생률과 관련이 있다고 했으므로 건강에 영향을 주지 않는다는 (d)의 설명은 사실과 다르다.

3. 호르몬을 'trigger'한다는 것은 '유발'한다는 뜻이므로, 몸속에 화학 물질을 생성시킨다는 (b)가 정답이 된다. (a)는 'trigger'의 근원적 의미인 총의 방아쇠를 당긴다는 뜻에서 'shoot'이라는 동사를 사용했지만, 이는 본문의 뜻과는 다르다.

4. 새들이 노래를 부르는 것은 짝을 찾기 위한 것이므로 (A)에는 mating이 적절하며, 식물이 광합성을 할 수 있는 것은 태양의 빛 에너지를 통해서 가능하므로 (B)에는 energy가 적절하다. 그리고 동물들은 지구상에 살면서 계절적 변화에 익숙해졌기 때문에 (C)에는 change가 와야 한다. 따라서 정답은 (a)가 된다.

정답 1.(a) 2.(d) 3.(b) 4.(a)

UNIT 20
Kimchi in space
우주식품

미국의 첫 우주인 존 글렌은 1962년 프렌드십 7호에 반유동체인 사과소스를 싣고 갔다. 우주에서도 하루 세끼를 먹는다. 남성에겐 보통 2,200kcal, 여성에겐 2,000kcal의 열량이 제공된다. 맛이나 식감은 대부분 일반식보다는 떨어진다. 우주 식품 제조 시 가장 먼저 고려하는 것은 경량화다. 1kg을 우주에 올리는 데 5,000만원이 들기 때문이다. 우주 식품을 동결건조·분말화하는 것은 이처럼 생산비 절감을 위해서다. 우주 식품에서는 위생도 중요하다. ISS 모듈엔 냉장고가 없어 많은 음식을 오래 두고 먹기 힘들어서다. HACCP(식품위해요소 집중관리기준)는 식품 안전과 소비자 보호를 위한 세계 최고 수준의 시스템이다. 그 기원은 우주 탐험에 뿌리를 두고 있으며, 유인 우주비행 시 먹을 음식 준비를 관리하기 위한 것이다. ISS 모듈에 냉장고가 없는 것은 전력이 부족하기 때문이다.

우주 식품의 제공은 미국과 러시아가 양분한다. 미국이 200가지, 러시아가 130가지의 식품·음료를 2008년 1월 국제우주식품 목록에 등록했다. 메뉴엔 별 차이가 없으나 포장재의 종류와 용기의 입구 부분이 다르다. 미국은 알루미늄 포일 등 빛이 통과하지 않는 포장재를, 러시아는 투명한 포장재를 쓴다. 미국산의 용기 입구는 LPG차의 가스 밸브, 러시아산은 휘발유차의 기름 밸브를 연상시킨다. 미국의 우주 식품은 러시아보다 더 잘 밀폐된 용기에 포장된다. 이들 경우에서 보듯이, 우주 식품을 준비하는 것이 지상의 음식 용기와 포장 기술에 큰 영향을 미쳤다.

해설

1. 이 글은 우주 식품에 관한 내용으로, 경량화나 위생 등에 대해 설명하고 있으며, 미국과 러시아의 우주 식품에 관해 비교하고 있다. 따라서 정답은 (c)가 된다.

2. 미국의 우주 식품이 러시아보다 종류가 많고, 더 잘 밀폐된 용기를 사용하므로, 러시아보다 미국의 우주 식품이 더 많이 사용될 것으로 추론할 수 있다. 따라서 정답은 (a)가 된다.

3. 차이가 나는 부분이 포장재 종류와 용기의 입구, 품목 수 등이었으므로 정답은 (d)가 된다. (d)는 언급되어 있지 않다.

4. 마지막 문장인 'the preparation of space foods has greatly contributed to improving the container and packaging technologies of foods on Earth.'를 보면 음식 용기와 포장 기술에 영향을 주었다고 했으므로 정답은 (b)가 된다.

정답 1.(c) 2.(a) 3.(d) 4.(b)

Part 4

UNIT 01

At Google, there is no manual
"구글에는 매뉴얼이 없습니다"

'이 곳'의 11개 식당에선 특급 주방장이 만드는 전 세계의 진수성찬을 맛볼 수 있다. 직원 본인은 물론 가족·방문객에게까지 무료다. 신선한 과일과 음료수도 무제한으로 제공된다. 트레이너가 항시 대기하는 체육관과 수영장, 그리고 마사지실과 스파도 있다. 업무 시간에 산책·일광욕을 즐기거나, 사무실에서 애완견과 함께 일해도 아무도 뭐라하지 않는다. '이 곳'은 미국 캘리포니아 마운틴뷰에 있는 구글 본사다.

마냥 느슨하고 내키는대로 일하라는 의미가 아니다. "직원들이 자유롭게 활동하는 시간과 터를 마련하면 그들은 거기서 해답을 찾고, 상상 속의 것을 실제로 만들어낸다"는 게 구글(메간 스미스 부사장)의 설명이다. 업무 집중도와 회사에 대한 만족도를 높이는 것이 생산성과 직결된다는 사실을 구글 경영진은 잘 알고 있었다.

이런 환경은 창의성을 끌어내는 기업문화로 이어진다. 구글의 회의는 항상 거침없는 질문과 열정으로 가득 차 있다. 말단 직원도 경영진에게 자유롭게 자신의 의견을 개진한다. 개인 근무시간의 20%는 맡은 업무와 관계없이 자신이 해보고 싶은 일을 해보라고 권장한다. 이른바 '20% 프로젝트'를 통해서 얻어지는 아이디어는 G메일·애드센스 등 혁신 사업으로 이어지곤 한다.

구글은 경영철학은 간단하다. '자율'과 '개방'이다. 감시·통제가 없어도 인재들은 자신의 업무를 100% 수행하고, 창의성과 열정, 그리고 주인의식을 발휘할 수 있다고 믿는다. 인재들을 자연스럽게 만족시키는 이런 조직문화는 구글을 '혁신의 아이콘'으로 만들었고, 구글의 진정한 경쟁력이 된 것이다.

해설

1. 구글의 생산성과 성공을 이끄는 혁신과 구글의 창의성을 이끌어내는 기업문화에 대한 글이다. 그러므로 정답은 (b)이다. 참고로 자율과 개방을 중시하고 창의성을 펼칠 공간을 제공하기 때문에, 단순히 싸워서 이기는 기업문화를 뜻하는 (a)는 올바른 내용이 아니다.

2. 구글의 조직 구조 내에서 서열은 일의 수행능력과 관련이 없다는 내용은 본문에서 없는 진술이다. 다만 '구글의 회의는 항상 거침없는 질문과 열정으로 인해, 말단 직원도 경영진에게 자유롭게 자신의 의견을 개진'할 수 있다고 언급했을 뿐이다. 그러므로 (a)는 틀린 진술이다. 이에 비해 구글은 '개인 근무시간의 20%는 맡은 업무와 관계없이 자신이 해보고 싶은 일을 해보라고 권장하며, 이른바 '20% 프로젝트'를 통해서 얻어지는 아이디어는 G메일·애드센스 등 혁신 사업으로 이어지곤 한다'는 진술로부터 구글의 성공적인 프로젝트 가운데 일부가 자유근무시간에 나왔다는 것을 끌어낼 수 있다. 그러므로 정답은 (c)가 된다.

3. '직원들이 자유롭게 활동하는 시간과 터를 마련하면 그들은 거기서 해답을 찾고, 상상 속의 것을 실제로 만들어낸다(when employees are provided with a workplace that allows them to work freely, they find answers and ideas that are beyond their normal imagination)'라는 진술로부터 구글은 재능이 있는 사람을 고용하여, 그가 자신의 방식대로 창의력을 발휘할 수 있는 장을 마련해 주면 성공할 수 있다는 사실을 알고 있다고 추론할 수 있다. 하지만 (b)처럼 단지 사람을 고용하여 독자적으로 일할 여지만 주면 성공이 무조건 뒤따라온다고 할 수는 없다.

4. 패러프레이즈의 핵심은 구조와 표현을 바꿔 내용의 동일성을 달성하면 된다. 즉 같은 내용을 다른 방식으로 전달하는 것이다. 본문의 '구글의 회의는 항상 거침없는 질문과 열정으로 가득 차있다'는 진술을 바꿔 쓰면 '구글은 사람들이 자신의 생각을 열심히 개진하는 생기넘치는 회의를 진행한다'는 의미로 볼 수 있다.

정답 1.(b) 2.(c) 3.(a) 4.(b)

UNIT 02

Candidate games
딜레마

딜레마는 진퇴양난 상황을 뜻한다. 딜레마 중 가장 유명한 것은 '죄수의 딜레마'로 게임이론의 일종이다. 위기의 상황에 처한 두 게임 참가자는 자신들의 의심과 이기심으로 최악의 선택을 하는 경향이 있다는 것이다. 경찰은 유죄를 입증할만한 충분한 증거가 없다. 그래서 경찰이 두 죄수를 분리 취조하면서 양자에게 같은 거래를 제안한다. (침묵 아니면 자백을 선택하게 한다.) 만약 한 명이 상대를 기소하는 데 유리한 증언을 하고 다른 한 명은 침묵을 지키면 밀고한 자는 풀려나지만 침묵을 지킨 공범자는 10년형을 받는다. 둘 다 침묵하면 1년, 둘 다 자백하면 각각 5년형을 받는다. 그렇지만 죄수들은 결국 모두 폭로를 택하고 5년형을 받는다.

이 '죄수의 딜레마'는 전후 냉전체제에 돌입한 미·소간 핵무기 개발 경쟁을 설명하는 근거가 되기도 했다. 자신이 새로운 핵무기 개발을 그만두면 상대방도 그럴 것이라는 것을 잘 알면서도, 양 군사대국은 상호 간의 불신과 두려움 때문에 더 많은 핵무기경쟁을 한 것이다. '죄수의 딜레마'와 마찬가지로 '치킨 게임'도 인간의 다양한 충돌을 설명하는 주요 모델이다. 젊은이들 사이에 크게 유행한 이 게임은 1955년 영화 '이유 없는 반항'으로 사람들의 주목을 받았다. 이 게임은 두 젊은이가 각자 자신의 차를 몰고 동시에 절벽을 향해 달리다가 가능한 한 마지막 순간에 차에서 뛰어 내리는 것이다. 먼저 차에서 뛰어내리는 쪽이 겁쟁이인 동시에 패자가 된다. 둘 다 패자·겁쟁이가 되지 않으려면 공멸하는 수밖에 없다.

해설

1. 본문은 딜레마에 관한 내용이다. 죄수의 딜레마라는 게임이론을 통해 서로에 대한 불신으로 인해서 자신들에게 가장 좋은 선택이 아닌 가장 좋지 않은 선택을 할 수밖에 없는 상황을 설명하고 있다. 따라서 정답은 미소의 군비경쟁이 필연적이었다고 설명한 (c)가 된다. 참고로 (b)의 경우 남보다 우월하고 싶다고 하였지 열등한 상황을 원하는 것은 아니므로 inferior는 완전히 틀린 진술이다.

2. 죄수의 딜레마를 작동시키는 기저에는 '상대에 대한 불신'이 자리 잡고 있다. 이를 달리 말하면 상대를 신뢰할 수 없으므로 스스로를 지키려는 (c)가 정답이 된다.

3. 죄수의 딜레마에는 양 측이 등장하며, 자신의 행동이 상대에게 영향을 미치는 상황이어야 한다. 정답은 (d)로 구명정에 탈 수 있는 사람들은 구명정에 탈 수 있는 사람들을 선택하는 사람에게 취할 수 있는 영향이 없기 때문이다.

4. (b)와 (d)는 지엽적이고, (c)는 본문과 무관하다. 정답은 (a)로 '죄수의 딜레마'나 '치킨 게임' 등에서와 같이 왜 사람들은 물러서지 않는가에 관한 의문을 제기하는 것으로 전체 내용을 축약해서 전달할 수 있다

정답   1.(c)   2.(c)   3.(d)   4.(a)

UNIT 03

Progress over product
GDP

    1989년 3월 알래스카에서는 유조선 엑손 발데즈호가 좌초돼 원유 4만㎥가 누출됐다. 2,000km의 해변이 오염됐고 기름 제거를 위해 많은 사람이 앵커리지 인근 프린스 윌리엄 해협으로 몰려들었다. 한적하던 레스토랑·호텔·주유소·상점은 갑자기 사람들로 북적대면서 전에 없는 호황을 누리게 됐다. 알래스카 지역의 국내총생산(GDP)도 덩달아 올라갔다. GDP가 늘어났다고 수많은 바닷새와 고래가 죽어나간 알래스카가 더 좋아졌다고 할 수 있을까?
    GDP는 생산 총량을 시장 가치라는 하나의 기준으로 평가하는 지표. 기본적으로 생산된 모든 것은 그 자체로 당연히 좋은 것이라고 가정한다. 지속 가능한 것과 지속 불가능한 것을 구별하지 못한다. 국민의 생활수준을 실제로 향상시키는 경제활동과 그렇지 않은 경제활동을 구별하지도 못한다. 자원 채굴, 삼림 남벌로 인해 자연의 가치가 줄어도 GDP는 늘어난다. 그래서 GDP는 덧셈만 하고 뺄셈을 하지 못하는 계산기라는 비판이 나온다.
    GDP는 1930년대 대공황 때 미국 상무부가 만들어 경제 회복을 측정하는 잣대로 사용했다. 하지만 실제 이를 만든 경제학자 사이먼 쿠즈네츠조차 "한 나라의 복지 상태를 국가 소득 합계에서 추정할 수 있는 경우는 거의 없다"면서 GDP 개념의 남용을 경계했을 정도다. GDP의 문제점이 대두되자 이를 대체할 새로운 지표를 개발하려는 노력이 이어지고 있다. 최근 새로 제시되는 지표 가운데 대표적인 것이 GPI(Genuine Progress Indicator, 진정한 진보 지표)다. GPI는 자원의 감소, 오염, 장기적인 환경피해, 가사노동처럼 GDP가 제외한 요소들까지 측정한다.

해설

1. 본문은 경제 현황을 측정해주는 기본 지표인 GDP에 대해 설명하면서 동시에 GDP가 지닌 한계점을 강조하고 있다. 따라서 1930년대 등장해 경제 부활의 지표 역할을 했던 GDP의 한계를 이제는 GPI 지표를 통해 개선하고 있다는 점에서 정답은 (b)가 적합하다.

2. GDP는 국민의 생활수준을 실제로 향상시키는 경제활동과 그렇지 않은 경제활동을 구별하지도 못하며, 첫 번째 문단에서 알래스카 지역이 유조선의 좌초로 오염됐지만 지역 GDP는 오히려 올라갔다는 내용을 통해 오염은 GDP에 산정되지 않음을 알 수 있다. 또한 마지막 문단의 경제학자 증언을 통해 한 나라의 복지 상태를 GDP에서 추정할 수 있는 경우는 거의 없다고 밝히고 있다. 따라서 정답은 (a)가 된다.

3. 유조선 엑손 발데즈호가 좌초되자 기름 제거를 위해 많은 사람이 몰리면서, 지역 경제가 전례 없는 호황을 누리게 됐다고 나온다. 따라서 정답은 기름 제거 작업에 모인 지원자들이 일종의 관광 산업을 일으켰다는 (a)가 정답이 된다.

4. GDP의 대안으로 GPI가 나온 것이므로 한 국가의 경제 상황을 보다 더 정확히 반영한다고 볼 수 있으며, 도입부에서는 발데즈호의 좌초로 수많은 바닷새와 고래가 죽어갔다고 밝히고 있다. (c) 또한 전체 내용을 통해 추론할 수 있다. 정답은 (d)로 알래스카의 지역 GDP가 늘어났지만 실제는 그렇지 않기 때문에 GDP 측정에 대한 비판적인 예로 사용된 것이므로, 실제 그곳 GDP는 높지 않을 것이라는 것을 짐작할 수 있다.

정답   1.(b)   2.(a)   3.(a)   4.(d)

UNIT 04

Respecting privacy v. Public interests
사생활 보호 v. 공익

일본 정부는 코로나19 확진자의 상세한 정보를 공개하지 않는다. 구(區) 단위의 거주지역과 연령대 정도만 공개한다. 확진자가 언제, 어디를 갔는지는 밝히지 않는다. 지자체에 따라 동네를 밝히는 경우도 있다. 확진의 경우, 회사가 홈페이지에 밝히지 않았다면 조용히 묻힐 비밀이었다. 정보공개 여부는 100% 기업 혹은 개인의 몫으로 넘긴 것이다.

명분은 '개인정보보호'다. 공개했을 경우 개인이나 기업이 입을 과도한 피해를 우려해서다. 실제로 확진자가 있었던 학교의 여학생들이 "코로나"라고 손가락질을 당했다는 뉴스도 있었다. 이런 피해를 원천적으로 막기 위해, 아예 공개를 하지 않는다는 게 일본 정부 기조다. (소수의 피해자를 만드느니) 깜깜이 상태에서 다수가 조심하는 쪽을 택한 것이다. 정부가 시민들의 휴대전화 정보를 확보하는 것도 일본에선 건드릴 수 없는 성역처럼 다뤄지고 있다. 전체주의적인 발상이 떠오른다는 이유에서다.

이런 기조는 한국과는 정반대다. 서울시는 이태원 클럽에서 확진자가 나오자, 행정력을 동원해 그 날 주변에 있었던 1만 여 명의 휴대전화 통신정보까지 뒤졌다. 원치 않게 신상이 공개돼 특정인에게 비난이 집중되는 부작용도 있었지만, 바이러스의 확산은 늦췄다. 결과적으로 한국은 감염경로를 파악하는 것이 일본에 비해 훨씬 더 성공적이다.

정부의 정보 통제와 감시에 대한 우려는 모든 나라가 고민하고 있는 지점이다. 그 지점에서 보다 안전하고 쾌적한 사회에 살고 싶다는 시민들의 자발적인 요구가 건전한 감시사회를 만들어 내고 있다. 많은 나라가 이 같은 흐름에 올라탔다. 감시를 허용할 것이냐의 문제가 아니라 정보를 공익적으로 사용하고 악용되지 않게끔 시스템을 갖추는 게 지금 논의할 일이다.

해설

1. Covid-19가 기승을 부리고 있는 상황에서 사생활과 개인의 정보 보호라는 사익과 국민의 알권리에 대한 공익의 충돌문제를 어떻게 처리할지가 글의 전반적인 내용이다. 그러므로 정답은 b)이다.

2. 확진 사례가 나오면 무조건 알려야 한다는 규정은 없으며, 일본 정부는 개인의 동선에 대해 구체적으로 알리지도 않는다. 개인정보를 보호하면 할수록 확진이 빠르게 멈춘다는 내용은 반대로 서술되었다. 오히려 개인정보를 공개할수록 감염의 확산을 늦출 수 있기 때문이다. 그러므로 개인 정보 접근의 용이성 때문에 한국은 일본보다 감염에 대해 더 잘 추적할 수 있다는 d)가 정답이다.

3. 밑줄 친 부분은 개인의 정보 남용을 방지하고, 공익을 위해서 정보를 이용할 수 있는 토대를 구축하는 게 중요하다는 게 핵심이다. 그러므로 '정부가 개인정보를 이용하는 것을 피하기 위하여, 모두의 보호를 위해 관련정보를 공유할 방법을 찾아야 한다.'는 d)의 내용과 일맥상통하므로 정답은 d)이다.

4. 일본 정부는 (소수의 피해자를 만드느니) 깜깜이 상태에서 다수가 조심하는 쪽을 택한 것이므로, 사생활과 건강 이라는 문제 사이에 선택이라면 일본은 건강보다는 사생활의 보호를 택한 것으로 볼 수 있다. 그러므로 정답은 a)이다. 참고로 언제 어디를 방문했는지 등은 상관없이 연령과 지역만 알고 있으면 동선 추적이 필요한 정보는 다 갖춘 것이라는 d)는 틀린 진술이다.

정답 1.(b) 2.(d) 3.(d) 4.(a)

UNIT 05

Just give them some fish
물고기를 줘라

"어떤 사람에게 물고기를 그냥 준다면 그를 하루만 배부르게 할 것이고, 물고기 잡는 법을 가르쳐준다면 평생을 배부르게 할 것이다." 익숙한 문구다. 선교단체나 개발기구, 비정부기구(NGO)에서는 일종의 선언문처럼 쓰이는 말이기도 하다. 원조나 복지가 누군가를 돕는 자선이 아니라 삶의 방식을 바꾸는 변화가 돼야 한다는 뜻이 담겨있다.

그런데 그게 정답일까. 제임스 퍼거슨 미국 스탠퍼드대 인류학과 교수는 저서 『분배정치의 시대』에서 오늘날 어업만 봐도 이 말이 더 이상 통하지 않는다고 지적한다. 기업들이 '떠다니는 공장'으로 불릴 만한 특수기술로 어업을 주도하면서 이제는 '물고기 잡는 사람'이 필요 없기 때문이다. "이 시대에 어떤 인간에게 물고기 잡는 법을 가르치는 것은 실업자 어부를 양산하거나 기껏해야 이미 경쟁이 포화상태인 분야에 초보자 한 명을 추가하는 것에 불과하다"고 그는 주장한다.

세상이 변했다. 오늘날 세계는 가난한 이들의 노동력 공급을 필요로 하지 않는다. 직업훈련에서 익힌 것을 써먹을 곳이 없다. 어차피 세계화, 디지털화로 완전 고용은 거의 불가능한 목표가 되고 있다. 그래서 어떤 이들은 가난한 이들에게 그냥 기본소득을 주라고 주장하기도 한다.

기본소득제에 대한 심리적 저항감은 엄청나다. 특히 정통 좌파일수록 거부감이 크다. '일하지 않은 자 먹지도 말라'는 철학에 배치되기 때문이다. 칼 마르크스는 정상적인 생산활동을 하지 않으면서 부유해지고 싶어 하는 무산계급을 '룸펜 프롤레타리아'라 칭하며 비판했다. 룸펜 프롤레타리아는 무산계급의 혁명을 방해할 뿐 아니라, 반동적 음모에 가담한다고 봤기 때문이다. 지금도 정통 좌파진영은 "기본소득제는 현금 지급으로 사람들을 신자유주의적 시장교환의 세계로 끌어들이는 것"이라며 거부한다.

해설

1. 가난한 자들을 위한 시스템 개선에 대한 논의가 진행되며, 그 가운데 기본소득제에 대한 얘기가 주류를 이룬다. 그러므로 이제 시스템 변화에 대하여 얘기할 시기가 되었고, 기본소득제에 대한 논의가 수면 위로 올라오고 있는 d)가 정답이다.

2. "어떤 사람에게 물고기를 그냥 준다면 그를 하루만 배부르게 할 것이고, 물고기 잡는 법을 가르쳐준다면 평생을 배부르게 할 것이다."라는 문구는 단기적으로 도움을 줄 것이 아니라 장기적인 관점에서 삶에 도움이 되는 방법을 모색하라는 뜻으로, 남을 도울 때는 단기적인 것보다 오래 지속되는 도움을 제공하는 것을 목표로 하라는 a)가 정답이다.

3. 칼 마르크스는 정상적인 생산활동을 하지 않으면서 부유하길 원하는 무산계급을 '룸펜 프롤레타리아'라 칭하며 비판(Karl Marx criticized the class who does not engage in proper production activities but wishes to become rich, calling it the "lumpenproletariat.")했기 때문에, 생산활동을 하지 않아도 주어지는 기본소득제에 대해서는 당연히 부정적인 입장이 되어야 한다. 그러므로 d)가 정답이다.

4. 직업훈련에서 익혔다 해도 그 기술을 사용할 데가 없다는 문장 뒤에 빈칸이 나오고, 그러므로(so) 가난한 이들에게 그냥 기본소득을 주라고 주장한다는 언급으로 이어진다. 만약 구직에 성공했다면 문제가 없겠지만, 그게 아닌 상황에서는 기본소득으로 소득을 채워줘야 한다는 논리이다. 빈칸에 들어갈 내용은 고용의 달성이 매우 어렵다는 진술이 나와야 한다. 그러므로 정답은 a)이다.

정답 1.(d) 2.(a) 3.(d) 4.(a)

UNIT 06

Dollar envy
시뇨리지

    1999년 미국 정부가 발행을 시작한 50개 주(states) 기념주화는 역사상 가장 성공적인 화폐 프로그램으로 꼽힌다. 미국 조폐국은 각 주를 상징하는 디자인을 넣은 25센트 동전을 해마다 5종씩 순차적으로 발매했다. 액면가로 유통된 이 기념주화는 폭발적 호응을 얻었다. 미국 인구의 절반 가량이 이 주화를 수집한 것으로 조폐국은 추산했다. 2008년을 끝으로 50종이 모두 나왔다.

    여기서 질문이 하나 떠오른다. "미국 정부는 주화 발행으로 얼마를 벌었는가?". 25센트 기념주화를 찍어 내는 비용은 5센트도 안 되기 때문이다. 그에 따른 수익은 2008년까지 벌써 46억 달러에 이른다. 이처럼 정부나 중앙은행이 화폐를 발행함으로써 얻는 이익을 시뇨리지(Seigniorage)라고 한다. 50개 주 기념주화처럼 시중에 유통되지 않고 수집품으로만 남는다면 액면가(25센트)와 발행비용(5센트)의 차액이 모두 시뇨리지가 된다. 하지만 지폐처럼 계속 유통되면서 몇 년 내로 닳아서 폐기되는 경우는 계산법이 조금 다르다. 중앙은행이 돈을 찍어 유통시키면서 획득한 금융자산의 운용수익이 시뇨리지가 된다. 연간 시뇨리지 총액은 시장 이자율에서 발행·유통비용을 빼고, 여기에다 현재 유통 중인 통화량을 곱해서 계산한다.

    시뇨리지는 달리 '인플레 세금'이라고도 부른다. 통화 공급을 늘려 인플레가 생기면 기존의 통화에서 실질가치가 줄어들고 그만큼의 부가 중앙은행에 이전되기 때문이다. 이것이 국내에서만 이뤄질 경우 부의 총량은 변하지 않는다. 하지만 국제 금융결제의 기축 통화, 미국 달러화의 경우는 문제가 달라진다. 미국이 발권량을 늘려 그로 인한 인플레가 생기면 전 세계의 달러 소유자로부터 줄어드는 실질 가치가 미국의 연방준비은행으로 이전하는 것이다. 제2차 세계대전 이후 달러가 국제 기축 통화로 결정된 이래 미국이 벌어들인 시뇨리지는 천문학적인 숫자가 될 것이다. 월요일에 미국과 유럽의 중앙은행들은 금융기업에 유동성을 공급하기 위해 미국 달러의 무제한 방출을 선언하였다. 미국의 연방준비위원회는 필요한 만큼 달러를 충분히 발행하고 중앙은행 간에 환율의 상환을 확대할 의도이다. 우리는 시뇨리지 효과를 누리며 국제통화의 기준이 되는 미국 달러가 부러울 뿐이다.

> **해설**
>
> 1. 정부나 중앙은행이 화폐를 발행함으로써 얻는 이익을 시뇨리지라고 한다. 기념주화를 찍어내거나 지폐처럼 계속 유통되는 주화를 찍어내는 것을 모두 포함하는 가장 올바른 진술은 (a)이다.
>
> 2. 기념주화가 가져온 이익, 시뇨리지의 계산법, 시뇨리지 효과와 국제시장 간의 관계 모두 언급하고 있으나 미국 정부가 힘이 없는 통화를 강하게 키울 수 있도록 도왔다는 것은 언급되어 있지 않다. 따라서 정답은 (b)이다.
>
> 3. 시뇨리지는 정부나 중앙은행이 화폐를 발행함으로써 얻는 이익으로 기념주화와 같이 수집품으로 퇴장당하면 액면가와 발행비용의 차액이 모두 시뇨리지가 되고, 지폐처럼 계속 유통되면 중앙은행이 돈을 찍어 유통시키면서 획득한 금융자산의 운용수익이 시뇨리지가 된다. 그러므로 이는 국가에 이득이 되는데, 실망스런 효과를 나타낼 뿐이라고 한 (c)가 정답이다. 참고로 (b)는 기념주화 발행이 시뇨리지가 증가하는 한 가지 예에 해당한다고 하였으므로 올바른 진술이다.
>
> 4. 인플레이션은 통화 공급이 늘어나서 화폐의 실질 가치가 숱어들게 되는 현상인데 이것이 일어나기 위한 원인이 될 수 있는 것은 통화의 공급이 증가하는 것이다. 보기 중 통화 공급이 증가할 수 있는 방안은 기념주화 생산밖에 없으므로 정답은 (b)이다.

정답   1.(a)   2.(b)   3.(c)   4.(b)

UNIT 07

More Sea Story blame game
정보의 비대칭성

아무리 민주적이고 투명한 사회라고 해도 불공평한 일은 늘 있기 마련이다. 그중에 가장 심각하면서도 해소하기 어려운 불공평은 아마도 정보의 배분일 것이다. 실생활에서도 정보의 불완전하고 불공평한 배분, 즉 정보의 비대칭성(information asymmetry) 때문에 많은 문제가 빚어진다. 대표적인 예가 중고차를 살 때다. 통상 중고차 판매상은 (팔려고 내놓은 차에 대해) 구매자보다 훨씬 더 잘 안다. 구매자가 차의 품질에 대해 잘 모르는 상황에서 판매상은 차를 실제 가치보다 비싸게 팔려는 유혹을 떨치기 어렵다. 구매자에게 바가지를 씌우는 것이다. 그러나 이런 일이 반복되면 구매자들도 더는 침묵하지만은 않는다. 평판이 나쁜 판매상과는 아예 거래를 하지 않는다. 몇몇 경우 판매자는 매장을 닫을 수도 있다. 그들이 정보의 우위를 이용해 한두 번 재미를 볼 수는 있겠지만 영원히 소비자를 속일 수는 없다.

클린턴 행정부 시절 백악관 경제자문위원을 지낸 조지 애컬로프 교수는 정보의 비대칭성을 바탕으로 한 이른바 레몬시장(Market for Lemons) 이론으로 노벨경제학상을 탔다. 레몬은 겉으로는 반짝반짝 광나는 중고차처럼 화려해 보이지만 안을 들여다보면 쓸모없는 상품을 의미한다. 정보의 비대칭성이 심각한 문제를 일으키는 장면은 주인-대리인 관계다. 사회가 복잡해질수록 전문가에게 판단과 의사결정을 맡기는 일이 잦아진다. 주주와 전문경영인의 관계가 대표적이다. 그런데 대리인이 진정으로 주인을 대신해서 성심성의껏 일한다는 보장이 없다. 일을 맡긴 주인은 그 분야와 관련된 지식을 전문가만큼 알 수가 없기에 제대로 감시·감독하기가 어렵다. 여기서 대리인의 도덕적 해이(moral hazard)가 발생한다. 자신의 이익을 앞세워 주인의 이익을 해칠 위험이 크다는 얘기다.

해설

1. 본문은 레몬시장, 주주-대리인 이론과 같은 예를 들면서 정보의 불공평한 배분인 정보의 비대칭성에 대해서 이야기하고 있다.

2. 판매자들이 정보의 우위를 이용해 품질을 속이고 비싸게 팔게 되면 처음 몇 번은 돈을 벌 수도 있지만 구매자들은 평판이 나쁜 판매자와는 거래를 하지 않고 심한 경우에는 문을 닫는 상황까지 일어날 수 있기 때문에 판매자가 성공하고자 한다면 소비자를 속여서는 안 된다는 것을 추론할 수 있다. 따라서 정답은 (b)이다.

3. 주인과 대리인 관계에서의 문제점은 주인이 대리인에게 맡긴 일의 내용을 전문가만큼 알 수 없기 때문에 즉, 정보의 비대칭성이 발생하기 때문에 제대로 감독하기가 어려워 대리인이 자신의 이익을 위해 주인의 이익을 해칠 수 있다는 점이다. 따라서 정답은 (c)이다.

4. 판매에 있어 평판은 큰 영향을 끼치며, 정보를 많이 가진 판매자는 정보가 없는 소비자를 속일 유혹을 받게 되며, 주주와 CEO는 주인-대리인 관계를 대표하는 사례이다. 레몬은 겉은 화려해 보이지만 실제로는 형편없는 제품을 의미한다. 그들이 해야 하는 직무에 대한 이해를 하지 못한 사람이라는 (b)는 틀린 진술이다.

정답 1.(c) 2.(b) 3.(c) 4.(b)

UNIT 08

Hierarchical incompetence?
피터원리

자리가 사람을 만든다는 말이 있다. 도저히 사람의 수준이 너무 낮지 않은 이상 일단 자리에 앉혀 놓고 보면 주어진 직무를 수행할 수 있다. 그러나 그 사람의 능력 수준과 너무 먼 자리에 가는 경우라면 얘기가 달라진다. 능력에 부치는 자리를 감당하지 못하는 본인도 버겁고, 그런 부조화의 고통을 견뎌야 하는 직원들도 괴롭다. 물론 무능한 인물을 잘못 기용한 조직이 먼저 비효율의 대가를 톡톡히 치러야 한다. 그런데 어떤 조직이든 인사철마다 무능하다고 여겨지는 사람이 승진대상 명단에는 꼭 낀다는 얘기가 나돈다. 왜 그럴까?

로렌스 피터는 무능력자의 승진이 위계조직에서 나타나는 보편적인 현상임을 밝혀냈다. 그는 1969년 이후 수백 건의 사례를 연구한 끝에 이러한 결론을 내리게 되었다. "조직체에서 모든 구성원은 자신의 무능력이 드러날 때까지 승진하려는 경향을 보인다"는 것이다. 이른바 '피터 원리(The Peter Principle)'다. 이 원리에 따르면 위계조직 내의 구성원은 자신의 무능력이 드러나는 단계까지 승진을 하게 된다. 자신의 능력을 넘어서는 자리로 승진한 사람은 직감적으로 그게 마지막 자리임을 안다.

그러나 절대로 그런 사실을 인정하거나 자발적으로 자리를 포기하지 않는다. 그 대신 자신의 무능을 감추기 위한 다양한 시도를 한다. 감추려는 일반적인 증상은 많다. 책상을 깨끗하게 정돈해야 안심이 되는 종이공포증, 바쁘게 보이려고 서류를 산처럼 쌓아놓는 문서 중독증, 무의미한 말을 장황하게 늘어놓는 만연체 화법, 부산하게 돌아다니는 책상 기피증, 끊임없이 (전화로 무언가를 떠들어대는) 전화 중독증, 업무성과를 가시적으로 보여줘야 직성이 풀리는 도표 집착증 등이다.

해설

1. 자리를 맡을 능력이 되지 않는 무능력한 사람이 그들 자신의 무능력이 드러날 때까지 승진하려는 경향이 있다는 것에 대해서 이야기하고 있다. 그들이 무능력을 감추기 위한 방법은 마지막 문단에서 소개되고 있으므로 전반적인 주제가 아니다. 따라서 정답은 (d)이다.

2. 피터는 위계조직에서 수백 건의 무능력 사례를 연구한 끝에 위계조직 내의 구성원은 자신의 무능력이 드러나는 단계까지 승진을 하게 된다는 것을 발견하였다. 이것이 바로 피터 원리이고, 정답은 (c)가 된다.

3. 자신의 능력을 넘어서는 자리로 승진한 사람은 그런 사실을 인정하거나 자발적으로 자리를 포기하지 않는다. 그 대신 무능을 감추기 위한 다양한 시도를 하면서 그의 무능이 알려지기 전까지는 계속 남아 있으려고 한다는 것을 추론할 수 있다. 유능해지기 위한 노력을 한다거나 무능에 대해 신경 쓰지 않거나 모른다고는 말할 수 없다. 따라서 정답은 (b)이다.

4. 무능력한 동료가 승진을 하게 되는 것을 받아들이는 것은 힘든 일일 것이며, 무능력함을 감추기 위한 방안으로 바쁘게 보이기 위해 서류를 산처럼 쌓아놓는 것이 언급되어 있다. 자신의 능력을 넘어서는 자리로 승진한 사람은 절대 무능력한 사실을 인정하거나 자발적으로 자리를 포기하지 않는다. 따라서 정답은 (c)이다.

정답 1.(d) 2.(c) 3.(b) 4.(c)

UNIT 09
Broken items
깨진 유리창

제과점 앞을 지나던 불량배가 유리창을 깼다. 놀란 가게 주인이 달려 나가서 쫓아갔지만 불량배는 달아났고, 피해는 생각보다 크지 않았다. 주인은 깨진 유리창을 종이로 적당히 가리고 그냥 넘어갔다. 얼마 후 가게 앞엔 쓰레기가 쌓이고, 벽에 낙서가 생겼다. 그러자 손님들이 점차 줄더니, 제과점 주변은 어느새 불량배들의 싸움판이 됐다. 미국의 범죄심리학자 제임스 윌슨과 조지 켈링은 이같은 도시범죄의 증폭 현상에 주목하고 1982년 '깨진 유리창'이란 논문을 발표했다. 건물 주인이 깨진 유리창과 같은 사소한 피해를 방치하면 절도나 폭력 같은 더 큰 강력범죄가 발생한다는 것이다. 깨진 유리창을 본 사람들은 건물주가 건물을 포기했다는 인상을 갖게 된다. 작은 무질서와 하찮은 범죄를 가볍게 여기면 심각한 사태로 발전한다는 이론이다.

홍보와 마케팅 전문가인 마이클 레빈은 이 이론을 경영학에 응용해 '깨진 유리창의 법칙'을 고안했다. 기업이 사소한 실수와 미비점을 방치하면 예기치 않은 손실과 치명적인 경영실패를 부른다는 것이다. 페인트 부스러기가 벗겨지면 화장실이 지저분해지고, 직원들을 불친절한 채로 방치하면 결국 거대기업의 몰락으로 이어질 수 있다는 얘기다. 범죄학이든 경영학이든 '깨진 유리창'은 바로바로 손봐야 한다는 메시지다.

경제학에선 일찍이 19세기 초반에 깨진 유리창을 둘러싼 논쟁이 벌어졌다. 프랑스 국가재건위원이었던 생샤망은 깨진 유리창을 갈아 끼우면 빵 가게 주인은 손해를 보겠지만 유리 가게주인이 그만큼 덕을 보기 때문에 국민경제적 손실은 없다고 단언했다. 그는 심지어 유리가게 주인의 지출로 새로운 소득이 창출되기 때문에 유리창을 깨는 것이 오히려 바람직하다는 주장을 폈다. 이에 대해 자유주의 경제학자 끌로드 프레데릭 바스티아는 유리창이 깨지지 않았다면 그 돈은 다른 곳에 쓰였을 것이라고 말했다. 그러므로 유리가게 주인의 이득은, 다른 업자의 기회손실에 불과하다고 논박했다. 바스티아에 따르면 파괴를 통해 부가 창출된다는 주장은 이른바 '깨진 유리창의 오류'에 빠진 허구라는 것이다.

해설

1. 깨진 유리창이나 기업의 사소한 실수이거나 방치해두면 예기치 않은 손실을 가져오게 된다는 '깨진 유리창' 이론에 대해 이야기하고 있으므로 정답은 (c)이다.

2. 범죄학이 다른 범죄를 유발하는 범죄들을 예측한다는 언급이 없으며 미국이 범죄율이 가장 높다는 것은 알 수 없으며 경제학자들 중 서로 반대되는 주장을 하는 사람들이 존재한다. 마지막 단락에 결국 파괴를 통해 부가 창출되는 것은 깨진 유리창의 오류라고 설명하고 있으므로 부정적인 상황으로부터 파생된 긍정적인 효과는 여전히 부정적이라는 것을 추론할 수 있다. 따라서 정답은 (b)이다.

3. 깨진 유리창 이론에 대해 경제학자인 생샤망과 끌로드 프레데릭 바스티아는 서로 반대되는 논의를 하고 있는 것을 알 수 있다. 따라서 정답은 (a)이다.

4. 깨진 유리창 이론은 작은 무질서와 같은 문제가 심각한 일로 발전한다는 이론으로써 사소한 문제가 생긴다면 그것을 즉시 고쳐야 하고 그렇지 않으면 더 큰 문제를 야기한다고 설명할 수 있다. 따라서 정답은 (d)이다.

정답 1.(c) 2.(b) 3.(a) 4.(d)

UNIT 10

Demonstrators in the dark
합리적 무시

1845년, 프랑스 경제학자 프레드릭 바스티아는 보호무역주의를 풍자하는 패러디를 썼다. 그의 이야기 속에서는 프랑스 양초제조업협회가 청원서 한 통을 의회에 제출했다. "우리 양초제조업자들은 우리보다 훨씬 나은 조건에서 조명기구를 생산하고 있는 외국 경쟁업체들과 감당할 수 없는 경쟁에 시달리고 있습니다. 이들은 엄청나게 낮은 가격으로 국내 시장을 잠식하고 있습니다. 태양과 다를 바 없는 이 경쟁 업체들이 무자비하게 국내 시장을 공략하고 있습니다." 프랑스 양초제조업자들은 외국산 양초의 수입 금지는 물론, 자연 채광마저 금지하는 입법에 매달렸다. '인위적인' 경쟁 배제와 수요 창출을 동시에 요구한 것이다. 그러나 이 청원은 '소비자의 이익을 무시했다'는 이유로 프랑스 의회에서 거부됐다.

미국의 경제·사회학자 맨슈어 올슨은 그의 책 『집단행동의 논리』에서 선별적이고 제한적으로 돌아가는 이익(혜택)은 집단지향으로 행동하는 잠재적인 집단의 합리적인 개인에게 자극이 될 것이라고 이론화했다. 집단행동에 나서는 사람들이 아무리 공익과 국익을 앞세워도 실은 철저하게 사적 이익을 추구할 뿐이란 얘기다.

걸린 이해가 클수록 이익집단의 응집력이 강해지고, 집단행동의 강도는 세다. 문제는 이익집단들의 집단행동에 대한 일반대중의 반발이 의외로 적다는 점이다. 왜 그럴까. 이익은 특정한 이익집단에 집중된 반면, 사회적 손실은 널리 분산되어 개개인에게 돌아오는 피해가 적기 때문이다. 이 경우 특혜를 받는 이익집단은 최소비용으로 최대의 이익을 얻겠다는 자신들의 합리적 판단에 따라 일반대중의 손해를 무시하게 된다. 이른바 '합리적 무시 이론'이다. 이를 뒤집으면 이익집단의 개별적인 손해를 줄이기 위해 아무리 큰 국가적 이익도 무시할 수 있다는 것이 된다.

해설

1. 합리적 무시 이론이 비즈니스에서 사람들이 따르는 보통의 정책이라는 것은 알 수 없다. 최소비용으로 최대의 이익을 얻겠다고 일반대중의 손해를 무시하는 이익집단으로부터 집단은 오로지 집단 내의 사람들의 이익만 생각한다는 것을 추론할 수 있다. 따라서 정답은 (c)이다.

2. 이익집단은 개별적인 손해를 최소화하기 위해 일반 대중의 손해를 무시한다고 한 점으로부터 그들이 최대한의 이익을 얻는다고 해도 최소한의 비용 이상을 받아들이지 않을 것임을 알 수 있다. 따라서 정답은 (a)이다.

3. 프랑스 양초제조업자들로부터 시작해 이익집단의 응집력과 집단행동에 관한 이야기를 다루고 있다. 최대의 이익과 최소의 비용과 단체교섭과 개인적 이익보다는 이익집단이라는 제목이 모든 것을 포괄한다고 할 수 있다. 따라서 정답은 (d)이다.

4. 외국산 양초의 수입은 물론 자연 채광마저 금지하는 입법에 매달리며 인위적인 경쟁 배제와 수요 창출을 요구했다는 것에서 자연 채광은 빛을 얻을 수 있는 원천이지만 촛불로부터 오는 것이 아니므로 인위적인 경쟁이라고 할 수 있다. 따라서 정답은 (b)이다.

정답 1.(c) 2.(a) 3.(d) 4.(b)

UNIT 11

An unbroken union
월마트

월마트에선 노동조합을 제외하고는 모든 것을 찾을 수 있다. 소매 거인인 월마트는 노조에 반대하는 정책으로 악명이 높다. 채용 때부터 미래의 노조원장이 될 만한 지원자를 걸러낸다. 1991년 작성된 내부 지침서엔 직원들의 노조 결성 낌새를 눈치채는 법 24가지가 적혀 있다. 직장 동료들 간 전화 통화가 늘어나거나, 회사 이익이나 정책에 대한 호기심이 많아지거나, 회의 때 과격한 질문이 많아지거나, 중재, 고충 처리, 근속 연수 등 노조 용어들이 자주 입에 오르내린다거나, 평소 안 친하던 직원들이 갑자기 자주 만난다는 조짐이 보이면 관리자는 본사 노조대책반에 알려야 한다. 대책반은 바로 전용기를 타고 문제의 지점으로 날아든다. 창업 40년이 넘도록 노조가 발 못 붙인 이유다. 꼭 한 차례, 2004년 캐나다 퀘벡주의 한 매장이 노조를 만든 적이 있지만, 월마트는 이듬해 매장을 아예 폐쇄해버렸다.

월마트의 무(無)노조 경영은 창업자 샘 월튼의 고객 철학에서 비롯했다. 월튼의 철학 제1조는 '고객은 항상 옳다'이다. 제2조는 '만약 고객이 옳지 않다면 제1조를 들여다보라'이다. 고객이 부당한 요구를 해도 화내면 안 된다. 고객이 불만을 제기하면 불려가 잔소리를 듣거나 사유서를 써야 한다. '열 걸음 지침'(Ten Foot Rule)은 필수다. 고객이 자신의 열 걸음 앞에 오면 항상 고객의 눈을 보고, 반갑게 인사하며, 도와줄 것을 물어야 한다. '묻지마 반품 정책'도 여기서 나왔다. 고객은 반품하고자 하는 이유를 설명할 필요도 없다. "마음이 변했다" 한마디면 족하다. 그러다 보니 몇몇 고객들은 캠핑 갔다 와서 텐트를 반품하고, 핼러윈 축제 후 파티복을 무르는 것과 같이 정책을 남용한다. 그런데 반품을 모두 받아주려니 돈이 많이 들고, 다른 곳에서 아낄 수밖에 없다. 그중 쉬운 게 임금 줄이기이고 이것이 무노조 경영의 이유 중 한 부분이다.

해설

1. 노조가 없다는 것으로 모든 직원이 작업 환경을 불행하게 여긴다고는 말할 수 없다. 월마트 창업자인 샘 월튼의 고객 철학 제1조는 '고객은 항상 옳다'이고, 제2조는 '만약 고객이 옳지 않다면 제1조를 들여다 보라'인 것을 보면 월마트는 무엇보다 고객을 가장 가치있게 여긴다는 것을 추론해 볼 수 있다. 따라서 정답은 (b)이다.

2. 월튼의 철학 제1조는 '고객은 항상 옳다', 제2조는 '만약 고객이 옳지 않다면 제1조를 들여다보라'인 것에서 결국 '고객이 옳다'라는 제1조로 이어진다는 것을 알 수 있다. 따라서 둘 사이에는 실제적인 차이가 없다는 (c)가 정답이다.

3. 월튼의 고객 철학과 다른 정책들로부터 그가 그의 직원들과 그들의 능력을 호의적으로 평가하지 않거나 존중하지 않는다고는 말할 수 없다. 따라서 정답은 (a)이다.

4. 둘째 문단에서 무조건적인 반품 정책으로 인해 절약해야 하는 부분이 임금을 줄이는 것이고 이것이 무노조 경영의 이유 중 한 부분이라고 나온 것으로 볼 때 다음 문단에서는 다른 부분의 무노조 경영의 이유가 나올 것이다. 따라서 정답은 (b)이다.

정답 1.(b) 2.(c) 3.(a) 4.(b)

UNIT 12
How the strong grew weak
강한 정부의 역설

    1970년대 오일쇼크가 일어났을 때 석유 수입국들의 대응 방식은 두 가지로 갈렸다. 대부분의 선진국은 즉각 석유류 가격의 인상을 허용한 반면, 많은 개발도상국은 국내 유가 통제에 나섰다. 전자는 석유 위기에 따른 조정을 시장 기능에 맡겼고, 후자는 정부가 시장에 직접 뛰어든 것이다. 과연 어느 쪽이 더 '강한 정부'일까. 외견상 유가 상승을 방치한 나라의 정부는 시장에 대한 영향력이 약하고, 유가를 통제한 나라의 정부가 힘이 센 것처럼 보인다. 결과는 거꾸로 나타났다. 기름값이 시장 원리에 따라 오른 나라에서는 소비자들이 스스로 에너지 절약에 나섰고, 에너지를 절감하거나 석유를 대체하는 기술 개발이 자발적으로 일어났다. 유가 급등의 충격을 막는다며 국내 기름 값을 묶은 나라에서는 석유 소비가 줄지 않았으며 오히려 가수요와 매점매석, 암거래가 성행했다. 그 후 선진국들의 석유 의존도는 크게 줄어든 반면, 개도국의 석유 의존도는 여전히 높았다.

    이른바 '강한 정부'는 시장이나 국민의 의사와 관계없이 독자적으로 국가 목표를 설정하고, 이를 실현할 수 있는 정책수단을 보유한 정부다. 석유파동이라는 위기가 발생하면 국내유가 안정이란 목표를 정하고, 시장에 직접 개입해 가격 통제에 나선다. 문제는 이처럼 정부가 힘을 발휘하면 할수록 시장의 기능은 쇠퇴하고, 정책의 효과는 크게 떨어진다는 점이다. '강한 정부'는 정책의 실패를 만회하기 위해 점점 더 가혹한 규제와 더 강한 행정력을 동원하는 악순환에 빠진다.

    정책 실패가 누적되다보면 정부는 시장과 국민으로부터 멀어지게 된다. 정부의 효율성과 영향력이 줄어들어 종국에는 경제 파탄이나 실권이라는 파국을 맞을 위험이 크다. 미국의 국제관계외교학자 존 아이켄베리는 이를 '강한 정부의 역설(irony of state strength)'이라고 했다. 강한 정부가 강력한 정책을 펼친 끝에 힘이 빠지고 국민으로부터 외면당하는 정부로 전락하고 만다는 것이다.

해설

1. 겉으로 보기엔 시장에 개입하는 정부가 강한 정부처럼 보이지만, 강한 정부는 결국 강력한 정책을 펼친 끝에 힘이 빠지고 국민으로부터 외면당하는 정부로 전락한다고 언급되어 있다. 시장이나 국민의 의사와 관계없이 독자적으로 국가 목표를 설정하고 실행하게 되었을 때 시장의 기능은 쇠퇴하고 정책의 효과는 떨어진다. 그러므로 진짜 강한 정부는 시장 원리에 따라 기능하도록 맡겨두는 정부임을 추론할 수 있다. 따라서 정답은 (b)이다.

2. 강한 정부는 시장 기능에 직접 나서서 영향을 미치는 정부가 아니라 수요와 공급의 균형을 유지하는 시장 원리에 따라 기능할 수 있도록 내버려두는 정부임을 이야기하고 있다.

3. 전체 지문은 겉으로 보기에 직접 관여하고 제어하는 정부가 '강한 정부'처럼 보이지만 실제로는 그렇지 않다는 이야기를 담고 있다. 마지막에 이를 '강한 정부의 역설'이라고 표하고 있으므로 제목으로는 '강한 정부의 역설, 겉으로 힘이 약해보이는 정부가 실제로는 아니다'가 가장 적절하다. 따라서 정답은 (b)이다

정답   1.(b)   2.(a)   3.(b)

UNIT 13

A crime of passion
'제2의 스위스' 된다는 영국의 망상

많은 심리학자들은 브렉시트를 '격정범죄(crime of passion)'로 분석하거나 분노와 같은 순간적 감정으로 장기적 판단을 거른 채 저지르는 불법행위로 해석한다. 브렉시트 역시 소외계층의 분노가 폭발해 이뤄진 근시안적이고 비합리적 결정이라는 것이다. 브렉시트 지지자들은 EU(유럽연합) 탈퇴가 번영을 가져올 거라고 믿는다. 그러면서 이들은 항상 예로 드는 게 스위스다. 영국독립당 나이절 패러지 당수는 스위스인은 자신의 방향을 스스로 결정했고 스위스인은 행복하다고 늘 강조했었다.

스위스가 1992년 국민투표에서 EU 전신인 EC(유럽공동체) 참가를 부결시켰지만 최고의 부국(富國)인 건 사실이다. 지난해 스위스의 일인당 국민소득은 8만675달러(9,460만원)로 룩셈부르크에 이어 세계 2위다. 영국(4만3771달러), 미국(5만5805달러)과 비교가 안 된다. 이에 대해 브렉시트 지지자들은 스위스의 번영이 EU로부터 독립한 덕이라고 주장한다. 천문학적 기여금을 낼 필요도 없는 데다 자신에 맞는 무역정책을 폈기 때문이라는 거다.

하지만 전문가들은 하나같이 고개를 젓는다. 스위스의 성공은 EU와의 결별이 아닌 유별난 근로정신 때문이라는 것이다. 실제로 지난 5일 스위스에서는 특별한 안건을 놓고 국민투표가 실시됐었다. 안건의 내용은 소비진작을 위해 일인당 월 2,500스위스프랑(300만원)씩을 무조건 나눠주자는 것이었다. 공돈을 준다는데 세상에 이렇게 좋은 정책이 있을 리 없다. 하지만 결과는 압도적 부결이었다. 열심히 일하려는 의욕을 꺾게 된다는 이유에서였다. 2014년에는 법정 유급휴가 기간을 4주에서 6주로 늘리자는 법안이 부결됐었다.

영국인들에게 이런 의식이 없는 한 EU에서 탈퇴한다고 해서 제2의 스위스가 될 턱이 없다. 홧김에 저지른 브렉시트가 '영국에게 도움이 되는 득점'이 될 것 같지 않아서 안타까울 뿐이다.

해설

1. 작가는 영국의 유럽연합 탈퇴에 대해 부정적인 입장을 갖는다. 또한 스위스인들의 근로정신은 영국인들과 다르게 때문에 영국의 탈퇴는 스위스처럼 긍정적인 효과를 불러일으키지 못할 것이라는 (d)가 정답이다.

2. 마지막 단락에서 영국인들은 이러한 (스위스인들의 유별난 근로정신) 윤리의식을 공유하고 있지 않기 때문에 유럽연합을 떠나는 것은 스위스와 다른 결과를 낳을 것이라는 내용으로 (d)가 올바른 추론임을 알 수 있다.

3. 6월 5일 있었던 국민투표에서 일인당 월 2,500스위스프랑을 무조건 나눠받는 안건이 열심히 일하려는 의욕을 꺾을 수 있다는 이유로 부결되었다. 어떠한 대가도 없이 받을 수 있는 돈이었지만 이러한 이유로 거부했다는 점에서 굉장히 놀라운 것이다.

4. (a)에서 브렉시트는 그저 반사적으로 나온 반응(knee-jerk reaction)이라는 부분이 밑줄 친 a spur-of-the-moment reaction에서 드러난다. 또한 둘 다 영국의 탈퇴에 관해 부정적인 입장을 보여준다는 점에서 일치한다.

정답 1.(d) 2.(d) 3.(c) 4.(a)

UNIT 14

A rational vote
투표의 경제학

민주사회에서 투표는 정치적 의사를 표현하는 핵심적인 수단이다. 투표 참여는 국민으로서 당연히 져야 할 의무라고 여겨지지만 모든 사람이 책임감만으로 투표에 참여하지는 않는다. 공공선택이론은 정치적 행위도 경제적 합리성을 좇아 이루어진다고 가정한다. 유권자는 투표에서 얻는 편익과 비용을 따져 예상되는 이익을 극대화하는 쪽으로 행동한다는 것이다.

단순히 경제적 득실만 따진다면 아예 투표를 하지 않는 편이 유권자가 취할 수 있는 최선의 선택이다. 한 사람의 투표가 선거 결과에 영향을 줄 수 있는 확률은 거의 제로에 가까운 반면, 투표를 하는 데 드는 수고는 적지 않기 때문이다. 그러나 이 이론은 여전히 사람들이 투표에 참여하는 이유를 설명하지 못한다. 그래서 경제학자들이 대안을 제시했다. 투표 행위에는 물질적 이득만이 아니라 비경제적인 편익도 중요한 요인으로 작용한다는 것이다. 예컨대 선거라는 중요한 정치과정에 참여하는 것이 수고가 아니라 뿌듯한 즐거움일 수 있다는 것이다. 현재의 정치상황에 대한 유권자의 평가와 판단도 투표율에 영향을 미친다. 선거에서 누가 승리하느냐에 따라 편익이 크게 달라진다면 투표에 참여하려는 동기가 더욱 강해지는 것이다.

장기적인 관점에서 투표 참여의 동기를 찾아야 한다는 주장도 있다. 기권은 민주주의 대신 다른 정치 체제를 원하는 것으로 보일 수 있다. 투표 참여는 민주 체제에 대한 적극적 지지를 표명하는 행위로 보일 수 있다. 기권과 정치적 무관심이 민주 체제의 기틀을 허물지 모른다면, 투표로부터 얻는 비용—편익의 계산이 확 달라지게 된다. 그래서 투표는 민주 체제를 지키는 행동인 것이다.

문제는 투표 제도가 항상 최선의 결과를 낳지 않는다는 점이다. 노벨 경제학상을 받은 케네스 애로우는 어떤 투표 제도도 일관성 있는 결과를 보장하지 못한다는 것을 증명했다. 민주적인 투표과정을 거쳤다고 해서 최고의 인물이 뽑힌다는 보장은 없다는 것이다. 그럼에도, 그보다 나은 대안이 없기 때문에 투표는 여전히 최선의 민주적 절차로 간주된다. 비록 불완전하지만 투표 제도는 투표과정의 공정성과 투표 결과에 대한 승복을 통해 정당성을 갖는다.

해설

1. 민주주의 체제에 대한 적극적 지지와 선거라는 중요한 정치과정에 참여하는 것이 뿌듯한 즐거움이라는 것, 최고의 경제 상황을 가져와 자신이 가질 편익이 클 후보를 선택하는 것이 투표에 참여하는 동기라고 언급되어 있다. 언급되어 있지 않은 것은 (a)이다.

2. 유권자들이 투표에 참여하는 이유, 참여로부터 무엇을 얻고 잃는지에 대한 동기에 관해서 전반적으로 다루고 있다. 경제적 합리성을 쫓는다는 가정, 이에 대해 경제학자들이 제안한 대안, 장기적인 관점에서의 동기를 찾는 것들이 차례대로 설명되어 있다. 따라서 정답은 (a)이다.

3. 유권자들이 기권을 하는 이유는 민주주의 대신 다른 정치 체제를 원하는 것으로 보일 수 있다는 설명으로부터 민주주의에 만족하지 않는 것을 보여주기 위한 행동이 기권임을 추론할 수 있다. 따라서 정답은 (b)이다.

4. 경제학자들이 제시한 경제적 합리성을 좇는 유권자들의 행동을 요약하면 그들에게 주어지는 경제적인 편익이 좋아질 것인가 나빠질 것인가를 판단해 후보자를 선정할 것이라는 것을 알 수 있다. 따라서 정답은 (d)이다.

정답 1.(a) 2.(a) 3.(b) 4.(d)

UNIT 15

In the interest of whom?
수쿠크

그리스 철학자 아리스토텔레스는 돈을 빌려주고 이자를 받는 것에 반대했다. 그는 어떤 교환이나 거래를 통하지 않고, 단순히 화폐가 화폐를 생산하는 것은 비정상적이라고 생각했다. 중세의 교황들도 그렇게 생각했다. "이자를 받지 말지니 곧 돈의 이자, 식물의 이자, 이자를 낼만한 모든 것의 이자를 받지 말라"는 성경의 가르침을 따른 것이다. 고리대금을 갚으라고 요구한 성직자들은 직책을 박탈당했다. 회개하지 않고 죽은 대금업자에겐 기독교식 매장을 허용하지 않았다. 하지만 이 시대에도 돈을 빌려주는 사람들은 이자를 수수(授受)했다. 돈을 빌리는 사람이 송금이나 환전에 대한 수수료를 내는 방법이 사용됐다.

500여 년 전 활동했던 일부 종교개혁가들도 대출에 대한 이자 금지를 주장했다. 독일의 종교개혁가 마틴 루터는 분노에 찬 목소리로 "원금보다 더 많이 돌려받는 것은 도둑질이다. 고리대금업자는 악에 깊이 물든 도둑들이다. 다리를 찢어 죽이는 거열형(車裂刑)에 처해야 한다."라고 했다. 그러나 화폐경제가 뿌리를 내리고 점점 더 많은 사람이 고리대금으로 얻은 수입에 의존해서 살게 되자, 교회는 이자를 합법적인 소득의 원천으로 인정하지 않을 수 없었다.

이슬람교는 여전히 이자(리바)를 엄격히 금지한다. 하지만 이슬람교도들도 이러한 종교적 규제를 회피하기 위한 방법을 고안해 냈다. 이슬람 채권인 수쿠크가 대표적이다. 수쿠크는 돈을 빌려주는 것이 아니라 이자를 금지하는 이슬람법을 회피하기 위해 거래되는 금융상품이다. 예를 들어 기계를 구매하기 위해 돈을 빌리려는 사람이 있다면, 은행은 돈을 빌려주고 이자를 받는 대신 직접 기계를 사서 이에 대한 사용료를 받는다. 사용료는 명목상 이자가 아니기 때문에 이자 금지에 어긋나지 않는다. 수쿠크는 금융 혁명을 이룩하는 데 큰 도움을 주었다고 평가되는 자산담보부증권(ABS)과 유사하다. ABS 역시 담보가 되는 자산을 바탕으로 채권을 발행하고, 자산에서 얻는 수익금을 채권 보유자에게 돌려주는 구조이기 때문이다.

해설

1. 본문은 이슬람의 수쿠크에 대해 설명하고 있으며, 이를 위해 고대의 아리스토텔레스에서 시작하여 중세의 종교개혁가들까지 이자를 반대한 사람들을 예로 들어 이슬람 문화권에서 수쿠크가 도입된 것을 설명하기 위한 자연스러운 전개를 취하고 있다. 이슬람교도들이 대금업자라고 하는 것이나, 대부업의 비도덕적 관행이나 고리대금업에 대한 처벌 등은 본문의 내용과는 거리가 멀다.

2. 본문에서 이슬람교도들은 이자를 금지하는 이슬람법을 회피하기 위해서, 사용자가 필요로 하는 자산을 직접 매입하여 임대하고, 이에 대한 사용료를 받는 '수쿠크'라는 방법을 고안했다고 설명하고 있다. 그러므로 정답은 (c)이다.

3. 본문 2번째 단락 끝부분에서 기존에 이자를 반대에 해왔던 교회가, 화폐경제가 뿌리내리고 이자 소득으로 생활하는 사람이 증가함에 따라 이자를 정당한 소득의 원천으로 인정할 수밖에 없었음을 설명하고 있다. 성경이 대금업을 할 수 있는 사람을 특정하고 있다거나, 마틴 루터가 대금업자들에게 측은함을 느꼈다는 말은 본문에 없다. 그리고 본문에서 이자를 요구하는 성직자는 그 지위를 박탈당했다고 쓰여있지만, 그런 일이 빈번했다는 말은 없다.

4. 고대의 아리스토텔레스가 대부업에 반대했고, 교회에서도 이를 비난하며 반대해 오다가 화폐경제가 발전되고 나서야 인정한 것을 고려하면 최초의 대금업자는 사회적으로 매우 멸시당했을 것이라 유추할 수 있다. 죽을 때까지 큰 부를 축적했을 것이라든가, 채권을 회수하기 위해 폭력을 행사하고, 비탄에 빠져있을 것이라는 것은 본문의 내용으로 유추할 수 없다. 따라서 정답은 (c)이다.

정답 1.(d) 2.(c) 3.(a) 4.(c)

UNIT 16
NGO: A dearth of humility
인본주의가 결여된 NGO

전설적인 퀀텀펀드의 공동 설립자 짐 로저스는 여러모로 독특한 인물이다. 오토바이와 자동차로 두 차례나 세계를 누볐다는 점도 차별화 요소다. 그 행로를 정리한 두 권의 여행기(『월가의 전설 세계를 가다』, 『어드벤처 캐피털리스트』) 역시 그러하다. 방문지의 경제 효율성 저해 요인을 지적한 여행기는 흔히 볼 수 있는 게 아니기 때문이다.

그 저해 요인에 선진국과 비정부기구(NGO)가 포함됐다는 점도 눈길을 끌었다. 이들의 '영혼 없는 원조'가 아프리카의 산업 경쟁력을 약화시켜 경제 발전을 가로막고 있다는 이유에서다. 원조 물품의 상당량이 빼돌려져 독재자와 중간 상인에게로 간다는 지적도 곁들였다. 특히 NGO에 대한 비판은 신랄하다.

로저스의 책에는 "이들은 에어컨이 나오는 사륜구동 자동차를 창문마저 꼭꼭 잠근 채 타면서 근사하게 살고 있다. 경비원이 지키는 출입구가 갖춰진 고급 주택 단지에서 위성 TV를 보면서 생활한다. 그러면서 가난한 현지인들에게 그들이 얼마나 바보 같은지를 설명하며 돌아다닌다. 원조가 중단되면 NGO는 아프리카에서 더는 일자리를 찾지 못할 것이다. NGO는 이제 큰 사업이 됐다. 부패한 정부로 인해 생겨나 막대한 자금 동원력을 갖게 된 NGO는 해외 원조와 부패한 정부 사이에 개입하는 수많은 중개인을 양산해냈다."고 적혀있다.

로저스는 말라위의 리조트에서 호화판 회의를 하면서 현지인 출입을 막은 독일 NGO 단체의 위선적 행태 등도 고발했다. 그러면서 "현지인들은 NGO에게 고마움이 아니라 모멸감을 느낀다. 이들을 새로운 식민주의자라 부르기까지 한다"고 주장했다.

물론 책이 나왔던 2000년대 초만 해도 말 그대로 '딴 나라 얘기'처럼 보였다. 당시는 한국의 NGO가 돈과 권력으로부터의 자유를 무기로 정·재계를 성역 없이 비판해 갈채를 받던 시절이기 때문이다. 하지만 불투명한 자금 관리, 조직 이기주의, 권력 영합, 비판정신 상실로 특징지어지는 현재의 한국 주류 NGO는 로저스가 했던 비판에 그리 멀어 보이지 않는다.

해설

1. 이 글은 짐 로저스의 NGO에 대한 비판이 주류를 이루고 있으며, 한국의 NGO를 이에 빗대어 역시 비난하고 있다. 그러므로 b)의 짐 로저스의 NGO에 대한 부정적인 의견이 정답이 된다.

2. NGO는 초기에는 좋은 의도로 시작했고, 성과도 냈지만, 차츰 변질되어 갔으며, 급기야는 조직이 부패하게 되었다. 그러므로 a)가 정답이다.

3. 로저스가 NGO로부터의 도움을 싫어하는 이유는 영혼 없는 원조로 인하여 동기가 저하되고 사람들 스스로 노력하려는 의욕을 꺾기 때문이다. 즉 '영혼 없는 원조'가 아프리카의 산업 경쟁력을 약화시켜 경제 발전을 가로막고 있다 (soulless aid weakens the industrial competitiveness of Africa and hinders economic development).

4. 한국의 경우 과거 NGO에 대해서는 이미지가 좋았지만, 지금은 그렇지 못하다는 이야기로 전개되어야 흐름이 맞는다. 짐 로저스는 NGO를 비판하고 있으므로, 한국의 NGO 역시 별반 다를 게 없다는 내용이 나오면 NGO에 대한 부정적인 내용으로 적절하게 이어진다. 그러므로 정답은 d)이다.

정답 1. b) 2. a) 3. c) 4. d)

UNIT 17

Populism's persuasiveness
상황주의

칠레는 자유선거로 사회주의 정권을 탄생시킨 최초의 나라다. 1970년 살바도르 아옌데가 당시 다국적 기업이 독점하고 있던 구리 광산을 국유화해 그 이익을 사회 환원하겠다는 공약으로 대통령에 당선됐다. 3년 만에 아우구스토 피노체트의 군사 쿠데타로 붕괴했지만 아옌데 정권은 '선거에 의한 사회주의 이행이 가능한지 여부에 대한 오랜 정치학 논쟁에 종지부를 찍었다. 칠레의 군부는 남미의 다른 국가들과 비슷했을지 몰라도, 사회 구조는 매우 독특했다. 19세기 초 이미 시민사회라 부를 만한 집단이 형성돼있었다. 사회갈등을 조절할 수 있는 정당 메커니즘이 작동했다. 남미의 고질병인 포퓰리즘(대중영합주의)이 칠레에서만 예외가 된 이유다.

흔한 선입견과는 달리 포퓰리즘은 진보, 좌파의 전유물이 아니다. 포퓰리즘을 가장 세련되게 써먹어 온 나라는 사실 미국이다. 심지어 포퓰리즘이란 단어도 미국에서 만들어졌다. 공화·민주 양당체제에 대항하는 인민당이 1891년 설립됐고, 은화의 무제한 주조 등 경제적 합리성을 무시한 정책을 주창했다. 포퓰리즘은 이러한 이데올로기에서 비롯됐다. 미국 사학자 마이클 카진은 『인민주의 신념(The Populist Persuasion)』에서 "미국 정치가 농민운동 같은 경제 포퓰리즘에서 사회 주류의 문화적 가치에 근거한 문화 포퓰리즘으로 대체되고 있다"고 지적한다.

민주당은 프랭클린 루스벨트 이후 수십 년 동안 중산층과 노동자 계층들을 부유한 공화당 지지세력과 맞서게 하는 경제 포퓰리즘으로 승리를 일궈냈다. 이어 공화당 또한 경제 포퓰리즘에 대적하는 방법을 터득했다. 로널드 레이건은 자신을 워싱턴의 기성 정치인 및 다양한 이익집단과 차별화하기 위해 문화적 포퓰리즘을 효과적으로 구사했다. 빌 클린턴은 백인 노동자층의 문화적 가치를 대변하면서 집권에 성공했다. 뉴욕타임스의 칼럼니스트 머린 도우는 네오 포퓰리즘의 특성을 상황주의로 설명했다. 포퓰리즘은 진실을 추구하는 대신 한 쪽의 이익을 위해 사용되고 있다.

해설

1. 본문에 의하면 포퓰리즘이라는 단어는 대중의 지지를 얻기 위해 은화를 무제한 주조하는 등 경제성 합리성을 무시한 정책을 주창하는 이데올로기에서 비롯됐다. 즉, 인기를 얻기 위해 비록 그것이 비합리적일지라도 그들이 원하는 것들을 수용하는 것을 의미한다. 이는 사람들을 속이거나 거짓된 모습을 보여주는 것과는 차이가 있다.

2. 뉴욕타임스의 칼럼니스트가 네오 포퓰리즘을 상황주의로 표현한 것을 고려하면, 현재 혹은 미래의 포퓰리즘은 상황을 고려하여 적합한 인기영합적 전략을 사용하는 것임을 유추할 수 있다. 또한 인기에 영합하려는 정치인들의 속성을 고려하면 미래에도 이러한 포퓰리즘이 계속되리라 생각할 수 있다. 포퓰리즘을 사용한 미국 대통령의 예시를 많이 들었지만, 미국의 모든 대통령이 인기영합주의적 정책을 폈다고 하는 것은 심한 비약이다.

3. 본문의 마지막이 네오 포퓰리즘을 소개하며 끝맺음하는 것을 보아 다음 단락에는 네오 포퓰리즘에 대한 이야기가 전개될 것임을 유추할 수 있다. 다른 보기는 본문에 언급된 내용들이지만 흐름상 마지막 단락 뒤에 올 수는 없다.

4. 본문에는 프랭클린 루스벨트 이후의 민주당과 로널드 레이건, 그리고 빌 클린턴 등이 포퓰리즘을 사용하여 집권에 성공해온 사례가 소개되어 있다. 칠레가 최근 다시 사회주의 국가가 되었다는 것이나 미국의 현 민주당 대통령이 문화 포퓰리즘을 이용한다는 내용은 본문에 나오지 않았다.

정답 1.(d) 2.(c) 3.(a) 4.(a)

UNIT 18

Korea lacks basic values
스마트 기업 50

'스마트·혁신·변화·창조'. 스타트업에서부터 대기업, 정부 할 것 없이 모든 조직이 탐내는 가치들이다. 그래서 이 가치에 누가 잘 다가가는지는 늘 관심사다. 매사추세츠공과대학(MIT) 테크놀로지 리뷰는 2010년부터 매년 이를 가늠케 하는 순위를 발표한다. '세계에서 가장 스마트한 기업 50'이 그것이다. '기술 관련 비즈니스를 새롭게 한 업체'를 최소 12개월 이상 분석하고 관찰해 뽑는다는 설명이다. 새 비즈니스 모델을 만들었거나 시장에 매력적인 기술을 선보인 기업이 리스트의 주인공이 된다. 매출이나 수익, 특허의 수와 같은 양적 지표는 고려되지 않는다.

당연히 절대적인 기준은 아니다. 그럼에도 매년 상당한 시사점을 준다. 올해는 지난해 상위에 있던 업체들이 대거 빠졌다. 지난해 2위였던 중국 샤오미의 부재가 가장 특징적이다. 지난해 "애플의 저렴이 버전'이라는 사업 모델을 넘어 반짝 할인과 모바일 메시지 플랫폼으로 성숙해가고 있다"고 판단해 혁신적이라고 평가받았지만 올해는 50위권 밖으로 빠졌다. 스마트폰 시장 내에서 새로움을 제시하지 못해서다. 경쟁사들도 같은 처지다. 애플도 지난해 16위였지만 올해는 빠졌다. 2014년 4위였던 삼성전자는 지난해에 이어 올해도 리스트에 없다.

올해의 1위는 아마존이다. "요구하면 인공지능(AI) 알렉사가 당신이 좋아하는 노래를 연주하고 피자도 주문해 줄 것이다". 아마존웹서비스(AWS)의 기업 클라우드 컴퓨팅 사업이 특히 유망하다"고 봤다. 2위는 바이두가 차지했는데, "중국의 선두 검색 엔진은 이제 무인자동차까지 개발하고 있다"고 소개했다. 바이두는 2014년 실리콘 밸리에 연구팀을 만들었고 올해 100명 이상의 무인자동차 연구원과 엔지니어를 고용할 계획이다. 화웨이(10위), 텐센트(20위), 디디추싱(21위), 알리바바(24위) 등 중국 업체들이 순위에 올라 있다. 한국 기업으로는 유일하게 쿠팡이 44위에 들었다.

해설

1. 본문은 '세계에서 가장 스마트한 기업 50'에 포함이 되었다가 순위에서 누락되는 기업들과 새로운 혁신적인 아이디어로 다시 리스트에 포함이 되는 기업들에 관해 이야기하고 있기 때문에 정답은 (d)이다. 리스트에 포함되는 기준에 새로운 비즈니스 모델과 기술은 고려되지만 매출이나 수익과 같은 양적 지표는 고려되지 않는다는 점에서 (a)가 될 수 없다.

2. 본래 샤오미가 '애플의 저렴이 버전' 비즈니스 모델을 넘어 더욱 성장하고 있다는 내용은 (a)의 내용과 동일한 의미이다. 애플의 저렴이 버전이라고 불렸지만 현재는 이를 넘어서고 있다는 것이다. 반면, (b)의 더 적은 예산으로 애플이 실현시키고자 하는 일을 샤오미가 더욱 잘 해내고 있다는 것은 애플의 목적이 무엇인지 언급되지 않고 비교대상이 샤오미의 이전 모델이 아니라 애플이기 때문에 틀린 답이다.

3. 세 번째 단락에서 당연히 양적 지표들을 고려하지 않고 새로운 비즈니스 모델과 기술로 평가되는 '세계에서 가장 스마트한 기업 50'은 절대적인 기준이 아니라는 점이 (d)가 답인 점을 뒷받침해준다.

4. 매출 혹은 수익, 그리고 특허의 수와 같은 양적 지표는 고려되지 않고 비즈니스 모델과 기술의 새로움 등의 질적 지표로 평가된다는 (a)가 정답이다. (b)는 본문의 내용과 반대 내용이고, (c)는 규모가 더 큰 기업이 리스트의 상위권에 든다는 점이 전제가 되어 틀린 것이다. 마지막으로 (d)는 평가를 받는 기간이 최소 12개월인 것이지 기업이 설립된 지 12개월 이하여야 한다는 의미가 아니므로 틀린 것이다.

정답 1.(d) 2.(a) 3.(d) 4.(a)

UNIT 19
Like Robin Hood, tax up to no good
부유세

17세기 영국의 윌리엄 3세 국왕은 전비(戰費) 마련을 위해 부자들에게 별도의 세금을 물렸다. 세금을 매긴 근거는 희한하게도 집 창문의 수였다. 당시 대부분 사람들은 추운 겨울에 열이 나가는 것을 막기 위해 봉쇄된 구조를 선택하였는데, 이때 부(富)의 상징 중 하나가 벽난로였다. 벽난로가 있는 집은 보통 창문을 많이 냈다. 차가운 공기가 창문을 통해 스며들어오긴 했지만 겨울에 벽난로가 집을 데워주었기 때문에 집 주인은 호사를 누릴 수 있었던 것이다. 그런데 벽난로가 부유하다는 상징이긴 하지만, 집에 벽난로가 있는지 정부가 엄청난 에너지와 시간을 들여서 일일이 확인하기가 어려웠다. 그래서 윌리엄 3세는 각 가정의 창문 수에 따라 이른바 '창문세'를 부과했다는 것이다. 창문세 도입 이후 일부 사람들은 창문세를 안 내려고 창문을 틀어막고 살았다고 한다.

이 사례는 오늘날의 부유세를 상기시킨다. 현대 국가에서의 부유세는 부의 분배의 불평등을 완화하자는 취지다. 그러나 이러한 세금은 의도하지 않은 여러 가지 부작용이 동반된다. 부유세 높기로 유명한 프랑스가 대표적 경우다. 2008년 프랑스 최고의 요리사 알랭 뒤 카스가 부유세를 피해 고국을 등지고 국적을 모나코로 옮겼는가 하면, 2006년엔 1억 장 이상의 앨범을 판 프랑스 가수 조니 알리데가 같은 이유로 스위스로 떠났다. 스웨덴의 세계적 가구업체 이케아(IKEA)의 캄프라드 회장도 외국에 설립한 재단에 상당한 재산을 빼돌려 부유세를 회피한 사례로 꼽힌다.

이러한 부유세는 영국 민담 속에 나오는 유명한 도망자의 이름을 딴 소위 '로빈 후드 효과(Robin Hood effect)'를 만들어낸다. 로빈 후드는 부자들의 재산을 빼앗아 가난한 사람들에게 나눠 준다. 그러나 현대의 일부 경제학자들은 로빈 후드가 사실은 가난한 사람들을 더 어렵게 만들었다고 말한다. 부유한 상인들이 자신들의 재산을 지키려고 다른 곳으로 이주하는 바람에 가게를 내고 운영할 여유가 있는 사람들이 적어져 물가를 끌어올렸다는 것이다.

해설

1. 사회의 빈부의 격차를 줄이기 위하여 어떤 조치를 취해야 하며, 그간의 부유세를 적용하는 과정에서 어떠한 문제점이 있었는지를 적고 있다.

2. 스웨덴의 세계적 가구업체 이케아(IKEA)의 캄프라드 회장도 외국에 설립한 재단에 230억 달러에 이르는 재산을 빼돌려 부유세를 회피한 사례로 꼽히지만, 캄프라드 회장은 프랑스인이 아니다. 그러므로 (a)가 정답이다.

3. 별도의 세금을 물렸다고 하였으므로, 이전 단락에서는 표준화된 세금을 어떻게 부과하였는지가 나와야 한다. 그래야 이어서 17세기는 어떠했고, 이후는 어떠했는지 서술된 것이 일관성을 지니게 된다.

4. 17세기에 일부 사람들은 창문세를 안 내려고 창문을 틀어막고 살았다는 것에서, 프랑스의 부자들이 세금을 안 내기 위해서 국적을 바꾸는 것들을 보면, 사람들은 세금을 내는 것을 좋아하지 않는다는 것을 추론할 수 있다. 참고로 (c)의 경우 물가가 오른 것이지 세금이 더 낸 게 아니다.

정답 1.(b) 2.(a) 3.(d) 4.(a)

UNIT 20

America's risky pot experiment
아슬아슬한 미국의 마리화나 실험

    2014년 3월 13일 미국 콜로라도주 덴버에선 마리화나(대마초) 취업박람회란 행사가 열렸다. 마리화나 재배와 유통, 여행상품과 관련한 12개 업체가 "유망 업종"이라며 홍보전을 펼쳤다. 박람회엔 5백 명이 넘는 구직자가 몰렸다. 올해 미국 최초로 오락용 마리화나까지 허용한 콜로라도주에서만 볼 수 있는 모습이다. 하지만 미국 사회 돌아가는 걸 보면 마리화나의 전면적 허용도 시간문제로 보인다. 현재 미국 20개 주에선 의료 목적에 한해 마리화나 사용을 승인하고 있다. 연방법상 마리화나는 마약류로 규정돼 처벌을 받지만, 오바마 행정부도 이런 흐름을 고려해 "이들 주의 마리화나 사용자들을 단속 목표로 삼지 말라"는 지침을 내렸다. 정말 중대한 변화는 콜로라도처럼 오락용도까지 허용하는 경우이다. 이미 워싱턴주는 허용했으며 애리조나, 알래스카주 등이 뒤를 따르고 있다.

    최근의 연구는 마리화나 합법화를 지지하는 것으로 보인다. 오바마 대통령도 "마리화나가 술보다 덜 해롭다"고 얘기할 정도이다. 최근 월스트리트저널 조사 결과 미국인들은 담배−술−설탕−마리화나 순으로 해롭다고 답했다. 설탕이 유해하다는 의견(15%)이 마리화나(8%)보다 배 가까이 많았다. 이번주 발표된 통계에서 콜로라도주가 1월 한달간 오락용 마리화나에서 거둬들인 세금은 2백억달러(20억원)가 넘었다. 디트로이트처럼 파산하는 시가 속출하는 상황에서 이런 수치는 주 정부들에게 매력적인 수입원이다. 마리화나가 보급되면 술 소비가 줄어들 거라는 연구까지 나왔다. 그렇게 되면 공공보건 차원에서 긍정적이라는 설명과 함께. 에릭 홀더 법무장관은 금요일 교도소의 수용인원을 줄이기 위해 "가벼운 마약 사범의 형량을 낮추는 데 동의한다"고 밝혔다.

    물론 마리화나 합법화를 찬성하는 측에서도 몇 가지 제한에 동의한다. 청소년들에게 무차별 전파되는 건 막아야 하고, 운전 등 안전과 관련한 행위엔 제한을 둬야 한다는 것 등이다. 하지만 미국 사회가 그런 정교한 규제 능력을 갖췄는가에 대해선 의문이다. 총기규제에도 불구하고 총기 사고가 빈번하게 발생한다. 많은 전문가들은 마리화나 허용이 중독자를 양산하고 다른 마약류에 대한 진입 장벽도 낮출 수 있고 걱정한다. 만약 그런 악순환과 고질적 총기 문제가 결합됐을 때 어떤 비극이 탄생할지 끔찍해진다. 지난 1월 콜로라도주의 한 경찰서가 시범적으로 실시한 단속에서 적발된 운전자 61명 중 31명이 마리화나를 피운 상태였다. 하지만 요즘 미국은 이런 복합적인 관계를 외면하는 듯 보인다.

해설

1. (d)의 내용처럼 오락용 마리화나를 허용하는 주가 증가하는 추세는 본문 첫 단락에 나온 내용을 근거로 올바른 진술이다. 참고로 (b)의 경우 본문에서는 마리화나가 술보다 덜 해롭다고 하였으므로 틀린 진술이다.

2. 문장의 빈칸에는 에릭 홀더 법무장관은 "가벼운 마약 사범의 형량을 낮추는 데 동의한다"고 밝힌 이유가 소개되어야 한다. 그러므로 '교도소의 수용인원을 줄이기 위해서'라는 근거가 들어가면 타당한 진술이 된다.

3. 마리화나 합법화로 인해 즉각적으로 경제가 활성화되는 것이란 근거는 없으며, 의학적 용도의 마리화나 허용도 아직 20여개 주에 불과한 실정이다. (c)의 내용은 본문에 근거가 없다. 미국 사회 돌아가는 걸 보면 마리화나의 전면적 허용도 시간문제로 보인다고 하였으므로 적절한 때가 되면 마리화나가 미국 전역에서 합법적으로 허용될 것이라고 추론할 수 있다. 그러므로 정답은 (d)이다.

4. 이 글의 저자는 총기 규제를 제대로 운용하지 못하는 예를 들면서 미국 사회가 그런 정교한 규제 능력을 갖췄는가에 대해선 의문이라고 하였다. 그러므로 미국은 마리화나의 합법화에 대해서 제대로 대처하기는 쉽지 않을 것이라는 (a)가 정답이다.

정답   1.(d)   2.(a)   3.(d)   4.(a)

Break Time

A homeless man asked a guy for 2 pounds.
"Are you going to buy liquor?" says the guy.
"No, I won't!" replies the homeless.
"Will you gamble it away?" asked the man.
"No, sor," said the tramp.
"Then will you come home with me?" said the man.
"so my wife can see what happens to a man who doesn't drink or gamble."

노숙자가 남자에게 2파운드를 달라고 했습니다.
"술이라도 사려는 건가?"라고 남자가 물었습니다.
"그럴리가요!" 노숙자는 대답했습니다.
"노름이라도 해서 다 써버릴 참인가?"라고 남자가 다시 물어봅니다.
"아니, 아니! 그런 일 없습니다."라고 대답하는 노숙자.
그러자 남자는 말합니다.
"그럼, 나와 같이 내 집에 가주지 않을텐가? 술도 마시지 않고 노름도 하지 않는 인간이 어떻게 되는지 내 마누라한테 보여주고 싶네."

gamble it away 도박으로 써버리다.
tramp 부랑자

MEMO

MEMO